The
Ultimate
DEHYDRATOR
Cookbook

The
Ultimate
DEHYDRATOR
Cookbook

Tammy Gangloff, Steven Gangloff & September Ferguson

STACKPOLE
BOOKS

Published by
STACKPOLE BOOKS
5067 Ritter Road
Mechanicsburg, PA 17055
www.stackpolebooks.com

Printed in the United States of America

First edition

Cover design by Caroline M. Stover
Photography by kc kratt photography: www.kckratt.com

Library of Congress Cataloging-in-Publication Data

Gangloff, Tammy.
    The ultimate dehydrator cookbook : the complete guide to drying food, plus 398 recipes, including making jerky, fruit leather & just-add-water meals / Tammy Gangloff, Steven Gangloff & September Ferguson.
        pages cm
    Includes index.
    ISBN 978-0-8117-1338-2
1. Dried foods. 2. Food—Drying. I. Gangloff, Steven. II. Ferguson,September. III. Title.
    TX609.G35 2014
    641.4'4–dc23

2014014848

To James Gangloff, my beloved husband and loving father of my children.

You believed I was wonderful. You believed everything I did was amazing, no matter how small. You showed me my wings and said I could fly, and I did and you smiled.

And when my wings were broken, you held me in your arms until they healed and I could soar again. I am because of you. I love you.

And to James, my beloved son and brother of my children.

Such a giving and loving heart only an angel could possess. The light came and took you home. The angels sang. I wept.

I was given a beautiful gift; that gift was to hold you in my arms. I was blessed. I love you.

Contents

Acknowledgments

Special thanks to Scott Gangloff for being a supporter and dedicated taste tester, and to Steve and Sue Ferguson for their love and support. Special thanks to Nancy Levensailor for her support. Also, to our photographer and to Stackpole Books and our editors for their time and efforts in making this incredible opportunity into a brilliant reality.

Introduction

With food dehydration you will embark on an incredible journey where you will learn to create delicious snacks and meals that will wow those around you. And because they are prepared using dehydrated ingredients, they will be faster and cheaper to make, as well as healthier. Follow me and I will show you the amazing benefits of dehydrating food. After that, there will be no stopping you.

WHY DRY?

Imagine placing your food into a state of suspended animation, perfectly preserved until it is needed. Picture effortlessly and quickly preserving your entire garden, using no unnatural additives or salt, and then storing those items five to ten times longer than possible with freezing or canning. Imagine lifting 50 pounds of potatoes with one finger, and five bushels of apples with another. This sounds unbelievable and yet, I have been doing this for years, and have only just begun to scratch the surface of the benefits of dehydrating food.

When I first started dehydrating, I was met with a lot of eye rolling and giggling. My children would look at me and say, "I'm not going to eat that." What they didn't know at the time, however, is that we all eat dehydrated foods every day without ever realizing it. Did you know that most restaurants use dehydrated foods? Have you noticed that over the past few years there are more and more packaged prepared dried items on the shelves of local stores compared to canned items?

Why, you might ask, has industry made this shift toward dried food? The foremost reason is its cost effectiveness. When you dry food, you remove nearly all the water it contains, significantly reducing it both in weight and size (volume). This allows you to store more food in a smaller space. Not to mention, less weight per item reduces transportation costs. Dehydrated foods do not require refrigeration, and the cost to produce a plastic bag to store dried foods is appreciably less than that of an aluminum can for canned foods. Additionally, the long shelf life of dried foods means less money sent down the drain due to spoilage. From factory to store, dehydrating foods saves money. Indeed, the food industry has utilized the benefits of dehydration for some time, but most people are not aware of just how many benefits can be reaped from home dehydration! All of the cost reductions seen by food companies can also be enjoyed by you!

The benefits of dehydrating foods are not just monetary. There are many nutritional benefits to using dehydrated foods. Dehydrated foods are salt free and have a higher nutritional value than the same foods canned or frozen. The water-free, air-free environment created by proper food dehydration impedes the growth of many contaminants that may be a problem with canning or freezing. Somewhere along the way, we have been taught to think that if something comes out of a can or if it's frozen, it is good. It is time to relearn what is "good." For an in-depth discussion of the safety and nutritional benefits of dehydrated foods see page 3.

You might be thinking, I don't have time to do this. Certainly, we all wish we had more free time. More time to spend with our families, more time to spend gardening or enjoying a good book, and more time to spend helping others or volunteering in our church or community. What if I were to tell you that using dehydrated foods could cut the time you spend in the kitchen in half, or more? Home dehydration allows you to create a stock of healthy ingredients that you will have on hand at all times. This means no more quick trips to the store to pick up those few ingredients missing to complete a new recipe or to replenish spoiled produce. Everything you need will be at your fingertips, stored properly to last a long time, and ready for cooking. With dehydration, even "out of season" produce will be ready whenever you are! No more food prep—washing, peeling, and chopping—for each and every meal; it has already been done! Just grab a handful of this, a pinch of that, and turn on the heat! If you pre-package your meals, preparing a delicious dinner can be as easy as opening a package, placing it in a slow cooker, adding liquid, and turning it on. All that is left to do is think about what you want to do with all of that extra time!

If you are a gardening enthusiast you are certainly familiar with this scenario: you have worked hard to nourish a large and beautiful garden you're proud of, but you soon find that this bounty of food has become too much to eat right away. Perhaps you try to can your excess produce, but you quickly come to realize the size of that sweat-inducing, labor-intensive task. What can you do to save your harvest from literally rotting on the vine? Dehydrating is a fast, easy, and simple way to solve this problem. In fact, you can preserve your entire garden and still have time and energy to tackle your neighbor's!

Because dehydrated foods have a long shelf life, it's a fast and affordable way to stock up and build a pantry that can sustain you and your family should you need it, whether because of the loss of a job, unexpected misfortune, hyperinflation, bad weather conditions, family and friends in need, or simply as a bridge when finances temporarily run short.

I had a dear friend quip back at me one day saying, "If there's an emergency, I have a huge freezer packed full of food." I replied, "Not if the electricity goes out." If your food is in the pantry and you lose electricity, your food is still safe. The great benefit of home-dehydrated products is you can cut the tethers binding you to environmental and mechanical mishaps.

This is just a glimpse at the possibilities home dehydration offers. Read on and I'll share with you the countless incredible and exciting things you can do with your dehydrator!

MY STORY

The passion I have for dehydrating came to me by way of another passion: cake decorating. I loved to design and bake fabulous cakes with intricate detailing. If someone needed a cake for a special occasion I would jump at the opportunity, and always strived to deliver a "WOW." I handmade all of my decorative pieces from fondant and gum paste. Depending on the size, most of these pieces would require at least a week to dry. Because of this, I couldn't accommodate requests on short notice. Searching for a better way, I decided to try using my oven instead of air-drying the pieces. I placed my fondant on a cookie sheet and then briefly heated it in my oven at 175°F (the lowest temperature it would allow) but once the pieces were dry, they were also discolored.

Finally, I learned about home dehydrators, and decided to give one a try. To my amazement, it worked beautifully. My pieces dried in hours, with no discoloration!

When Two Worlds Collide

Early on Saturday mornings, my husband and I would let our boys sleep in, and sneak off to the local farmers' market. Because this locally grown food offered a way to eat fresh, healthy, and untreated foods at a fraction of store prices, we were always eager to take advantage of buying in bulk. We would fill the back of our truck with bushels of apples, corn, potatoes, huge beets and carrots, collard greens, parsley, and more.

Returning home, Jim would kick back in his reclining chair and I would start canning and pickling. Hours I worked, through steam and sweat, diligently laboring over my pressure cooker. Try as I did, I could never finish canning our haul from the farmers' market, and would end up giving a good portion away each time to neighbors.

But each Saturday, Jim and I would be right back at the farmers' market, repeating the events of the week before. One Saturday, after having recently purchased a dehydrator for my cake fondant, I decided to give it a try with some of the produce my husband was lugging into the kitchen. I was skeptical as to how dehydrated food would taste, and doubtful that it would ever hold a candle to my canning.

The first item I dehydrated was collard greens. Holding a large leaf by the stem, I dropped it into boiling water for a couple minutes, then placed it flat on the dehydrator rack. Around six hours later, the collard leaf was completely dehydrated. First I must say, I am a collard green lover, so there was nary a person more qualified to put this petrified leaf to the test. I placed the dehydrated collard leaf into a pot of boiling water for about ten minutes, removed it, and plated it with a little lemon butter and salt. To my surprise and excitement, the rehydrated product tasted fresh, alive, and fabulous!

From that moment I threw myself into researching, experimenting with, and developing the art of dehydrating. I dehydrated everything in sight. If I came across a problem, I would not let go until I found the answer. I tried many different methods of prepping, storing, and cooking each item. I dehydrated truckloads upon truckloads of food, canning a distant memory in my rearview mirror.

Wake Up, Everyone, There's a New Way

My children, on the other hand, were less than enthusiastic about this new turn of events. "I'm not going to eat that *dry* food," my youngest would whine. I was lucky to have the support of my husband, an incredible man, who thought everything I made was delicious, and was willing to try anything new. His encouragement kept my persistence with my children strong; I knew that there was some way I could use my motherly ingenuity to get my children to try this just once. One evening, after preparing a meal nearly entirely of dehydrated foods, my youngest asked, as he always did, "Mom is there dried-up food in my dinner?" I looked at my husband, who was fighting a smile, and back at my son. "No, there isn't," I said calmly. After all, I reasoned to myself, the food was rehydrated, so it wasn't dry . . . *anymore.* It wouldn't be until much later that I revealed my sneaky ploy to my children. The funny thing is, no one ever noticed. When I later told my sons that many of their meals had been reconstituted dry foods, they were surprised, but didn't mind. It was delicious all the same. As the years passed, dehydrated foods became a staple in our home.

A moment that stands out was the day my grown daughter September requested that I bring her more dehydrated foods. "I'm all out!" she pleaded. I had frequently brought dehydrated items over to her house, but I wasn't sure if she was cooking with them or simply taking them to be kind, and stockpiling them in her basement. I was so happy that I ran around gathering tons of different items for her. Who knew she would soon become a dehydration expert as well?

I developed a tremendous appreciation for dehydrated foods and wanted to "ring the bell" to all my friends and family. I wanted to show them a better way of preserving foods, building their pantries, and making meals in a snap. I started inviting them into my home, where I would cook up a storm. "How do those carrots taste?" I would ask, "They're huge, aren't they?"

I would then pass around a small jar holding the dehydrated carrots. This little jar, I would explain, contains the equivalent of 5 pounds of fresh carrots. My "students" would rattle the dried carrots around in the jar and marvel at their miniscule size. "These tiny, dry morsels were used in your meal to make the plump tender carrots slices you are enjoying," I would say with a smile.

It was my son Steven, who was fourteen at the time, who suggested I share my knowledge about food dehydration with the world by producing instructional videos on YouTube. And share I did; those videos have now been viewed by millions of people in all corners of the earth. From there, Dehydrate2Store.com was born, an instructional source for people like me, who are interested in learning the fascinating art of dehydration. I developed my own techniques, and gained recognition as a dehydration expert. Nevertheless, to this day, many years after my first introduction to the dehydrator, I am still learning and experimenting, and have not lost my wide-eyed curiosity and excitement about food dehydration and storage.

A Brisk Reality

A few years ago we had a horrible storm that took out all of the electrical power lines in our area. Some people were deprived of electricity for weeks. Two days after the storm, purely out of curiosity since I already had everything I needed, I walked into a nearby grocery store. The store was dimly lit, run solely on generators. The shelves were almost bare, frantic customers grabbing whatever was left. *This is nuts,* I thought. If everyone kept a stocked pantry and practiced self-reliance this craziness wouldn't exist.

We practice escape routes with our children in case of a fire, we purchase homeowner's and life insurance, and save money for a rainy day, but talk about food storage in case of an emergency and people look at you like you just landed a spaceship.

Why the big disconnect? I believe that it stems from several common misconceptions about food storage. Food storage and dehydration are not about digging a hole and burying it, or yourself, in the backyard. Storing food is not about preparation for a zombie apocalypse or futuristic robotic takeover. To put it simply, dehydration is a fast, easy, healthy, and economical way to preserve food, with a longer shelf life and higher nutritional value than other methods, using no preservatives. As an added bonus, it allows us to build our pantries at a very low cost and to make delicious meals and creative treats in a snap.

So, when people think you're crazy for dehydrating and cooking with dehydrated foods, just smile and offer up a sample. They are sure to change their tune with their first bite.

How Dehydration Works

Welcome to your introductory course to the fascinating science behind food dehydration! If you broke into a sweat and started having high school flashbacks when you saw the word "science," have no fear. We're going to keep this course short, as well as fun and instructive. What you need to know is that it is very important to understand the science behind food dehydration to ensure your final dehydrated and stored products are of expert quality.

So let's begin our class by jumping into our souped-up and sporty time-mobile. Our time travel budget is a bit tight, so we will have to rely on "imagination" for this next part.

"ZZZAP!" The time-mobile flashes us to ancient Egypt. Endless rolling golden dunes of sand stretch out to the horizon to your right, and ahead you spot a city. At its center, you watch as workers prepare a tomb to receive the mummified body of the recently deceased pharaoh, King Drymesumcinnamon. Unnoticed, we sneak into the tomb below. Gold and priceless gems are everywhere; but that's not why we are here. Then we spot it. The real treasure: the pantry! Jars upon jars of dried spices and honey line the walls. These items were stored here, deep in this dry, sandy tomb, to accompany the king on his journey into the afterlife and sustain him. Quickly, before anyone can see, we snatch a jar of honey, and two of spices, and we frantically escape back to the time-mobile.

"ZZZAP!" Back in the lab we examine our find. Much to our astonishment, these herbs and spices look perfectly preserved. Even the aroma of a jar of dried pomegranate is alive and exuberant. To test your find, you whip together a tea from the pharaoh's spices, and sip deeply. "Delicious!" you exclaim. (See page 110 for our recipe for Pharaoh's Tea.)

I take a sample of honey and smear it onto a microscope slide. Using special stains and high magnification, I look into the sticky sweet substance. Much to my surprise, it is sterile! There are no bacteria, no mold spores, and no fungi to be found. The herbs are also devoid of mold. How can this be?

HOW DEHYDRATION WORKS

Food dehydration uses gentle temperatures (90° to 125°F for most items) and an even airflow to slowly remove the moisture from foods through the process of evaporation. We say an item is "dried" when we remove any amount of moisture from it, but for something to be considered "dehydrated," 95% or more of its moisture must be removed.

The foundational purpose of food dehydration is to prevent food from spoiling and extend shelf life (although, as you will discover in this book, dehydration can be used for so much more). The main degrading agents to food are microorganisms (bacteria, fungi, and mold), oxygen, heat, moisture, and light. Through the process of dehydration, moisture is removed at the same time it creates an environment uninhabitable to most organisms. Through proper storage, exposure to degrading levels of oxygen, heat, and light can be eliminated.

PROPER FOOD DEHYDRATION

It is important to understand how proper dehydration and storage work in order to effectively create an expert finished product. Properly dehydrated and stored items will have the longest shelf life possible, will contain the highest possible levels of nutrients, and will have the best taste. Using the proper techniques when dehydrating will preserve the compounds that give your food its aroma, taste, and appearance.

As mentioned, an item is considered dehydrated when approximately 95% of its moisture has been removed. Since you have no way to test for this percentage at home, however, you will need to develop an experienced eye, ear, and hand. In general, properly dehydrated items are not sticky or tacky, do not feel moist or soft, and often will snap or crunch easily when broken. You will learn more about the specifics of each particular food item in the chapters that follow.

Many foods need special preparation before dehydrating, which can include blanching in boiling water, steaming, spraying with lemon juice, as well as others. These techniques also help to deter bacterial growth and preserve nutrients.

Lemon juice (and ascorbic acid, which works the same way), for example, is important to add to many foods before dehydrating for a few reasons. First, it prevents the browning that can occur when certain fruits and vegetables are cut. Cutting ruptures cells, which causes various enzymes to be released. These enzymes can react with compounds in the produce, such as phenols, to produce brown pigments. Enzymes function only in relatively narrow windows of temperature, pH (a measure of acidity), and salt content. If you expose them to high acidity or high heat, some can be deactivated. The application of lemon juice to the cut surfaces of fruit like apples or avocadoes plays just such a role.

Another beneficial function of lemon juice is that it has antibacterial properties. Most bacteria that are pathogenic (cause disease) to humans thrive around a pH of 7.4, while the pH of lemon juice is between 2 and 3. This is sufficient to inhibit the growth of many bacteria including some pathogenic strains of *E. coli* and *Salmonella* (the culprits behind food poisoning), and *L. monocytogenes* (which causes listeriosis). Finally, the application of lemon juice provides an additional boost of vitamin C. As you will soon learn, vitamin C is one of the few nutrients that are difficult to preserve.

THE EFFECT OF DEHYDRATION ON NUTRIENTS

In any type of food processing, from boiling and canning to simply cutting with a knife, nutrients are going to be lost to some degree. The unique technique of dehydration, which exposes food to a minimally elevated temperature over a long period of time, is ideal for maximum retention of nutrients. Compared to canning and freezing, dehydration comes out on top in regard to the conservation of nutrients. The United States Department of Agriculture indicates that on average 40% to 60% of nutrients are lost when food is frozen for storage, while canning can result in a whopping 60% to 80% loss. Home food dehydration, however, produces only an average nutrient loss of 3% to 5%!

The secret is in the temperatures employed in each process. Both the very low temperatures of freezing and the high temperatures of canning cause the cells of fruits, vegetables, and greens to break open, spilling out their precious nutrient cargo. The temperatures used in dehydration don't wreak this havoc.

Here is how dehydration affects certain nutrients:

Calories: Dehydrating has no effect on the calorie content of a specific item, say a slice of apple or a broccoli floret. However, dehydrated foods have more calories *per weight* because removing the water shrinks the food and makes it lighter without removing any calories. The condensed product is consequently more calorie dense, meaning there is huge calorie difference between 1 ounce of fresh apples and 1 ounce of dried apples.

Carbohydrates and other sugars: As with calories, dehydration has no effect on the carbohydrate or sugar content of a specific piece

HOME DRYING VS. COMMERCIAL DEHYDRATION

Commercially dried fruit is usually treated with preservatives and sweeteners, which changes its nutrition content. Additionally, many companies juice the fruits before dehydrating them, resulting in a less colorful, less aromatic, and less flavorful product. Just one more reason to jump on the home dehydrator bandwagon!

of food. However, dehydrated fruit will be sweeter than non-dried fruit, since the removal of the water concentrates the sugar in the fruit into a smaller volume and weight. Again, there is a significant difference in the carbohydrates contained in 1 ounce of fresh grapes versus 1 ounce of raisins. This kind of concentration is a boon to hikers or athletes who may need a quick energy boost from a lightweight and portable food, but it can be problematic for dieters, if you're not mindful.

Fiber: Dehydrating food has no effect on total fiber content. Fiber is a plant material that aids with digestion.

Minerals: Minerals, such as iron, are not affected by food dehydration.

Proteins: Dehydration has no effect on total protein content.

Vitamin A (beta-carotene): Beta-carotene (responsible for the brilliant orange color in foods like carrots and sweet potatoes), which is converted to vitamin A in the body, is destroyed by contact with air. You can actually watch this happen. Leave carrots out in the open, and as the vitamin A begins to deplete, the color of the carrots will fade. Luckily, this can be avoided by blanching before dehydrating. Doing this changes the chemical structure of the food slightly, preventing this loss and in fact increasing the quantity of beta-carotene it contains. As an experiment, dehydrate some uncooked carrots and some blanched carrots and set them side by side. The dehydrated blanched carrots will not only be a much brighter orange, but over time their color will not fade compared to carrots that have not been subject to blanching.

Vitamin B: B vitamins are water-soluble; because of this, they can be lost if steamed or blanched. However, they will not evaporate along with the water when you dehydrate.

Vitamin C: Vitamin C is a delicate flower, sensitive to exposure to light and air. The best way to prevent or minimize the loss of vitamin C is to remove both—air by using vacuum sealing and oxygen absorbers, and light by storing foods in Mylar bags or away from light. In addition, spraying appropriate items with lemon juice prior to dehydrating will add a blast of vitamin C.

KEEPING THE BUGS AT BAY: BACTERIA, MOLD, AND FUNGI

At some point, whether it is refrigerated or left at room temperature, fresh food will begin to degrade. The prime culprits are bacteria, mold, and fungi. Canning, freezing, and dehydration are all attempts to stave off rot and to preserve food for future healthy (and one hopes tasty!) consumption. Proper dehydration (and subsequent storage) is the most successful of these processes because it virtually eliminates what these little pests and other contaminants like best.

Temperature: Most bacteria that are pathogenic (cause disease) to humans thrive at human body temperature (98.6°F). Once the temperature begins to rise above that temperature, the growth of many bacteria begins to slow, and some even die; hence the effectiveness of having a fever when you are sick. Some common foodborne bacteria include *Clostridium botulinum* (which causes botulism) and *Salmonella* and *Campylobacter* or *E. coli* (food poisoning). The growth of nearly all strains of these bacteria slows between 98.6° and 112°F or higher. Most foods are dehydrated at 120° to 125°F, except meat, where higher temperatures are used (155° to 160°F).

Air (oxygen): Some pathogenic bacteria are aerobic (thrive in the presence of oxygen), and some are what are known as obligate aerobes (they will die without oxygen). As such, air removal via vacuum sealing (our preferred method for storing dehydrated foods) inhibits the growth of, or kills, some pathogenic bacteria. Furthermore, a properly sealed vacuum bag will prevent new bacteria from landing on and colonizing your food.

Moisture: The most important deterrent to the growth of contaminants is the removal of water. If performed properly, dehydration should remove at least 95% of the moisture the food originally contained. Most bacteria, mold, and fungi cannot grow, and often die, below 10% water content. Food storage techniques such as freezing and canning, where the food is exposed or stored in contact with liquid, pose an increased risk for food illnesses if not performed properly.

Common Foodborne Illnesses You Want to Avoid

Campylobacter: One of the leading causes of food poisoning (fever and abdominal distress), this bacterium is commonly associated with undercooked chicken and grows best between 98.6° and 108°F; it is destroyed at temperatures above 120°F. These bacteria are fragile and cannot tolerate drying.

Clostridium perfringens: This is typically only associated with raw meats, and therefore is not a prime concern with food dehydration. The organisms are killed at 150°F, and do not replicate in a moisture-free environment.

Salmonella: This bacterium causes salmonellosis ("salmonella poisoning"); victims experience fever, vomiting, and abdominal discomfort. *Salmonella* is often spread through polluted water, and commonly associated with uncooked eggs, undercooked chicken, and reptiles. Since we do not recommend the dehydration of raw eggs—or reptiles—the risk is reduced. The bacterium is not destroyed by freezing, and requires high temperatures to kill it. Luckily, the temperatures used in the dehydration of jerky (155° to 160°F) are sufficient to destroy the organism. For added safety, make sure to wash your hands and utensils prior to dehydrating, and make sure your chicken is dehydrated thoroughly.

Clostridium botulinum: Although botulism is rare these days in the U.S., it is important to include on this list because of its history with food canning, and because it is especially dangerous. This organism is waterborne, and many of its outbreaks have been attributed to home canning. Home canning uses hot liquids to store food long term. If done improperly, or if a seal breaks, this bacterium can infect the food items once they cool. As it grows, *C. botulinum* produces a neurotoxin that causes paralysis, resulting in respiratory and other problems. The growth of *C. botulinum* is abruptly halted by removing moisture from foods, and therefore has not been an issue in home dehydration. *C. botulinum* also cannot grow in honey due to its viscous state and lack of water. Although it cannot replicate, the toxin/spores of botulinum *can* be found in honey in small amounts. These small amounts are only dangerous to infants, and therefore it is not recommended to feed honey to infants less than one year old. It is important to note that the association of botulism with canning is mostly a historic one, and that recent data from the CDC shows that home canning–associated botulism cases are now very rare.

Bacteria in Infused Oils

If you have made infused oils at home using fresh herbs, flowers, fruits, or vegetables, you know that they go rancid quickly. In fact, it is recommended that you keep these infused oils for only about one week *in the refrigerator.* Why is that? Oil, like honey, is a viscous solution, a difficult environment for bacteria to inhabit, as they need water and many also require oxygen. However, when you add fresh ingredients to oil, you are also adding water. These leaves, flowers, or bits of fruit or vegetables provide small pockets of moisture ideal for bacterial growth.

If, however, you infuse your oils with properly dehydrated ingredients, you eliminate this problem entirely. Infused oils made with dehydrated items will last up to ten times longer than those prepared with fresh ingredients, and are equally delicious! For more on making infused oils with dehydrated ingredients, see page 170.

As you can see, the common bacterial causes of food illness are not a significant cause for concern with food dehydration. The risk of this kind of contamination in properly dehydrated foods is extremely low, and significantly lower than canning and freezing, making it the safest food storage method of the three. In fact, the highest risk for contamination of your dehydrated foods is insects! To prevent an infestation, simply make sure all of your food items are in sealed vacuum bags, Mylar bags, or tightly sealed buckets, and that your storage bags are not punctured.

However, home dehydration does pose a risk in regards to milk and eggs, as salmonella and staphylococcus can grow in these items quickly, even during the dehydration process. Because of this, we do not recommend trying to home dehydrate milk or uncooked eggs. If you wish to store them long term, purchase commercially prepared powdered milk and powdered eggs.

GENERAL SANITATION

Although the risk of foodborne illness resulting from dehydrated foods is extremely low, it is important to always practice proper hygiene and sterile technique to avoid the introduction of any contamination. Sterile technique is simple. Wash all items with soap and water, or rinse with water before dehydrating. Make sure all kitchen surfaces and utensils are clean. Wearing latex or vinyl gloves will also help prevent the introduction of oils from your hands into your foods.

GOOD BACTERIA

As you may know, a lot of bacteria are good! Our body is filled with a vibrant landscape of bacteria that we call our "normal flora." These bacteria are important for the production of compounds we need for food digestion. This population is so abundant, in fact, that we contain more bacterial cells in our body than human cells! Spooky!

Furthermore, small exposures to bacteria and viruses throughout our lives help to build up a strong and responsive immune system, and even reduce the occurrence of immune hyper-reactive processes such as asthma.

With the recent emphasis on probiotics in the media, we have been asked, since food dehydration kills or causes many bacteria to go dormant, will consumption of dehydrated foods interfere, reduce, or kill this normal flora, making us ill and prone to infection? The answer, of course, is no.

The vast majority of our flora is established when we are very young. Our floral changes throughout life are minimal, and the relationship between diet and floral changes is not fully understood. The different *types* of bacteria in our flora change, although the abundance is always high. Natural exposures to bacteria in our daily lives—in our water, on surfaces, in the air, etc.—serve as immune and floral support.

Our flora is typically only radically changed as a result of more extreme medical interventions, such as certain medications, chemotherapy and radiation therapy, and gastrointestinal surgery. Your physician may recommend ways to supplement this bacterial loss, but likely your flora will simply repopulate itself on its own from regular daily exposures.

In summary, some good bacteria will be lost from food during dehydration, but even a diet consisting solely of dehydrated foods is not likely to disrupt your normal flora.

SAFE REHYDRATION

Since you are reintroducing water during rehydration, you can potentially create an environment where new bacteria, or dormant bacteria, can grow (just like if you left wet food in the open). Studies show that if you rehydrate foods for 30 minutes or less at room temperature, the risk of harmful levels of bacterial growth is essentially absent. Rehydrating while heating for longer periods (such as when making soups) is also safe since high temperatures hinder bacterial growth. Similarly, rehydrating in the refrigerator (see page 25 for more information on this), which may take up to 24 hours, is also fine since the lower temperature slows or halts bacterial growth. In summary, you should never rehydrate in room-temperature water on the countertop for more than a half hour. If the item is expected to take longer than 30 minutes to rehydrate, put it in the refrigerator to rehydrate, or use boiling water.

Congratulations on completing the course! You are now an expert in the science of food dehydration, and on your way to building a delicious pantry of food that can sustain you, your family, and your friends for years to come.

2

Your Dehydrator Toolbox

It is often said that a carpenter is only as good as his tools, and this saying holds true for home dehydration as well. In this chapter we'll cover what to look for in a dehydrator that will serve your particular needs, as well as the other tools, utensils, and equipment that will make the process easier, more time efficient, and help yield the best possible results.

THE DEHYDRATOR

A commercially produced electric dehydrator for home use (which is what I recommend and use) is a small cube- or cylinder-shaped container, usually constructed from metal and sturdy plastic. They range in size somewhat but typically are about the size of a microwave. If you were to take apart your dehydrator, you would find that it contains very few parts, primary of which are shelves, typically mesh-lined, for the food; a fan; and a convection heating unit of some sort, usually heated coils. The concept is simple: the dehydrator maintains a low but consistent heat through these coils, and uses the fan to distribute that heat evenly to your foods. Dehydration is accomplished through low heat and long drying times, as opposed to an oven, whose higher temperatures result in food being cooked instead of dried.

Because there are so few parts, you need to pay special attention to each one when you go shopping for a dehydrator, as well as a few other features.

Size: Dehydrator size is determined by the number of trays it contains, typically ranging from four trays up to nine or more. Economically, the smart choice would be to purchase the largest model. The

DEHYDRATING AND YOUR OVEN

Some people try to dehydrate using their home oven, and some models even have a "dehydrate" feature built in. I do not recommend either of these. Conventional and convection ovens do not offer adequate airflow, and the lowest temperature setting is typically around 150°F; far too high for dehydrating most items. A dehydrator is one of the few absolutely necessary tools for safe, effective, and efficient home dehydration.

purchase price will be more, but if you become a dehydrator enthusiast, I guarantee you will kick yourself if you don't opt for the largest size available from the start. Suffice to say, I own three 9-tray dehydrators that I run at the same time, and all of the time.

The fan: Placement of the fan on your dehydrator is key to proper dehydration. The fan should be affixed to the back wall of the dehydrator; this arrangement will create an even airflow that pushes horizontally across each shelf of food, expelling the moisture it picks up from the food out the front and sides of the dehydrator. Some dehydrators, typically the cylindrical ones, have the fan on the bottom or top of the device. This forces air through each layer of food *vertically*, creating poor air circulation since the air is impeded by the food it is supposed to be drying. As a result, foods closest to the fan will dry first, while those farther away remain moist. As such, you will have to rotate your trays periodically to ensure even drying. This problem is eliminated by placing the fan in the back (this feature is most typically available in cube-shaped models)

Trays/shelving: Dehydrators typically contain multiple removable trays, which come in two basic styles. The frame of the tray may be either plastic or metal, and does not make a difference. The top of the tray, which is where you will place your food, may also be metal, often shot through with numerous small holes, or a plastic mesh. Trays with plastic mesh tops are a far better choice; metal tray tops will retain heat, which can burn the bottom of your food. I recommend you purchase a model with plastic mesh tray tops that are removable and flexible, not permanently attached to the tray framework. This will make for easy removal and cleaning of your trays. Additionally, if the mesh tray tops are flexible, you can bend them to fit into your sinks for soaking and cleaning. You will find, also, that the ability to bend and contort your plastic mesh tray tops will make the removal of dried foods from the trays easier.

Temperature control: All food dehydrators should have a temperature control. I have received thousands upon thousands of emails from people with questions and concerns regarding their dehydrators. To my horror, many people have purchased dehydrators without a temperature control. As sad as it is to say, my only response is to "toss it in the garbage!" Different foods require different temperatures to be dehydrated properly; if you can't precisely control the temperature in the dehydrator, you can't dehydrate effectively or safely. To get maximum use from your dehydrator, look for one that will go as low as 90° and as high as 150°F (if you want to be able to make jerky).

Timer: I find this to be a completely unnecessary feature that only serves to up the price of the dehydrator. You never want your dehydrator to shut off after a specified time because once the dehydrator turns off, your food will immediately begin to reabsorb moisture from the air. Remember, you can under-dehydrate, but you cannot over-dehydrate!

As you can see, there are numerous methods to dehydrate food at home. However, it is imperative that your food be dehydrated efficiently and properly for a finished product that is not only delicious, but also safe. The best way to do this is with a commercially produced electric dehydrator capable of heat control and even air circulation.

OTHER USEFUL EQUIPMENT AND SUPPLIES

Buying a quality dehydrator suited to your needs is of primary importance, but there are a number of tools and products that can help increase your efficiency and the quality of your dehydrated food.

Apple peeler: This item will help you peel, core, and evenly slice an entire apple in just seconds. With most models, you can easily remove the corer and use it to peel potatoes as well. Various models allow you to stabilize the device during use with either suction cups or a clamp. Keep in mind that a clamp, though a sturdy option, may scratch some surfaces. Slicing evenly is important for even drying, and speed and efficiency will make you a dehydrating master. For these reasons, an apple peeler is an amazing tool to have!

Ascorbic acid/lemon juice: Ascorbic acid is another name for vitamin C. Many food items require pre-treatment with a vitamin C-based item prior to dehydrating to prevent browning. Ascorbic acid can be purchased as a powder and then dissolved in water to use as a soak or spray. Be sure you follow the manufacturer's directions for using ascorbic acid, as using too much can burn your food. Alternatively, which I prefer, you can simply use lemon or another citrus juice to spritz those items requiring vitamin C pre-treatment.

Bean frencher: If a recipe calls for frenched beans you will need this device, which will cut the beans into thin strips from top to tail. Simply feed the green beans through the frencher, either one by one or using the faster hand-crank models.

Blender: You will need a blender if you want to make fruit leathers, baby foods, and breadcrumbs, or to turn your dehydrated food into powders or sugars.

Cherry pitter: These come in all sizes and prices. A small hand-held pitter will pit one cherry at a time, while a larger one will pit a handful all at once while turning a handle or lever. It beats cutting the pits out one by one with a knife.

Disposable latex or vinyl gloves: It is important to wear disposable gloves when handling dried food in order to prevent the transfer of oil or moisture from your hands to the food, which can end up resulting in spoilage. If you choose not to wear gloves, make sure any hand lotions are thoroughly washed away, and your hands are completely dry prior to handling your food.

Drying sheets: Use these reusable or disposable sheets of silicone, Teflon, or other nonstick material to line your drying trays when you are dehydrating very small items that might fall through mesh trays, or sauces, purees, or fruit leathers. These can be purchased online. Alternatively, you can use a nonstick oven liner trimmed to the size of your dehydrator tray. Parchment paper also works but because it's lightweight, it may get blown around by the fan in the dehydrator. You can secure the paper by weighing down the corners with medium-sized flat stones.

Food processor: This is great when you need to grate carrots, zucchini, or potatoes, or slice and chop fruit and vegetables to the same size and thickness.

Kitchen scissors: Once your food has been dehydrated, it is far easier and safer for your fingers to cut it with scissors than a knife.

Meat slicer: This tool is not just for meats! You have the ability to select a desired thickness, and quickly and evenly slice meats, fruits, or vegetables. If you make our signature Crazy Fruits (page 27) or fruit and vegetable chips they must be cut very thin, and this is most easily done with a meat slicer. A mandoline is another good choice for slicing vegetables and fruits very thinly.

Rolling pin: This is a useful tool when preparing pumpkin, squash, and sweet potatoes for dehydration. After cooking these items (see their individual entries for particulars), reduce them to a puree, cover with a sheet of parchment paper, and then spread them over the drying sheets using a rolling pin before dehydrating.

Spray bottle: Many food items need to be soaked or sprayed with lemon juice or a solution of ascorbic acid prior to dehydration to prevent browning. Spraying is less messy and generates less waste than soaking, and a food-grade spray bottle makes doing this a snap.

Squeeze bottles: These come in handy when making leathers (see Chapter 6). Fill the bottles with the purees and you can squeeze the puree directly onto drying sheets, mixing different purees together in colorful designs. Be sure to buy food-grade bottles.

Stainless steel knives: When dehydrating, all knives and all cutting tools should be stainless steel. Using a utensil that is not stainless steel could discolor some items.

Tea infuser, sealable tea bags, and tea press: Dehydrated herbs, flowers, and fruit ground into tea make fabulous gifts. *Sealable tea bags* come in multiple sizes and are easily filled and sealed with an iron, vacuum sealer, clam sealer, or even a curling iron. I recommend larger tea bags because they are easier to fill. *Tea infusers* come in many different styles, from a small round ball that you fill for one serving at a time, to a small teapot for many servings. A *tea press* is a small cylindrical container with a plunger/strainer that is used after steeping to push herbs to the bottom of the container. These are fast and easy to fill with your dehydrated herb mixtures.

3

Dehydration 101

I n this chapter we will cover everything you need to know about dehydrating. We'll guide you step by step through the process so you can achieve the best possible end product.

SETTING UP THE DEHYDRATOR

Always preheat your dehydrator. This should be done about 15 minute before filling. Depending on how much you will be dehydrating, you can turn it on, then do your food prep while it preheats.

If you'll be dehydrating items that have been minced, grated, or chopped into tiny pieces that may fall through the holes of the dehydrator trays, fit the trays with drying sheets. You should also use drying sheets when dehydrating purees or anything that might drip. When making jerky with a jerky gun (in which the meat is like a ground beef, hamburger texture with brine mixed in) using a drying sheet will make it easy to remove and provides a non-textured surface, resulting in a smooth jerky.

FOOD PREP

When cutting and prepping your food before dehydration, think about how you plan on using that item. In my pantry, for example, I keep dehydrated sliced carrots, shredded carrots, chopped carrots, and whole baby carrots, so that I am ready for whatever a particular recipe may call for. Think about doing this as a time-saving measure for the food items you use most frequently in cooking. The exceptions, though, are herbs and garlic. To preserve the best flavor, dehydrate

AVERAGE DEHYDRATING TEMPERATURES

- 90°–110°F for herbs
- 125°F for fruits and vegetables
- 155°–160°F for meats

13

INVEST IN DISPOSABLE GLOVES

Disposable vinyl or latex gloves are indispensable:

1. If working bare-handed, the lotions, moisture, and natural oils on your skin can quickly be absorbed by your dehydrated foods.
2. Peter Pepper prepped a pack of pickled peppers for preserving without proper protection, and suffered second-degree burns on his hands.
3. Many different fruits and vegetables will stain your fingers and nails unflattering colors.
4. Lemon juice is used frequently to prep dehydrated foods. If you have a cut, lemon juice is the last thing you want coming into contact with it.
5. Rinsing, scrubbing, and prepping produce without gloves can turn your hands to sandpaper.

herb leaves whole and garlic in slices, and then crush, chop, or mince when needed.

There are many fruits and vegetables that discolor once cut and exposed to air. To prevent this, they should be sprayed with lemon juice or an ascorbic acid solution as soon as possible after being cut. It also gives them a welcome shot of vitamin C. In the individual produce entries, I specifically indicate which can benefit from this application. Take note that leafy greens, herbs, and broccoli should never be sprayed in this way—the acid will turn them brown.

I highly recommend that you use only stainless steel knives when cutting. Certain foods, like bananas, will discolor if you use anything but stainless steel to slice them. The food is still good to eat, just less appetizing looking.

Tips to Save Nutrients and Reduce Your Workload

We know that dehydration is the best method of food preservation when it comes to retaining nutrients. Here are some steps you can take for even better nutrient retention, as well as saving yourself some work.

- Leaving the skin and stem on while steaming, blanching, boiling, or baking fruits or vegetables headed to the dehydrator will help to hold in nutrients that would otherwise leak out. It will also make the skin softer and easier to remove. For example, carefully place an entire pumpkin in a large pot of boiling water, stem and all. Cover and cook until tender, then remove and place in a sink filled with ice water to cool. Now marvel as the pumpkin casing simply cracks off or peels away with ease, revealing a beautifully soft and vibrant sphere, most all of its nutrients left intact.
- Cherries and grapes can go into a pot with their stems, which act as little plugs, holding the nutrient-rich juices inside. Make sure to cool fully before removing the stems.
- Some produce that will be dehydrated raw, such as herbs and greens, can be dehydrated whole, then chopped or crushed after drying. Doing this will retain nutrients as well as flavor.

ITEM PLACEMENT IN THE DEHYDRATOR

When placing items on the dehydrator trays, it is typically okay to pile on the smaller items like peas, beans, corn kernels, or smaller chopped items such as carrots or celery, or herbs and leafy items like spinach. The rule typically is, if it is sliced, it should not overlap but for anything else it is usually okay. The reason you would not want to overlap your sliced items is so they do not become fused together. The exception to this rule is when you are making our Crazy Fruits (page 27), where the goal is for the items to become fused.

It's fine to dehydrate different vegetables and fruit in the same dehydrating load even if their dehydrating times are not the same—you can always remove items from a load that have completely dehydrated. However, you do not want to add undehydrated items to a partially dehydrated load. The moisture from the newly introduced items will add humidity, causing the other items to absorb that moisture and extending the total time needed for complete dehydration.

When mixing different items in your dehydrator, it is a good idea to place juicier items (unless they can be placed skin side down) on the lower racks and less juicy items on the higher racks in case of dripping. For example, if you place a tray of beets above a tray of white potatoes, you could end up with purple polka-dotted potatoes. Mushrooms can get discolored in the same way. With fruits, it's the blueberry that needs to be placed on the lowest trays, and raspberries and blackberries should go on the top rack when mixed with other items that could drip. The reason for this is that drippings can cause blackberries to deflate, leaving you with a deformed berry.

DRYING TIMES

For every food we cover in this book, we provide an approximate time needed to dehydrate the item; note the word "approximate." Because so many variables can affect the drying time, these times can and will vary. Here are the factors that can affect drying times:

Region and variety: All tomatoes (and other produce) are not created equal. There are literally hundreds of varieties of tomatoes, each with distinguishing characteristics of color, texture, and flavor. Some are better used in sauce, some for eating fresh, some are lower in acid, some are better for long-term storage. All of these traits can impact precisely how long it might take to dehydrate a particular tomato. Now layer on top of that the impact of where precisely your tomato was grown and when it was harvested. If you're only dehydrating produce coming from your own garden or a local CSA, this won't be an issue for you. But if you're buying in bulk from the supermarket, or you frequent different farmers' markets, you may notice a difference in the time it takes to dehydrate, say, a Brandywine tomato you bought at a local produce stand versus one from a larger supermarket that is having the tomatoes shipped in from another area.

Age of the item: Over time, enzymes break down the starch in fruits into simple sugars. Unlike starch, these sugars are water soluble, and therefore attract water, making the fruit larger (if vine-ripened), softer, and juicier. This higher sugar and water content can increase the item's drying time.

ODOR CONTROL

Using your dehydrator is like having a wonderful scented air freshener, filling your home with enticing aromas of different fruits, herbs, and flowers.

I have dehydrated many different items at once and have never had the scents transfer from one item to another. When the fan is located at the back of the dehydrator, it pushes the air across the food and out the front.

The one exception to this are onions. If you dehydrate raw onions with other food items, a slight onion smell and taste can transfer. You can avoid this by dehydrating onions on their own or blanching them before dehydration (the latter will also speed the drying process). Be aware that filling your entire dehydrator with raw onions can be a tearful event. In such a case, I would strongly recommend that you place your dehydrator in the garage or enclosed porch on a dry day.

THE 5 GOLDEN RULES OF DEHYDRATING

1. **A Carpenter is Only as Good as His Tools**
   Having a good-quality dehydrator is the key to dehydrating success. Choose one with a reputation for durability and a design that facilitates even, uninterrupted airflow.

2. **Say No to the Timer**
   Some dehydrators offer a timer as a feature. To that I say, "Just say no." Even if your dehydrator has a timer, do not use it. A steady and constant airflow is good for your dehydrated foods; it moves moisture out and away from your food. The timer will automatically shut off your machine while you are away, allowing moisture from the air to seep back in. This moisture creates a fertile environment for bacteria and will result in the spoilage of your food.

3. **Start Me Up Before You Go Go.**
   Start your dehydrator while you are preparing your food so it can reach the desired drying temperature prior to placing the food inside. Once you wash, cut, and prep your food, place it immediately in the dehydrator; don't let it sit out at room temperature for any length of time.

4. **When in Doubt, Keep Drying It Out!**
   It is not possible to overdry your food. If you are at all uncertain, keep going, even if you are beyond our recommended drying time.

5. **You Cannot Overdry!**
   I promise that no matter how long you dry your food, it will not turn to dust. Under-drying is your enemy, and will leave your food prone to molding and spoilage.

How the item is cut: Whether your food item is sliced, grated, cubed, or not cut at all will affect drying time. Typically, thinly sliced or shredded items dry the quickest, while cubed or chunked items take longer.

How the item was prepped: Some items should be blanched prior to dehydrating, while others are dehydrated raw. Blanched items will take less time to dehydrate than raw.

Density of the food on the drying rack and in the dehydrator: Are you using all the dehydrator trays? Are they fully loaded or partially loaded? The more items in the dehydrator, the longer it will take to thoroughly dehydrate them.

Type of dehydrator: Using a dehydrator with a back-mounted fan (see page 10) will significantly reduce your drying time. Dehydrators with a floor- or top-mounted fan will take longer to dry the same food, and may require periodic tray rotation for faster and more even drying.

Humidity level: If it's a humid day (regardless of the temperature), it will take slightly longer for your dehydrator to do its job.

Average Dehydrating Times

This list will give you a sense, in the most general way, of approximate drying times for different categories of food. We provide drying times and temperatures throughout the book for specific items.

- **8–10 hours:** Frozen vegetables (placed directly onto trays while frozen)
- **8–10 hours:** Mushrooms and onions (sliced or chopped)
- **8–15 hours:** All fresh vegetables, excluding potatoes or sweet potatoes and yams
- **12–15 hours:** Sweet and white potatoes (thinly sliced or chopped)
- **12–15 hours:** Fruits, cut into ¼-inch slices or ½-inch cubes
- **15+ hours:** Fruit leathers
- **15–24 hours:** Grapes
- **18–24 hours:** Blueberries, raspberries, whole cranberries
- **24–36 hours:** Chopped dried dates for date sugar

APPROXIMATE WEIGHT CONVERSION CHART

The amount of water lost in dehydration is pretty amazing. Check out the chart below for some examples of fresh vs. dehydrated weight.

Produce	Weight Fresh (lbs.)	Weight Dehydrated (lbs.)
Apples	20	6.5
Beans	20	3
Carrots	20	3
Cherries	20	7
Corn	20	6
Onions	20	3
Peaches	20	6.5
Pears	20	6.5
Peas	20	5
Prunes	20	7.5
Squash	20	2

WHEN IN DOUBT . . .

If you are uncertain if something is completely dry, place the item in question in a ziptop plastic bag for a day or so, making sure the bag is completely sealed. If it's completely dried, it will still be paper-dry or brittle when you check back on it. If it has become sticky and wet, place it back in the dehydrator.

HOW DO YOU KNOW IT'S DEHYDRATED?

All food must be dry, dry, dry. I cannot stress this enough. It may take some practice and experience to know when your items are completely dehydrated. In general, a properly dried item will not feel sticky or tacky to the touch, and there should be no sign of moisture. Many items should also have an audible snap or crumble when broken if properly dehydrated, but some will simply be bendable and feel dry to the touch. Lower-sugar items (like raw onions or raw papaya slices), in general, will be bendable and tear easily like paper, while those higher in sugar (figs, dates, and apricots, for instance) are also bendable but difficult to tear. In contrast, some smaller high-sugar items,

NEVER, EVER, EVER:

- Never use granulated sugar in blended items such as fruit leathers. The sugar will crystallize over time. Instead, use honey or corn syrup.
- Lemon juice is great for prepping many items. However, do not spray lemon juice on broccoli, leafy greens, or herbs prior to dehydrating. The acid will turn them brown.

like grapes and cherries, will be hard and unbending and make a clicking sound when dropped on the counter. When a handful of these items are squeezed, they should not clump together. Properly dried food items should pop and peel off the dehydrator trays with ease. If you are pulling and prying at your food only to leave pieces stuck behind, it is not dehydrated and should be placed back in the dehydrator.

In each of the individual ingredient entries and throughout the book, we describe how particular items should look, feel, and/or sound when properly dehydrated.

TIPS TO HELP SPEED UP THE DEHYDRATING PROCESS

Dehydrating isn't something you can rush. However, there are a few things you can do to help the process along while maintaining a good end product, if you like.

- When dehydrating fruits with a high sugar content, such as apricots, blueberries, dates, grapes, or cherries, or overripe items, remove the items from the trays when they are almost dry (about three-quarters of the way through the dehydrating process), transfer them to a clean, dry tray, and place them back in the dehydrator.
- If you have a lot of small items such as corn kernels, blueberries, etc., stir them up and move them around a little on the trays halfway through the drying time.
- If you have a humidifier running, turn it off while dehydrating.
- Refrain from canning or boiling large pots of water while dehydrating.
- If it is hot and humid outside, run the air-conditioning or turn on ceiling fans.
- If your dehydrator is completely full with fruits and/or vegetables, kick the temperature up to 135°F for 1 to 2 hours only, then back it down to 125°F.

STORAGE

Properly dehydrated foods can last for years! To maximize shelf life, you must provide your foods with the best possible environment for storage.

There are six environmental enemies of food storage. If you can eliminate them or minimize your food's exposure to them, you will maximize shelf life.

1. Moisture: Moisture creates a playground for bacteria and mold in food. For that reason, you want to make sure that your items are completely dehydrated, meaning that 95% or more of their moisture has been removed. While we can't measure the actual degree of dehydration at home, if you follow the visual, touch, and sound tests we've given you, you can be confident in your own evaluation of each item. And remember Golden Rule #5: You Cannot Overdry. When in doubt, keep drying it out. We promise your food will not turn to dust!

Once the moisture is removed, the next task is to keep away the moisture. There is moisture everywhere, even in the air and on our skin. When we touch our dehydrated foods, they will suck that moisture up instantly, along with the oils on our hands. For these reasons I recommend not leaving your dehydrated items out in the open for extended periods and wearing gloves whenever handling your dehydrated foods, if you intend to put them back into storage.

2. Heat: Exposure to even slightly elevated heat over weeks or months can destroy many of the nutrients in your food! It is recommended that you store your food in a cool, dry place, such as a dry basement. The temperature at which you store your food can not only change its taste, color, and nutritional value, but it can also affect shelf life. A temperature increase of just 10 degrees can take a year off the shelf life of your food.

3. Oxygen: Oxygen is a natural, and powerful, degrading agent. It is involved in a process called oxidation, which alters the chemical structure of items, from sliced apples (browning) to sheets of iron metal (rusting). In food, this alteration will result in a loss of nutrients over time, as well as changing the taste and appearance of the food. Eliminating exposure to oxygen as much as possible when storing dehydrated food will prevent or minimize such degradation; it will also prevent some species of bacteria from growing. To that end, wherever possible vacuum seal your food in heavy-duty vacuum bags. Items that are especially fragile, such as large collard leaves and large eggplant slices, should not be vacuum sealed if you wish to keep them whole, as the vacuum process will break them into pieces. For these items, store in airtight containers with an oxygen pack, which will remove any residual oxygen that may be present. For short-term storage, you can also use glass jars, but don't forget to add an oxygen pack.

4. Microorganisms: Some types of bacteria, mold, and fungi can be harmful to humans, while others contribute to the degradation and decay of food. Practicing sanitary technique in the kitchen prevents the addition of bacteria, and pretreating foods with lemon juice or blanching them in boiling water prior to dehydration removes bacteria as well. The gentle heat of dehydration kills other microorganisms, while removing oxygen through vacuum sealing prevents others from growing. However, the greatest aid to prevention is the removal of moisture. Without moisture, most microorganisms will die, or will stop growing.

5 STEPS TO SUCCESSFUL STORAGE*

1. Let the food cool for about 3 minutes after being dehydrated.
2. Place the food in ziptop plastic bags or canning jars and seal.
3. Check the items in the next day or two for dryness; if they are not completely dry, toss them back into the dehydrator until dry.
4. When assured that the items are completely dry, place into canning jars with oxygen packs or vacuum seal with an oxygen pack, then double-bag in Mylar bags and heat seal.
5. Label everything with the contents and the date dehydrated.

*This does not include jerky; see page 117 for storage instructions.

5. Light: The energy in light has the ability to alter the chemical structure of many compounds, thus changing the nutritional value and appearance of your foods in a very short period of time. Certain nutrients, such as vitamins A, C, and E, are especially impacted by exposure to light. Double-bagging your vacuum-sealed long-term storage items inside Mylar bags is an effective way to block light, as Mylar is a light- and heat-reflective material.

6. Other pests: Always keep in mind that you're not the only living thing that likes to eat! Rodents and insects can get into your food if it is not stored properly. To prevent this, use good-quality heavy-duty plastic bags or buckets to store your food. Mylar bags are especially tough, impervious to tears even from the hungriest scavenger.

Storage Supplies

For proper storage, you need the proper equipment and supplies.

Weight scale: If you choose to measure your prepackaged dehydrated items by weight instead of volume, this will be a needed item.

Disposable latex or vinyl gloves: It is important to wear disposable gloves when handling dried food for storage in order to prevent the transfer of oil or moisture from your hands to the food, which can end up resulting in spoilage.

Canning jars with lids: Traveling back and forth to Pennsylvania, I would frequently stop at estate sales. One thing I always had my eye out for were Ball Heritage Blue jars.

In Buffalo, New York, around 1885, the Ball brothers started a canning jar business. In 1890, Ball Jar Company purchased sand from Lake Michigan for their glass. Because of the minerals in the sand and the amount of oxygen that was in the furnace, the glass turned blue.

So what does any of this have to do with dehydrated foods?

Over time light breaks down the nutrients in our food, limiting its shelf life. Being conscientious about keeping light, heat, moisture, and oxygen away from dehydrated items can preserve its quality and extend shelf life. The Ball Heritage Blue jars do not keep all light out, but because of the darker glass they do reflect back much of it.

Because of my Buffalo roots, I am quite partial to the Ball brand jars, but other brands, such as Mason, work just the same. Whatever the brand, it is ideal to use a tinted glass, if available, especially if storing food for longer periods of time.

Make sure to flip your lid: New Ball jar lids will fit most of the Ball Blue jars, so if using old jars be sure to purchase new lids to ensure a good airtight seal. The new lids, however, will not properly fit jars made from 1890 to 1910, but if you do come across those they are worth some money, so don't toss them out! Ball Brothers only made these blue jars from 1890 to 1937, and in 1975–77 they made a limited bicentennial production run. Every so often, Ball will release a limited edition blue jar. They are more expensive than their clear counterparts, but cheaper than the vintage ones.

Plastic buckets and other containers: Plastic 5-gallon buckets with lids make food storage easy. Dehydrated food is practically weightless. After filling a bucket, you can literally lift it with one finger, and stack one on top of another.

Bakeries and donut shops ship their frostings and fillings in 5-gallon buckets, and throw them away when finished. In most cases, if you ask a manager to put these empty buckets aside they will. Simply wash the bucket thoroughly with hot water and dish soap, and dry completely before using.

Make sure all plastic containers that come in contact with your foods are food safe. Containers that are not food safe can leach chemicals, plastics, and dyes into your food when stored long term. A general way to determine if a container is food safe (or "food grade") is to look on the container for the recycling symbol (three arrows in a triangle with a number in the center). In general, numbers 1, 2, 4, and 5 are food safe, as well as some containers with the number 7. To be extra certain that your container is food grade, you can check the price tag/label, which will often state "food grade," or you can contact the manufacturer. The container should also be opaque to deter light. Here is another good rule: If you can see through it, light can get to it. The containers must also have an airtight rubber seal.

Bucket opener: A bucket opener looks like a large plastic wrench and is used to remove the lids from plastic storage buckets with ease. No more breaking nails with this handy tool!

Ziptop plastic freezer bags: Good quality plastic ziptop bags are a necessity when dehydrating. Because dehydrated foods can have sharp edges, opt for the heavier plastic of the freezer-style bags for better protection against punctures. Although I do not recommend them for long-term food storage, they work great for short-term storage of dehydrated items. Keep plenty on hand.

Vacuum sealer and bags: If you decide to become a serious pantry packer, you will want to invest in a quality vacuum sealer. A vacuum sealer, along with specialized vacuum bags, stores your food items in an air-free environment, while also packing the items into a smaller volume. This increases food shelf life and allows for more compact storage. A vacuum sealer is great for use with dehydrated foods, refrigerated fresh foods, and frozen foods.

It's also great for preserving many nonfood items that you want to protect from water or moisture like medications, soaps, important papers, blankets, or matches. You can even use it to make handy mini emergency packs for your backpack or purse.

I recommend purchasing a high-quality and durable vacuum sealer with dual (or double piston) suction motors, instead of brands

AVERAGE SHELF LIFE

When stored properly, fruits, vegetables, and herbs can be stored between 5 and 20 years.

that have only one suction motor. Dual motors provide powerful suction, with no need for a cool-down time between sealing.

No matter what kind of vacuum sealer you have, your vacuum bags must be at least 2 ply and 3 millimeters (mil) in thickness. Do not settle for a cheaper product. Even if you are using the most expensive vacuum sealer on the market, if you are using low-quality bags, your storage efforts will be futile. Bags of poor quality do not allow for complete air removal, frequently leak, and easily puncture. If you find your bags do leak, suspect the bags before the sealer. I recommend channeled (aka embossed, textured, or microchannel) bags of 3 mil or higher thickness. "Channeled" bags contain grooves that allow for streamlined air removal and a tighter seal.

Mylar bags: These silver bags are made of smooth, durable Mylar material. Their purpose is to reflect heat and light away from the food. By reducing heat and eliminating light, two powerful food-degrading agents, you extend the shelf life of your dehydrated product. Mylar bags also serve as a tough durable outer jacket for vacuum-sealed food, protecting against puncture from external objects or rodents. Mylar bags cannot be vacuum-sealed directly. You must vacuum seal your food in a vacuum bag, and then double-bag it in a Mylar bag, which will then be heat sealed to close (an iron works fine). They are also reusable, making them very effective.

Oxygen absorbers/packs: Oxygen is one of the four agents that you need to keep away from your dehydrated food in order to maintain a long shelf life. I recommend placing oxygen absorbers (aka oxygen packs) in any glass jars or buckets containing dehydrated foods. As the oxygen absorber removes the oxygen from the glass jar you will hear the lid pop down the same way it would with canning. Each time you open the jar you should hear a suction release. When you no longer hear this, it is time to replace the oxygen pack.

Although vacuum sealing removes most of the air from vacuum bags, a small amount of residual oxygen will be present around the creases and crevices of your foods. Placing an oxygen pack in your vacuum bag will remove this oxygen, and further protect and preserve your dehydrated items. Oxygen absorbers are safe and will not cause harm to you or your dehydrated foods.

Oxygen packs are made for use with dry foods and should not be used in liquids. Because the absorbers remove oxygen, you should not let children play with them.

Oxygen packs come in different sizes:

- A 12- to 24-ounce jar with a lid requires one 100 cc pack.
- A 1-gallon Mylar bag or vacuum bag requires one 100 cc pack.
- A 5-gallon bucket will need one 2,000 cc pack. An oxygen pack should not be placed directly in a bucket; it will cause the bucket to collapse. Rather, put your food in a 5-gallon Mylar

bag, insert the oxygen pack, heat-seal the bag, then place it in the bucket.

Desiccant packs: A desiccant pack is different from an oxygen pack in that it removes moisture from containers. Desiccant packs are typically made from silica gel and/or other materials and chemicals. As such, it is important that you make sure the packs are FDA approved for contact with foods and medications prior to use. However, if you follow proper dehydration techniques, placing a desiccant pack in with your food should not be necessary. However, you may wish to use these inside large containers, especially if they are permeable, if you are storing the items in a humid or moist location.

Labels: All items should be labeled and dated. Mylar bags are not transparent, and it is important to keep track of what each bag contains and how long it's been stored. You can write directly on the Mylar; if you do it at the very top of the bags, you can store the bags in a filing cabinet for swift and easy selection. In addition, when you cut the Mylar bag with scissors to open it, you will cut off the old label, so you can reuse and re-label the bag over and over again until it's too small. I recommend stocking items from the back, so that your older items are pushed to the front of your storage shelves for earlier consumption.

Storage Systems

When you start dehydrating, it can seem almost impossible for it to take over your pantry, let alone your home, because it is such a space saver. However, dehydrating can become somewhat addictive. The next thing you know, you're trying to dehydrate anything that is not nailed down! So here are a couple storage tips for when you find yourself knee deep in vacuum-sealed bags of dehydrated food:

- Try using a shelf system. Since dehydrated food is virtually weightless, any kind of shelving unit will handle the load. Just place the bags like you would books on a book shelf. Don't forget to date and label your bags.
- Try using plastic totes. Plastic totes are great because they stack on top of each other and are waterproof, rodent proof, and insect proof. Using these totes also makes it easy to categorize your product. Don't forget to date and label your bags as well as your totes.

WHAT COULD GO WRONG?

Dehydrating is a simple process but you can sometimes run into problems. Here are some common ones, with suggested solutions.

The outside of the food is hard but the inside is still moist: Called *case hardening*, this can occur if the temperature used to dehydrate is too high. The outside of the food quickly hardens, trapping moisture inside. When this happens, the moist food will sour, become rancid over time, and have to be thrown away. Case hardening is most common with potatoes, but can occur in any item. Once dehydrated, potatoes should be translucent in the center. If case hardening has occurred, the center will be more opaque, and over time may even become black. The center may also appear thicker than the rest of the item. If you suspect case hardening, simply snap the item in half and look for moisture inside.

To try to fix case hardening, cut the pieces in half or put a slit in the top of each piece before placing them back in the dehydrator. This will allow the trapped moisture to escape. For sliced potatoes with case hardening, I simply poke them with a sharp knife and put them back in the dehydrator. It is very difficult to rescue small cubes of case-hardened potatoes; in that case, my recommendation would be to cook them up and eat them. Case-hardened items can still be rehydrated, cooked, and eaten, but you do not want to store them long term.

Dehydrated items stored in jars start to feel tacky: This is caused when the lid has been left off for a period of time. Sometimes when using items from jars, we tend to get caught up in our cooking and forget to check that the lids have been properly closed. If it is very humid in the kitchen, the dehydrated items will absorb ambient moisture; it will not be immediately noticeable but rather the tackiness will become apparent a day or two after resealing the jar. As long as you do not see any mold growing, simply toss the items back in the dehydrator for 2 to 3 hours to eliminate the moisture.

Dehydrated white potatoes turn black or gray: This happens when an uncooked or partially cooked potato is dehydrated. As awful as they look, they are safe to eat. For a prettier dehydrated potato, cook it all the way through before dehydrating.

Dehydrated white mushrooms turn black: If the mushrooms you dehydrate are not fresh or have been soaked in water or gotten wet prior to dehydration, they will turn an unattractive grayish-black color. For beautiful white mushrooms, only dehydrate the freshest product and simply wipe them with a damp rag to clean, and no more, before dehydration.

But don't throw out those discolored dehydrated mushrooms. Add them to a soup or stew and no one will notice the color difference.

REHYDRATING

The true wonder of dehydration lies in rehydration. Rehydration brings a dehydrated product, which is often very small, shriveled, and hard or brittle, back to its original large, plump, soft self! When you rehydrate, you are adding back the water you removed in dehydration because you are ready to eat or cook with the ingredient. There are several methods for doing this.

Quick soak: Some items require only a brief dip in boiling water to rehydrate. For example, Dehydrated Apple-Potato Cakes (page 135) need only to be dipped in boiling water for less than 10 seconds before placing them in a hot frying pan to heat through and crisp up. This is also the case with greens like spinach and collard greens.

15-minute soak: Most dehydrated fruits and vegetables require a only a soak of 15 minutes or more in a covered bowl of boiling water to rehydrate prior to their use in a recipe. To save time, this can be done while you prep other parts of the recipe.

Rehydration by refrigeration: This method is great to use when you want your dehydrated ingredients ready to go when you get home from work. Place $1\frac{1}{2}$ cups of a dehydrated sliced item such as beets, apples, peaches, or zucchini in a 24-ounce canning jar. (If using small or chopped items such as peas, corn kernels, or onions, use about $\frac{2}{3}$ cup of the dehydrated item.) For dehydrated vegetables, fill the jar to the top with **boiling** water. For dehydrated fruits, fill to the top with **lukewarm** water, fruit juice, or a spiced water. For the vegetables, after the water cools, place the jar in the refrigerator for 24 hours (put fruit immediately into the fridge). The rehydrated items are a delicious snack right out of the jar. If you rehydrate cucumber spears or chips or other vegetables in brine this way, you will have the easiest pickles ever—crunchy, cold, and ready to eat the next day! See page 291–92 for some of my favorite pickle recipes.

In all of my recipes calling for dehydrated ingredients that require rehydration before being added, I tell you specifically how to rehydrate them.

Now that we have gone over the basics of dehydrating, you are ready to dive right in and start dehydrating. So, what will be your first dehydrated item? In the following chapters we will not only walk you through the step-by-step process of whichever item you choose to dehydrate, but we will also give you plenty of recipes to use your dehydrated items. Now, preheat that dehydrator and let's get started!!

4

Dehydrating Fruits & Nuts, A–Z

SAY NO TO AVOCADO

Because of its very high oil content, the avocado is not recommended for dehydration, as dehydrated avocados will go rancid very quickly.

In this chapter you will find specific guidelines for dehydrating most any fruit you can think of, as well as special drying instructions for nuts and seeds.

In many of the references I have consulted over the years, the recommended temperature for dehydrating fruit is 135°F. My experience, however, is that this temperature is simply too high. I have found that a slightly longer drying time at 125°F is optimal for most fruit. Nuts should be dehydrated at 100°F.

DEHYDRATING FROZEN FRUITS

The same fruit dehydrated will last 10 to 15 times longer than frozen. So if your supermarket is running a great sale on frozen fruits, buy them up—but instead of putting them in the freezer when you get home, crank up the dehydrator.

The beauty of dehydrating frozen fruits is that, pretty much without exception, all the prep work has been done for you. (You'll want to slice frozen whole strawberries before dehydrating them. Run cool water over them for just a few seconds, place on a cutting board, and slice as desired.) Simply open the bag and spread the frozen items onto the dehydrating trays. Dehydration time will depend on the item and the size of the cut. In general, frozen foods will have approximately the same drying time as their fresh counterpart.

DEHYDRATING CANNED FRUITS

Canned fruit can be drained and pureed to make quick fruit leathers (see page 86), minus adding the corn syrup called for in the recipe if the fruit is packed in syrup.

However, I am not a proponent of doing this. Through the canning process, these foods have lost a lot of their nutrients. Also, most canned items contain a large amount of salt, which means, if dehydrated, they will take a lot longer to rehydrate.

Crazy Fruit

The entries that follow address dehydrating a single fruit at a time. Crazy Fruit are thin fruit chips made up of multiple fruits and we love them at our house! To make Crazy Fruit, use a mandoline, meat slicer, or food processor to very thinly and evenly slice the fruits of your choice, then spray them lightly with lemon juice or an ascorbic acid solution. On the dehydrator tray, pile different fruit slices on top of each other, in stacks of two or three. If you like, sprinkle a little colored sugar on top to add more pizzazz! Then dehydrate (use the timing for the fruit that takes the longest); the fruit slices will fuse together, creating a one-of-a-kind treat that the whole family will go "crazy" for!

Here are a few of my favorite combinations to get you started:

- Mango and honeydew melon
- Kiwi and strawberry
- A lengthwise banana slice topped with a thin wedge slice of cantaloupe, sprinkled with chopped maraschino cherries
- Watermelon and apple
- Cucumber and strawberry
- Pineapple and banana, sprinkled with shredded coconut

STORING DEHYDRATED FRUITS AND NUTS

For optimal long-term shelf life, fruits and nuts should be completely dehydrated and stored so as to prevent contact with oxygen, moisture, light, high heat, and insects/rodents. If you are unsure if the item is dehydrated, follow the dryness test provided in every entry for each particular fruit. Once completely dried, most items should be vacuum-sealed in vacuum bags along with an oxygen pack to remove any residual oxygen, and then double-bagged in Mylar to protect them from sunlight, heat, and insects.

APPLES

If you're lucky enough to find yourself with a bushel of apples, consider prepping them for dehydration in multiple ways, according to how you might end up using them. Apple chips make a delicious snack as is. Use dehydrated apple slices in pies and crisps; chopped apples are perfect for use in soups, salads, side dishes, and stuffings; and shredded apples can be added to gelatin, cakes, muffins, pancakes, and much more. If you prefer your apples peeled, you can still make use of that beautiful apple skin; dehydrate the peels, then powder them and use to add to teas or potpourri or to sprinkle on top of muffins. You can even dehydrate whole apples for use as doll heads! And if you love your applesauce, I recommend you make it first, then dehydrate it.

Dehydrating temperature: 125°F

Preparation: Wash with soap and water, especially if you intend to dehydrate the peelings. Have a spray bottle of lemon juice or ascorbic acid solution on hand.

Apple chips: Core and, leaving the peel on, cut across into ⅛-inch-thick slices. Spray lightly with lemon juice and sprinkle with sugar and/or ground cinnamon, cloves, or allspice. Spread evenly on dehydrator trays and dehydrate for 10 hours.

Apple slices: Core, then peel and cut across into ¼-inch-thick slices. Cut the slices in half. Lightly spray with lemon juice, spread evenly on dehydrator trays, and dehydrate 10 to 12 hours.

Chopped or cubed apples: Core, then peel the apples. Working with one apple at a time, place it in a food processor or vegetable chopper and chop or cube. Lightly spray with lemon juice, spread evenly on dehydrator trays, and dehydrate 10 to 12 hours. When dehydrated, chopped or cubed apples develop a hard outer coating and will click when dropped on the counter. They will not stick if squeezed together in your hand.

Shredded apples: Core, then peel the apples. Working with one apple at a time, place it in a food processor and shred. (You can also do this by hand using the largest holes on a box grater.) Lightly spray with lemon juice, spread evenly on dehydrator trays, and dehydrate 10 to 12 hours.

Apple peels: Spray apple peels with lemon juice, pile on dehydrator trays, and dehydrate 10 to 12 hours.

Dryness test: Unless otherwise indicated, the dehydrated product should be brittle, feel dry to the touch, and snap in half easily.

Storage: See Storing Dehydrated Fruit (page 27).

APRICOTS

You can dry apricots with or without their skin—your choice. If you know that you are going to eventually puree the fruit, dehydrating them without their skins makes sense.

Dehydrating temperature: 125°F

Preparation: Have a spray bottle of lemon juice or ascorbic acid solution on hand.

Halved, skin on: Using apricots with the skins on is great for preparing many different dishes. The skins are soft and edible and it is not necessary to remove them. Blanch apricots in a large pot of boiling water for 30 seconds only. Remove from the pot with a slotted spoon or strainer, and place in a bowl full of ice water. Cut apricots in half, remove the kernel, lightly spray with lemon juice, and place on the dehydrator tray skin side down. Dehydrate 12 hours, then, wearing disposable gloves, push each apricot inside out, return it to the tray (skin side down), and dehydrate for another 12 hours.

Halved, peeled: Blanch the apricots in a large pot of boiling water until the skins blister, which should only take about 1 minute. Remove from the pot with a slotted spoon or strainer and place in a bowl full of ice water. Slide the skins off the fruit, and then cut in half and remove the kernel. Spray with lemon juice, arrange spread on dehydrator trays, and dehydrate for 12 hours.

Dryness test: Should feel dry like paper and be flexible.

Storage: See Storing Dehydrated Fruit (page 27). If you want to store your apricots chopped and ready to add straight to a recipe, chop them after dehydration, then add ¼ cup granulated sugar per 1-quart jar and shake; this will keep the small pieces from sticking together.

BANANAS

Tips

- For a crisp banana chip, do not use bananas that are too ripe; I recommend using ones that still have a little green on the peel.
- Bananas will discolor if you don't cut them with a stainless steel knife or blade.
- Make sure not to let the banana slices overlap one another on the dehydrator tray, otherwise they will fuse together.

When prepping bananas for the dehydrator, you can slice them ⅛ inch thick for chips (great for snacking as is, added to granola, or to use to make smoothies or pies) or ¼ inch thick. I like to rehydrate and fry the thicker slices or dip them as is into chocolate.

Dehydrating temperature: 125°F

Preparation: Have a spray bottle of lemon juice or ascorbic acid solution on hand.

Banana chips: Peel the banana and cut across into ⅛-inch-thick slices. Lightly spray with lemon juice, spread on dehydrator trays, and dehydrate for 10 hours.

Banana slices: Peel the banana and cut in half lengthwise. Cut across into ¼-inch-thick slices. Lightly spray with lemon juice, spread on dehydrator trays, and dehydrate for 12 hours.

Dryness test: Should be brittle, feel dry to the touch, and snap in half easily.

Storage: See Storing Dehydrated Fruit (page 27).

BLACKBERRIES & RASPBERRIES

Tip

When dehydrating frozen blackberries or raspberries, line the dehydrator tray with a drying sheet, in case there is bleeding.

Have these on hand to add to yogurt, pies, muffins, and more.

Dehydrating temperature: 125°F

Preparation: If you don't have to rinse your berries off, then don't. If you do need to rinse them, it is important that you *air-dry* them completely before dehydration. You can do this by using a small fan, or your dehydrator set to Cool. If you place wet berries in a hot dehydrator, they will flatten like pancakes. Line the berries up in rows on the dehydrator trays, with the pointed apex of the berry facing up; they will look like rows of little traffic cones. Dehydrate for 18 to 20 hours.

Dryness test: You can easily crush a berry into powder with your fingers.

Storage: See Storing Dehydrated Fruit (page 27).

BLUEBERRIES

Dehydrated blueberries are a wonderful addition to muffins, pancakes, granola, and your morning yogurt.

Dehydrating temperature: 125°F

Preparation: Place the blueberries in a large strainer and dip the strainer into a large pot of boiling water for 30 seconds. Remove and dip the strainer into a large bowl of ice water until the berries cool. Shake to remove as much water as possible. Pour the blueberries onto a rimmed baking sheet and arrange so they are not touching; place in the freezer until frozen, which will take about 2 hours. Arrange the frozen blueberries on dehydrator trays and dehydrate for 12 hours; check your blueberries. Some will appear swollen and plump like small balloons; use a toothpick to prick them, then dehydrate another 12 hours.

Dryness test: Dehydrated blueberries develop a hard outer coating and will click when dropped on the counter. The berries should not stick together when squeezed in your hand.

Storage: See Storing Dehydrated Fruit (page 27).

Tips

- Freezing the blueberries speeds up their dehydration time but isn't a necessary step. Just be aware they'll take a lot longer to dry.
- If you are dehydrating store-bought frozen blueberries, line the dehydrator tray with a drying sheet.
- If you plan to dehydrate blueberries with other items at the same time, place them on the bottom tray so they do not bleed blueberry juice on your other foods.

CHERRIES

Tip

Leave the stems on cherries when blanching them. They serve as little plugs, keeping valuable cherry juices from leaking out into the pot. Remove the stem during pitting.

Dehydrated cherries are wonderful to have on hand to add to pies, breads, muffins, and fruit salad.

Dehydrating temperature: 125°F

Preparation:

Fresh cherries: Place the cherries (leave any stems on) in a strainer and dip the strainer into a large pot of boiling water for 30 seconds. Remove and dip the strainer into a large bowl of ice water until the cherries cool. Drain, then remove the stems and pits, and lightly spray with lemon juice or an ascorbic acid solution. Spread, skin side down, on dehydrator trays and dehydrate for 24 hours.

Jarred Maraschino cherries: Pour the cherries into a strainer set over the sink and rinse under cool running water. Drain on paper towels. Break the cherries in half and place on dehydrator trays. Dehydrate for 10 to 12 hours.

Dryness test: Dehydrated cherries develop a hard outer coating and will click when dropped on the counter. The cherries should not stick together when squeezed in your hand.

Storage: See Storing Dehydrated Fruit (page 27). If you want to store your cherries chopped, chop them in a food processor after dehydration, then add ¼ cup granulated sugar per 1-quart jar and shake; this will keep the small pieces from sticking together.

CITRUS FRUITS

All citrus fruits (lemons, limes, oranges, grapefruit, and kumquats) can be handled in a similar manner when it comes to the dehydrator. You can dehydrate them with their peels on (citrus chips make a lovely garnish floated in a pitcher of water or iced tea) or off (powder the dried slices to make lemonade or a piquant sauce). Citrus peels and zest can be dehydrated on their own for use in potpourri and all sorts of savory and sweet preparations.

Dehydrating temperature: 125°F

Preparation: Wash thoroughly if dehydrating slices with peel on or the zest separately.

Citrus chips, with peel: Cut across into ⅛-inch-thick slices. Spread evenly on dehydrator trays and dehydrate 8 to 10 hours.

Citrus chips, peeled: Peel the fruit and set peelings aside to be dehydrated separately. Pull away every bit of the woolly white pith. Slice citrus crosswise ¼ inch thick and then into chunks, if desired. If you want to dehydrate wedges, take a sharp knife and completely cut away the outer membrane of the citrus fruit (except for kumquats). Then, cutting into the fruit, cut the wedge away from the membrane that would hold the section together on each side. Do this over a bowl to catch the juice and the wedges as they fall away. Spread the slices, chunks, or wedges on dehydrator trays and dehydrate 10 to 12 hours.

Peel or zest: If the citrus has a thin layer of pith, you may place the entire peeling on a dehydrator tray. If the pith of the fruit is thick, before peeling, remove just the zest by grating it. Using a microplane makes this very easy. Spread the zest on a drying sheet set in a dehydrator tray. Dehydrate the zest for 4 hours and peelings 10 to 12 hours. If you want to use the dehydrated peeling for zest, coarsely grind it in a blender.

Dryness test: Should be brittle, feel dry to the touch, and easily snap in half.

Storage: See Storing Dehydrated Fruit (page 27).

Tips

- Over time dehydrated citrus fruits will darken in color. This is a normal process and the foods will regain their proper color when rehydrated.
- If dehydrating slices with the rind attached, choose a fruit with thin pith (the white and bitter area between the rind and pulp). Fruit with a thick layer of pith should be peeled prior to dehydrating.

COCONUTS

Dehydrating fresh coconut at home is a great way to save money and get a healthier product. Store-bought shredded coconut is often pressed to remove oils in order to speed the drying process, and is exposed to chemicals and high heat. Though you can sometimes find frozen unsweetened coconut, it is typically sold sweetened (with the addition of corn syrup) in the baking aisle.

Chopped dehydrated sliced coconut is great to use in parfaits, crackers, granola, cakes, and pies. Use dehydrated shredded coconut as you would store-bought.

Dehydrating temperature: 125°F

Preparation: On the shell of a coconut are three round indentations ("eyes") that resemble finger holes on a bowling ball. Use a screwdriver and hammer to puncture the three holes. (Please be careful!) Tip the coconut upside down over a cup to drain the coconut water, and set aside to be used for coconut leather; refrigerate or freeze it if you won't be using it immediately. With the hammer, tap the shell until it cracks into several pieces. Use a flexible frosting knife as a wedge to pry the coconut meat from the shell. Place the pieces of coconut in a food processor and either shred or slice them, whichever you prefer. Line the dehydrator tray with a drying sheet and evenly spread the coconut on top. Dehydrate for 10 hours.

Dryness test: Should be brittle, feel dry to the touch, and easily snap in half.

Storage: See Storing Dehydrated Fruits (page 27).

Tips

- If you like, you can dehydrate store-bought dried coconut (sweetened or unsweetened), which will extend its shelf life. Line a dehydrator tray with a drying sheet, spread the coconut over it, and dehydrate for 8 hours. Your final product with be crunchy and crispy, a great sweet snack to eat as is or sprinkle over the top of yogurt and desserts!

- Many recipes that use coconut call for toasting it. You can have ready-made toasted coconut at your fingertips! Once you've sliced or shredded the fresh coconut, spread it over a rimmed baking sheet and bake in a preheated 350°F oven until golden brown, 10 to 15 minutes. Then proceed with dehydrating as directed. You can also toast store-bought coconut before dehydrating.

- After dehydrating fresh coconut, you can return it to the food processor to achieve a finer texture, if desired, before storing it.

CRANBERRIES

Cranberries dehydrate quickest when chopped but it's also nice to have dehydrated whole cranberries on hand to make a traditional whole-berry cranberry sauce or for use in a pie. Store-bought dried cranberries are also a candidate for the dehydrator!

Dehydrating temperature: 125°F

Preparation: Pick over fresh cranberries for any stems. Rinse well under running water and drain on paper towels.

Chopped cranberries: Place the cranberries in a blender or food processor and chop. Once evenly chopped, spread on dehydrator trays and dehydrate 8 to 10 hours.

Whole cranberries: Place the cranberries in a strainer and dip the strainer into a large pot of boiling water until their skins crack open. The cracking of the skins makes a slight popping noise and the white center of the cranberry will become visible. Remove immediately and plunge the strainer into a large bowl of ice water. When the berries are cool, shake off as much water as possible, spread on dehydrator trays, and dehydrate 12 to 15 hours.

Dried cranberries: Store-bought sweetened dried cranberries (such as Craisins) can be dehydrated to extend their shelf life. Spread on dehydrator trays and dehydrate 8 to 10 hours. When dehydrated, they will no longer feel sticky or moist, and if you squeeze a handful of them together, they won't stick together.

Dryness test: Unless otherwise indicated, you can easily crush the berries into powder between your fingers.

Storage: Dehydrated whole cranberries are fragile, so do not vacuum seal them. However, dehydrated chopped cranberries are not as fragile because they are not blanched; therefore they can be vacuum sealed. Place in ziptop plastic freezer bags and seal, trying to get as much air out as possible, then double-bag inside a Mylar bag, or store in a canning jar with a lid and oxygen pack. Dehydrated store-bought dried cranberries can be vacuum sealed, but they will stick together. When you are ready to use them, they can be pulled apart easily.

DATES

Tip

See the recipe for date sugar on page 167.

Because of their high sugar content, dates take a long time to dehydrate, even if you start with store-bought dried dates. Dehydrating dried dates will significantly extend their shelf life.

Dehydrating temperature: 125°F

Preparation:

Fresh dates: Place the dates in a strainer and dip in a pot of boiling water until their skins blister, then plunge into a large bowl of ice water until the dates are cool. Drain, cut the dates in half, and remove the pits. Arrange the dates on dehydrator trays, skin side down. Dehydrate for 24 hours. Wearing disposable gloves, cut the dates into smaller pieces with clean kitchen scissors, spread evenly over clean dehydrator trays, skin side down, and dehydrate for another 24 hours.

Halved dried dates: Cut store-bought dried dates in half, place them skin side down on dehydrator trays, and dehydrate 48 hours.

Chopped dried dates: Cut dried dates in half, place them skin side down on dehydrator trays, and dehydrate for 24 hours. Wearing disposable gloves, chop the halves into small pieces, spread over the trays, and dehydrate another 24 hours. When dehydrated, chopped dates develop a hard outer coating and will click when dropped on the counter. They will not stick together when squeezed in your hand.

Dryness test: Unless otherwise indicated, should feel dry like paper and be flexible.

Storage: See Storing Dehydrated Fruit (page 27). However, when storing dehydrated dates in canning jars, over time they can get sticky because of their high sugar content. If that happens, you can add ¼ cup granulated sugar per 1-quart jar and shake. This will eliminate the stickiness.

DRAGON FRUIT

Dragon fruit is a beautiful fruit, with a bright pink skin and white flesh studded with small black seeds. If you're lucky enough to find it in your area, buy them up. When dehydrated, dragon fruit tastes and crunches just like a Rice Krispy treat. It's also wonderful added to gelatin.

Dehydrating temperature: 125°F

Preparation: Wash fruit thoroughly, slice ¼ inch thick, spread on dehydrator trays, and dehydrate for 10 hours.

Dryness test: Should feel dry like paper, be flexible, and tear easily.

Storage: See Storing Dehydrated Fruit (page 27).

> ## Tip
>
> Leaving the skin on the fruit helps to hold the slices together.

FIGS

If you have a fig tree, the dehydrator will be your salvation when all that fruit comes ripe at the same time!

Dehydrating temperature: 125°F

Preparation:
   Fresh figs: Wash the fruit thoroughly and remove any stems. Cut into quarters, wedges, or thin slices, as you prefer. Place quartered figs skin side down on dehydrator trays. If thinly sliced or in wedges, arrange, without much overlapping, on the trays. Dehydrate for 18 hours. When dehydrated, fresh figs should be hard and feel dry, but still be somewhat flexible.
   Dried figs: Dehydrating dried figs will extend their shelf life. Cut in halves or quarters, place on dehydrator trays, and dehydrate for 10 hours. When dehydrated, dried figs should be leathery but still somewhat pliable.

Storage: See Storing Dehydrated Fruit (page 27). However, when storing dehydrated figs in canning jars, over time they can get sticky because of their high sugar content. If that happens, you can add ¼ cup granulated sugar per 1-quart jar of figs and shake. This will eliminate the stickiness.

> ## Tips
>
> - When cutting figs into thin slices, a meat slicer, mandoline, or food processor works well. Otherwise, be sure to use a very sharp knife.
> - Do not remove the skin from figs.

GRAPES

Tips

- Leave grapes on their stems when blanching; this will preserve the juice within the grapes.
- Transferring the grapes to a clean tray three quarters of the way through dehydrating them keeps them from sticking and speeds up the process.
- You can use grape leaves in savory recipes but the ground dehydrated leaves make a nice tea.

Dehydrated fresh grapes are not the same as raisins; when fresh grapes are dehydrated, they become hard and crunchy, with none of the chewiness of raisins. That said, you can use dehydrated fresh grapes and raisins interchangeably in recipes. If you grow your own grapes, try drying the leaves as well and use them crushed in teas or as a wrap.

Dehydrating temperature: 125°F for grapes, 100°F for leaves

Preparation:

Fresh grapes: Working with one cluster of grapes at a time, blanch them in a large pot of boiling water for just less than 1 minute. Remove and let cool enough so you can handle them. Remove the grapes from their stems and spread over dehydrator trays. Dehydrate for 18 hours and transfer the partially dehydrated grapes to clean, dry dehydrator trays. Dehydrate for another 6 hours. Dehydrated grapes develop a hard outer coating and will click when dropped on the counter. They should not stick together when squeezed in your hand.

Raisins: Dehydrate store-bought raisins to extend their shelf life. Spread on dehydrator trays and dehydrate 10 to 12 hours. When dehydrated, raisins should not feel sticky or moist, and they should not stick together when squeezed in your hand.

Grape leaves: Wash the leaves and pat dry, then lay flat on dehydrator trays. Dehydrate 8 to 10 hours. The dehydrated leaves should be brittle, feel dry to the touch, and crumble easily.

Storage: For dehydrated grapes and raisins, see Storing Dehydrated Fruit (page 27). The dehydrated leaves are fragile, so do not vacuum seal unless you plan to crush them for tea. Place in ziptop plastic freezer bags and then double-bag inside a Mylar bag, or store inside a canning jar with a lid and oxygen pack.

KIWI FRUIT

Dried kiwi slices are a wonderful addition to salads and smoothies; I also love to include them in Crazy Fruit (page 27).

Dehydrating temperature: 125°F

Preparation: With a paring knife or vegetable peeler, peel the kiwis and slice as thinly as you can. Lightly spray with lemon juice or an ascorbic acid solution, spread on dehydrator trays, and dehydrate for 12 hours.

Dryness test: Should feel dry like paper, be flexible, and tear easily.

Storage: Dehydrated kiwi slices are fragile, so do not vacuum seal. Place in ziptop plastic freezer bags and seal, trying to remove as much air as possible. Double-bag inside a Mylar bag, or store inside a canning jar with a lid and oxygen pack.

Tips

- Having a meat slicer or a mandoline can make short work of slicing kiwi; both tools will also allow you to cut the kiwi paper-thin.
- Fun fact: Fresh kiwi contains an enzyme that makes it impossible to use with gelatin. Once it's dehydrated, though, it works fine!

MANGO

Mangoes are great for snacking or using in salads, gelatins, cakes and smoothies.

Dehydrating temperature: 125°F

Preparation: Peel the mango; then, from top to bottom, cut the flesh off the large, flat seed on both sides. Cut the large pieces into wedges, or thinly slice if making mango chips, or chop. Lightly spray with lemon juice or an ascorbic acid solution. Spread on dehydrator trays and dehydrate 10 to 12 hours.

Dryness test: Should feel dry like paper, be flexible, and tear easily.

Storage: See Storing Dehydrated Fruit (page 27).

Tip

You can also dehydrate the peel of the mango to use in tea (see my recipe for Tropical Tea on page 111). Spread the peel on the dehydrator tray, skin side down, and dehydrate 8 to 10 hours.

MELONS (Cantaloupe, Honeydew, and Watermelon)

Dehydrated melon slices make a great snack—if you dry them in long, thin wedges, the consistency is almost exactly like that of fruit leather. They're also a tasty addition to salads and parfaits.

Dehydrating temperature: 125°F

Preparation: Cut the melon in half or wedges (however it's easiest to work with and depending on what size slices you want). Remove the seeds, then cut the flesh from the rind. (If working with watermelon with seeds, you can remove them or leave them in; it's up to you.) Cut the melon into ¼-inch-thick slices, spread on dehydrator trays, and dehydrate for 16 hours.

Dryness test: Should feel dry like paper, be flexible, and tear easily.

Storage: See Storing Dehydrated Fruit (page 27).

NECTARINES & PEACHES

Tip

Soft nectarines and peaches are perfect for making fruit leather. Use firmer fruit when you intend to use it in pies or to add to yogurt.

Have these on hand to add to fruit salad, granola, or yogurt, or to use in pies or cakes.

Dehydrating temperature: 125°F

Preparation: Peel before slicing. If the skin won't come off easily, blanch the fruit in boiling water until the skin blisters, about 1 minute. Remove from the water using a slotted spoon or strainer and transfer to a bowl full of ice water. When cool enough to handle, slip the skins off. Cut into ½-inch-thick or less slices and lightly spray with lemon juice or an ascorbic acid solution. Spread on dehydrator trays and dehydrate 12 to 14 hours.

Dryness test: Should feel dry like paper and be flexible.

Storage: See Storing Dehydrated Fruit (page 27).

NUTS AND SEEDS

If you buy nuts/seeds in bulk from the store, you know they can go rancid if they're not stored in the refrigerator or freezer. When dehydrated, you can store them long term at room temperature. See page 34 for coconuts and page 78 for water chestnuts.

Dehydrating temperature: 100°F

Preparation:

Raw nuts and seeds: Cover the nuts or seeds with warm water and let soak for at least 8 hours and up to 24 hours. If you'd like your nuts/seeds to be salted, you can add salt to the soaking water; this will also aid in removing phytic acid. Drain, then spread the nuts/seeds on a drying sheet set in a dehydrator tray, and dehydrate for 24 hours.

Bulk nuts and seeds: Much of the nuts and seeds that you would buy at the grocery store in bulk have already been soaked, then dried or roasted. For long-term storage, we still recommend you dehydrate them to remove any remaining moisture, which can take up to 12 hours.

Dryness test: Should have a good crunch when you bite down on them.

Storage: See Storing Dehydrated Fruits and Nuts (page 27).

Tip

We recommend soaking raw nuts and seeds like pumpkin and sunflower before dehydrating them. Certain compounds that naturally form on the surfaces of seeds and nuts, such as phytic acid, bind to and prevent the absorption of important minerals like iron, zinc, calcium, and magnesium. Protein absorption may also be interfered with by certain enzyme inhibitors present on the seeds' surface. Soaking the seeds and nuts will help to gently remove some of these "anti-nutrients."

OLIVES

Tips

- Because olives are high in oil content, they are not recommended for long-term storage, even when dehydrated. Storage life is about 1 year.
- You can dehydrate whole olives, but they must be pitted.

Dehydrating cured olives allows you to keep on hand longer and ready at a moment's notice types of olives that might not be available canned.

Dehydrating temperature: 125°F

Preparation: Drain the olives and spread on dehydrator trays. Dehydrate 10 to 12 hours.

Dryness test: Should feel dry like paper and be somewhat flexible but will snap if bent in half.

Storage: See Storing Dehydrated Fruit (page 27).

PAPAYA

Tip

If you are planning on using your dehydrated papaya with gelatin, you must steam it prior to dehydration or the gelatin will not set. Like pineapple, papaya contains an enzyme that digests proteins, including those that give gelatin its structure. By cooking it briefly, you denature (deactivate) this enzyme.

Dehydrated chopped papaya makes a great snack on its own, and is a tasty addition to any trail mix. Steam papaya prior to dehydrating if you plan to use it for baking or with gelatin. Dehydrated raw papaya is preferable for use in salads or snacking.

Dehydrating temperature: 125°F

Preparation: Peel the papaya and clean out the seeds, then chop or slice as desired. If you know you will be using the papaya with gelatin or in baking, steam it over boiling water for 1 to 2 minutes. Otherwise, lightly spray with lemon juice or an ascorbic acid solution, spread on dehydrator trays, and dehydrate 12 to 14 hours.

Dryness test: Dehydrated steamed papaya develops a hard outer coating, will click when dropped on the counter, and will be dark red-orange in color. Pieces should not stick together when squeezed in your hand. Dehydrated raw papaya should feel dry like paper, be somewhat flexible, and will be a dull peach color.

Storage: See Storing Dehydrated Fruit (page 27).

PEARS

Prepare pears according to how you think you might be using them: pear chips are great for snacking on as is and used as a garnish; use rehydrated sliced pears in pies, cakes, and salads; chopped pears work great in muffins and gelatin; and I like to use shredded pears when making quick breads.

Dehydrating temperature: 125°F

Preparation: Have a spray bottle of lemon juice or ascorbic acid solution on hand.

Pear chips: Wash the fruit thoroughly. Without peeling or coring, slice the pears across into ⅛-inch-thick disks. Lightly spray with lemon juice or an ascorbic acid solution, spread evenly on dehydrator trays, and dehydrate 10 to 12 hours. When dehydrated, pear chips are brittle, feel dry to the touch, and will snap in half.

Pear slices: Peel the pears and cut across into ¼-inch-thick slices. Cut the slices across to make half moons. Lightly spray with lemon juice, spread evenly on dehydrator trays, and dehydrate 10 to 12 hours. When dehydrated, pear chips are brittle, feel dry to the touch, and will snap in half.

Chopped or cubed pears: Peel the pears, and place the pear whole in a food processor or vegetable chopper to chop or cube. Lightly spray with lemon juice, spread evenly on dehydrator trays, and dehydrate 10 to 12 hours. When dehydrated, chopped pears feel dry like paper and the pieces are somewhat flexible.

Shredded pears: Peel the pears. Place the pear whole in a food processor and shred. Lightly spray with lemon juice, spread evenly on dehydrator trays, and dehydrate 10 to 12 hours. When dehydrated, shredded pears feel dry like paper and the pieces are somewhat flexible.

Storage: See Storing Dehydrated Fruit (page 27).

PINEAPPLE

Unless you're planning only to enjoy your dehydrated pineapple as a snack or in powder form (see page 81), for best results you need to steam it before dehydration.

Dehydrating temperature: 125°F

Preparation:

Steamed pineapple: Peel the pineapple; coring is optional. Slice, cube, chop, or shred the pineapple as you prefer. Steam over boiling water the pineapple until bright yellow and tender, 3 to 5 minutes. Spread on dehydrator trays and dehydrate for 12 to 15 hours. When dehydrated, steamed pineapple will develop a hard outer coating, will click when dropped on the counter, and be bright yellow. Pieces of it will not stick together when squeezed in your hand.

Pineapple chips (raw): Peel and core the pineapple. Cut across into paper-thin rings, spread on dehydrator trays, and dehydrate 8 to 10 hours. Dehydrated raw pineapple feels dry like paper, is flexible, tears easily, and is pale yellow in color.

Storage: See Storing Dehydrated Fruit (page 27). However, when stored in canning jars, over time dehydrated steamed pineapple can get sticky (cooking the pineapple elevates its already high sugar content). If that happens, you can add ¼ cup granulated sugar per 1-quart jar of pineapple and shake. This will eliminate the stickiness.

PLANTAINS

Enjoy the dehydrated chips as is for a tasty snack, or rehydrate to use in recipes or fry.

Dehydrating temperature: 125°F

Preparation: Peel the plantains, then cut across into ⅛-inch-thick rounds. Lightly spray with lemon juice or an ascorbic acid solution, spread on dehydrator trays, and dehydrate for 12 hours.

Dryness test: Should be brittle, feel dry like paper, and snap in half.

Storage: See Storing Dehydrated Fruit (page 27).

Tips

- A food processor, mandoline, or meat slicer will make short work of slicing plantains.
- Plantains are denser than bananas; the same size dehydrated plantain chip will be a little heavier than a banana chip.

PLUMS

Plums are great in both sweet and savory recipes.

Dehydrating temperature: 125°F

Preparation: Blanch the plums in a large pot of vigorously boiling water for 30 seconds. Remove with a slotted spoon or strainer and cool in ice-cold water. Slice in half, remove the pit, and lightly spray with lemon juice or an ascorbic acid solution. Lay the halved plums on dehydrator trays, skin side down. Dehydrate for 12 hours; then, wearing disposable gloves, push the plums inside out. Return them to the dehydrator trays, skin side down, and dehydrate for another 3 to 4 hours.

Dryness test: Should be very dark black-purple in color and feel dry and hard, though still be somewhat flexible.

Storage: See Storing Dehydrated Fruit (page 27).

Tip

Use very ripe plums (no matter the variety) for best results when dehydrating.

POMEGRANATES

Because of the abundance of seeds in pomegranates, the only purpose for dehydrating the inside of the fruit is for use in herbal teas. Otherwise, you can juice pomegranates and combine the juice with fruit purees to make fruit leather (see page 86).

Dehydrating temperature: 125°F

Preparation: Cut the pomegranates in half, and with a spoon remove the seeds and flesh to a bowl. When ready, spread this on a dryer sheet set on a dehydrator tray. Dehydrate for 10 hours.

Dryness test: Should feel hard and dry and the seeds will click when dropped on the counter.

Storage: See Storing Dehydrated Fruit (page 27).

RHUBARB

Rhubarb is primarily used in pies and breads. Our recipe for Orange-Rhubarb Bread (see page 150) is a must-try!

Dehydrating temperature: 125°F

Preparation: Completely trim the leaves away from the rhubarb stalks (the leaves contain high amounts of oxalic acid, which can make you very sick if eaten). Wash the stalks, then cut them into 1-inch cubes and place in a strainer. Dip the strainer in a large pot of boiling water and blanch the cubes for 1 minute. Dip the strainer in a large bowl of ice water, shake to drain, and empty the cubes onto a dehydrator tray. Spread out the cubes and dehydrate 10 to 12 hours.

Dryness test: Dehydrated rhubarb develops a hard outer coating and will click when dropped on the counter. Pieces of it should not stick together when squeezed in your hand.

Storage: See Storing Dehydrated Fruit (page 27).

STAR FRUIT

Dehydrate star fruit? You bet! It's wonderful as is for a snack, and it makes a beautiful garnish. It also looks and tastes wonderful in gelatin.

Dehydrating temperature: 125°F

Preparation: Wash, then cut into thin slices and lightly spray with lemon juice or an ascorbic acid solution. Spread on dehydrator trays and dehydrate for 10 hours.

Dryness test: Should feel dry like paper, be flexible, and tear easily.

Storage: See Storing Dehydrated Fruit (page 27).

STRAWBERRIES

Enjoy dehydrated strawberries as is for snacking or rehydrated in salads, pies, cakes, smoothies, and much, much more.

Dehydrating temperature: 125°F

Preparation: Wash and hull the berries, then cut them in half or into thin slices and lightly spray with lemon juice or an ascorbic acid solution. Spread on dehydrator trays (strawberry halves should be placed cut side up) and dehydrate thinly sliced strawberries for 8 hours, halved strawberries 16 to 18 hours.

Dryness test: Should feel dry like paper and be somewhat flexible.

Storage: See Storing Dehydrated Fruit (page 27).

5

Dehydrating Vegetables, Greens, & Mushrooms, A-Z

Many people recommend a dehydrating temperature of 135°F or more for vegetables. However, it has been my experience that this is too high. For the best finished product, 125°F is optimal for most vegetables, and even lower (110°F) for certain leafier items. Drying longer at a lower temperature will preserve nutrients and prevent burning and case hardening, a particular problem for potatoes.

DEHYDRATING FROZEN VEGETABLES

The same vegetable dehydrated will last 10 to 15 times longer than frozen. So if your supermarket is running a great sale on frozen vegetables, buy them up but instead of putting them in the freezer when you get home, crank up the dehydrator.

The beauty of dehydrating frozen vegetables is that, pretty much without exception, all the prep work has been done for you. (In the case of certain brands of frozen cauliflower or broccoli, I find that the pieces are on the large side. In these cases, run cool water over the top of the frozen item for just a few seconds, place on a cutting board, and slice as desired.) Simply open the bag and spread the frozen items onto the dehydrating trays. Dehydration time will depend on the item and the size of the cut. In general, frozen foods will have approximately the same drying time as their fresh counterpart.

DEHYDRATING CANNED VEGETABLES

You can dehydrate store-bought canned vegetables and beans by simply draining off the packing water and placing the items on dehydrator trays.

However, I am not a proponent of doing this. Through the canning process, these foods have lost a lot of their nutrients or those nutrients have been transferred to the liquid the produce is packed in, which for vegetables gets poured down the drain when you're going to dehydrate them. Also, most canned items contain a large amount of salt, which means, if dehydrated, they will take a lot longer to rehydrate. That said, you'll find a few canned items in this chapter that I think give good results when dehydrated.

STORING DEHYDRATED VEGETABLES

For optimal long-term shelf life, the vegetables should be completely dehydrated and stored so as to prevent contact with oxygen, moisture, light, high heat, and insects/rodents. If you are unsure if the item is dehydrated, follow the dryness test provided in every entry for each particular vegetable. Once completely dried, most items should be vacuum-sealed in vacuum bags along with an oxygen pack to remove any residual oxygen, and then double-bagged in Mylar to protect the items from sunlight, heat, and insects.

SAY NO

There are very few things you can't dehydrate when it comes to produce, but here are two:

- **Lettuce:** There is no value in dehydrating lettuce. The finished product cannot be rehydrated or doesn't have much use or flavor used in its dehydrated state.
- **Sprouts:** We are often asked if it is possible to dehydrate sprouts. You can, but it really doesn't make sense. If you love sprouts, then have plenty of dried beans on hand and keep a sprouting tray going in your kitchen. Wheatberries work well too.

ARTICHOKES

If you've never grown artichokes and live in the right climate, please give them a try. The artichoke is a beautiful plant, plus dehydrating your own is a lot cheaper than buying frozen or canned artichoke hearts.

Dehydrating temperature: 125°F

Preparation: Bring a large pot of water to a boil, add the artichokes, and cook until the leaves are soft and easily removed from the base of the artichoke. The stem can be left on, as it is a part of the artichoke heart. Drain and transfer the artichokes to a large bowl of ice water until cool. Drain again, then remove all the leaves until you reach the center core (heart) of the plant. You may eat the bases of each artichoke leaf as you remove them, but the remainder of the leaf is not edible. When you reach the heart, you will find a fuzzy, hair-like thistle structure on the top of the heart. This is the "choke" of the plant, and is not edible. Use a spoon to scrape it off. Once you expose the heart, lightly spray the entire surface with lemon juice or an ascorbic acid solution, as artichokes will oxidize and brown very quickly once cut. Slice or cube the hearts, spray with lemon juice again, arrange on dehydrator trays, and dehydrate 10 to 12 hours.

Dryness test: Should feel dry like paper and be flexible.

Storage: See Storing Dehydrated Vegetables (page 49).

ASPARAGUS

Asparagus makes a great side dish or is great in soups.

Dehydrating temperature: 125°F

Preparation: Wash, remove the tough end, then boil or steam asparagus just until you can pierce the thick end with a knife; don't let it get mushy. Drain, then plunge into a large bowl of ice water until cool. Cut thick stalks into 1- to 3-inch pieces; thin stalks can be left whole. Spread over dehydrator trays and dehydrate for 12 hours.

Dryness test: Should feel dry like paper and be somewhat flexible.

Storage: See Storing Dehydrated Vegetables (page 49).

Tip

Bend your asparagus and it will automatically snap in the exact spot where the tender part of the stalk meets the tough end.

BEANS, GREEN AND YELLOW

These beans are great for casseroles, soups, and side dishes.

Dehydrating temperature: 125°F

Preparation: Leave beans whole or cut/french to the desired size, usually between 1 and 4 inches. Boil or steam the beans just until tender. Drain and place in a large bowl of ice water until cool. Drain, spread on dehydrator trays, and dehydrate 8 to 12 hours.

Dryness test: Should feel dry like paper and be somewhat flexible.

Storage: See Storing Dehydrated Vegetables (page 49).

Tip

If you want to french the beans, do that before blanching.

BEANS, SHELL (Black, Kidney, Navy, Pinto, Soy)

Tip

If you dehydrate shelled fresh beans, remember that they will need to be soaked like store-bought dried beans before cooking.

Also known as legumes, these are beans that are shelled. Even if you don't grow your own beans or have access to them through a CSA or farmers' markets, you can take advantage of what your supermarket has to offer. Dehydrating canned beans will save valuable storage space. Or you can cook, then dehydrate, store-bought dried beans; they'll take up even less storage space and be already cooked through when rehydrated. For directions on how to dehydrate garbanzo beans (chickpeas), see the entry for Peas.

Dehydrating temperature: 90°F for shelled fresh beans, 125°F for cooked beans, and 135°F for soybeans (to make soy nuts)

Preparation:

Shelled fresh beans: Shell the beans, rinse, spread on dehydrator trays, and dehydrate at 90°F for 24 hours. Dehydrated fresh shell beans develop a hard outer coating and will click when dropped on the counter.

Cooked whole dried beans: Soak dried beans in water and cover for up to 24 hours, depending on the type. Drain, then bring to a boil in a generous pot of fresh water and simmer until tender. Drain, spread on dehydrator trays, and dehydrate at 125°F for 18 hours; they will crack and pop open while dehydrating. When dehydrated, they will feel hard and dry to the touch.

Dried soybeans: Make your own soy nuts! Soak the dried beans in water and cover overnight. Drain, then place in a pot with generously salted water (1 cup soy beans per 5 cups water). Bring to a boil and let boil until tender and swollen, about 2 hours. Drain, then pour the beans into a large bowl of ice water to cool. Drain again and spread over dehydrator trays. Sprinkle with salt and dehydrate at 135°F for 12 hours.

Canned whole beans: Drain the beans, then rinse under cold running water. Spread over dehydrator trays and dehydrate at 125°F for 18 hours; they will crack and pop open while dehydrating. When dehydrated, they will feel hard and dry to the touch.

Storage: See Storing Dehydrated Vegetables (page 49).

BEETS & BEET GREENS

Beets are a double source of goodness—you can dehydrate both the beet root and the beet greens with great results. Be sure to separate them, though, as they require different timing in the dehydrator.

Dehydrating temperature: 125°F

Preparation: Cut the greens 5 inches from the top of the beet.

Beets: Place the whole beets in a large pot of boiling water and boil until you can easily pierce them with a sharp knife or skewer. Drain and place in a large bowl of ice water to cool, then slide the skins and tops off the beets by rubbing them with your hands (no knife is needed). Slice, cube, chop, shred, or french the beets, spread on dehydrator trays, and dehydrate 12 to 14 hours. Dehydrated beets should feel dry like paper and be somewhat flexible.

Beet greens: Wash the greens well to remove any grit. Spread on dehydrator trays and dehydrate for 8 hours. Dehydrated beet greens will feel dry to the touch; they are also brittle and will easily crumble in your hands.

Storage: For beet root, see Storing Dehydrated Vegetables (page 49). The dehydrated beet leaves are fragile, so do not vacuum seal. Place in ziptop plastic freezer bags and then double-bag inside Mylar or store in a canning jar with a lid and oxygen pack.

BROCCOLI

Tip

The rehydrated puree made from broccoli stalks is the perfect base for a cream of broccoli soup.

Dehydrating broccoli allows you to use every bit of the head—even the stalks!

Dehydrating temperature: 125°F

Preparation: Steam or boil heads of broccoli whole just until you can pierce the florets with a sharp knife or skewer; don't let them get soft. The color of the cooked broccoli should be a vibrant green. (Steaming yields a better result than boiling.) Drain, then plunge the broccoli into a large bowl of ice water to cool.

Florets: After cooking, cut the florets off; set the stalks aside. Arrange the florets on dehydrator trays and dehydrate 10 to 12 hours.

Stalks: Continue to boil the stalks until they are very tender. Drain and puree in a blender. Line the dehydrator trays with drying sheets. Working with 1 cup of puree at a time, spread it in a strip ¼ inch thick, leaving space between the strips on each drying sheet. Dehydrate for 12 hours.

Dryness test: Should be dark green, brittle, and feel dry to the touch.

Storage: See Storing Dehydrated Vegetables (page 49).

BRUSSELS SPROUTS

Tip

If you're dehydrating your Brussels sprouts to enjoy as a snack, you can salt the cooked Brussels prior to dehydrating them.

Dehydrate Brussels sprouts to enjoy as a crispy snack as is, or to rehydrate and prepare using your favorite recipe.

Dehydrating temperature: 125°F

Preparation: Trim the stems of the Brussels sprouts and remove any wilted or damaged outer leaves. Boil or steam them whole until you can pierce them with a sharp knife or skewer. Drain and place the sprouts in a large bowl of ice water until cool. Cut each sprout vertically in half through the stem and spread on dehydrator trays, cut side up. Dehydrate for 12 hours.

Dryness test: Should feel dry to the touch and be crunchy.

Storage: See Storing Dehydrated Vegetables (page 49).

CABBAGE

Cabbage is so nutritious. Dehydrate shredded cabbage, and you can add a handful of it to most any soup, stew, or casserole! Dehydrate the whole leaves and making cabbage rolls is a snap. The preparation outlined here works for all kinds of cabbage, including Napa and Chinese.

Dehydrating temperature: 125°F

Preparation:

Whole leaves: Core the cabbage, then cut it in half, if you like. Boil or steam the cabbage halves or whole head until the leaves are tender and fall away from the head. Cool the cabbage in a large bowl of ice water, then pull the leaves away from the head. Spread the leaves on dehydrator trays and dehydrate 8 to 10 hours.

Shredded or chopped cabbage: Core the cabbage, then cut into ½-inch-thick slices. Boil or steam 2 to 3 minutes. Drain and place in a large bowl of ice water until cool. Drain, then chop the cabbage, if you like, or loosen the shreds with your fingers and pile it onto dehydrator trays. Dehydrate 8 to 10 hours.

Dryness test: Should feel dry like paper and be flexible.

Storage: See Storing Dehydrated Vegetables (page 49).

Tip

A meat slicer makes short work of shredding cabbage.

CARROTS

Carrots are 88% water, so they will reduce in size dramatically when dehydrated. Upon rehydration, however, they will enlarge like a sponge back to their full size! I love showing people dehydrated and rehydrated carrots side by side because the difference is so remarkable! Make sure you're fully stocked with dehydrated carrots prepped every way you're likely to use them—sliced, chopped, shredded, even whole baby carrots.

Dehydrating temperature: 125°F

Preparation: Trim the carrots and peel (this isn't necessary for baby carrots). Blanch whole in a large pot of boiling water for 5 minutes, and no longer (they are ready when they turn bright orange). Drain and place in a large bowl of ice water to cool. You can dehydrate the carrots whole or slice, chop, or shred as it suits your planned use for them. Lightly spray with lemon juice or an ascorbic acid solution, spread on dehydrator trays, and dehydrate 10 to 12 hours.

Dryness test: Should feel hard and dry to the touch, but still be somewhat flexible.

Storage: See Storing Dehydrated Vegetables (page 49).

Tips

- Because carrots lose so much water when dehydrated, be sure to add extra liquid to any recipe you add dehydrated carrots to.
- Carrots cooked prior to dehydration will retain their beautiful vibrant orange color over time; if they are dehydrated raw, they will take on an unappealing color and continue to fade over time. This is due to a provitamin in carrots called beta-carotene, which gives the vegetable its orange color, and is converted to vitamin A in the body. A brief heating releases the beta-carotene from cell walls, thus increasing its bioavailability. In addition to it resulting in better color for the dehydrated product, it will also allow the beta-carotene to be more efficiently absorbed by the body. A further benefit to precooking is that it will cut the rehydration time.

CAULIFLOWER

Add rehydrated cauliflower to soups, stews, and side dishes.

Dehydrating temperature: 125°F

Preparation:
Florets: Steam or boil the cauliflower in large pieces (or you can leave the head whole) until tender and place in a large bowl of ice water to cool. Cut the cauliflower into 1- to 3-inch florets, spread on dehydrator trays, and dehydrate 12 to 14 hours. The dehydrated florets will become dark yellow brown and feel hard and dry to the touch.

Stalks: Continue to boil the stalks until they are very tender. Drain and puree in a blender. Line the dehydrator trays with drying sheets. Working with 1 cup of puree at a time, spread it in strips ¼ inch thick on the sheets, leaving space between them. Dehydrate the strips 12 hours. They should be brittle and feel dry to the touch.

Storage: See Storing Dehydrated Vegetables (page 49).

Tips

- Dehydrated cauliflower turns a light yellow to brown color. Don't worry, the natural color will return when it is rehydrated.
- The rehydrated puree made from cauliflower stalks is a great base for cream of cauliflower soup.

CELERY

With dehydrated chopped celery in your pantry, there is no need for a bunch of fresh celery to wilt away in your vegetable crisper again!

Dehydrating temperature: 125°F

Preparation: Wash and trim the stalks (but don't trim away the leaves). Chop the celery into ½-inch or smaller pieces and boil or steam for no longer than 1 minute. Drain and place in a large bowl of ice water until cool. Drain again, spread on dehydrator trays, and dehydrate 10 to 12 hours.

Dryness test: Should feel hard and dry to the touch.

Storage: See Storing Dehydrated Vegetables (page 49).

Tip

Do not precook celery if you are going to make celery powder with it.

COLLARD GREENS

Tip

For chopped collards, wait until after dehydrating the whole leaves to cut them with kitchen scissors or break them into pieces with your hands. This will ensure maximum nutrient retention.

Substitute whole collard leaves for cabbage for a new spin on stuffed cabbage. Dehydrated chopped collards can be added directly to soups and stews.

Dehydrating temperature: 125°F

Preparation: Working with one leaf at a time, dip into a pot of boiling water for 15 to 30 seconds, then plunge into a large bowl ice water until cool. Place on a clean, dry kitchen towel to drain. Trim away the stem. Arrange the leaves on dehydrator trays and dehydrate 6 to 8 hours.

Dryness test: Should be brittle, crumble easily in your hands, and feel dry to the touch.

Storage: The dehydrated leaves are fragile, so do not vacuum seal. Place in ziptop plastic freezer bags and then double-bag inside a Mylar bag or store inside a canning jar with a lid and oxygen pack. For chopped collards, see Storing Dehydrated Vegetables (page 49).

CORN

Buy ears of corn in bulk when it's in season in your area. Enjoy it fresh but then dehydrate the rest to have sweet corn on hand all year round. And though I'm not normally a fan of dehydrating canned vegetables or fruits, corn offers up some options that work well in the dehydrator—whole kernels, baby corn, and creamed corn.

Dehydrating temperature: 125°F

Preparation:

Fresh corn kernels: Shuck the ears and carefully clean the corn of the silk. Place the ears in a large pot of boiling water, making sure the water completely covers the corn. Cook until tender, approximately 8 minutes. Transfer the ears to a large bowl of ice water until cool. Working over a bowl, cut the kernels from the cobs using a decobber or sharp knife. Pour the kernels onto dehydrator trays and dehydrate 10 hours. Dehydrated corn kernels are darker yellow in color than fresh, develop a hard outer coating, and will click when dropped on the counter.

Canned baby corn: Boil or steam until tender, 3 to 4 minutes. You can leave the cobs whole or slice lengthwise down the middle. Spread on dehydrator trays and dehydrate 10 to 12 hours. Dehydrated baby corn will feel dry like paper and still be somewhat flexible, but will break if bent in half.

Canned corn kernels: Drain and rinse the corn, then pour it onto the trays and dehydrate 8 to 10 hours. Dehydrated corn kernels are darker yellow in color than fresh, develop a hard outer coating, and will click when dropped on the counter.

Storage: See Storing Dehydrated Vegetables (page 49).

Tips

- Don't worry about evenly spreading the kernels across the dehydrator tray; uneven piles of corn will dehydrate just fine.
- Frozen corn kernels will take 8 to 10 hours to dehydrate.

CUCUMBERS

Dehydrate cucumber spears and chips you'll never buy pickles again! Check out my no-muss, no-fuss refrigerator pickle recipes on pages 291–92.

Dehydrating temperature: 125°F

Preparation:

Fresh cucumbers: If you don't plan to peel the cucumbers, blanch the whole unpeeled cucumbers in a large pot of boiling water for exactly 30 seconds, and no longer. (This will remove the wax from the cucumbers and soften the skins.) Otherwise, peel the cucumbers. Cut the cucumbers in slices or spears as you prefer, spread on dehydrator trays, and dehydrate 8 to 10 hours.

Crispy pickle chips or spears: You can dehydrate drained store-bought pickle slices or spears for a crunchy, salty snack. The brine from the jar will remain on the pickles, giving the dehydrated product a kick of pickle flavor. Spread on dehydrator trays and dehydrate for 10 hours.

Dryness test: Should be brittle, feel dry to the touch, and snap in half.

Storage: Dehydrated pickles and cucumbers are fragile and should not be vacuum sealed. Place in ziptop plastic freezer bags and double-bag inside a Mylar bag, or store inside a canning jar with a lid and oxygen pack.

EGGPLANT

Dehydrate your eggplant and you'll never have to salt it before cooking again! Keep your pantry stocked with eggplant prepped the way you use most—sliced, chopped, cubed—and getting dinner on the table just got that much easier!

Dehydrating temperature: 125°F

Preparation: If you don't plan on peeling the eggplant before dehydration, blanch the entire eggplant in a large pot of boiling water for 15 seconds or less, then transfer it to a large bowl of ice water until cool. Otherwise, peel the eggplant. Cut the eggplant up as you prefer (see Tip on this page), spread on dehydrator trays, and dehydrate 10 to 12 hours.

Dryness test: Should be brittle, feel dry to the touch, and snap in half.

Storage: See Storing Dehydrated Vegetables (page 49).

Tip

You can slice, cube, dice, or chop the eggplant prior to dehydration as you prefer, but whatever the cut, make sure the eggplant is no more than ¼ to ½ inch thick.

FENNEL

Tip

As long as you keep the temperature at 90° F and no higher when dehydrating fennel seeds, they will still germinate when planted.

Dehydrated fennel bulb is delicious as is—it's a crispy chip, with a distinctive anise-like (licorice) flavor. In addition to the bulb, the aromatic stalks and leaves can be dehydrated for use in teas, potpourri, and infused oils. Fennel seeds can also be dehydrated—why pay a premium price for it in the spice section?

Dehydrating temperature: 90°F for seeds, 90° to 100°F for stalks and leaves, and 125°F for bulbs

Preparation: Wash, then cut the stalks from the bulb.

Stalks and leaves: Blanch the stalks (with their leaves left on) in boiling water for no more than 1 minute. Drain, then place in a large bowl of ice water until cool. Spread the stalks and leaves on dehydrator trays and dehydrate at 90° to 100°F for 12 hours. When dehydrated, the leaves will be brittle, feel dry to the touch, and crumble easily. The stalks will feel hard and dry but still be somewhat flexible.

Fennel bulb: Set a mandoline or meat slicer to its thinnest setting and slice the bulb. Blanch the slices in boiling water for 1 minute. Drain, then place in a large bowl of ice water until cool, Drain, then spread on dehydrator trays and dehydrate at 125°F for 12 hours. Dehydrated fennel bulb should feel hard and dry to the touch and snap in half.

Fennel seeds: See Dehydrating Herb Seeds (page 103).

Storage: See Storing Dehydrated Vegetables (page 49).

GARLIC

After dehydrating and using a lot of garlic, I have found that it's best to dehydrate garlic slices, and to crush or chop them afterwards. You end up with a much more robust flavor than if you dehydrated chopped garlic, plus doing it this way minimizes the odor and increases nutrient retention. And if you're a fan of roasted garlic, why not roast multiple heads at once, use one, and dehydrate the rest?

Dehydrating temperature: 125°F

Preparation:

Fresh garlic: Peel the cloves and slice (a food processor will make short work of this). Spread on dehydrator trays and dehydrate for 8 hours.

Roasted garlic: Slice off the tops of the garlic heads so the cloves are exposed. Roast the heads in a preheated oven at 400°F or on the grill with the lid down until the cloves feel soft when you squeeze them, about 30 minutes. Once the garlic has cooled enough to handle, squeeze the cloves out of their peels directly onto a drying sheet set on a dehydrator tray and mash. Dehydrate 8 to 10 hours.

Dryness test: Should be brittle and feel dry to the touch; dehydrated garlic slices should snap in half and crush into a powder, and roasted garlic should easily break apart in your hands.

Storage: See Storing Dehydrated Vegetables (page 49).

Tips

- See page 80 for how to make your own garlic powder and garlic salt.
- To dehydrate jarred chopped garlic, drain, then spread on a drying sheet set on a dehydrator tray and dehydrate for 8 hours, until the garlic is brittle and dry to the touch.

GINGER

Tips

- A meat slicer or food processor is handy for the slicing, as ginger is pretty fibrous.
- If you want to reduce dehydrated ginger to a powder for use in cooking, be aware that because it's so fibrous, no matter how long you whir it in the blender, you will not end up with a fine powder. So be reassured, that a coarse, even chunky, powder is fine.
- Don't use your home-made ground ginger as a 1:1 substitute for store-bought. The flavors are not exactly alike, so experiment first.

Make your own ground ginger—simply throw it in the blender after dehydrating it. Dehydrated ginger is also nice used in tea.

Dehydrating temperature: 125°F

Preparation: Thinly slice (no need to peel the ginger first). Spread on a dehydrator tray and dehydrate 8 to 10 hours.

Dryness test: Should be brittle, feel dry to the touch, and snap in half.

Storage: See Storing Dehydrated Vegetables (page 49).

KALE

You'll never have to buy expensive kale chips again! And you'll always have super-nutritious kale on hand to add to soups, stews, and more.

Dehydrating temperature: 125°F

Preparation: Wash the leaves well and pat dry.

Kale chips: Cut the center stems from the leaves. Slice the leaves into 4 x 3-inch rectangles. If you like, blanch the kale in a large pot of gently boiling water for 15 seconds, then remove and shock it in a large bowl of ice water (see Tip). If you wish, you can salt the boiling water or lightly salt the kale prior to dehydrating to add a little flavor. Tossing the kale with sesame seeds and soy sauce prior to dehydration is another tasty option. Spread the kale on dehydrator trays and dehydrate 4 to 5 hours.

Kale leaves: Cut the center stems from the leaves, blanch for 15 seconds in boiling water, then shock them in a large bowl of ice water. Spread on dehydrator trays and dehydrate 6 to 8 hours.

Dryness test: Should be brittle, feel dry to the touch, and easily break apart in your hands.

Storage: The dehydrated product is fragile, so do not vacuum seal. Place in ziptop plastic freezer bags and then double-bag inside a Mylar bag, or store inside a canning jar with a lid and oxygen pack.

Tip

Blanching kale flattens the leaf, making for a nicer chip. However, you can dehydrate the kale without taking this step if you choose.

LEEKS

Tip

Take extra care when washing leeks, as they tend to be sandy near the roots.

Next time you have to buy a bunch of leeks when you only need one, dehydrate the rest and you'll have them on hand to add to soups and stews.

Dehydrating temperature: 125°F

Preparation: Trim the roots from the leeks, as well as the dark green portion, and discard. You can either cut them across into thin rounds or lengthwise into strips. Place them in a large bowl of water and agitate well to dislodge any dirt. With your hands or a strainer, remove from the water to clean, dry kitchen towels and pat dry. If the leeks haven't already separated themselves, pull any remaining slices into ringlets. Spread on dehydrator trays and dehydrate 8 to 10 hours.

Dryness test: Should feel like paper to the touch and be flexible.

Storage: See Storing Dehydrated Vegetables (page 49).

MUSHROOMS

Dried mushrooms add great depth of flavor to soups, stews, risottos, and so much more. Try to keep a variety of different types on hand. And dehydrating whole portobello mushroom caps means you can make yourself a mushroom burger any time you want!

Dehydrating temperature: 125°F

Preparation: Clean the mushrooms (see Tip).

Whole mushrooms (except portabellos): Trim the bottom of the stem (for shiitakes, remove the stem entirely). Spread on dehydrator trays and dehydrate 10 to 14 hours depending on size.

Whole portabello mushrooms: Discard the stems. Place the caps, stem side down, on dehydrator trays, and dehydrate 12 to 14 hours.

Sliced mushrooms: Trim the bottom of the stem (for shiitakes, remove the stem entirely). Slice the mushrooms, spread on dehydrator trays, and dehydrate for 8 hours.

Dryness test: Should be brittle, feel dry to the touch, and snap in half.

Storage: See Storing Dehydrated Vegetables (page 49).

Tips

- If you soak or wash mushrooms in water prior to dehydrating, they will turn an unattractive gray color. These are still fine to eat and cook with, but for a nice-looking dehydrated product, simply clean your mushrooms by wiping them with a damp cloth. Pre-cleaned or pre-sliced mushrooms purchased from the store will turn out perfect.
- Due to the thickness of some mushrooms, you might have to remove the dehydrator tray above for them to fit.

OKRA

Sliced okra is a delicious addition to soups (it's a traditional ingredient in gumbo) and it's particularly delicious when it's rehydrated, tossed in cornmeal, and fried up crisp.

Dehydrating temperature: 125°F

Preparation: Place the okra pods in a strainer and dip into a large pot of boiling water for no more than 10 seconds; remove, and dip in a large bowl of ice water until cool. Trim ¼ to ½ inch from the bottom of each pod, then cut the rest of the pod into rounds of whatever size you prefer. Spread on dehydrator trays and dehydrate 8 to 10 hours.

Dryness test: Should be brittle, feel hard and dry to the touch, and crush easily.

Storage: The dehydrated product is fragile, so do not vacuum seal. Place in ziptop plastic freezer bags and then double-bag inside a Mylar bag, or store inside a canning jar with a lid and oxygen pack.

ONIONS (Yellow, White, and Red)

Buy onions in bulk when they're on sale and stock your dehydrator pantry!

Dehydrating temperature: 125°F

Preparation:

Raw onions: Peel away the outer skin, then slice, chop, or mince the onions. If sliced, separate the slices into rings. Spread on dehydrator trays (if the onions are minced, first line the tray with a drying sheet) and dehydrate 12 to 14 hours. Dehydrated raw onions will feel dry like paper and be flexible.

Blanched onions: Peel, then cut the onions as directed above. Place in a strainer and dip in a large pot of boiling water 15 to 30 seconds, then place into a large bowl of ice water until cool. Shake to remove as much water as possible, then spread on dehydrator trays and dehydrate 8 hours. Dehydrated blanched onions will be brittle, feel dry to the touch, and snap in half.

Storage: See Storing Dehydrated Vegetables (page 49).

Tips

- If cutting onions makes you cry, place them in the freezer for one hour before slicing and chopping.
- Blanching onions prior to dehydrating will also reduce the pungency, as well as cut the dehydrating time significantly.
- A meat slicer or mandoline will slice your onions up in no time.

- You can mince your onions prior to dehydration but I prefer to do that once the onions are dehydrated; the more you chop onions prior to dehydration, the greater the flavor loss.
- Onions with a high sugar content (like Vidalia, Maui, or 1015 Sweets) will turn pink when dehydrated. That color goes away once the

onions are rehydrated. If you blanch the onions before dehydration, the color change won't occur.
- Do not dehydrate onions with other foods, as they may take on the onions' strong odor.
- Dehydrated blanched onion slices are yummy to eat as as snack and taste like onion rings without the fat.

ONIONS & SHALLOTS
(Green Onions, Scallions, Shallots, Pearl Onions, Cipolline)

Scallions are particularly nice to have on hand to add to Asian-inspired dishes.

Dehydrating temperature: 125°F

Preparation:

Green onions and scallions: Wash, then trim the root end and any damaged greens. Cut across into thin rings or into lengths, as you prefer. Spread on dehydrator trays and dehydrate 8 to 10 hours.

Pearl onions, cipolline, and shallots: Peel, then cut into thin slices. Pull the slices apart into rings. Spread on dehydrator trays and dehydrate 8 to 10 hours.

Dryness test: Should feel dry like paper and be flexible.

Storage: See Storing Dehydrated Vegetables (page 49).

PARSNIPS & TURNIPS

Tip

With dehydrated mashed parsnips and turnips in your pantry, all you need to do is add water for an almost-instant side dish!

Parsnips and turnips are a tasty change from carrots.

Dehydrating temperature: 125°F

Preparation: Peel the parsnips and turnips, if you like. Add the whole parsnips or turnips to a large pot of boiling water and cook until tender all the way through, 35 to 40 minutes. Drain and place in a large bowl of ice water until cool. Drain, then cut out the fibrous core and slice, cube, chop, shred, or mash as you prefer and spread on dehydrator trays. (For mashed turnips, working with 1 cup of puree at a time, spread it ¼ inch thick in strips on drying sheets set in the trays.) Dehydrate for 12 hours.

Dryness test: Should feel dry like paper and be somewhat pliable but will break apart.

Storage: See Storing Dehydrated Vegetables (page 49). For the dehydrated mashed turnips, break each strip into pieces and bag separately, so that you know that amount will rehydrate to 1 cup of puree.

PEAS & CHICKPEAS
(English, Sugar Snap, Snow, & Garbanzo Beans)

Canned peas and chickpeas are exceptions to my usual preference to not dehydrate canned vegetables (see page 49). But fresh is always best!

Dehydrating temperature: 125°F

Preparation:

English peas: Remove the peas from their pods, place in a strainer, and steam or boil until dark green and tender, about 5 minutes. Set the strainer in a large bowl of ice water until cool. Shake to remove as much water as possible, spread on dehydrator trays, and dehydrate 8 to 10 hours.

Sugar snap and snow peas: Wash the peas, then boil or steam until tender, about 5 minutes. Drain and place in a large bowl of ice bath until cool. Drain, spread on dehydrator trays, and dehydrate 8 to 10 hours. Dehydrated sugar snap and snow peas will be a translucent dark green, be brittle, feel dry to the touch, and snap in half.

Canned peas or chickpeas: Drain and rinse the peas, spread on dehydrator trays, and dehydrate 8 to 10 hours.

Dryness test: Unless otherwise indicated, should feel hard and dry, and will reduce to powder if struck with a kitchen mallet.

Storage: See Storing Dehydrated Vegetables (page 49).

PEPPERS, BELL & CHILE

Tips

- You can grill or broil peppers before dehydration for extra flavor. Broil or grill the peppers whole until the skins are blackened on all sides. Remove to a bowl and cover with plastic wrap for 10 minutes, then remove the skins, which should just slip off. Cut the peppers in half, and remove the stems and seeds. Cut the peppers up as you prefer and dehydrate pepper pieces as directed.

- When working with hot peppers, it's a good idea to wear disposable gloves to keep your skin from coming into contact with capsaicin, the active ingredient in chiles that causes that sought-after burn. Also, be vigilant about not touching your face or eyes.

Have fun and fill your garden with an enormous selection of the incredible variety of bell peppers and chiles now available as seeds. Then you can have at your fingertips, ready for rehydration, whole bell peppers in red, yellow, purple, orange, and green to use for stuffed peppers, or chiles from the mildest to the most incendiary to customize the heat of your favorite spicy dishes.

Dehydrating temperature: 125°F

Preparation: Wash thoroughly.

Whole bell peppers: Cut off the tops and remove the seeds and white membranes. Place on their sides on dehydrator trays, with the insides of the peppers facing the fan of the dehydrator. Dehydrate for 8 hours, then, wearing disposable gloves, push the peppers inside out. Return them to the trays, placing them cut side down. Dehydrate another 6 to 8 hours. To rehydrate, soak them inside out in boiling water for 20 to 30 minutes, then push them right side out.

Whole chile peppers: Do not remove the stems; pierce with a toothpick or sharp knife (this facilitates air flow and helps the drying process along). Spread on dehydrator trays and dehydrate up to 24 hours, depending on the size of the chiles, periodically turning them as they dehydrate. When dehydrated, they will be brittle and the seeds will rattle when shaken.

Pepper pieces: Cut off the stems and remove the seeds and white membranes. Slice, chop, or mince as you prefer, or leave the peppers in halves. Spread on dehydrator trays (if dehydrating halves, place them skin side down) and dehydrate for 10 hours.

Dryness test: Unless otherwise indicated, should be brittle, feel dry to the touch, snap in half, and can be easily crumbled between your fingers.

Storage: See Storing Dehydrated Vegetables (page 49).

POTATOES

I have dehydrated a lot of potatoes, so let me save you some grief—do not try dehydrating baking potatoes (Idahos, russets, etc.). They simply do not dehydrate well. Instead, use the denser waxy varieties, like Yukon Gold or the ubiquitous red potato. Also, don't waste time and potatoes trying to dehydrate mashed potatoes; getting the quality found in store-bought instant mashed potatoes requires special commercial equipment. I have found that it is near impossible to get the lumps out when you use home-dehydrated mashed potatoes.

Dehydrating temperature: 125°F

Preparation: Potatoes must be cooked all the way through before dehydrating. You can cook them whole, then cut them up, or cut them up first and then cook them. Here are the methods I use.

Cooking whole potatoes: You can boil them or bake them before cutting them up. *To boil,* bring the whole potatoes (with or without their peels) to a boil in a generous pot of water. Continue to boil just until you can easily insert a skewer into the centers of the potatoes. Drain and place in ice water to stop the cooking. Drain again. *To bake,* wrap each potato in aluminum foil and bake at 350°F until tender, about 1 hour. Let cool to room temperature with the foil still on. Either way, refrigerate the potatoes overnight to firm up, then peel off the skin with a knife and cut into slices or cubes no more than ⅓ inch thick, chop, or shred as desired. Spread on dehydrator trays and dehydrate 12 to 15 hours.

Cooking cut-up potatoes: Wash the potatoes if you intend to leave the skins on. Otherwise, peel them. Slice, cube, chop, or shred them as you prefer. Place the cut potatoes in a strainer, set in a large pot of water, bring to a boil, reduce the heat to medium-low, and cook until tender (if the cut potatoes are cooked at a rolling boil, they will fall apart, so make sure to reduce heat). Run the potatoes under cold water. Spread on dehydrator trays and dehydrate 12 to 15 hours.

Oven-baking sliced potatoes: Place potatoes sliced no more than ⅓ inch thick in a deep baking pan, cover with water, and bake in a preheated 350°F oven until tender, about 1 hour. Remove from the oven, drain, let cool, then spread on dehydrator trays and dehydrate 12 to 15 hours.

Dryness test: All properly dehydrated potatoes should be hard and will break in half with significant force. They also must be completely transparent through the middle. If you see any solid

Tip

- All potatoes need to be cooked before dehydration, white-fleshed potatoes in particular, because otherwise they will turn dark gray or black. But do not overcook them or they will fall apart.
- Potatoes are susceptible to case hardening when dehydrated, which can turn the inside of the potato piece black. To try to keep this from happening, your potato slices and cubes should be no more than ⅓ inch thick.

white spots in the center, the potato is not completely dehydrated and should be dehydrated longer. If the center of a potato cube or slice is black, this is a sign of case hardening, and these potatoes should NOT be stored long-term. See page 23–24 for tips on how to try to reverse case hardening.

Storage: See Storing Dehydrated Vegetables (page 49).

PUMPKIN & WINTER SQUASH

> ## Tip
>
> Pumpkin and other winter squash need to be cooked before dehydration and I like cooking them whole if possible for two reasons:
>
> 1. The skin creates a protective shield that helps keep the nutrients and flavor in.
> 2. They're much easier to peel and cut when cooked.

The best way to dehydrate pumpkin and other winter squash (with the exception of spaghetti squash—see below) is to reduce it to a puree, which you can then use in pies, cakes, side dishes, and much more.

Dehydrating temperature: 125°F

Preparation: Place the whole pumpkin or squash on a rack set in a large pot over boiling water and steam until tender, about 1 hour (check by inserting a skewer; it should go in without resistance). Transfer the whole pumpkin/squash to a sink of ice water. Once cool, let the water drain from the sink. Working in the sink, take a knife and gently cut away the skin. Carefully remove the peeled whole pumpkin/squash from the sink and place on a cutting board. Cut in half and remove all the seeds. Using a large spoon, scoop the flesh into a measuring cup and smoosh it down until you have 2 cups. Transfer this to a sheet of wax paper, and place another sheet of wax paper on top. Lightly roll the flesh with a rolling pin until it is as thin as a pie crust. Remove the top sheet and turn the other sheet upside down onto a dehydrator tray. Peel off the wax paper. With a pizza wheel, lightly wheel across the pumpkin, making a patchwork of 1-inch squares. Repeat until the trays are full. Dehydrate 10 to 12 hours. When dehydrated, it should feel dry like paper and be somewhat flexible and easy to break into squares.

Spaghetti squash: Cut the squash in half lengthwise, place cut side down on a baking sheet, and bake in a preheated 350°F oven until tender, 30 to 35 minutes. Let cool. Take a fork and gently shred the long strands from the middle of the squash. Spread them on dehydrator trays fitted with drying sheets and dehydrate 8 to 10 hours. Dehydrated spaghetti squash should be brittle and feel dry to the touch.

Storage: See Storing Dehydrated Vegetables (page 49).

RADISHES

Have these on hand in your dehydrator pantry to rehydrate and enjoy in salads and as a chip for dip.

Dehydrating temperature: 125°F

Preparation: Wash the radishes, then slice. Spread on dehydrator trays and dehydrate 6 to 8 hours.

Dryness test: Should be brittle, feel dry to the touch, and snap in half.

Storage: See Storing Dehydrated Vegetables (page 49).

Tips

- Thinly sliced radishes will curl up when dehydrated, but will straighten out again when rehydrated.
- If you want smaller pieces of radish, I recommend dehydrating radish slices, then chopping them in a blender or food processor after dehydration.

RUTABAGA

Rutabaga is a nice addition to soups and stews.

Dehydrating temperature: 125°F

Preparation: Place whole rutabagas in a large pot of water and bring to a boil. Continue to boil just until you can pierce easily with a skewer, 40 to 50 minutes. Transfer to a sink of ice water and let cool. Peel off the skin and cut into quarters.

Chopped rutabaga: Chop in a food processor. Spread on drying sheet set in a dehydrator tray and dehydrate for 12 hours.

Mashed rutabaga: Reduce to a smooth puree in a blender or food processor, or use a potato masher. Working with 1 cup of puree at a time, spread it ¼ inch thick in strips on drying sheets set in the trays. Dehydrate for 12 hours.

Dryness test: Should feel hard and dry, but still be somewhat flexible.

Storage: See Storing Dehydrated Vegetables (page 49).

Tip

For best results, it's important to cook the rutabaga all the way through before dehydration.

SPINACH

Tip

- Always chop spinach **after** it has been dehydrated for maximum flavor and nutrient retention.

Having dehydrated spinach on hand means you don't need to worry about spoilage again. You can dehydrate baby spinach as well as mature leaves.

Dehydrating temperature: 110°F

Preparation: Wash well to get rid of any grit. Spread the leaves on dehydrator trays and dehydrate 8 to 10 hours.

Dryness test: Should be brittle, feel dry to the touch, and easily break apart in your hands.

Storage: Dehydrated whole spinach leaves are fragile, so do not vacuum seal. Place in ziptop plastic freezer bags and then double-bag inside a Mylar bag, or store inside a canning Mason jar with a lid and oxygen pack.

SWEET POTATOES & YAMS

Tip

Like regular potatoes, sweet potatoes and yams must be cooked prior to dehydration or they will turn black.

Sweet potatoes and yams are botanically distinct but they are handled the same way in the dehydrator.

Dehydrating temperature: 125°F

Preparation: You can boil or bake sweet potatoes and yams. *To boil,* bring the whole potatoes/yams to a boil in a generous pot of water. Continue to boil just until you can easily insert a skewer into the centers of the potatoes. Drain and place in ice water to stop the cooking. Drain again. *To bake,* wrap each potato in aluminum foil and bake 350°F until tender, about 1 hour. Let cool to room temperature with the foil still on. Either way, refrigerate overnight to firm up, then peel off the skin with a knife.

Sliced sweet potatoes/yams: Cut the peeled potatoes/yams into ¼-inch rounds. Spread the slices on dehydrator trays and dehydrate 12 to 14 hours.

Mashed sweet potatoes/yams: Mash the peeled potatoes/yams until smooth. Working with 1 cup of mash at a time, spread ¼ inch thick on drying sheets, then using a pizza cutter, cut into 1-inch squares. Dehydrate for 14 hours.

Dryness test: Should feel hard and dry, and be somewhat flexible (both sliced and mashed).

Storage: See Storing Dehydrated Vegetables (page 49).

SWISS CHARD

Swiss chard is a tasty and nutritious addition to soups and stews.

Dehydrating temperature: 125°F

Preparation: Wash the leaves to get rid of any grit and trim the stems. Dip the leaves into a large pot of boiling water for 1 second and place on dehydrator trays. Dehydrate 6 to 8 hours.

Dryness test: Should be brittle, feel dry to the touch, and easily break apart in your hands.

Storage: See Storing Dehydrated Vegetables (page 49).

Tip

For the best nutrient retention, slice or chop Swiss chard after dehydration.

TOMATOES

Make the most of your garden surplus or summer sales when local tomatoes hit the market.

Dehydrating temperature: 125°F

Preparation: Wash the tomatoes.
Cherry or plum tomatoes: Cut in half, place on dehydrator trays skin side down, and dehydrate 10 to 16 hours. When dehydrated, they should feel hard and dry but still be somewhat flexible.
Chopped or sliced tomatoes: If slicing, cut the tomatoes ⅛ to ½ inch thick, as you prefer (I usually cut mine ¼ inch thick). Place the sliced or chopped tomatoes on dehydrator trays and dehydrate 10 to 12 hours. When dehydrated, they should feel dry like paper, and be flexible but easily torn.

Storage: See Storing Dehydrated Vegetables (page 49).

Tip

You can remove the skins if you like, but it's optional. To make this easier, dip the tomatoes in boiling water until the skins blister, about 1 minute. Place them in ice water and you should be able to slip the skins right off.

WATER CHESTNUTS

Canned water chestnuts are a good candidate for the dehydrator. That way you can use just what you need without worry of spoilage.

Dehydrating temperature: 125°F

Preparation: Drain water from the can. If the chestnuts are whole cut them into ¼-inch-thick slices. Spread the slices on dehydrator trays and dehydrate for 10 hours

Dryness test: Should feel very hard and dry, and snap in half with significant force.

Storage: See Storing Dehydrated Vegetables (page 49).

ZUCCHINI & OTHER SUMMER SQUASH

When your garden is overflowing with summer squash, your dehydrator can come to the rescue. Dehydrate the squash in slices to enjoy as a side dish later on, or shredded to add to muffins and quick breads, or even squash blossoms!

Dehydrating temperature: 100°F for squash blossoms and 125°F for sliced, shredded, or baby squash

Preparation:

Sliced or shredded squash: Wash, then cut into ¼-inch-thick slices or shred. Spread on dehydrator trays and dehydrate at 125°F for 10 to 12 hours.

Baby squash: Cut them in half lengthwise (if the squash is more than 1½ inches thick, cut lengthwise into thirds instead of halves, to ensure proper dehydration). Spread on dehydrator trays skin side down and dehydrate at 125°F for 8 hours. Turn the halves skin side up, score the skin with a sharp knife, and dehydrate for another 6 hours. These are delicious rehydrated in brine and then grilled.

Squash blossoms: Carefully wash the blossoms and spread over the dehydrator tray, and dehydrate at 110°F for 10 to 12 hours. The dehydrated flowers should be straw-like in texture.

Dryness test: Unless otherwise indicated, should be brittle, feel dry to the touch, and snap in half. Whole baby squash will be somewhat pliable.

Storage: See Storing Dehydrated Vegetables (page 49).

Tip

The fastest way to get even pieces is to use a food processor.

6

Powders & Leathers

Why include powders and leathers in the same chapter? Because they dehydrate in the same way—as a puree spread on drying sheets set in dehydrator trays. After dehydration, they go in two different directions, but both are invaluable in the dehydrator pantry.

POWDERS

Why reduce dehydrated fruits and/or vegetables to powder? If it is a fruit or vegetable you intend to use as a puree (say pumpkin puree for a pie, or rutabaga puree for a side dish, or any fruit or vegetable if you want to make baby food), powdering the produce after dehydration will allow for much more efficient storage. These powders can also be used as an ingredient in smoothies and soups, as a puree for making instant baby food or a quick and easy side dish, or be added as a flavoring to flour, bread crumbs, salt, or sugar. And why pay the high price of buying ground pure chile powder, onion powder, or garlic powder at the store when you can make your own? In addition to the money you'll save, you'll also get a more flavorful, potent product.

Not all produce are alike when preparing powders. Follow the template directions below.

Vegetable powder: All vegetables (with the exception of mushrooms) must be cooked until tender before dehydration, then pureed until smooth (do not add salt, sugar, or corn syrup to the puree) and spread on drying sheets set in dehydrator trays, spread no more than 1/4 inch thick. Dehydrate at 125°F for 12 to 15 hours. The dehydrated puree will be hard and though it might be somewhat pliable, it will break easily. This can then be ground into a fine powder using a blender, stone grinder, or mortar and pestle. *Note:* You cannot grind dehydrated cooked potatoes into a powder to make instant mashed potatoes; for more on why, see the entry for dehydrating potatoes on page 73.

Fruit powder: Fruit does not need to be cooked before dehydration when making powders. Peel and pit/core the fruit if needed, then puree until smooth. If puree is too thick to spread thinly on the drying sheet in the dehydrator, add water to thin. (You can also use 100% pure fruit juice, with no added sugars.) If the puree is too thin, add cornstarch (you'll have to experiment with the amount you need to get the right consistency) and heat in a saucepan over medium heat, stirring, until thick. Do not add any salt, sugar, or corn syrup to the puree. Spread the puree no more than ¼ inch thick on the drying sheet and dehydrate at 125°F for 12 to 15 hours. The dehydrated puree will be hard and break easily. It can then be powdered using a blender, stone grinder, or mortar and pestle. If the fruit used to make the powder is especially high in sugar (dates, grapes, cherries, apricots), the powder should be tossed with a little granulated cane sugar prior to storing to prevent clumping.

Powder from herbs and flowers: These items do not need to be cooked prior to dehydration. Simply follow the directions on page 102–05 for dehydration, then grind them into a powder once dry using a blender, stone grinder, or mortar and pestle.

Storing Powders

Powders are best stored in canning jars with an oxygen pack or, for longer-term storage, vacuum sealed with an oxygen pack, then double-bagged in Mylar and stored in a cool, dry place. Stored this way, powders should keep for five years or more. When stored long term in a vacuum-sealed bag, powder can become compacted. If it does, just sift or reblend it before use.

Rehydrating Powders

Since powdering condenses the dehydrated item, you will need to use 5 to 20 times more water for rehydration than needed to rehydrate the item chopped or shredded. For example, ¼ cup powdered pumpkin requires 2 cups of boiling water for rehydration, whereas 2 cups water would be sufficient to rehydrate an entire cup of dehydrated pumpkin flakes, both of which will end up yielding the same amount of puree.

There is no table I can provide for exactly how much water to add to how much powder to rehydrate for the simple reason that it depends. It depends on how finely you've ground the item (the finer the powder, the more water it will require) and the desired thickness

---

INSTANT SIDE DISHES FROM POWDERS

With powders on hand, you can have a beautiful vegetable puree on the table in just a few minutes. Rehydrate, season to taste, and it's ready to serve! Veggies that work particularly well this way include:

- Parsnips
- Rutabagas
- Sweet potatoes
- Turnips

Also keep in mind that these powders can be used as the basis for creamed soups—cream of broccoli, cream of mushroom, cream of asparagus—the garden's the limit!

of the puree you want. To use pumpkin as an example again, for a pie filling, I rehydrate ¼ cup powder with 2 cups boiling water. However, to make pumpkin soup, I will rehydrate that same ¼ cup powder with 6 to 8 cups of boiling water. It also depends on the item itself. In contrast to pumpkin, ¼ cup of powdered dehydrated peas requires only 1 cup of boiling water to rehydrate to a puree. When using the powders in your own recipes, you'll need to experiment with the amounts of water and powder to get the thickness you like for the particular preparation.

Vegetable Stock Powder

Having this powder on hand allows you to have flavorful vegetable stock in an instant. You can also use it as the foundation for crafting your own instant soup mix (see page 82).

Makes ⅔ cup powder

> 4 cups water
> 1 cup chopped fresh onion
> 4 fresh garlic cloves, peeled
> 1 fresh green bell pepper, cut in half and seeded
> 1 fresh red bell pepper, cut in half and seeded
> 1 teaspoon chopped fresh thyme
> 1 teaspoon chopped fresh rosemary
> 1 teaspoon chopped fresh tarragon
> 1 tablespoon cornstarch

1. In an uncovered stockpot, combine all the ingredients except the cornstarch and bring to a boil. Reduce the heat to a simmer and cook until all the vegetables are tender and three quarters of the water has evaporated.
2. Using an immersion blender, blend the stock until all the solids are pureed. Stir in the cornstarch and let simmer, stirring until thickened.
3. Pour the puree on a drying sheet set on a dehydrator tray. Slap the tray on the counter a couple times to level the liquid. Dehydrate at 125°F for 10 hours. The dehydrated stock will brittle.
4. Break the dehydrated stock into pieces, place in a blender, and reduce to a powder. Store in a canning jar with an oxygen pack or a vacuum-sealed bag with an oxygen pack and double-bag in Mylar. Stored this way, it will keep 5 or more years.
5. **To rehydrate,** add 1 tablespoon powdered dehydrated vegetable stock powder per 1 cup boiling water.

Making Instant 100% Natural Baby Food from Powders

A wonderful use of vegetable and fruit powders is in making your own instant baby food; just add boiling water, cool, and eat!

Important Note: If you are going to make instant baby food, the produce you use must be cooked until very tender before dehydration (even if, in the directions above for powders, it is indicated that cooking is not necessary before dehydration).

Here are the steps for making your own instant baby food:

1. Prior to dehydration, cook the produce until very tender—you can boil, steam, or bake as you wish. Be sure not to use any added oil or fat when cooking.
2. Puree the produce until smooth. Do not add anything to the puree at this point, including sugar or salt.
3. Pour the puree onto drying sheets set in dehydrator trays to a thickness of about ¼ inch. Dehydrate at 125°F for 8 to 15 hours (see the time guidelines for the particular fruit or vegetable). When completely dehydrated, the puree should be hard and break easily.
4. Break the puree into pieces, place in a blender, and process into a fine powder.
5. Store the powder in canning jars with an oxygen pack, or vacuum seal with an oxygen pack and double-bag in Mylar. When stored in this way, these powders should keep for 5 years or more.

To Rehydrate Powders into Instant Baby Food

As a general rule, add ¼ cup boiling water per 1 tablespoon vegetable powder and stir, letting it cool before feeding it to baby. Fruit powders have more variability in the water they require. Powders made from juicier fruits will require more water. For example, peach powder will require ⅓ cup boiling water per 1 tablespoon powder, whereas only ¼ cup boiling water is needed per 1 tablespoon apple powder. I recommend starting with ¼ cup boiling water per 1 tablespoon powder, and adding more water if needed to reach the desired consistency.

Part of the fun of making your own baby food from powders is that it's so easy and convenient to mix and match flavors. Here are a few of our favorite combinations.

Zucchini and Summer Squash Baby Food

Makes 1 to 2 servings

1½ teaspoons powdered dehydrated zucchini
1½ teaspoons powdered dehydrated yellow summer squash
¼ cup boiling water

Stir together the ingredients, let cool, and serve. Will keep, tightly covered, in the refrigerator for up to 3 days.

Apple and Sweet Potato Baby Food

Makes 1 to 2 servings

2 teaspoons powdered dehydrated cooked apples
1 teaspoon powdered dehydrated cooked sweet potatoes
⅓ cup boiling water

Stir together the ingredients, let cool, and serve. Will keep, tightly covered, in the refrigerator for up to 3 days.

Peaches and Tapioca Baby Food

Makes 2 servings

1 tablespoon powdered dehydrated cooked peaches
1 tablespoon powdered quick-cooking tapioca
½ cup boiling water

Stir together the ingredients, let cool, and serve. Will keep, tightly covered, in the refrigerator for up to 3 days.

Peach and Mango Baby Food

Makes 1 to 2 servings

1½ teaspoons powdered dehydrated mangoes
1½ teaspoons powdered dehydrated peaches
⅓ cup boiling water

Stir together the ingredients, let cool, and serve. Will keep, tightly covered, in the refrigerator for up to 3 days.

Banana and Blueberry Baby Food

Makes 1 to 2 servings

2 teaspoons powdered dehydrated bananas
1 teaspoon powdered dehydrated blueberries
¼ cup boiling water

Stir together the ingredients, let cool, and serve. Will keep, tightly covered, in the refrigerator for up to 3 days.

Pineapple-Orange-Banana Baby Food

Makes 1 to 2 servings

1 teaspoon powdered dehydrated pineapple
1 teaspoon powdered dehydrated oranges
1 teaspoon powdered dehydrated banana
⅓ cup boiling water

Stir together the ingredients, let cool, and serve. Will keep, tightly covered, in the refrigerator for up to 3 days.

LEATHERS

There is a whole crazy and delicious world of leathers out there. They can be made with vegetables, fruit, or both. Leather can be chunky, smooth, or even crunchy. You can make big round circles, small squares, or little tiny drops. You can go crazy with color and swirls, or make funny faces. No matter how you color it, shape it, or flavor it, fruit leather is fun and delicious!

Leathers can be eaten as is for a quick and nutritious snack, or can be reconstituted to be used as an ingredient in another recipe.

To make a leather (or roll-up), the fruit or vegetable is washed and peeled if desired. (I recommend that you try making the same leather with and without the peel and see which you prefer. Leaving the skin on apples, for instance, will add great color and nutrients, as well as enhance the texture of the leather.)

The fruit or vegetable is then pureed along with cornstarch and very often lemon juice. The addition of cornstarch will prevent the leather from cracking, a very common problem. The lemon juice enhances the final color and also provides a boost of vitamin C. You also add corn syrup if you would like to be able to roll up the final leather. The flexibility of a leather depends largely on its sugar content, and the presence of corn syrup ensures that your leather will be flexible rather than hard like candy. Lack of flexibility is a bigger problem with vegetable leathers, which are naturally a bit more brittle. Adding corn syrup, or even a little pureed fruit, when making a vegetable leather can help improve the flexibility of the final product.

If the puree is too thick, like the consistency of a thick milkshake, add a little water or 100% pure juice while blending until you achieve a smoothly flowing, but not watery, puree, similar to the consistency of applesauce.

For the best results, all fruit and vegetable purees should be transferred to a saucepan and then brought to a boil. Immediately reduce the heat to a simmer and let it gently bubble for 2 minutes. This will help to create a more pliable and translucent leather.

Cooking the puree is optional in most cases (exceptions include carrots, potatoes, spinach, and cucumbers). If you do skip this step, the resulting leathers will be brittle and crunchy, especially if the item is low in sugar and pale in color.

You can also use some partially processed items to make leathers. Applesauce simply needs to be spread on drying sheets and then placed in the dehydrator to create an applesauce leather. Dehydrate canned fruit in the same way, first pureeing it with a little of its packing syrup to thin it to a spreadable consistency. Refried beans and canned whole beans can be handled in the same manner, pureeing them with their packing liquid (rehydrated, you can use them as a quick bean dip). You can also dehydrate store-bought salsa or chili sauce or your own homemade salsa (see page 98).

You can even make leathers out of sauce; they rehydrate in minutes, ready to be heated up and served with chicken, pork, or beef. I've included some of my favorite recipes here.

Storing Leathers

Leather can be rolled up in plastic wrap or parchment paper (this is best done while the leather is still warm) or can be placed flat in an individual ziptop plastic bag. Or you can stack multiple leathers in a large ziptop bag or airtight container, with sheets of parchment paper inserted between them to keep them from sticking. Store in a cool, dry place; they will keep for up to a year.

Rehydrating Leathers

Leathers can be eaten as is, or you can rehydrate them for use in other recipes, like sauces or soups. Place the leather in a small bowl with a little boiling water, let sit for 2 minutes, and stir.

TIPS FOR LEATHER SUCCESS

- Never use powdered or granulated sugar in your leathers, as it will crystallize over time. Use honey, corn syrup, or stevia.
- Add an extra tablespoon of corn syrup to leathers containing lemon, lime, or grapefruit to balance the sourness.
- You can place different purees in plastic squeeze bottles and use them to create mixed fruit or vegetable leathers, swirling them together directly on the drying sheets. You can also use the bottles to create leather "drops" on the sheets or other shapes, including smiley faces and fun animals.

- For some added texture and flavor zing, sprinkle the puree on the drying sheet with grated citrus zest before dehydrating.
- To make leather, you'll need to line your dehydrator trays with drying sheets, which can be purchased from the company that made your dehydrator or online. There are disposable and reusable options. Less expensive alternatives to drying sheets are oven liners trimmed with scissors to fit your trays, or large ziptop plastic bags, cut open to make one large sheet. You'll need to weight the corners down with flat stones so

the plastic doesn't blow into the leather as it is drying. If there is any print on the bag, face it away from the food, otherwise it will transfer to the leather when it is peeled away from the plastic.
- A spatula is indispensable for spreading the puree on the sheets and for helping lift off the finished leather.
- Slapping the dehydrator trays on the counter prior to dehydrating will help to level the puree and create leathers of a more even thickness.

Basic Fruit or Vegetable Leather

Makes 4 leathers

> 4 cups pureed raw or cooked fruits or vegetables (carrots, potatoes, spinach, and cucumbers must be cooked)
>
> 2 tablespoons corn syrup
>
> 1 tablespoon lemon juice
>
> 1 to 2 teaspoons cornstarch (start with 1 teaspoon and add the second if necessary for the right consistency)
>
> Water or fruit juice as needed (optional)

1. In a blender, combine the puree, corn syrup, lemon juice, and cornstarch and blend until smooth. Keep in mind, you may need to add water, fruit juice, or more corn syrup depending on the desired vegetable and/or fruit combination until you reach an applesauce-like consistency.
2. If needed or preferred, pour the puree into a small saucepan, bring to a boil, reduce the heat to medium, and let simmer for 2 minutes.
3. Let cool, then pour 1 cup of puree per leather in strips on a drying sheet set in a dehydrator tray. Slap the tray on the counter a couple times to level the liquid. Dehydrate at 125°F until the leathers easily peel off the drying sheet, 10 to 12 hours.
4. At this point, peel the leathers off the drying sheets and place them on the mesh rack of the dehydrator tray itself, then place back into the dehydrator for another 2 to 3 hours. This will help to remove any remaining tackiness.
5. Remove from the tray, roll up in wax or parchment paper while still warm, and store as directed (page 87).

Red Hot Cherry Leather

Makes 2 leathers

> 3 cups fresh cherries, pitted
>
> ½ fresh chile pepper, seeded
>
> 2 tablespoons lemon juice
>
> 1 teaspoon cornstarch

1. In a blender, combine the ingredients and blend until smooth, with an applesauce-like consistency.
2. Pour the puree into a small saucepan, bring to a boil, reduce the heat to medium, and let simmer for 2 minutes.
3. Let cool, then pour 1 cup of puree per leather into strips on a drying sheet set in a dehydrator tray. Slap the tray on the counter a couple times to level the liquid. Dehydrate at 125°F until the leathers easily peel off the drying sheet, 10 to 12 hours.
4. Peel the leathers off the sheet and place them on the mesh rack of the dehydrator tray, then place back into the dehydrator for another 2 to 3 hours. Store as directed while warm (page 87).

Strawberry Leather

Makes 2 leathers

    4 cups hulled ripe strawberries
    ½ to 1 cup water, as needed
    1 tablespoon corn syrup
    1 tablespoon lemon juice
    1 teaspoon cornstarch

1. In a blender, combine the ingredients, starting with ½ cup water, and blend until smooth; add more water if needed to get the proper applesauce-like consistency.
2. Pour the puree into a small saucepan, bring to a boil, reduce the heat to medium, and let simmer for 2 minutes.
3. Let cool, then pour 1 cup of puree per leather in strips on a drying sheet set in a dehydrator tray. Slap the tray on the counter a couple times to level the liquid. Dehydrate at 125°F until the leathers easily peel off the drying sheet, 10 to 12 hours.
4. Peel the leathers off the drying sheet and place them on the mesh rack of the dehydrator tray itself, then place back into the dehydrator for another 2 to 3 hours. Store as directed while warm (page 87).

Raspberry Leather

Makes 4 leathers

    4 cups fresh raspberries
    2 tablespoons corn syrup
    1 tablespoon lemon juice
    1 teaspoon cornstarch

1. In a blender, combine the ingredients and blend until smooth, with an applesauce-like consistency.
2. Pour the puree into a small saucepan, bring to a boil, reduce the heat to medium, and let simmer for 2 minutes.
3. Let cool, then pour 1 cup of puree per leather in strips on a drying sheet set in a dehydrator tray. Slap the tray on the counter a couple times to level the liquid. Dehydrate at 125°F until the leathers easily peel off the drying sheet, 10 to 12 hours.
4. Peel the leathers off the sheet and place them on the mesh rack of the dehydrator tray, then place back into the dehydrator for another 2 to 3 hours. Store as directed while warm (see page 87).

Blueberry and Cantaloupe Leather

Makes 2 leathers

> 1 cup fresh blueberries, picked over
> 1 cup ½-inch cantaloupe cubes
> 1 tablespoon lemon juice
> 1 tablespoon corn syrup
> 1 teaspoon cornstarch

1. In a blender, combine the ingredients and blend until smooth, with an applesauce-like consistency.
2. Pour the puree into a small saucepan, bring to a boil, reduce the heat to medium, and let simmer for 2 minutes.
3. Let cool, then pour 1 cup of puree per leather in strips on a drying sheet set in a dehydrator tray. Slap the tray on the counter a couple times to level the liquid. Dehydrate at 125°F until the leathers easily peel off the drying sheet, 10 to 12 hours.
4. Peel the leathers off the sheet and place them on the mesh rack of the dehydrator tray, then place back into the dehydrator for another 2 to 3 hours. Store as directed while warm (page 87).

Cranberry Leather

Makes 5 leathers

> 4 cups fresh cranberries, picked over
> 2 cups water
> 1 cup corn syrup
> 1 tablespoon lemon juice
> 1 teaspoon cornstarch

1. In a blender, combine the ingredients and blend until smooth.
2. Pour the puree into a small saucepan, bring to a boil, reduce the heat to medium, and let simmer until thickened to an applesauce-like consistency, 15 to 20 minutes.
3. Let cool, then pour 1 cup of puree per leather in strips on drying sheets set in dehydrator trays. Slap the trays on the counter a couple times to level the liquid. Dehydrate at 125°F until the leathers easily peel off the drying sheets, 10 to 12 hours.
4. Peel the leathers off the sheets and place them on the mesh racks of the dehydrator trays, then place back into the dehydrator for another 2 to 3 hours. Store as directed while warm (page 87).

Cranberry-Apple Leather

Makes 4 leathers

3 apples, cored (peeling is optional)
½ cup fresh cranberries, picked over
1 cup apple juice, cranberry juice cocktail, or water
2 tablespoons corn syrup
2 tablespoons lemon juice
1 teaspoon cornstarch

1. In a blender, combine the ingredients and blend until smooth, with an applesauce-like consistency.
2. Pour the puree into a small saucepan, bring to a boil, reduce the heat to medium, and let simmer for 2 minutes.
3. Let cool, then pour 1 cup of puree per leather in strips on a drying sheet set in a dehydrator tray. Slap the tray on the counter a couple times to level the liquid. Dehydrate at 125°F until the leathers easily peel off the drying sheet, 10 to 12 hours.
4. Peel the leathers off the sheet and place them on the mesh rack of the dehydrator tray, then place back into the dehydrator for another 2 to 3 hours. Store as directed while warm (page 87).

Apple Leather

Red apples will make red leather, green apples will make green leather, and yellow apples will make yellow leather. You can make tricolored apple leather by putting the different-colored apple purees in squeeze bottles and swirling them together directly on the drying sheet.

Makes 4 leathers

4 apples, cored but not peeled
1 cup apple juice or water
2 tablespoons corn syrup
1 tablespoon lemon juice
1 teaspoon cornstarch

1. In a blender, combine the ingredients and blend until smooth, with an applesauce-like consistency.
2. Pour the puree into a small saucepan, bring to a boil, reduce the heat to medium, and let simmer for 2 minutes.
3. Let cool, then pour 1 cup of puree per leather in strips on a drying sheet set in a dehydrator tray. Slap the tray on the counter a couple times to level the liquid. Dehydrate at 125°F until the leathers easily peel off the drying sheet, 10 to 12 hours.
4. Peel the leathers off the sheet and place them on the mesh rack of the dehydrator tray, then place back into the dehydrator for another 2 to 3 hours. Store as directed while warm (page 87).

Candy Apple Leather: Follow the directions for Apple Leather, adding 8 hard cinnamon candies to the puree when it is transferred to the saucepan. Stir as the mixture heats up until the candies have melted.

Apple Mint Leather: Follow the directions for Apple Leather, adding 2 tablespoons chopped fresh mint to the blender.

Apple and Spinach Leather

This is a great way to get your kids to eat their spinach—all you taste are the apples.
Makes 2 leathers

> 2 apples, cored (peeling is optional)
> ½ cup cooked spinach
> ½ cup apple juice or water
> 2 tablespoons corn syrup
> 2 tablespoons lemon juice
> 1 teaspoon cornstarch

1. In a blender, combine the ingredients and blend until smooth, with an applesauce-like consistency.
2. Pour the puree into a small saucepan, bring to a boil, reduce the heat to medium, and let simmer for 2 minutes.
3. Let cool, then pour 1 cup of puree per leather in strips on a drying sheet set in a dehydrator tray. Slap the tray on the counter a couple times to level the liquid. Dehydrate at 125°F until the leathers easily peel off the drying sheet, 10 to 12 hours.
4. Peel the leathers off the sheet and place them on the mesh rack of the dehydrator tray, then place back into the dehydrator for another 2 to 3 hours. Store as directed while warm (page 87).

Apple and Zucchini Leather

Another sneaky way to get kids to eat their vegetables!

Makes 4 leathers

> 2 cups shredded zucchini (don't peel)
> 2 cups shredded green apples (don't peel)
> 1 cup apple juice
> ¼ cup corn syrup
> 1 tablespoon lemon juice
> 1 teaspoon cornstarch

1. In a blender, combine the ingredients and blend until smooth, with an applesauce-like consistency.
2. Pour the puree into a small saucepan, bring to a boil, reduce the heat to medium, and let simmer for 2 minutes.
3. Let cool, then pour 1 cup of puree per leather into strips on a drying sheet set in a dehydrator tray. Slap the tray on the counter a couple times to level the liquid. Dehydrate at 125°F until the leathers easily peel off the drying sheet, 10 to 12 hours.
4. Peel the leathers off the sheet and place them on the mesh rack of the dehydrator tray, then place back into the dehydrator for another 2 to 3 hours. Store as directed while warm (page 87).

Lemon Leather

This also works with limes.

Makes 2 leathers

> 4 lemons, peels and seeds removed
> ½ cup corn syrup
> 2 teaspoons cornstarch

1. In a blender, combine the ingredients and blend until smooth, with an applesauce-like consistency.
2. Pour the puree into a small saucepan, bring to a boil, reduce the heat to medium, and let simmer for 2 minutes.
3. Let cool, then pour 1 cup of puree per leather into strips on a drying sheet set in a dehydrator tray. Slap the tray on the counter a couple times to level the liquid. Dehydrate at 125°F until the leathers easily peel off the drying sheet, 10 to 12 hours.
4. Peel the leathers off the sheet and place them on the mesh rack of the dehydrator tray, then place back into the dehydrator for another 2 to 3 hours. Store as directed while warm (page 87).

Orange Leather

Makes 2 leathers

> 4 navel oranges, peeled and sliced
> ¼ cup corn syrup
> 1 tablespoon cornstarch

1. In a blender, combine the ingredients and blend until smooth, with an applesauce-like consistency.
2. Pour the puree into a small saucepan, bring to a boil, reduce the heat to medium, and let simmer for 2 minutes.
3. Let cool, then pour 1 cup of puree per leather into strips on a drying sheet set in a dehydrator tray. Slap the tray on the counter a couple times to level the liquid. Dehydrate at 125°F until the leathers easily peel off the drying sheet, 10 to 12 hours.
4. Peel the leathers off the sheet and place them on the mesh rack of the dehydrator tray, then place back into the dehydrator for another 2 to 3 hours. Store as directed while warm (page 87).

Piña Colada Leather

Makes 2 leathers

> 1 cup coconut slices
> 1 cup chopped pineapple
> 1 cup coconut water
> 1 tablespoon lemon juice
> 2 tablespoons corn syrup
> 1 teaspoon cornstarch

1. In a blender, combine the ingredients and blend until smooth, with an applesauce-like consistency.
2. Pour the puree into a small saucepan, bring to a boil, reduce the heat to medium, and let simmer for 2 minutes.
3. Let cool, then pour 1 cup of puree per leather in strips on a drying sheet set in a dehydrator tray. Slap the tray on the counter a couple times to level the liquid. Dehydrate at 125°F until the leathers easily peel off the drying sheet, 10 to 12 hours.
4. Peel the leathers off the sheet and place them on the mesh rack of the dehydrator tray itself, then place back into the dehydrator for another 2 to 3 hours. Store as directed while warm (page 87).

Chocolate-Banana Leather

Makes 2 leathers

4 ripe bananas, peeled
1 cup apple juice or water
1 tablespoon lemon juice
1 tablespoon corn syrup
1 tablespoon unsweetened cocoa powder
1 teaspoon cornstarch

1. In a blender, combine the ingredients and blend until smooth, with an applesauce-like consistency.
2. Pour the puree into a small saucepan set over medium heat, bring to a simmer, and let simmer for 2 minutes. Do not boil.
3. Let cool, then pour 1 cup of puree per leather in strips on a drying sheet set in a dehydrator tray. Slap the tray on the counter a couple times to level the liquid. Dehydrate at 125°F until the leathers easily peel off the drying sheet, 10 to 12 hours.
4. Peel the leathers off the sheet and place them on the mesh rack of the dehydrator tray itself, then place back into the dehydrator for another 2 to 3 hours. Store as directed while warm (page 87).

Peach-Mango Leather

Makes 4 leathers

2 cups chopped peeled ripe peaches
2 cups chopped peeled ripe mangoes
2 tablespoons corn syrup
1 tablespoon lemon juice
1 teaspoon cornstarch

1. In a blender, combine the ingredients and blend until smooth, with an applesauce-like consistency.
2. Pour the puree into a small saucepan, bring to a boil, reduce the heat to medium, and let simmer for 2 minutes.
3. Let cool, then pour 1 cup of puree per leather into strips on a drying sheet set in a dehydrator tray. Slap the tray on the counter a couple times to level the liquid. Dehydrate at 125°F until the leathers easily peel off the drying sheet, 10 to 12 hours.
4. Peel the leathers off the sheet and place them on the mesh rack of the dehydrator tray, then place back into the dehydrator for another 2 to 3 hours. Store as directed while still warm (page 87).

Apricot and Chile Pepper Leather

Makes 2 leathers

2 cups chopped fresh apricots
¼ cup water or as needed
½ fresh chile pepper, seeded
2 tablespoons lemon juice
1 teaspoon cornstarch

1. In a blender, combine the ingredients and blend until smooth, with an applesauce-like consistency.
2. Pour the puree into a small saucepan, bring to a boil, reduce the heat to medium, and let simmer for 2 minutes.
3. Let cool, then pour 1 cup of puree per leather into strips on a drying sheet set in a dehydrator tray. Slap the tray on the counter a couple times to level the liquid. Dehydrate at 125°F until the leathers easily peel off the drying sheet, 10 to 12 hours.
4. Peel the leathers off the sheet and place them on the mesh rack of the dehydrator tray, then place back into the dehydrator for another 2 to 3 hours. Store as directed while warm (page 87).

Watermelon and Kiwi Leather

Makes 2 leathers

1 cup cubed seeded watermelon
3 kiwi fruits, peeled
1 tablespoon lemon juice
2 teaspoons cornstarch

1. In a blender, combine the ingredients and blend until smooth, with an applesauce-like consistency.
2. Pour the puree into a small saucepan, bring to a boil, reduce the heat to medium, and let simmer for 2 minutes.
3. Let cool, then pour 1 cup of puree per leather in strips on a drying sheet set in a dehydrator tray. Slap the tray on the counter a couple times to level the liquid. Dehydrate at 125°F until the leathers easily peel off the drying sheet, 10 to 12 hours.
4. Peel the leathers off the sheet and place them on the mesh rack of the dehydrator tray, then place back into the dehydrator for another 2 to 3 hours. Store as directed while warm (page 87).

Carrot Cake Leather

Makes about 4 leathers

2 cups chopped cooked carrots (be sure to cook them until they're very soft)

2 cups chopped raw apples (peeling is optional)

½ cup apple juice or water

2 tablespoons dehydrated shredded coconut

2 tablespoons corn syrup

2 tablespoons lemon juice

1½ teaspoons pumpkin pie spice

1 teaspoon cornstarch

1 tablespoon dehydrated grapes, finely chopped

1. In a blender, combine all ingredients, except the grapes, and blend until smooth, with an applesauce-like consistency.
2. Pour the puree into a small saucepan, bring to a boil, reduce the heat to medium, and let simmer for 2 minutes.
3. Let cool, then pour 1 cup of puree per leather in strips on a drying sheet set in a dehydrator tray. Sprinkle each leather puree with the chopped grapes. Slap the tray on the counter a couple times to level the liquid. Dehydrate at 125°F until the leathers easily peel off the drying sheet, 10 to 12 hours.
4. Peel the leathers off the sheet and place them on the mesh rack of the dehydrator tray, then place back into the dehydrator for another 2 to 3 hours. Store as directed while warm (page 87).

Papaya and Peas Leather

The peas supply added sweetness in this unusual and surprising flavor combination.

Makes 2 leathers

2 cups chopped peeled papaya

½ cup cooked peas

¼ cup water or as needed

2 tablespoons lemon juice

1 tablespoon corn syrup

1 teaspoon cornstarch

1. In a blender, combine the ingredients and blend until smooth, with an applesauce-like consistency.
2. Pour the puree into a small saucepan, bring to a boil, reduce the heat to medium, and let simmer for 2 minutes.
3. Let cool, then pour 1 cup of puree per leather into strips on a drying sheet set in a dehydrator tray. Slap the tray on the counter a couple times to level the liquid. Dehydrate at 125°F until the leathers easily peel off the drying sheet, 10 to 12 hours.

4. Peel the leathers off the sheet and place them on the mesh rack of the dehydrator tray, then place back into the dehydrator for another 2 to 3 hours. Store as directed while warm (page 87).

Green Pea Leather

You can enjoy it as is or process it into a powder to add to soups or sauces or rehydrate into instant baby food.

Makes 3 leathers

> 2 cups cooked peas
> 1 cup water
> 1 tablespoon lemon juice
> 1 teaspoon cornstarch

1. In a blender, combine the ingredients and blend until smooth, with an applesauce-like consistency.
2. Pour 1 cup of puree per leather into strips on a drying sheet set in a dehydrator tray. Slap the tray on the counter a couple times to level the liquid. Dehydrate at 125°F until the leathers easily peel off the drying sheet, 10 to 12 hours.
3. Peel the leathers off the sheet and place them on the mesh rack of the dehydrator tray, then place back into the dehydrator for another 2 to 3 hours. This leather will be brittle.

Fresh Salsa Leather

Rehydrate into instant salsa any time you like!

Makes 2 to 3 leathers

> 4 large ripe tomatoes, cut into chunks
> 1 green bell pepper, cut in half and seeded
> 1 red bell pepper, cut in half and seeded
> 4 garlic cloves, peeled
> 1 large chile pepper, cut in half and seeded
> 1½ teaspoons cornstarch
> 1 medium onion, cut into chunks
> 2 stalks celery, cut into chunks
> 3 tablespoons chopped fresh parsley

1. In a blender combine half of the tomatoes, bell peppers, garlic, and chile pepper and all the cornstarch. Blend until smooth, with an applesauce-like consistency.
2. Chop the onion, celery, and remaining tomatoes, bell peppers, garlic, and chile.
3. Transfer the puree to a medium saucepan, bring to a boil, and reduce the heat to medium. Stir in the chopped vegetables and parsley and simmer for 2 minutes, no longer.

4. Let cool, then pour 1 cup of puree per leather in strips on drying sheets set in dehydrator trays. Slap the trays on the counter a couple times to level the liquid. Dehydrate at 125°F until the leathers easily peel off the drying sheets, 10 to 12 hours.

5. Peel the leathers off the sheets and place them on the mesh racks of the dehydrator trays, then place back into the dehydrator for another 2 to 3 hours.

6. **To rehydrate,** take one salsa leather, place it in a small heatproof bowl, and pour 1 cup boiling water over it. Let sit for a few minutes, then stir, cover, and refrigerate until chilled. One leather will make 1 cup salsa.

Even Quicker Salsa Leather: Dehydrate store-bought salsa instead of homemade. Pour it straight from the jar into strips onto the drying sheet and dehydrate at 125°F for 8 to 10 hours. Leather made from store-bought salsa will have a consistency similar to that of homemade fruit leather, whereas a leather made from homemade salsa will be brittle.

Tomato Puree Leather

This is a great way to take care of a surplus of garden tomatoes.

Yield is variable

Tomatoes
Cornstarch

1. In a large, heavy saucepan, combine 1 tablespoon cornstarch per 6 tomatoes reduced to a puree in a blender. Cook over medium heat until thick, 10 to 15 minutes. Remove from the heat and let cool.

2. Pour 1 cup of puree per leather in strips on a drying sheet set in a dehydrator tray. Slap the tray on the counter a couple times to level the liquid. Dehydrate at 125°F until the leathers easily peel off the drying sheet, for hours. When dehydrated, it will be brittle, feel dry, and break apart easily in your hands. Store in canning jars or vacuum seal with an oxygen pack and double-bag in Mylar.

3. **To rehydrate,** take one leather, place it in a small heatproof bowl, and pour 1 cup boiling water over it. Let sit 15 to 20 minutes. One leather will make 1 cup tomato puree.

Hummus Leather

You can also enjoy this dried as a snack, if you like, though it does crumble easily.

Makes 1 leather

> 1 cup cooked chickpeas
> 1 cup water
> 2 garlic cloves, peeled
> 1 chile pepper, seeded and chopped

1. In a blender, combine the ingredients, except the chile, and blend until smooth, with an applesauce-like consistency. Stir in the chile.
2. Pour 1 cup of puree per leather in strips on a drying sheet set in a dehydrator tray. Slap the tray on the counter a couple times to level the liquid. Dehydrate at 125°F until the leathers easily peel off the drying sheet, 10 to 12 hours.
3. Peel the leathers off the sheet and place them on the mesh rack of the dehydrator trays, then place back into the dehydrator for another 2 to 3 hours. The hummus will crumble when dehydrated. Store in canning jars or vacuum seal with an oxygen pack and double-bag in Mylar.
4. **To rehydrate,** in a small heatproof bowl, combine ¼ cup crumbled dehydrated hummus and ½ cup boiling water. Let sit a couple of minutes, then stir, cover, and refrigerate for 2 hours. It will thicken as it chills. Stir in 1 tablespoon extra virgin olive oil before serving. This will yield ½ cup hummus.

Zesty Orange Sauce for Chicken or Pork

A time-saving shortcut for weeknight cooking.

Makes 2 leathers; each leather is enough to sauce 3 boneless skinless chicken breast halves or 1 small (1½ pounds) pork loin when rehydrated

> 3 navel oranges, peeled
> 1 garlic clove, peeled
> 1 teaspoon soy sauce
> 2 teaspoons coarsely ground dehydrated ginger
> ¼ cup molasses
> 1 teaspoon cornstarch
> ½ dehydrated chile pepper, crumbled
> 1 tablespoon grated fresh orange zest

1. Place the oranges, garlic, soy sauce, ginger, molasses, and cornstarch in a blender and puree until smooth. Stir in the chile pepper and orange zest.
2. Transfer the puree to a small, heavy saucepan and heat, stirring, over medium heat until thickened. Remove from the heat and let cool a few minutes.

3. Pour 1 cup of puree per leather into strips ⅛ to ¼ inch thick on a drying sheet set in a dehydrator tray. Slap the tray on the counter a couple times to level the liquid. Dehydrate at 125°F for 12 hours. When dehydrated, the leathers will be pliable but break when bent.

4. **To rehydrate the sauce,** after browning your meat on all sides in a skillet, add 1 cup water per number of leathers you intend to use. Over medium-high heat, scrape up all the browned bits from the bottom of the skillet. Add the leather(s), reduce the heat to medium, and stir until dissolved and well mixed. Return the meat to the pan and let simmer in the sauce until fully cooked through and glazed with the sauce.

Strawberry Sauce Leather

Rehydrate this for a delicious sauce to pour over cake or ice cream.

Makes 4 leathers

> 4 cups sliced ripe strawberries
> ½ cup corn syrup
> ¼ cup lemon juice
> 1 tablespoon cornstarch

1. In a blender, combine the ingredients and blend until smooth, with an applesauce-like consistency.

2. Pour the puree into a small saucepan, bring to a boil, reduce the heat to medium, and let simmer for 5 minutes to thicken.

3. Let cool, then pour 1 cup of puree per leather into strips on a drying sheet set in a dehydrator tray. Slap the tray on the counter a couple times to level the liquid. Dehydrate at 125°F until the leathers easily peel off the drying sheet, 10 to 12 hours.

4. Peel the leathers off the drying sheets and place them on the mesh rack of the dehydrator tray itself, then place back into the dehydrator for another 2 to 3 hours. Store as directed while warm (page 87).

5. **To rehydrate,** combine one leather and 1 cup boiling water in a small heatproof bowl and let sit a few minutes. Pour into a blender and process until smooth. Enjoy warm or let cool completely.

7

Dehydrating Herbs & Flowers & Making Tea Blends

With a home dehydrator and a kitchen herb garden, there's no need to spend money on expensive little bottles of dried herbs again. You can also experiment with drying all sorts of edible flowers. Then you'll have all the ingredients you need to make your own tea blends, flavor rubs (page 163), flavored oils (page 170), potpourri (page 184), and more. Enjoy your creativity!

STORING DEHYDRATED HERBS AND FLOWERS

How you store your dried herbs and flowers depends on how you intend to use them. Once dehydrated, they are very fragile. If you vacuum pack them, the leaves/flowers will be crushed. If you are fine with that, then vacuum pack them and double-bag in Mylar. If you want them to remain whole, then store in canning jars with an oxygen pack. Stored in this way, they should retain their flavor for five years or more.

HERB LEAVES

This category includes those herbs that are used predominantly for their leaves, including basil, sage, oregano, marjoram, and others. Though most of these herbs dehydrate in 10 to 12 hours, there are exceptions, which are noted below. It's a good idea when dehydrating an herb for the first time to check on it regularly, and then note the dehydration time for future reference.

Dehydrating temperature: 90°F for lighter, finer leaves (like dill or thyme) and 110°F for more substantial or resinous leaves (like bay and rosemary).

Preparation: Trim the herbs of roots or wilted leaves, then rinse thoroughly and pat dry. Spread on dehydrator trays. Most herbs dehydrate in 10 to 12 hours but basil, some mints, and bay leaves can take up to 18 hours, while chives will be ready in about 4 hours.

Dryness test: Leaves are brittle and will crumble or break easily.

Tip

Drying the leaves while still on their branches or stalks will yield the best flavor. After dehydrating, strip the leaves from the stalks, then store.

HERB SEEDS

This category includes the seeds from such herbs as fennel, dill, flax, and caraway.

Dehydrating temperature: 110°F

Preparation: Put the herb seeds in a drawstring nylon mesh bag (or you can use reusable tea bags; fill, then press and seal). This will prevent the seeds from blowing around. Place the bag(s) on dehydrator trays and dehydrate 10 to 12 hours.

HERB BERRIES

Tip

Place smaller lightweight berries in a drawstring nylon mesh bag (or you can use reusable tea bags; fill, then press and seal) so they don't get blown around.

This includes barberries, juniper berries, and rose hips.

Dehydrating temperature: 110°F

Preparation: Wash thoroughly, then pat dry. Spread on dehydrator trays in a single layer; do not allow the berries to overlap or they will not dry properly. Dehydrate 8 to 12 hours.

Dryness test: Should be hard and will click when dropped on the counter.

HERB ROOTS

This category includes roots like burdock and horseradish (used in cooking) and ginseng (used medicinally).

Dehydrating temperature: 110°F

Preparation: Cut the root from the stalk and wash thoroughly. If the root is more than ½ inch thick, cut it lengthwise in half or across into slices less than ¼ inch in thickness. Spread on dehydrator trays and dehydrate 14 to 18 hours.

Dryness test: Some roots will become leathery and others will break easily. It is best to break or cut open a root to check that the inside is not wet.

LEMONGRASS

Being a stalk, lemongrass is in its own class

Dehydrating temperature: 110°F

Preparation: Trim the roots, then make a lengthwise slit down the stalk and peel away the tough, fibrous outer layers. Spread the stalks on dehydrator trays and dehydrate 10 to 12 hours.

Dryness test: Should be brittle and break easily.

Tip

Chop lemongrass after dehydration for better flavor.

EDIBLE FLOWERS

Do not assume a flower is edible; please check a reputable source to confirm that a flower is indeed edible or you could make yourself very sick. Among those that are edible are bee balm, lavender, chrysanthemum, pansies, marigold, honeysuckle, geranium, echinacea, rose, and daylily.

Dehydrating temperature: 110°F

Preparation: Gently rinse the flowers, then pinch them from their stems. Spread on dehydrator trays and dehydrate 10 to 12 hours. If you are going to remove the petals always remove after dehydrating.

Dryness test: Should be dry and straw-like in texture.

Tips

- Be particularly mindful of the source of your flowers in regard to possible exposure to poisonous pesticides if you intend to use them in food preparation. This can be the case with flowers harvested on the roadside or those purchased as cut flowers from the supermarket or florist.
- If you intend to remove the petals from the flowers, do that after dehydration.

HAVE IT HOT OR COLD!

You can steep these teas, then enjoy them hot or refrigerate to chill and make a delicious iced tea!

MAKING YOUR OWN TEA BLENDS

With food dehydration you have the unique opportunity to build an extensive pantry of dehydrated herbs and flowers. One of the exciting things you can do with them is create delicious teas. Imagine, no more overpriced store-purchased teas in the same old flavors!

Start first with ingredients that you know, love, and understand. Then slowly spread those wings and become an amazing tea maker, exploring new ingredients and combinations. Dehydrated leaves, herbs, fruit, fruit peels, flowers, and spices are at your fingertips, offering up their fantastic natural flavors as well as their medicinal benefits, vitamins, and nutrients.

Brewing Tea

You have a number of different options in regard to actually making yourself a cuppa.

Tea press: Also known as a coffee press or French press, it can be used to brew coffee as well. To make a pot of tea using a press, place your dehydrated loose herbs and ingredients in the bottom of the beaker. Fill with boiling hot water, let steep as directed in the particular recipe, then press down on the plunger, which will push the loose ingredients to the bottom of the beaker. Pour into cups and serve.

Press-and-seal bags: These disposable bags are commonly used to make your own tea bags. I recommend the larger 5-inch bags (they can be filled with enough of your dry tea blend to yield 2 to 4 servings) because I find the smaller single-serving bags are hard to fill. You place the dehydrated ingredients of your choice into the bag and seal, using an iron or even a curling iron. Place the bag in a teapot, pour in the boiling water, and let steep as directed in your recipe. Pour into cups and serve. Throw away the used tea bag when done.

Reusable tea bags: These are not only great for the environment but they are also great for the budget. These tea bags are muslin bags that you fill with the dehydrated ingredients of your choice, then tie closed with the pull string at the top. Put the bag in your teapot, pour in the boiling water, and let steep according to the recipe. To wash these bags for reuse, simply turn them inside out, rinse out the herbs, and let soak in boiling water for a bit—do not use soap on them. Air-dry the bags or place them on a dehydrator tray at 135°F until dry.

Tea infuser: Tea infusers are small mesh or perforated metal containers that you fill with your dehydrated ingredients, then place in a cup or pot to steep tea. Depending on the size of your infuser, it may be used to make single or multiple servings. Once used, simply open the container and rinse to clean.

To get your creativity moving, here are some of our favorite teas!

Chamomile-Ginger-Orange-Honey Tea

This tea is hot, spicy, and sweet. It will warm you up and energize you better than a strong cup of coffee—and without the caffeine!

Makes 4 servings

> 2 tablespoons dehydrated chamomile flowers
> 1 tablespoon coarsely ground dehydrated ginger
> ½ teaspoon powdered dehydrated orange zest
> 4 cups boiling water
> Honey

Place the chamomile, ginger, and orange zest in your tea apparatus of choice. Pour in the boiling water and let steep 3 to 7 minutes. Pour into cups and add honey to taste.

Rosemary and Lemon Tea

I am sitting here and typing while drinking my rosemary tea with a half slice of dehydrated lemon. It's simply heaven and takes little effort to prepare!

Makes 2 servings

> 2 teaspoons dehydrated rosemary leaves
> ½ slice dehydrated lemon
> 2 cups boiling water

Place the rosemary and lemon in the tea apparatus of your choice. Pour in the boiling water and let steep for 5 minutes or more. Pour into cups and serve.

Minty Alfalfa-Anise Tea

A wonderfully light and refreshing holiday herbal tea.

Makes 2 servings

> 1 teaspoon dehydrated alfalfa leaves
> ½ teaspoon dehydrated peppermint leaves
> ½ teaspoon dehydrated anise leaves
> 2 cups boiling water

Place the leaves in the tea apparatus of your choice. Pour in the boiling water and let steep 15 to 20 minutes. Reheat if necessary and serve piping hot.

Marigold Round Tea

The marigold provides fragrant floral notes, with a sweet, tangy flavor.

Makes 4 to 5 servings

> 1 tablespoon dehydrated lemon balm leaves
> 1 tablespoon dehydrated marigold flowers
> ½ teaspoon powdered dehydrated orange zest
> ½ teaspoon dehydrated stevia leaves
> 4 to 5 cups boiling water

Place the lemon balm, marigold, orange zest, and stevia in the tea apparatus of your choice. Pour in the boiling water and let steep for 20 minutes. Reheat if necessary and serve piping hot.

Sweet Potato Pie Tea

This tea has a sweet Southern charm that keeps you going back for more.

Makes 4 to 5 servings

> 2 tablespoons dehydrated parsley leaves
> 2 teaspoons powdered dehydrated sweet potato
> ½ teaspoon dehydrated stevia leaves
> 1 whole clove
> 4 to 5 cups boiling water

Place the parsley, sweet potato, stevia, and clove in the tea apparatus of your choice. Pour in the boiling water and steep for 20 minutes. Reheat if necessary and serve piping hot.

Beet-Red Tea

This beautiful, deep red tea, with a hint of raspberry and little bit of heat from the chile, will warm you up and energize you!

Makes 4 to 5 servings

> 2 tablespoons dehydrated raspberry leaves
> 2 teaspoons powdered dehydrated beets
> ¼ teaspoon crushed dehydrated chile pepper
> 4 to 5 cups boiling water

Place the raspberry leaves, beets, and chile pepper in the tea apparatus of your choice. Pour in the boiling water and let steep for 20 minutes. Reheat if necessary and serve piping hot.

Parsley and Pineapple Tea

This sweet and tangy tea is loaded with antioxidants.

Makes 6 servings

2 tablespoons dehydrated parsley leaves
2 tablespoons powdered dehydrated pineapple
6 cups boiling water

Place the parsley and pineapple in the tea apparatus of your choice. Add the boiling water and let steep for 20 minutes. Reheat if necessary and serve piping hot.

Rosemary, Sage, and Cinnamon Tea

This tea tastes of spice and earth (in a good way), with just a hint of sweetness from the honey.

Makes 2 servings

1 teaspoon dehydrated rosemary leaves
1 dehydrated sage leaf
2 cups boiling water
1 teaspoon honey
2 small cinnamon sticks

Place the rosemary and sage in the tea apparatus of your choice. Add the boiling water and let steep for 20 minutes. Add the honey, reheat if necessary, and serve piping hot, with each cup getting its own cinnamon stick.

Cranberry, Stevia, and Cinnamon Tea

Tart and sweet.

Makes 2 servings

1 teaspoon dehydrated chopped cranberries
1 teaspoon dehydrated stevia leaves
2 cups boiling water
2 small cinnamon sticks

Place the cranberries and stevia in the tea apparatus of your choice. Pour in the boiling water and let steep 15 minutes. Reheat if necessary and serve piping hot, with each cup getting its own cinnamon stick.

Rose Hips and Chamomile Tea

The flavor of rose hips reminds me of strawberry lemonade, a perfect balance of sweet and tart.

Makes 2 servings

> 1 teaspoon dehydrated rose hips
> 1 teaspoon dehydrated chamomile flowers
> 2 cups boiling water

Place the rose hips and chamomile in the tea apparatus of your choice. Add the boiling water and steep for 15 minutes. Reheat if necessary and serve piping hot.

"Bluegrass" Tea

It's the marriage of lemongrass and blueberries that makes this tea memorable.

Makes 2 servings

> 1 tablespoon dehydrated blueberries
> 1 tablespoon dehydrated chopped lemongrass
> 2 cups boiling water

Place the blueberries and lemongrass in the tea apparatus of your choice. Add the boiling water and steep for 15 minutes. Reheat if necessary and serve piping hot.

Pharaoh's Tea

This wonderful tea includes some of the dried herbs and food items that have been found stored in pharaohs' tombs throughout Egypt: licorice (anise), orange, olives, and honey. The strong kick of licorice is balanced by the sweetness of honey and slight bitter notes from the olive leaves. If you aren't lucky enough to have access to olive leaves, you can substitute grape leaves.

Makes 2 servings

> 1 tablespoon dehydrated anise leaves
> 1 tablespoon dehydrated orange zest
> 1 tablespoon dehydrated olive leaves
> 2 cups boiling water
> ½ tablespoon honey

Place the dehydrated items in the tea apparatus of your choice. Pour in the boiling water and let steep for 15 to 20 minutes. Reheat if necessary, then stir in the honey and serve piping hot.

Tropical Tea

This tea holds the sweet and exotic flavors of a tropical island.

Makes 4 to 5 servings

>   1 tablespoon powdered dehydrated mango peel
>   1 tablespoon powdered dehydrated papaya peel
>   1 tablespoon powdered dehydrated pineapple
>   1 tablespoon dehydrated honeysuckle flowers
>   4 to 5 cups boiling water

Place the powdered fruit and honeysuckle in the tea apparatus of your choice. Pour in the boiling water and let steep for at least 20 minutes—the longer it steeps, the stronger the flavor. Reheat if necessary and serve piping hot.

Tahiti Tea

Sweet and tart, with just a hint of raspberries from the leaves.

Makes 4 to 5 servings

>   2 tablespoons dehydrated raspberry leaves
>   1 tablespoon powdered dehydrated pineapple
>   1 tablespoon chopped dehydrated coconut
>   1 to 2 teaspoons date sugar (page 167), to taste
>   4 to 5 cups boiling water

Place the raspberry leaves, pineapple, coconut, and date sugar in the tea apparatus of your choice. Pour in the boiling water and let steep for at least 20 minutes— the longer it steeps, the stronger the flavor. Reheat if necessary and serve piping hot.

Autumn Tea

The taste and aroma of cinnamon and apples are the perfect combination for a cool autumn day. The dandelion leaves provide a welcome offsetting note of bitterness.

Makes 2 servings

>   2 tablespoons dehydrated dandelion leaves
>   1 tablespoon powdered dehydrated apple peels
>   1 teaspoon coarsely ground dehydrated ginger
>   ½ teaspoon ground cinnamon
>   2 cups boiling water

Place the dandelion, apple peel, ginger, and cinnamon in the tea apparatus of your choice. Pour in the boiling water and let steep for 15 minutes. Reheat if necessary and serve boiling hot.

Chamomile and Apricot Tea

Sweet and relaxing.

Makes 2 servings

2 tablespoons dehydrated chamomile flowers
1 tablespoon finely chopped dehydrated apricot
1 teaspoon fennel seeds
1 teaspoon coriander seeds, crushed
1 teaspoon dehydrated orange zest
2 cups boiling water

Place the chamomile, apricot, fennel and coriander seeds, and orange zest in the tea apparatus of your choice. Pour in the boiling water and let steep for 15 minutes. Reheat if necessary and serve piping hot.

Peppy Patty Tea

The decadent flavor of chocolate meets mint in this delicious tea.

Makes 2 servings

2 tablespoons dehydrated peppermint leaves
2 teaspoons unsweetened cocoa powder
½ teaspoon dehydrated stevia leaves
2 cups boiling water

Place the peppermint, cocoa, and stevia in the tea apparatus of your choice. Pour in the boiling water and let steep for 15 minutes. Reheat if necessary and serve piping hot.

Lemony Lavender and Honeysuckle Tea

A cup of sweet citrus tranquility.

Makes 2 servings

1 tablespoon dehydrated lavender flowers
1 tablespoon dehydrated lemon balm leaves
1 tablespoon dehydrated honeysuckle flowers
1 teaspoon dehydrated stevia leaves
2 cups boiling water

Place the herbs in the tea apparatus of your choice. Pour in the boiling water and let steep for 15 minutes. Reheat if necessary and serve piping hot.

Spearmint and Dandelion Tea

This tea is warm and refreshing in the same sip!

Makes 4 servings

2 tablespoons dehydrated spearmint leaves
1 tablespoon dehydrated dandelion leaves
1 teaspoon dehydrated stevia leaves
4 cups boiling water

Place the spearmint, dandelion, and stevia in the tea apparatus of your choice. Pour in the boiling water and let steep for 15 minutes. Reheat if necessary and serve piping hot.

Sunshine Tea

Bring balance to your world with this citrus floral tea.

Makes 4 to 5 servings

1 tablespoon dehydrated honeysuckle flowers
1 tablespoon dehydrated chrysanthemum flowers
1 tablespoon dehydrated lemon zest
4 to 5 cups boiling water
1 tablespoon honey

Place the honeysuckle, chrysanthemum, and lemon zest in the tea apparatus of your choice. Pour in the boiling water and let steep for at least 20 minutes—the longer it steeps, the stronger the flavor. Reheat if necessary. Right before serving, stir in the honey.

8

Making Jerky and Dehydrating Tofu, Eggs & Dairy

This chapter will explore the options for dehydrating meat, eggs, and dairy along with the meat substitute tofu. We will walk you through the steps for producing a safe and delicious jerky as well as discussing the various health concerns associated with dehydrating meat.

JERKY

Jerky is one of those things that seem to get eaten up as fast as you can make it! It is a salty and chewy snack that is high in protein and is easy to take with you just about anywhere. Jerky isn't just for the meat lovers anymore; you can even make tofu jerky! Jerky is something everyone can truly enjoy.

Before I go on, let me make the distinction between jerky and freeze-dried meats. Jerky is not meant for long-term pantry storage. At most, vacuum-sealed beef jerky can be stored in the pantry for up to one month; beyond that time, it needs to go in the refrigerator or freezer. If you want to include meat in your long-term storage pantry, purchase commercially prepared freeze-dried meats.

Do It Right

Due to potentially harmful organisms often found in animal proteins, it is very important to prepare jerky properly.

1. Pre-freeze for safety. Putting your meat in the freezer for two months will kill many harmful organisms, pathogens, and parasites, including tape- and trichina worms (those responsible for trichinosis), salmonella, listeria, and *E.coli.*

2. Keep it clean. Thoroughly wash your hands and all surfaces and utensils that will come in contact with the meat. Keep meat properly refrigerated until you are ready to prep it, then place immediately in the dehydrator or refrigerate until you are ready to do so.

3. Slice thinly. Thin slices will allow the heat to reach the center of the meat. Cut meat with the grain for a chewy jerky or cut meat against the grain for tender and brittle jerky.

4. Marinate. Marinades, with their flavorful combinations of spices, vinegars, and salts, can help destroy pathogens and surface bacteria; also, salt aids in the dehydrating process.

5. Bring on the heat. Always dehydrate meat at the recommended temperature of 160°F for a minimum of 6 hours. This temperature is adequate to kill most pathogenic bacteria. If your dehydrator does not go as high as 160°F and does not have a fan, for safety reasons, the dehydrator should not be used to dehydrate meat.

6. Dry completely. Give your jerky a final drying by arranging in a single layer on baking sheets and putting it in a preheated 275°F oven for 15 minutes. Let it cool completely before storing it. Your finished product should be fairly firm and not moist. You should be able to shred or tear the pieces easily, with no residual moisture.

Choosing Your Meat

You can make jerky from just about any animal protein you want, including beef, pork, lamb, poultry, fish, shrimp, and game. The leaner the protein is, the better the jerky. Fat does not dry and can cause jerky to spoil much faster.

For beef, New York strip, bottom round, and flank and skirt steaks are great cuts to use, as are sirloin and top round. For pork, use the loin; for lamb, filet.

When making jerky from turkey or chicken, use the breast because it is the leanest. Jerky made from dark meat can be very tough and hard to chew.

When making jerky from fish, I recommend you stay away from freshwater fish, as they are exposed to too many parasites to make dehydration a safe option. Ocean fish are a much safer choice. I particularly like using salmon for jerky, but bass, pike, cod, and trout are other flavorful options.

If you intend to make jerky from game you or a friend have killed, be sure that the animal or bird is cleaned properly and that the meat you use has not come into contact with the viscera. Use the leanest cuts possible. Because of its high fat content, bear is not a candidate for making jerky.

Preparing the Meat

Trim the meat of any visible fat or skin (in the case of poultry of fish). Thinly slice the meat, ideally ¼ inch thick for meat and poultry, ¼ to ½ inch for fish. This is a lot easier to do if you partially freeze the meat first; it will allow you to cut straight and even slices with a sharp knife or meat slicer. For tender cuts, slice with the grain for a more durable product. Cutting against the grain is ideal for tougher, chewier cuts but will result in a more shredded and crumbly product. Try cutting both ways and see which you prefer.

If you want to flavor the meat, you can use either a rub (see pages 163–66) or a marinade. I find it easiest to place the meat strips in a large ziptop plastic freezer bag and add the rub or pour in the marinade. Knead the slices with the rub or marinade to make sure you've got good coverage, zip it up, then refrigerate. Marinating times can range from just a couple hours for fish to up to at least 24 hours for red meat; meats like beef and bison should marinate until they are no longer red.

Dehydrating the Meat

When you're ready, drain the marinade, if necessary, then line the strips in a single layer on dehydrator tray, leaving space between them to allow for good air flow, and dehydrate at 160°F until firm and not moist or overly pliable, 6 to 8 hours; meat treated with a dry rub tends to take less time than marinated meat.

MAKING DRIED SHRIMP

When dehydrating shrimp, use medium to large shrimp (jumbo shrimp are not recommended because they end up being too tough to eat after dehydration). Peel and devein the shrimp, then cut them in half lengthwise. Drop them in boiling salted water for 2 to 3 minutes (no more!), then drain and immediately drop into ice water to stop the cooking. Drain again and pat dry. Put the shrimp in a ziptop plastic bag, add the rub of your choice (I like to use Jerk Rub, on page 164), seal the bag, and shake until the shrimp are coated evenly. Refrigerate for 1 hour. (You can use a marinade instead if you like but avoid any that contain citrus juice or vinegar because they will toughen the shrimp.) If using a marinade, drain the shrimp and place in a single layer on dehydrator trays and dehydrate at 160°F for 6 hours. Remove the jerky from the dehydrator, arrange on baking sheets in a single layer, and place in a preheated 275°F oven for 15 minutes. When dehydrated, the shrimp will be salty and chewy. Remove from the oven and let the jerky cool completely. Vacuum seal and place in the refrigerator for best results, where it will keep for up to 3 months.

Storing Jerky

Jerky cannot be dehydrated at home for long-term storage. It can, however, be dehydrated for short-term consumption and will keep for up to 1 month in the pantry, 6 months in the refrigerator, or 1 year in the freezer, except for salmon, which will keep for 1 month in the refrigerator and 6 months in the freezer.

Let the meat cool completely before storing it in an airtight container. Vacuum-sealed bags with oxygen packs will provide the best results. Jerky will stay freshest if placed in the refrigerator or freezer until it is ready to eat.

Classic Jerky

This works well with beef, lamb, and venison.

Makes ½ pound jerky

1½ pounds boneless beef (preferably eye of round), lamb, or venison
¼ cup soy sauce
⅓ cup Worcestershire sauce
1 tablespoon steak sauce
1 teaspoon liquid smoke
½ teaspoon black pepper
½ teaspoon garlic powder
½ teaspoon onion powder
½ teaspoon salt

1. Trim the meat of any visible fat, then partially freeze. Cut into ¼-inch-thick slices or strips across the grain using a very sharp knife or meat slicer. Try to cut the meat as uniformly as possible for even drying. Place the strips in a large ziptop plastic freezer bag.
2. Whisk the remaining ingredients together in a small bowl and carefully pour over the strips in the bag. Squish everything around to coat, then seal the bag and refrigerate until the meat is no longer red, about 24 hours, turning and squishing the bag about halfway through to ensure even coverage with the marinade.
3. Drain off the marinade and place the strips in a single layer on dehydrator trays. Dehydrate at 160°F for 6 to 8 hours. When done, the jerky should bend but not snap, and should show no signs of redness.
4. Remove the jerky from the dehydrator, arrange on baking sheets in a single layer, and place in a preheated 275°F oven for 15 minutes. Allow the jerky to cool completely before placing in an airtight container.

Sweet and Spicy Pepper Beef Jerky

This is sweet and tangy with a kick. It also works well with poultry and pork.

Makes ½ pound jerky

 1½ pounds beef eye of round
 ½ cup pineapple juice
 ¼ cup firmly packed brown sugar
 ¼ cup soy sauce
 1 tablespoon crushed dehydrated jalapeños
 1 teaspoon hot sauce

1. Trim the meat of any visible fat, then partially freeze. Cut into ¼-inch-thick slices or strips across the grain using a very sharp knife or meat slicer. Try to cut the meat as uniformly as possible for even drying. Place the strips in a large ziptop plastic freezer bag.
2. While the meat freezes, combine the remaining ingredients in a small saucepan. Place over medium heat and stir until the sugar dissolves. Let cool, then carefully pour over the strips in the bag. Squish everything around to coat, then seal the bag and refrigerate until the meat is no longer red, about 24 hours, turning and squishing the bag about halfway through to ensure even coverage with the marinade.
3. Drain off the marinade and place the strips in a single layer on dehydrator trays. Dehydrate at 160°F for 6 to 8 hours. When done, the jerky should bend but not snap, and show no signs of redness.
4. Remove the jerky from the dehydrator, arrange on baking sheets in a single layer, and place in a preheated 275°F oven for 15 minutes. Allow the jerky to cool completely before placing in an airtight container.

Maple Salmon Jerky

This warm maple marinade, spiced with black and cayenne pepper, also works well with duck and goose.

Makes ½ pound jerky

 1½ pounds salmon fillets, skin and pin bones removed
 ¼ cup maple syrup
 4 slices dehydrated garlic, crushed
 ¼ cup tamari (see Note on next page)
 2 teaspoons salt
 2 teaspoons black pepper
 ½ teaspoon cayenne pepper

1. Partially freeze the fillets, then cut across into ¼- to ½-inch-thick slices or strips using a very sharp knife or meat slicer. Try to cut the salmon as uniformly as possible for even drying. Place the strips in a large ziptop plastic freezer bag.

2. Whisk the remaining ingredients together in a small bowl and carefully pour over the strips in the bag. Squish everything around to coat, then seal the bag and refrigerate for 3 to 6 hours (no longer, or you run the risk of the salmon becoming mushy), turning and squishing the bag about halfway through to ensure even coverage with the marinade.
3. Drain off the marinade and place the strips in a single layer on dehydrator trays. Dehydrate at 160°F for about 6 hours. When done, the jerky should bend but not snap.
4. Remove the jerky from the dehydrator, arrange on baking sheets in a single layer, and place in a preheated 275°F oven for 15 minutes. Allow the jerky to cool completely before placing in an air-tight container.

Note: It's important to use tamari, not soy sauce, for this recipe, Using soy sauce could make the jerky too salty and overpower the maple flavor. If you can't find tamari, substitute low-sodium soy sauce and omit the salt.

Smoky Salmon Jerky

This also works well with beef, poultry, and wild game.

Makes 1/2 pound jerky

  1½ pounds salmon fillets, skin and pin bones removed
  ½ cup soy sauce
  1 tablespoon molasses
  1 tablespoon lemon juice
  1 tablespoon Worcestershire sauce
  2 teaspoons black pepper
  1 teaspoon liquid smoke

1. Partially freeze the fillets, then cut across into ¼- to ½-inch-thick slices or strips using a very sharp knife or meat slicer. Try to cut the salmon as uniformly as possible for even drying. Place the strips in a large ziptop plastic freezer bag.
2. Whisk the remaining ingredients together in a small bowl and carefully pour over the strips in the bag. Squish everything around to coat, then seal the bag and refrigerate for 3 to 6 hours (no longer, or you run the risk of the salmon becoming mushy), turning and squishing the bag about halfway through to ensure even coverage with the marinade.
3. Drain off the marinade and place the strips in a single layer on dehydrator trays. Dehydrate at 160°F for about 6 hours. When done, the jerky should bend but not snap.
4. Remove the jerky from the dehydrator, arrange on baking sheets in a single layer, and place in a preheated 275°F oven for 15 minutes. Allow the jerky to cool completely before placing in an air-tight container.

Spicy Sriracha Turkey Jerky

You can also use this peppy marinade with pork.

Makes ½ pound jerky

1½ pounds boneless, skinless turkey breast, trimmed of all visible fat
⅔ cup soy sauce
3 tablespoons honey
¼ cup sriracha
2 teaspoons red pepper flakes

1. Partially freeze the turkey breast, then cut into ¼-inch-thick slices or strips using a very sharp knife or meat slicer. Try to cut it as uniformly as possible for even drying. Place the strips in a large ziptop plastic freezer bag.
2. Whisk the remaining ingredients together in a small bowl and carefully pour over the strips in the bag. Squish everything around to coat, then seal the bag and refrigerate for 12 hours, turning and squishing the bag about halfway through to ensure even coverage with the marinade.
3. Drain off the marinade and place the strips in a single layer on dehydrator trays. Dehydrate at 160°F for 6 to 8 hours. When done, the jerky should just bend but not snap.
4. Remove the jerky from the dehydrator, arrange on baking sheets in a single layer, and place in a preheated 275°F oven for 15 minutes. Allow the jerky to cool completely before placing in an airtight container.

Teriyaki Chicken Jerky

This Asian-inspired sauce is sweet and tangy. You can also use it with beef, pork, and game.

Makes ½ pound jerky

1½ pounds boneless, skinless chicken breasts, trimmed of all visible fat
⅔ cup teriyaki sauce
½ cup root beer
¼ cup water
1 tablespoon honey
1 tablespoon soy sauce
1 tablespoon firmly packed brown sugar
1 teaspoon liquid smoke
1 teaspoon onion powder
½ teaspoon garlic powder
½ teaspoon salt
¼ teaspoon black pepper

1. Partially freeze the chicken breasts, then cut into ¼-inch-thick slices or strips using a very sharp knife or meat slicer. Try to cut them as uniformly as possible for even drying. Place the strips in a large ziptop plastic freezer bag.

2. Whisk the remaining ingredients together in a small bowl and carefully pour over the strips in the bag. Squish everything around to coat, then seal the bag and refrigerate for at least 12 hours, turning and squishing the bag about halfway through to ensure even coverage with the marinade.

3. Drain off the marinade and place the strips in a single layer on dehydrator trays. Dehydrate at 160°F for 6 to 8 hours. When done, the jerky should just bend but not snap

4. Remove the jerky from the dehydrator, arrange on baking sheets in a single layer, and place in a preheated 275°F oven for 15 minutes. Allow the jerky to cool completely before placing in an airtight container.

Sweet and Sour Chicken Jerky

This marinade also pairs well with pork and fish.

Makes ½ pound jerky

> 1½ pounds boneless, skinless chicken breasts, trimmed of all visible fat
> ¼ cup firmly packed brown sugar
> ¼ cup distilled white vinegar
> ¼ cup pineapple juice
> 1 tablespoon powdered dehydrated onions
> 4 fresh garlic cloves, peeled and crushed
> 1 tablespoon soy sauce

1. Partially freeze the chicken breasts, then cut into ¼-inch-thick slices or strips using a very sharp knife or meat slicer. Try to cut them as uniformly as possible for even drying. Place the strips in a large ziptop plastic freezer bag.

2. Whisk the remaining ingredients together in a small bowl and carefully pour over the strips in the bag. Squish everything around to coat, then seal the bag and refrigerate for at least 12 hours, turning and squishing the bag about halfway through to ensure even coverage with the marinade.

3. Drain off the marinade and place the strips in a single layer on dehydrator trays. Dehydrate at 160°F for 6 to 8 hours When done, the jerky should just bend but not snap.

4. Remove the jerky from the dehydrator, arrange on baking sheets in a single layer, and place in a preheated 275°F oven for 15 minutes. Allow the jerky to cool completely before placing in an airtight container.

Smoky Hot Jerky

This is my go-to marinade for beef and game.

Makes ¾ pound jerky

> 2 pounds flank steak
> 1 cup soy sauce
> ½ cup Worcestershire sauce
> 2 fresh jalapeño peppers, seeded and chopped
> 1 teaspoon liquid smoke

1. Trim the meat of any visible fat, then partially freeze. Cut into ¼-inch-thick slices or strips across the grain using a very sharp knife or meat slicer. Try to cut the meat as uniformly as possible for even drying. Place the strips in a large ziptop plastic freezer bag.
2. While the meat freezes, combine the remaining ingredients in a small saucepan. Place over medium heat and stir until the sugar dissolves. Let cool, then carefully pour over the strips in the bag. Squish everything around to coat, then seal the bag and refrigerate until the meat is no longer red, about 24 hours, turning and squishing the bag about halfway through to ensure even coverage with the marinade.
3. Drain off the marinade and place the strips in a single layer on dehydrator trays. Dehydrate at 160°F for 6 to 8 hours. When done, the jerky should bend but not snap, and should show no signs of redness.
4. Remove the jerky from the dehydrator, arrange on baking sheets in a single layer, and place in a preheated 275°F oven for 15 minutes. Allow the jerky to cool completely before placing in an airtight container.

Duck Jerky

This marinade is a delicious combination of sweet, salty, and hot. It's also a great choice for goose.

Makes 1 pound jerky

> 3 pounds boneless duck breasts, all skin and fat removed
> ⅔ cup soy sauce
> ½ cup sherry
> ½ cup honey
> 2 tablespoons grated fresh ginger
> 1 tablespoon meat tenderizer
> 8 fresh garlic cloves, peeled and crushed
> 1 fresh chile pepper, seeded and chopped

1. Partially freeze the duck breasts, then cut into ¼-inch-thick slices or strips using a very sharp knife or meat slicer. Try to cut them as uniformly as possible for even drying. Place the strips in a large ziptop plastic freezer bag.

2. Whisk the remaining ingredients together in a small bowl and carefully pour over the strips in the bag. Squish everything around to coat, then seal the bag and refrigerate for at least 12 hours, turning and squishing the bag about halfway through to ensure even coverage with the marinade.

3. Drain off the marinade and place the strips in a single layer on dehydrator trays. Dehydrate at 160°F for 6 to 8 hours When done, the jerky should just bend but not snap.

4. Remove the jerky from the dehydrator, arrange on baking sheets in a single layer, and place in a preheated 275°F oven for 15 minutes. Allow the jerky to cool completely before placing in an air-tight container.

Spicy Ginger Jerky

I love using this marinade with flank steak but it also works with pork and fish. Grinding the meat will give the jerky a different texture—less tough and easier to chew. You'll need a jerky gun for this. It works much like a pastry bag (which you can use instead), in that you fill it with the ground meat mixture and can then squeeze it out into thin strips or sticks in a uniform manner, making a more attractive jerky stick.

Makes ½ pound jerky

> 1½ pounds flank steak
> 1 cup ginger ale
> 2 tablespoons brown sugar
> 1 tablespoon salt
> 2 teaspoons dry mustard (like Colman's)
> 1 teaspoon cayenne pepper
> 1 teaspoon liquid smoke

1. In a meat grinder or food processor, grind the flank steak until it has the consistency of ground beef. Transfer to a large bowl and add the remaining ingredients. Mix until well blended.

2. Place the mixture in a jerky gun or pastry bag fitted with a ¼- or ½-inch tip. Line the dehydrator trays with drying sheets. Squeeze the gun or bag to create lines of the mixture on the drying sheets that are ½ inch wide and 8 inches long. Lightly pat them so they are flat, and not round like a Tootsie roll. Dehydrate at 160°F for 6 to 8 hours. When done, the jerky should just bend but not snap.

3. Remove the jerky from the dehydrator, arrange on baking sheets in a single layer, and place in a preheated 275°F oven for 15 minutes. Allow the jerky to cool completely before placing in an air-tight container.

DEHYDRATING TOFU

Tofu, or soybean curd, is very nutritious. A half-cup serving of firm tofu contains no cholesterol (because it is plant-based), 10 grams of protein (twice the amount of protein you would get from a half cup of dairy milk), 22% of the recommended daily value of calcium, and has less than a third of the calories and a third of the fat found in ground beef. It also tastes great in a variety of dishes, from stir-fries and soups to homemade tofu nuggets. And the great news is that you can dehydrate tofu!

Tofu comes in a variety of textures. Semi-firm, firm, and extra-firm textures work best when dehydrating because they contain less water and are easier to work with.

To dehydrate tofu, first drain any excess water, then cut the tofu into ¼- to ½-inch-thick strips or chunks.

You can dehydrate tofu plain or, for a flavorful and healthy jerky-like snack, soak the tofu in your favorite marinade in the refrigerator for several hours or toss it with your favorite seasoning mixture before dehydrating.

Let the tofu come to room temperature, then arrange in a single layer on dehydrator trays, spacing the chunks to allow for airflow. You might want to consider first fitting the trays with drying sheets; this will prevent sticking and keep any marinade from dripping and creating a mess in the dehydrator. Dehydrate at 150° to 155°F for 3 to 6 hours. Tofu is dehydrated when it is dry, brittle, and snaps in half. Tofu that is vacuum sealed and double-bagged in Mylar will keep for 5-plus years in the pantry.

To rehydrate tofu, you can soak it in a brine or marinade overnight in the refrigerator or pour boiling water over it and let it sit for 20 minutes.

EGGS AND DAIRY

Dehydrating eggs and dairy products such as milk and cheese for storage outside of the refrigerator is not recommended; that includes finished dishes that contain eggs and/or dairy. Eggs and dairy products contain organisms that may not be completely eliminated through dehydration alone. You are best served by purchasing powdered eggs, milk, and cheese from companies that have the appropriate equipment to process and offer up for sale a reliable, safe dried product.

Making Yogurt

Though I don't recommend dehydrating dairy, it turns out that you can make delicious homemade yogurt in your dehydrator. With your choice of fresh ingredients, you can make your own custom blends at a fraction of the cost!

Tips

- See the yogurt drop recipe on page 128.
- Yogurt drops and leathers containing yogurt must be dehydrated at 135–145°F and stored in the refrigerator.

To make yogurt, in addition to your dehydrator, you'll need:

- 4 half-pint canning jars with lids
- Candy/deep-fryer thermometer
- Hand/immersion blender

To make 4 cups yogurt, you'll need:

4 cups fat-free milk
½ cup powdered milk
1 heaping tablespoon plain yogurt (any level of fat—including nonfat— is fine but make sure it contains an active culture)

1. Preheat the dehydrator to 115°F (no higher!). Sterilize the canning jars and lids.
2. In a microwave-safe medium bowl, whisk together the liquid and powdered milks until thoroughly blended. Microwave the milk until it starts to boil (or heat it on the stovetop, if you prefer). Remove the bowl from the microwave and insert a candy or deep-fry thermometer. Watch until the temperature of the milk drops below 120°F, but is still above 100°F. As soon as it drops just below 120°F, add the yogurt, then blend with a hand blender for a few seconds. This yogurt provides the "starter culture" needed to facilitate the growth of the *Acidophilus* bacteria.
3. Carefully pour or ladle the mixture into the sterilized jars and put the lids on. Remove all the trays but the bottom one from the dehydrator, and place the jars on that tray. Dehydrate for 6 hours, then transfer to the refrigerator and chill for 6 to 8 hours before enjoying. Your plain yogurt will keep in the refrigerator for up to 1 month.
4. When ready to eat, remove a jar from the refrigerator and fold in your favorite fresh or dehydrated fruits, nuts, and/or date sugar to taste.

YOGURT RULES FOR SUCCESS

1. Yogurt cultures will die if the temperature exceeds 120°F and will grow too slowly if the temperature drops below 100°F.
2. It is important to sterilize the jars to avoid the growth of any unwanted bacteria.

Your yogurt can be used as the culture to start a new batch of yogurt, but it needs to used within seven days for that purpose.

9

Backpacking and Camper Food

TEA TO GO

Don't forget to pack in some of your tea blends (pages 106–13) to warm you up on chilly nights!

If you are an avid backwoods camper or backpacker and looking for an alternative to expensive freeze-dried foods, the dehydrator is your answer. In this chapter you'll find a starter collection of recipes perfect for the great outdoors. When you're packing in, we know you want to keep fuel use to a minimum, as well as prep. All these recipes require only boiling water, and the veggie and rice cakes a quick fry-up in a skillet. You'll be eating well in a matter of minutes.

In addition to these recipes, also check out our instant soup mixes (pages 172–74), grab-and-go snacks (page 171), and fruit leathers (page 88). Also consider bringing vegetable powders (page 80)—just add boiling water and you can have an instant vegetable puree side dish.

WHAT YOU SHOULD KNOW BEFORE YOU START

When dehydrating fully cooked dishes that contain dairy, oil, meat, seafood, or poultry for backpack/camping use, after dehydration, these items must stay refrigerated until your trip. Once removed from the refrigerator, these items will only be good for five days.

Please feel free to experiment with dehydrating dishes of your own making or your favorite prepared canned foods. Just follow these temperature guidelines for safety:

- If there is meat, seafood, or poultry in the dish, dehydrate at 155°F.
- If the dish is prepared with commercially powdered eggs, dehydrate at 145° to 155°F. We do not recommend dehydrating anything prepared with fresh eggs.
- If there is dairy in the dish, dehydrate at 135°F.

Important: When dehydrating dishes that contain meat/poultry/seafood, dairy, or oil, after four hours, when the top of the item is dry, flip the drying sheet over onto the dehydrating rack and peel away and discard the sheet. When dehydrating at these higher temperatures, case hardening can occur (see page 23) and this will help prevent it, allowing the item to dry all the way through. When dehydrated, the item should be dry and brittle, and break or crumble easily.

Here are some tips for dehydrating for the trail:

- **For camping, canned is good:** When I am storing food for home or long-term storage, I prefer to use fresh or frozen fruits and vegetables because they have a higher nutritional value than the same produce canned. However, dehydrating canned items can be very beneficial when backpacking or camping. Since they are cooked before being canned, they rehydrate faster and require only a heat-up, and no additional cooking. Some other canned or jarred items that dehydrate nicely are tuna (water packed, not oil packed), creamed corn, refried beans, applesauce, condensed soups, split pea soup, and chili.
- **Make use of quick-cooking products:** When creating your own dishes, incorporate quick-cooking ingredients like minute rice, couscous, rice noodles, angel hair pasta, and shredded potatoes or carrots.
- **Use store-bought powdered eggs, milk, and cheese:** Home-dehydrated egg and milk products are truly inferior to commercially prepared. Buy it from the store; your stomach will thank you.
- **Ziptop freezer bags are your friend:** Freezer bags are heavier-duty than regular plastic bags. In fact, they are so sturdy that you can pour the boiling water needed to rehydrate some of these dishes directly into the bag. If you want these items to have a longer shelf life, you can vacuum pack them with an oxygen pack and double-bag in Mylar.
- **Label, label, label:** No, you will not recognize what it is later on, or remember how much water you were supposed to add to it. Label every bag with what it contains and how to prepare it.
- **Double-bag in Mylar:** When backpacking, place the dehydrated food you're bringing in Mylar bags; this will protect it from light, heat fluctuations, and any creepy-crawlies. Several plastic bags can go into each Mylar bag. Mylar has the added benefit that, if you rehydrate your food right in the bag, you can zip it up, put it in Mylar, and it will retain its heat for quite a while, allowing you to get some camp chores done before sitting down to a hot meal.

OATMEAL YOUR WAY

Oatmeal is a great choice when you're camping. All you need to do is bring along individual packets of your favorite instant oatmeal. But don't forget to also include your favorite dehydrated fruits to add to your morning bowl. Just be sure to chop up larger pieces before packing them. To prepare, follow the oatmeal packet directions, also adding 1 tablespoon fruit plus an extra tablespoon of boiling water to compensate for the moisture the dehydrated fruit will absorb. Instead of berries or chopped fruit, you could also try adding 1 teaspoon powdered dehydrated pumpkin or sweet potatoes plus a sprinkling of pumpkin pie spice and 2 additional tablespoons of water instead of one.

Yogurt Drops

Makes a great snack on the go.

Makes 40 drops

> 1 cup fruit yogurt of choice (if it has chunky fruit, puree in a blender)
> ½ cup crispy rice cereal, coarsely crushed

1. In a small bowl, mix the yogurt and cereal together, then place in a pastry bag with the tip of your choice. On drying sheets set in dehydrator trays, squeeze out dots the size of a quarter. Dehydrate at 135°F for 10 to 12 hours. When dehydrated, the drops should be dry like paper and somewhat flexible.
2. If you vacuum seal with oxygen absorbers, the drops will keep up to 1 month in the pantry, 6 months in the refrigerator, or 1 year in the freezer. If stored in ziptop plastic freezer bags, they will keep in the refrigerator for 1 month and will be good for 5 days after being removed from the refrigerator if kept cool and dry

Peach Rice Cakes

Enjoy these tasty rice cakes for breakfast.

Makes ten 3½-inch cakes

> 1 cup chopped ripe peaches
> ½ cup unsweetened applesauce
> 2 tablespoons chopped fresh parsley
> 2 cups cooked long-grain white rice
> ¼ cup lemon juice

1. In blender, combine the peaches, applesauce, and parsley and blend until smooth. Pour the puree into a medium bowl and add the remaining ingredients. Mash for 1 minute with a potato masher to combine (do not use a blender or mixer).
2. Using a ¼-cup measure, scoop the mixture onto drying sheets set on dehydrator trays. With the potato masher, lightly tap each cake 4 to 5 times to flatten it down and form a 3½-inch diameter cake. Dehydrate at 125°F for about 12 hours; flip the cakes over onto the dehydrator trays after 6 hours; remove and discard the drying sheets. When dehydrated, the cakes will be hard, completely dry, and snap when bent.
3. Store in canning jars or vacuum seal with one 100 cc oxygen pack, and double-bag in Mylar until needed. Stored this way, they will keep 5 or more years.
4. **To prepare:** Dip each cake in boiling water for 15 seconds and no more. Heat 1 tablespoon cooking oil in a skillet over medium-high heat. Place the cakes in the hot skillet and cook for 30 seconds on each side.

Raspberry Rice Cakes

Makes ten 3½-inch cakes

> 2 cups cooked long-grain white rice
> 1 cup fresh raspberries, pureed
> ½ cup unsweetened applesauce
> ¼ cup lemon juice
> 1 tablespoon chopped fresh parsley

1. In a medium bowl, combine the ingredients and mash for 1 minute with a potato masher to combine (do not use a blender or mixer).
2. Using a ¼-cup measure, scoop the mixture onto drying sheets. With the potato masher, lightly tap each cake 4 to 5 times to flatten it down and form a 3½-inch diameter cake. Dehydrate at 125°F for about 12 hours; flip the cakes over onto the dehydrator trays after 6 hours; remove and discard the drying sheets. When dehydrated, the cakes will be hard, completely dry, and snap when bent.
3. Store in canning jars or vacuum seal with one 100 cc oxygen pack, and double-bag in Mylar until needed. Stored this way, they will keep 5 or more years
4. **To prepare:** Dip each cake in boiling water for 15 seconds and no more. Heat 1 tablespoon cooking oil in a skillet over medium-high heat. Place the cakes in the hot skillet and cook for 30 seconds on each side.

Veggie Egg Scrambler

Makes 1 serving

> ¼ cup store-bought powdered eggs
> 1 tablespoon dehydrated mixed chopped bell peppers
> 2 dehydrated tomato slices, crumbled

1. Combine all the ingredients. If you vacuum seal with an oxygen absorber, it will keep up to 6 months in the pantry, 1 year in the refrigerator, or 2 years in the freezer. If stored in a ziptop plastic freezer bag, it will keep in a cool, dry place for 1 month.
2. **To prepare:** Add ½ cup warm water to the bag, seal, and let sit for 3 minutes. Spray a skillet with cooking spray, heat over the fire, add the mixture, and scramble as you prefer.

Veggie Hash Browns

Makes 1 serving

> ½ cup dehydrated shredded potatoes
> 4 dehydrated tomato slices, crumbled
> 1 tablespoon dehydrated mixed chopped green and red bell peppers

1. Combine all the ingredients. If you vacuum seal with an oxygen absorber, it will keep for 5 or more years in a cool, dry place. If stored in a ziptop plastic freezer bag, it will keep for 1 month.
2. **To prepare:** Add ½ cup boiling water to the bag, seal, and let sit for 10 minutes. Heat 1 teaspoon cooking oil in a skillet over the fire, add the mixture, and fry until browned and heated through.

"Just Add Water" Blueberry Pancakes

Pancakes are great for breakfast whether you are at home or camping!

Makes 4 pancakes

> ½ cup store-bought "just add water" pancake mix
> 2 tablespoons dehydrated blueberries

1. Combine the ingredients. If you vacuum seal with an oxygen absorber, it will keep up to 1 year in a cool, dry place. If stored in a ziptop plastic freezer bag, it will keep for 1 month.
2. **To prepare:** Add ½ cup boiling water to the bag and lightly squeeze the bag to mix everything up. Heat 1 teaspoon cooking oil in a skillet over the fire, then pour the batter directly from the bag into the skillet to make 4 pancakes. Cook until golden, 2 to 3 minutes per side.

Variations: Don't stop at blueberries! You can substitute dehydrated sliced strawberries, shredded or chopped apples, raspberries, sliced bananas or peaches, chopped pineapples, apricots, cranberries or, 1 tablespoon powdered dehydrated sweet potatoes or pumpkin. Create and enjoy!

Easiest Camper Soup

Avail yourself of store-bought condensed soup and you can sustain yourself for an entire trip without repeating a flavor once! You need only to simmer the soup a few minutes with a little cornstarch added to thicken it up; otherwise the broth will run off the drying sheet in the dehydrator.

Makes 2 servings

> 1 (10.5-ounce) can condensed soup of your choice
> 2 teaspoons cornstarch

1. In a small saucepan, combine the condensed soup (do not add water) and cornstarch and simmer over medium heat until thick, 2 to 3 minutes.
2. Let cool until warm to the touch. Pour onto a drying sheet set in a dehydrator tray to make one leather and dehydrate at 155°F for 8 to 10 hours. After 4 hours, when the top of the soup is dry, it is important to flip the drying sheet over onto the dehydrating tray and peel the drying sheet away. Because of the higher temperature used to dehydrate this, case hardening can occur (see page 23 for more details) and this will help prevent that from happening, allowing the soup to dry all the way through. When dehydrated, it should be dry and brittle, and break or crumble easily.
3. If you vacuum seal with an oxygen absorber, it will keep up to 1 month in the pantry, 6 months in the refrigerator, or 1 year in the freezer. If kept in a ziptop plastic freezer bag, it will keep in the refrigerator for 1 month and be good for 5 days once removed from the refrigerator if kept cool and dry.
4. **To prepare:** Pour 2 cups boiling water over the leather, cover, and let stand for 10 minutes. Stir and enjoy.

Tuna and Apricot Salad

Yes, you can dehydrate canned tuna! You can switch out the apricots for another dehydrated fruit, chopped onions or celery, or even chopped dehydrated bread-and-butter pickles. Do not try to dehydrate oil-packed tuna (or salmon, for that matter). Only water-packed will work.

Makes 1 serving

> 1 (5- to 6-ounce) can water-packed tuna, drained
> 2 teaspoons Vegetable Stock Powder (page 82)
> 2 slices dehydrated apricots, cut into small pieces

1. Spread the tuna on a drying sheet set in a dehydrator tray and dehydrate at 155°F for 8 to 10 hours. When dehydrated, it will be dry and brittle, and break or crumble easily.
2. Combine the dehydrated tuna with the remaining ingredients. If you vacuum seal with an oxygen absorber, it will keep up to 1 month in the pantry, 6 months in the refrigerator, or 1 year in the freezer. If kept in a ziptop plastic freezer bag, it will keep in the refrigerator for 1 month and be good for 5 days once removed from the refrigerator if kept cool and dry.
3. **To prepare:** Pour 1/3 cup boiling water into the bag, squish around to mix, seal, and let sit for 10 minutes. You can eat it right out of the bag or enjoy on crackers.

Dehydrated Veggie Burgers

This is a powder that will transform into a veggie burger in minutes. If you like, sprinkle the patties with sesame seeds on both sides prior to frying.

Makes ¾ cup, or enough for 6 burgers

> 1 cup crumbled dehydrated refried beans
> 1 cup dehydrated sliced zucchini
> 3 dehydrated mushrooms
> 1 tablespoon Vegetable Stock Powder (page 82)
> 1 (½-inch) piece dehydrated chile pepper

1. Combine the ingredients in a blender and process into a fine powder. Store in ¼-cup increments (enough to make two burgers). If you vacuum seal with an oxygen absorber, it will keep for 5 years or more in a cool, dry place. If stored in a ziptop plastic freezer bag, it will keep for 1 month.
2. **To prepare:** Add ¼ cup boiling water to the bag, carefully squish around to mix, seal, and let sit for 2 to 3 minutes. If the mixture is really thick, you can add an extra tablespoon of water. Form the mixture into two even-sized balls, then press each down into a hot, well-greased skillet. Fry until nicely browned and heated through, about 2 minutes per side.

Turkey Sloppy Joe

Sloppy Joes, the healthy way!

Makes 5 to 6 servings

> 1 pound lean ground turkey
> 1 small onion, chopped
> 1 medium green bell pepper, seeded and chopped
> 1 medium red bell pepper, seeded and chopped
> 1 garlic clove, crushed
> 1 cup tomato sauce of your choice
> 2 tablespoons brown sugar
> 1 tablespoon Worcestershire sauce
> 2 teaspoons chili powder
> 2 teaspoons cornstarch

1. Spray a large skillet with cooking spray, then heat over medium-high heat for a couple of minutes. Add the turkey and cook, breaking up any clumps, until no longer pink. Drain off any fat. Add the onion, bell peppers, and garlic and cook, stirring a few times, until softened, 3 to 4 minutes. Stir in the remaining ingredients, bring to a gentle boil, reduce the heat to low, and simmer until nicely thickened, about 30 minutes. If it is still loose, add another teaspoon of cornstarch. It should be thick and not runny.

2. Working with ½ cup at a time (enough for one serving), spread in round patties on drying sheets set in dehydrator trays. Dehydrate at 155°F for 11 to 12 hours. After 5 to 6 hours, when the top of the sloppy Joe mixture is dry, flip the drying sheet over onto the dehydrating tray and peel the drying sheet away. Because of the higher temperature used to dehydrate this, case hardening can occur (see page 23 for more details); this will help prevent that from happening, and allow the mixture to dry all the way through. Continue to dehydrate until dry and brittle.

3. Crumble each of the leathers (they should measure to ¼ cup) and store. If you vacuum seal with oxygen absorbers, it will keep up to 1 month in the pantry, 6 months in the refrigerator, or 1 year in the freezer. If kept in a ziptop plastic freezer bag for easy access, it will keep in the refrigerator for 1 month and be good for 5 days once removed from the refrigerator if kept cool and dry.

4. **To prepare:** Pour ½ cup boiling water into the bag, squish around to mix, seal, and let sit for 5 minutes. Serve on a hamburger roll.

Ready to Heat and Eat Dehydrated Spaghetti

When making spaghetti for dehydration, it is best to use a fine pasta like angel hair because it will rehydrate faster. You can make this with the tomato sauce of your choosing, including a meat-based sauce. If you do make it with a meat sauce, use the leanest meat possible for best dehydration results.

Makes 4 servings

> 8 ounces (½ box) angel hair pasta
> 2 cups tomato sauce of your choice

1. Cook the pasta according to package directions until tender, about 5 minutes. Drain, then add to the sauce. Stir and toss until the sauce covers all of the pasta. Using a fork, remove one quarter of the pasta with the sauce clinging to it to a drying sheet set in a dehydrator tray. Twirl the pasta in a bird's nest with the fork, then lightly tap the nest with a rubber spatula or the fork to flatten it a bit. If you like, add an extra tablespoon of sauce on top. Repeat with remaining pasta and sauce, for 4 birds' nests. Dehydrate at 135°F if using a vegan sauce (no meat or dairy, including butter or oil) or 155°F for 8 to 10 hours if the sauce contains meat and/or dairy. After 4 to 5 hours, when the top of the mixture is dry, flip the drying sheet over onto the dehydrating tray and peel the drying sheet away. Because of the higher temperature used to dehydrate this, case hardening can occur (see page 23 for more details) and this will help prevent that from happening, allowing the mixture to dry all the way through. Continue to dehydrate until dry and brittle.

2. Store each bird's nest individually in its own small ziptop freezer bag. If vacuum sealed with an oxygen absorber, those made with a meat- and/or dairy-based sauce will keep up to 1 month in the pantry, 6 months in the refrigerator, or 1 year in the freezer; if kept in a ziptop plastic freezer bag, it will keep in the refrigerator for 1 month and be good for 5 days once removed from the refrigerator. Those made with a vegan sauce (and no oil) will keep in a cool, dry place for 5 or more years in a vacuum-sealed bag with an oxygen absorber; if stored in a ziptop plastic freezer bag, it will keep for 1 month.

3. **To prepare:** Add ¼ cup boiling water to the bag, seal, and let sit 3 to 4 minutes before enjoying.

Camper Chili

Follow these directions using any of the chili recipes in this book, your own favorite recipe, and even chili from a can.

1. If the chili you're using is runny, add a little cornstarch and cook until the liquid has thickened to the point that it will not run off the drying sheets. With a fork, mash any pieces of meat until they are the size of large grains of rice. Beans can be left whole or cut in half.
2. Working with 1 cup of chili at a time, spread it in strips on drying sheets set in dehydrator trays. Dehydrate at 135°F for a vegan chili (no meat, dairy, or oil) or 155°F (if it contains meat) for 8 to 10 hours. For a meat-based chili, after 5 to 6 hours, when the top of the chili is dry, flip the drying sheet over onto the dehydrating trays and peel the drying sheet away. Because of the higher temperature used to dehydrate this, case hardening can occur (see page 23 for more details) and this will help prevent that from happening, allowing the chili to dry all the way through. Continue to dehydrate until dry and brittle.
3. Crumble each of the leathers (they should measure to 1 cup) and store individually. If vacuum sealed with an oxygen absorber, a meat-based chili will keep up to 1 month in the pantry, 6 months in the refrigerator, or 1 year in the freezer; if kept in a ziptop plastic freezer bag, it will keep in the refrigerator for 1 month and be good for 5 days once removed from the refrigerator if kept cool and dry. A vegetarian chili will keep in a cool, dry place for 5 or more years in a vacuum-sealed bag with an oxygen absorber; if stored in a ziptop plastic freezer bag, it will keep for 1 month.
4. **To prepare:** Add 1¼ cups boiling water to the bag, squish around to mix, seal, and let sit 3 to 5 minutes.

Hot Apples and Mangoes with Raisins

A hot fruit side dish for cool nights.

Makes 2 servings

½ cup dehydrated sliced apples (with or without peels)
2 tablespoons dehydrated date sugar (page 167)
1 tablespoon dehydrated grapes
1 tablespoon dehydrated sliced mango cut into ½-inch pieces
2 teaspoons cornstarch

1. Combine all the ingredients. If you vacuum seal with an oxygen absorber, it will keep for 5 years or more in a cool, dry place. If stored in a ziptop plastic freezer bag, it will keep for 1 month.
2. **To prepare:** Add ⅔ cup boiling water to the bag, seal, and let sit for 15 minutes.

Creamy Cheesy Shredded Potatoes

All the comforts of home in this quick and easy side dish.

Makes 1 serving

½ cup dehydrated shredded potatoes
¼ cup store-bought powdered milk
2 teaspoons store-bought powdered cheese
1 teaspoon dehydrated chopped onions

1. Combine all the ingredients. If you vacuum seal with an oxygen absorber, it will keep up to 1 year in a cool, dry place. If stored in a ziptop plastic freezer bag, it will keep for 1 month.
2. **To prepare:** Pour ⅔ cup boiling water into the bag, seal, and let sit for 5 minutes in a Mylar bag. Squish around to mix again, then let sit another 10 minutes in the Mylar. If it seems to have lost too much heat, drop the plastic bag in hot water for 2 minutes, then serve.

Apple-Potato Cakes with Sweet Pepper and Parsley

These rehydrate in literally seconds—they're a great choice for camp cooking. Enjoy them with a dollop of sour cream or applesauce.

Makes eighteen 3½-inch cakes.

4½ to 5 cups shredded potatoes (peeling is optional)
½ cup shredded green bell peppers (do this in the food processor)
½ cup shredded onions
1½ cups unsweetened applesauce
¼ cup chopped fresh parsley
1 tablespoon dehydrated chile pepper, crushed

1. Place the shredded potatoes, bell peppers, and onions in a large saucepan and cover with water (do not add salt). Bring to a boil, then reduce the heat to low and simmer until tender, about 5 minutes.
2. Drain in a colander, transfer to a large bowl, then stir in the applesauce, parsley, and chile. Using a potato masher, lightly mash ingredients together for just 1 minute. (You don't want to turn the mixture into mashed potatoes; you want most of the potatoes to still remain shredded.)
3. Using a ¼-cup measure, scoop the mixture onto drying sheets set in dehydrator trays. With the potato masher, lightly tap each cake 4 to 5 times to flatten it down and form a 3½-inch diameter cake. Dehydrate at 125°F for about 12 hours; flip the cakes over onto the dehydrator trays after 6 hours; remove the drying sheets. When dehydrated, the cakes will be hard, completely dry, and snap when bent.
4. Store in canning jars or vacuum seal with one 100 cc oxygen pack, and double-bag in Mylar until needed. Stored this way, they will keep 5 or more years.
5. **To prepare:** Dip each cake in boiling water for 3 seconds and no more. Heat 1 tablespoon cooking oil in a skillet over medium-high heat. Place the cakes in the hot skillet and cook for 30 seconds on each side.

Lemon-Garlic-Parsley Rice Cakes

Makes eight 3½-inch cakes

> 2 cups cooked long-grain white rice
> ½ cup unsweetened applesauce
> ¼ cup lemon juice
> 2 tablespoons chopped fresh parsley
> 1 fresh garlic clove, crushed

1. In a medium bowl, combine all the ingredients and mash for 1 minute with a potato masher (do not use a blender or mixer).
2. Using a ¼-cup measure, scoop the mixture onto drying sheets set in dehydrator trays. With the potato masher, lightly tap each cake 4 to 5 times to flatten it down and form a 3½-inch-diameter cake. Dehydrate at 125°F for about 12 hours; flip the cakes over onto the dehydrator trays after 6 hours; remove the drying sheets. When dehydrated, the cakes will be hard, completely dry, and will snap when bent.
3. Store in canning jars or vacuum seal with one 100 cc oxygen pack, and double-bag in Mylar until needed. Stored this way, they will keep 5 or more years.
4. **To prepare:** Dip each cake in boiling water for 15 seconds and no more. Heat 1 tablespoon cooking oil in a skillet over medium-high heat. Place the cakes in the hot skillet and cook for 30 seconds on each side.

Orange-Garlic-Ginger Rice Cakes

Makes ten 3½-inch cakes

> 1 navel orange, peeled
> 1 garlic clove, peeled
> 1 teaspoon coarsely ground dehydrated ginger root
> 2½ cups cooked long-grain white rice
> ½ cup unsweetened applesauce
> 1 teaspoon grated fresh orange zest

1. In a blender, combine the orange, garlic, and ginger and blend until smooth. Pour the puree into a medium bowl, add the remaining ingredients, and mash for 1 minute with a potato masher to combine (do not use a blender or mixer).
2. Using a ¼-cup measure, scoop the mixture onto drying sheets set in dehydrator trays. With the potato masher, lightly tap each cake 4 to 5 times to flatten it down and form a 3½-inch-diameter cake. Dehydrate at 125°F for about 12 hours; flip the cakes over onto the dehydrator trays after 6 hours; remove the drying sheets. When dehydrated, the cakes will be hard, completely dry, and snap when bent.
3. Store in canning jars or vacuum seal with one 100 cc oxygen pack, and double-bag in Mylar until needed. Stored this way, they will keep 5 or more years.

4. **To prepare:** Dip each cake in boiling water for 15 seconds and no more. Heat 1 tablespoon cooking oil in a skillet over medium-high heat. Place the cakes in the hot skillet and cook for 30 seconds on each side.

Raspberry-Coconut Pudding

Great for a quick snack or a sweet treat.

Makes 2 to 3 servings

    1 cup dehydrated raspberries (crush half the berries and leave the other half whole)
    1 cup store-bought powdered milk
    ⅓ cup sugar
    2 tablespoons cornstarch
    1 tablespoon dehydrated shredded coconut
    2 teaspoons store-bought powdered eggs

1. Combine all the ingredients. If you vacuum seal with an oxygen absorber, it will keep up to 1 month in the pantry, 6 months in the refrigerator, or 1 year in the freezer. If stored in ziptop plastic freezer bags, it will keep in the refrigerator for 1 month and will be good for 5 days once removed from the refrigerator if kept cool and dry.
2. **To prepare:** In a pot, combine with 2½ cups water. Bring to a boil over the fire and cook until thick, 2 to 3 minutes. Remove from the fire, cover, and let sit for 5 minutes.

Banana-Raisin Rice Pudding

A perfect choice for dessert or even breakfast!

Makes 2 servings

    ½ cup minute rice
    3 tablespoons store-bought powdered milk
    ⅛ cup dehydrated sliced bananas
    1 tablespoon dehydrated grapes
    1 tablespoon brown sugar
    2 teaspoons store-bought powdered eggs

1. Combine all the ingredients. If you vacuum seal with an oxygen absorber, it will keep up to 1 month in the pantry, 6 months in the refrigerator, or 1 year in the freezer. If stored in ziptop plastic freezer bags, it will keep in the refrigerator for 1 month and will be good for 5 days once removed from the refrigerator if kept cool and dry.
2. **To prepare:** In a pot, combine with 1¼ cups water. Bring to a boil over the fire and cook until thick, 2 to 3 minutes. Remove from the fire and enjoy warm or cold.

Banana Rice Cakes

Delicious for dessert, you can also enjoy these cakes for breakfast.

Makes ten 3½-inch cakes

> 2 ripe bananas, peeled
> 2 cups cooked long-grain white rice
> ½ cup unsweetened applesauce
> 2 tablespoons lemon juice
> 2 teaspoons apple pie spice

1. In a medium bowl, mash the bananas with a potato masher into a smooth puree. Add the rice, applesauce, and lemon juice and mash for 1 minute to combine (do not use a blender or mixer).
2. Using a ¼-cup measure, scoop the mixture onto drying sheets set in dehydrator trays. With the potato masher, lightly tap each cake 4 to 5 times to flatten it down and form a 3½-inch-diameter cake. Sprinkle the cakes with the apple pie spice. Dehydrate at 125°F for about 12 hours; flip the cakes over onto the dehydrator trays after 6 hours; remove the drying sheets. When dehydrated, the cakes will be hard, completely dry, and snap when bent.
3. Store in canning jars or vacuum seal with one 100 cc oxygen pack, and double-bag in Mylar until needed. Stored this way, they will keep 5 or more years
4. **To prepare:** Dip each cake in boiling water for 15 seconds and no more. Heat 1 tablespoon cooking oil in a skillet over medium-high heat. Place the cakes in the hot skillet and cook for 30 seconds on each side.

Berry Rice Cakes

Makes twelve 3 1/2-inch cakes

> 1/2 cup fresh blueberries, picked over
> 1/2 cup sliced ripe strawberries
> 2 1/2 cups cooked long-grain white rice
> 1/2 cup unsweetened applesauce
> 2 tablespoons lemon juice
> 1 teaspoon crumbled dehydrated stevia leaves or 1 tablespoon sugar

1. In blender, combine the berries and blend until smooth. Pour the puree into a medium bowl and add the remaining ingredients. Mash for 1 minute with a potato masher to combine (do not use a blender or mixer).
2. Using a 1/4-cup measure, scoop the mixture onto drying sheets set in dehydrator trays. With the potato masher, lightly tap each cake 4 to 5 times to flatten it down and form a 3 1/2-inch diameter cake. Dehydrate at 125°F for about 12 hours; flip the cakes over onto the dehydrator trays after 6 hours; remove the drying sheets. When dehydrated, the cakes will be hard, completely dry, and snap when bent.
3. Store in canning jars or vacuum seal with one 100 cc oxygen pack, and double-bag in Mylar until needed. Stored this way, they will keep 5 or more years.
4. **To prepare:** Dip each cake in boiling water for 15 seconds and no more. Heat 1 tablespoon cooking oil in a skillet over medium-high heat. Place the cakes in the hot skillet and cook for 30 seconds on each side.

10

Bread & Crackers

Making your own bread is quick and easy. Whether it is yeast bread or quick bread, we will show you how to create a delicious work of art using the different dehydrated fruits, vegetables, and herbs you have on hand. And for those times when you have too much bread on hand, we show you how to use your dehydrator to make dried bread cubes (perfect for stuffing and bread pudding) and breadcrumbs, along with flavored options. We will even show you how to make crackers. Your dehydrator is not just for fruits, veggies, and herbs—did you know that you can use your dehydrator to speed up the rising process when making bread or that you can use dehydrated ingredients to make your own yeast? In this chapter, we will explore all of these possibilities!

YEAST BREADS

Mixing dehydrated fruits, veggies, and herbs into your yeast breads is an excellent way to enhance taste and aroma. There are two ways you can do it.

Powdered dehydrated ingredients (see page 80) can be stirred into the water, yeast, and sugar mixture prior to mixing in the flour. Powders I particularly like to use in my yeast breads are tomato, beet, sweet potato, pumpkin, pineapple, date sugar, onion and garlic, chile peppers, and dill, but the possibilities are limitless. Using powders can add a lovely color to your bread.

Dehydrated chopped ingredients can also be used. In that case, add them to the dough prior to kneading. Unlike in quick breads, where items like berries tend to sink as baking occurs, the strands of gluten in a yeast bread will capture the chunks of dehydrated items and hold them in place while the dough bakes.

Basic Bread Dough Recipe

This basic recipe is tasty as is but below you'll find a selection of my favorite dehydrated add-ins.

Makes two 9 x 5-inch loaves

> 2 (¼-ounce) packages active dry yeast
> ½ cup sugar
> 2 cups warm water (110° to 115°F)
> 6 to 6½ cups all-purpose flour
> ¼ teaspoon salt
> ¼ cup cooking oil of your choice, plus extra to coat the dough

1. In a small bowl, stir the yeast, sugar, and water together and let sit until it begins to bubble.
2. In a large bowl, whisk 6 cups of the flour and the salt together. Add the yeast mixture and oil and mix until it forms a dough that easily pulls away from side of the bowl, adding as much of the remaining ½ cup flour as needed.
3. On a lightly floured work surface, knead the dough for 10 minutes. Lightly oil the dough and cover with a damp cloth. Let the dough rise in the dehydrator at 110°F until doubled in size, 30 to 45 minutes, or in an area that is slightly warmer than room temperature for 1 to 2 hours.
4. Punch the dough down, divide in half, lightly oil each half, and place into two greased 9 x 5-inch loaf pans. Cover with a damp cloth and let rise again until the dough doubles in size, 30 to 45 minutes in the dehydrator or 4 hours on the counter.
5. Once risen, place the pans in a preheated 350°F oven and bake until golden brown, about 30 minutes.
6. Immediately turn the bread out of the pans onto clean dish towels. Let cool completely before slicing. The bread can be frozen; if stored in a ziptop freezer bag, it will keep in the freezer for 2 weeks. If frozen, then vacuum sealed, it will keep in the freezer up to 6 months.

Tomato-Herb Bread: Add to the flour-and-salt mixture in step 2, 2 cups dehydrated sliced Roma tomatoes, chopped in a blender, and 1 teaspoon dehydrated oregano, crushed.

Peaches-and-Cream Bread: With kitchen scissors, cut 2 cups dehydrated sliced peaches into ¼-inch pieces. Heat ½ cup half-and-half and pour over the peaches. Cover and let sit 15 to 20 minutes; do not drain. Add to the flour in step 2 along with the yeast mixture and oil.

Piña Colada Bread: Mix 2 tablespoons powdered dehydrated raw pineapple and 1 tablespoon powdered dehydrated coconut powder in with the flour in step 2.

Cucumber-Herb Bread: Place 2 cups dehydrated sliced cucumbers, 1 tablespoon dehydrated thyme, and 4 dehydrated garlic slices in a blender. Stir into the flour in step 2, and add ¼ cup water along with the yeast mixture and oil.

Onion-Garlic Bread: Add ¼ cup powdered dehydrated onion and 1 teaspoon powdered dehydrated garlic to the flour in step 2.

Beet Bread: Add 2 tablespoons powdered dehydrated beets to the flour mixture in step 2.

Sweet Potato Bread: Add ¼ cup dehydrated powdered sweet potatoes to the flour mixture in step 2.

Cranberry-Apple Bread: Soak ¼ cup dehydrated chopped apples in boiling water, covered, for 15 minutes. Drain, then add, along with ¼ cup dehydrated chopped cranberries (they do not need soaking) to the flour mixture in step 2. Then add yeast mixture and oil and proceed as directed.

Carrot-and-Zucchini Bread: Combine ½ cup each dehydrated shredded carrots and shredded zucchini and pour enough boiling water over to cover the vegetables. Cover and let soak 15 minutes. Drain, then chop in a blender or food processor. Add to the flour with the yeast mixture and oil, along with ¼ cup water, in step 2.

Cabbage-and-Garlic Bread: Chop 2 cups dehydrated shredded cabbage and 4 dehydrated garlic slices in a blender or food processor. Add to the flour with the yeast mixture and oil, along with ¼ cup water, in step 2.

Spinach Bread: Powder 2 cups dehydrated spinach in a blender. Stir into the flour. Add ¼ cup water along with the yeast mixture and oil in step 2

TROUBLESHOOTING TIPS FOR YEAST BREAD

- **The bread is too heavy:** Flour is your most important ingredient. Different kinds of flours will deliver different results in the rising and texture of bread. Knowing your flour will help put your bread-baking worries at ease. Whole wheat flour is heavy and difficult to rise, delivering a heavy bread. Adding equal portions (50:50) of all-purpose flour or bread flour to the wheat flour is the best way to create light and fluffy bread. No matter what kind of flour you choose, using the 50:50 Rule can save the day.

- **The bread is flat:** The older we get, the less active we become; this same rule applies to yeast. Using old yeast will cause your finished bread to be flat. Give your yeast the Active Yeast Test: place it in lukewarm water (hot water will kill the yeast) with a little sugar or honey and wait a few minutes. If the yeast is active, it will ferment the sugar and honey, producing bubbles of carbon dioxide. If you do not see bubbles, your yeast is no longer active and should not be used.

- **The bread is misshapen:** You must knead your dough for 10 to 15 minutes to get a nicely shaped round top on your bread. If your bread comes out of the oven looking like something from an alien invasion, perhaps knead your dough a little longer next time.

- **The bread is yeasty and heavy tasting:** I was always taught; let it rise, punch it down, and let it rise again. If dough is not allowed to rise long enough, your bread may end up tasting yeasty and heavy. But watch the dough: If you let it rise too much, you can end up with large holes in the finished bread.

- **The bread is too doughy:** There are two possibilities: (1) An oven temperature that is too high will cause the crust of your bread to cook faster than the inside, creating a doughy bread. (2) If you cut the bread before it cools down you can cause the bread to mash together into a doughy center.

Spicy Fruit and Nut Bread

Makes two 9 x 5-inch loaves

1 cup apple juice

3 cups total assorted dehydrated fruits (apples, apricots, peaches, pears, and dehydrated grapes are nice choices), chopped in a blender or food processor into ¼-inch pieces

2 tablespoons active dry yeast

1½ cups warm water (110° to 115°F)

¾ cup (1½ sticks) margarine or butter, melted

½ cup wheat germ

¼ cup firmly packed light brown sugar

¼ cup honey

1 tablespoon anise seed

1 teaspoon ground cinnamon

1 teaspoon salt

½ teaspoon ground cloves

7 cups all-purpose flour, or as needed

1 cup dehydrated chopped dates

½ cup chopped walnuts

½ cup chopped almonds

1. In a medium saucepan, bring the apple juice to just under the boiling point. Remove from the heat, stir in the dehydrated fruit, cover, and let soak 15 to 20 minutes.

2. In a stand mixer bowl, soften the yeast in ½ cup of the warm water for 5 minutes. Stir in the remaining 1½ cups warm water, ½ cup of the melted margarine, the wheat germ, brown sugar, honey, anise, cinnamon, salt, and cloves. Gradually add 3½ cups of the flour and mix at medium speed for 5 minutes. Mix in another 1½ cups flour. Slowly add as much of the remaining 2 cups flour as needed until the dough is no longer sticky and pulls away from bowl, making a large ball. Continue to mix until the dough is soft and springs back when pushed down.

3. Remove the dough from the mixer, place in a greased bowl, turn to grease the top, and cover with a damp cloth. Let the dough rise in the dehydrator at 110°F until doubled in size, 30 to 45 minutes, or, in an area that is slightly warmer than room temperature, about 1½ hours.

4. Add the dates and nuts to the rehydrated fruit mixture. Punch down the dough and divide into two equal pieces. Place one piece on a lightly floured work surface. Flatten to a ½-inch-thick circle. Place half of the fruit-and-nut mixture on top and gradually work it throughout the dough, adding only enough flour to prevent the dough from sticking. Shape the dough into a loaf. Repeat with the remaining dough and fruit-and-nut mixture.

5. Place the loaves in two well-greased 9 x 5-inch loaf pans, cover with a damp cloth, and let rise in the dehydrator at 110°F until doubled in size, 30 to 45 minutes, or, in an area that is slightly warmer than room temperature, about 1 hour.

6. Brush the loaves with the remaining ¼ cup melted margarine and bake in a preheated 350°F oven until the bread pulls away from the sides of the pans, about 1 hour. If it seems to be browning too fast, cover with aluminum foil.

7. Immediately turn the bread out of the pans onto clean dish towels. Let cool completely before slicing. The bread can be frozen; if stored in a ziptop freezer bag, it will keep in the freezer for 2 weeks. If frozen, then vacuum sealed, it will keep in the freezer up to 6 months.

A QUICK-RISE SHORTCUT: THE DEHYDRATOR

If you have a dehydrator that is large enough, placing your bread dough in the dehydrator will help speed up the rising process, cutting back rising times that are normally 1 to 2 hours to 30 to 45 minutes. Preheat the dehydrator to 110°F. Remove the dehydrator trays, set a dish of warm water in the bottom of the dehydrator, and place a dehydrator tray directly above it. After kneading your dough, place it in a well-greased bowl or loaf pan. Cover with a damp cloth and set on the tray in the dehydrator. Check the dough in 30 to 45 minutes.

California Fruit Yeast Rolls

Makes about 10 rolls

> ½ cup dehydrated grapes
> ½ cup dehydrated steamed chopped pineapple
> ¼ cup dehydrated dates, chopped
> ¼ cup dehydrated cranberries, crushed
> 1 tablespoon dehydrated orange zest
> 2 cups boiling water
> ⅔ cup milk
> ½ cup sugar
> 2½ teaspoons active dry yeast
> 3½ cups all-purpose flour
> 2 teaspoons ground allspice
> ¼ teaspoon salt
> ½ cup (1 stick) butter, softened
> 1 large egg
> ½ cup raw sunflower seeds
> 2 tablespoons olive oil

1. In a medium heatproof bowl, combine the dehydrated fruit and orange zest and boiling water, cover, and let sit for 15 minutes to rehydrate. Drain any remaining water.
2. Warm the milk until it is just lukewarm (no hotter than 100° to 115° F). Add the sugar and yeast and stir until dissolved. Set aside.
3. In a large bowl, sift the flour, allspice, and salt together. Add the butter and egg and work into the flour mixture until crumbly. Stir in the rehydrated fruit, orange zest, and sunflower seeds. Add the yeast mixture and stir until well combined.
4. Place the dough on a lightly floured work surface and knead until it forms a soft dough. Gather together into a ball, place in a clean bowl, cover with a damp cloth, and let it rise in the dehydrator at 110°F until doubled in size, 30 to 45 minutes, or in an area that is slightly warmer than room temperature, about 2 hours.
5. Grease a 12-inch round baking pan with 1 tablespoon of the oil.

6. Punch down the dough and evenly divide it into small balls (you should have about 10). Arrange the balls in the pan. Brush the tops of the balls with the remaining 1 tablespoon oil. Cover and let the dough rise in the dehydrator at 110°F until doubled in size, 30 to 45 minutes, or in an area that is slightly warmer than room temperature, about 1 hour.

7. Place the pan in a preheated 350°F oven and bake the rolls are until golden brown, about 50 minutes.

MAKING YOUR OWN YEAST

Not only can you make satisfying yeast breads using dehydrated ingredients, you can grow your own yeast!

Important Note: Never use kiwi, pineapple, or papaya when making yeast because they contain protein-degrading enzymes (actinidain, bromelain, and papain) that will break down the dough. Bananas are another bad choice, as they turn into more of a sludge than a yeast. My top dehydrated produce picks for making yeast are raisins, peaches, sweet potatoes, and beets.

Preparation: Start with a sterile 24-ounce (1½-pint) canning jar with a lid. Add ¼ cup of the dehydrated produce (½ cup if they are large slices). Bring a pan of water to a rolling boil, then let the water cool until lukewarm. Pour the water over the dehydrated produce, leaving just 1 inch of headspace at the top. Add 2 tablespoons of sugar or honey. Secure the lid and lid ring tightly on the jar, tighten the jar lid, and shake. Loosen the lid ring and store on a shelf out of direct sunlight for 7 days. When you notice many bubbles on the surface of the water and a faint scent of wine, fermentation has begun, which means yeast is alive and well in your jar. Strain the liquid from the solids, discard the solids, and place the liquid in a clean bottle with a cork. Store in the refrigerator and use 1 cup of liquid per every 2 loaves of bread. This bottle of active yeast is good in the refrigerator for 2 to 3 weeks.

How does this work? Most fruits and vegetables, especially those that are high in sugar content, naturally contain yeast, a living single-celled fungal organism. The dehydration process causes the yeast to go dormant. Once you reintroduce water, and add sugar or honey for the yeast to consume, the fermentation process can begin. Fermentation is the conversion of sugar to alcohol and gas. In baking, the alcohol evaporates and the gas (carbon dioxide) helps bread to rise.

QUICK BREADS, SAVORY AND SWEET

Quick breads contain a leavening agent, like baking powder and/or baking soda, instead of yeast, so you can get your delicious bread to the table faster. The variety of dehydrated fruits and vegetables you have in your pantry will allow you to develop endless creative and exciting quick breads to impress your family and friends. Here are some of my favorite recipes.

Quick Bread Mix

I use this mix as the basis for a lot of my quick bread recipes. It's also delicious mixed up just as is. Vacuum seal the mix in one-loaf quantities, or put it in canning jars, with the directions for finishing and baking the loaf on a decorative label, for a lovely gift at holiday time.

Makes enough for three 9 x 5-inch loaves

> 8 cups all-purpose flour
> 1½ cups firmly packed brown sugar
> 1 cup store-bought powdered milk
> 3 tablespoons ground cinnamon
> 5 teaspoons baking soda
> 5 teaspoons baking powder
> 2 teaspoons salt
> ½ teaspoon ground ginger
> ½ teaspoon ground cloves
> ½ teaspoon ground allspice

1. In a large bowl, whisk together all the ingredients for several minutes until thoroughly blended.
2. Place 3¼ cups of mix into three separate vacuum bags (each bag will make one loaf). Put one 100 cc oxygen pack in each bag and vacuum seal.
3. On each vacuum bag write the following directions:

   Add 1 cup water, ⅓ cup neutral vegetable oil, and 2 large eggs. Blend until smooth, pour into a greased 9 x 5-inch loaf pan, and bake in a preheated 350°F oven until golden brown and springs back when touched, about 50 minutes.

Variation: For a less spicy bread, you can omit the cinnamon, cloves, allspice, and ginger.

Quick Apple-Raisin Bread

Makes one 9 x 5-inch loaf

> ½ cup dehydrated white grapes
> ½ cup dehydrated chopped or shredded apples
> 2 cups boiling water
> 1 vacuum-sealed bag (3¼ cups) Quick Bread Mix (recipe above)
> 2 large eggs, beaten
> 1 cup water
> ⅓ cup vegetable oil
> ½ cup chopped nuts of your choice (optional)

1. Preheat the oven to 325°F. Spray a 9 x 5-inch loaf pan with cooking spray.
2. In a medium bowl, place the dehydrated grapes and apples, cover with boiling water, cover, and let soak for 15 minutes. Drain any remaining water.

3. Pour the Quick Bread Mix into a large bowl. Add the eggs, 1 cup water, and oil and mix until smooth. Stir in the rehydrated fruit and nuts, if using. Pour the batter into the loaf pan. Bake until golden brown and springs back in the center when pushed down, about 50 minutes. Let cool completely in the pan before removing and slicing.

Quick Banana-Nut Bread

Makes one 9 x 5-inch loaf

 1 cup dehydrated banana chips
 1 cup boiling water
 2 large eggs, beaten
 1 cup water
 1/3 cup vegetable oil
 1 vacuum-sealed bag (3 1/4 cups) Quick Bread Mix (page 146)
 1/2 cup chopped nuts of your choice

1. Preheat the oven to 325°F. Spray a 9 x 5-inch loaf pan with cooking spray.
2. In a medium bowl, combine the dehydrated banana chips and boiling water, cover, and let sit for 15 minutes to rehydrate. Drain any remaining water and transfer to a blender. Add the beaten eggs, water, and oil and blend into a smooth puree.
3. Pour the batter into a medium bowl, add the Quick Bread Mix, and stir until thoroughly combined. Stir in the nuts. Pour the batter into the loaf pan and bake until golden brown and the center springs back when pushed down, about 50 minutes.
4. Immediately turn the bread out of the pan onto a clean dish and let cool completely before slicing.

Quick Blueberry Bread

Makes one 9 x 5-inch loaf

 2/3 cup dehydrated blueberries
 2 cups boiling water
 1 vacuum-sealed bag (3 1/4 cups) Quick Bread Mix (page 146)
 2 large eggs, beaten
 1 cup water
 1/3 cup vegetable oil

1. Preheat the oven to 325°F. Spray a 9 x 5-inch loaf pan with cooking spray.
2. In a medium bowl, combine the dehydrated blueberries and boiling water, cover, and let sit for 15 minutes to rehydrate. Drain any remaining water.
3. Pour the Quick Bread Mix into a large bowl. Add the eggs, 1 cup water, and oil and mix until smooth. Stir in the rehydrated berries. Pour the batter into the loaf pan. Bake until golden brown and the center springs back when pushed down, about 50 minutes. Let cool completely before slicing.

Quick Pineapple-Pine Nut Bread

Makes one 9 x 5-inch loaf

> 1 cup dehydrated steamed cubed pineapple
> 2 cups boiling water
> 1 vacuum-sealed bag (3¼ cups) Quick Bread Mix (page 146)
> 2 large eggs, beaten
> 1 cup water
> ⅓ cup vegetable oil
> ½ cup pine nuts

1. Preheat the oven to 325°F. Spray a 9 x 5-inch loaf pan with cooking spray.
2. In a medium heatproof bowl, combine the dehydrated pineapple and boiling water, cover, and let sit for 20 minutes to rehydrate. Drain off any remaining water.
3. Pour the Quick Bread Mix into a large bowl. Add the beaten eggs, water, and oil and mix until smooth. Stir in the rehydrated pineapple and pine nuts until well mixed. Pour the batter into the loaf pan and bake until golden brown and the center springs back when pushed down, about 50 minutes.
4. Immediately turn the bread out of the pan onto a clean dish and let cool completely before slicing.

Date-Nut Bread

This bread freezes well.

Makes two 9 x 5-inch loaves

> 3 cups all-purpose flour
> 1 teaspoon baking powder
> 1 teaspoon baking soda
> 1 teaspoon salt
> ¼ teaspoon ground nutmeg
> 1 cup (2 sticks) butter, softened
> ½ cup granulated sugar
> ½ cup date sugar (page 167)
> 3 large eggs
> 1 teaspoon vanilla extract
> 1½ cups milk
> ½ cup dehydrated chopped dates
> ½ cup chopped walnuts

1. Preheat the oven to 350°F. Spray two 9 x 5-inch loaf pans with cooking spray.
2. In a medium bowl, whisk the flour, baking powder and soda, salt, and nutmeg together.

3. In a large bowl, beat the butter and both sugars together until smooth. Add the eggs, one at a time, beating well after each. Add the vanilla and milk and beat well. Stir in the flour mixture until well mixed. Stir in the dehydrated dates and walnuts. Divide the batter evenly between the two loaf pans. Bake until golden brown and the center springs back when pushed down, about 55 minutes.

4. Immediately turn the breads out of their pans onto clean dish towels and let cool completely before slicing.

Brown Sugar Pumpkin Bread

Makes one 9 x 5-inch loaf

2 tablespoons powdered dehydrated pumpkin
1 cup boiling water
1½ cups all-purpose flour
2 teaspoons pumpkin pie spice
1½ teaspoons baking powder
1 teaspoon baking soda
½ teaspoon coarsely ground dehydrated ginger
½ cup (1 stick) butter, softened
1 cup firmly packed brown sugar
2 large eggs, beaten

1. Preheat the oven to 350°F. Spray a 9 x 5-inch loaf pan with cooking spray.

2. In a small heatproof bowl, whisk the pumpkin powder and boiling water together, cover, and let sit for about 20 minutes to rehydrate to an applesauce-like consistency (do not drain off any extra water).

3. In a medium bowl, whisk together the flour, pumpkin pie spice, baking powder and soda, and ginger.

4. In a large bowl, beat the butter and brown sugar together until smooth. Add the eggs and beat until smooth, then the rehydrated pumpkin puree. Stir in the flour mixture until smooth. Pour the batter into the loaf pan. Bake until golden brown and the center springs back when pushed down, about 50 minutes.

5. Immediately turn out of the pan into a clean dish towel and let cool completely before slicing.

Orange-Rhubarb Bread

Makes one 9 x 5-inch loaf

Bread:

3/4 cup dehydrated chopped rhubarb
1 1/2 cups boiling water
2 1/4 cups all-purpose flour
1 teaspoon baking powder
1/2 teaspoon salt
1/4 teaspoon baking soda
1 cup sugar
1/2 cup (1 stick) butter, softened
2 large eggs
1/3 cup orange juice

Crumb topping:

1/4 cup firmly packed brown sugar
1/4 cup all-purpose flour
2 tablespoons butter
2 teaspoons ground cinnamon

1. Preheat the oven to 350°F. Spray a 9 x 5-inch loaf pan with cooking spray.
2. In a medium heatproof bowl, combine the dehydrated rhubarb and boiling water, cover, and let sit for 15 minutes to rehydrate (do not drain any remaining water).
3. In a small bowl, whisk the flour, baking powder, salt, and baking soda together.
4. In a large bowl, beat the sugar and butter together until smooth. Add the eggs, one at a time, beating well after each. Beat in the orange juice. Stir in the flour mixture until well combined. Stir in the rehydrated rhubarb. Pour the batter into the loaf pan.
5. In a small bowl, cut the crumb topping ingredients together. Sprinkle the crumb topping on top of the batter.
6. Bake until golden brown and the center springs back when pushed down, about 50 minutes. Immediately turn the bread out of the pan onto a clean dish towel and let cool completely before slicing.

Spiced Apple Bread with Apple Peel Topping

Makes one 9 x 5-inch loaf

Bread

- 1 cup dehydrated shredded apples
- 1 cup boiling water
- 2 cups all-purpose flour
- 1 teaspoon coarsely ground dehydrated ginger
- 1 teaspoon baking powder
- ½ teaspoon baking soda
- ½ teaspoon salt
- ¾ cup granulated sugar
- ¼ cup cooking oil
- 2 large eggs
- 2 tablespoons lemon juice
- ½ teaspoon almond extract

Apple Peel Topping

- ½ cup confectioners' sugar
- 2 tablespoons dehydrated apple peels cut into small bits with kitchen scissors
- 2 teaspoons butter, softened

1. Preheat the oven to 350°F. Spray a 9 x 5-inch loaf pan with cooking spray.
2. In a small heatproof bowl, combine the dehydrated apples and boiling water, cover, and let sit for 10 minutes to rehydrate (do not drain any remaining water).
3. In another small bowl, whisk the flour, ginger, baking powder and soda, and salt together.
4. In a large bowl, whisk the granulated sugar, oil, eggs, lemon juice, and almond extract together until smooth. Add the flour mixture and stir until well combined. Stir in the rehydrated apples. Pour the batter into the loaf pan and bake until golden brown and the center springs back when pushed down, about 50 minutes. Immediately turn the bread out of the pan onto a clean dish towel and let cool completely before slicing.
5. While the bread bakes, mix the topping ingredients together. Sprinkle the topping over the bread while the bread is still warm.

Kim's Monkey Bread

Makes one 9 x 5-inch loaf

> ½ cup dehydrated sliced bananas
> 1 cup boiling water
> 1 teaspoon baking soda
> ¼ cup sour cream
> 1⅓ cups sugar
> ½ cup (1 stick) butter, softened
> 2 large eggs
> 1½ teaspoons vanilla extract
> 1½ cups all-purpose flour
> 1 cup chopped nuts

1. Preheat the oven to 350°F. Spray a 9 x 5-inch pan with cooking spray.
2. In a small heatproof bowl, combine the dehydrated bananas and boiling water, cover, and let sit for 15 minutes to rehydrate. Drain any remaining water, transfer to a blender, and process into a smooth puree.
3. Stir the baking soda into the sour cream.
4. In a large bowl, beat the sugar and butter together until smooth. Add the eggs, one at a time, beating well after each. Stir in the sour cream mixture and the vanilla. Stir in the banana puree until well combined. Add the flour and stir until well combined. Stir in the nuts. Pour the batter into the loaf pan. Bake until golden brown and the center springs back when pushed down, about 1 hour.
5. Immediately turn the bread out of the pan onto a clean dish towel and let cool completely before slicing.

Double Corn Bread with Chile Peppers

Half-and-half is poured over the batter of this spicy corn bread right before it going into the oven, resulting in a cream cheese-like top layer.

Makes 8 servings

> 1¼ cups all-purpose flour
> ¾ cup yellow cornmeal
> 2 tablespoons crumbled dehydrated chile peppers
> 1 teaspoon baking soda
> ¼ teaspoon salt
> 1 cup milk
> 2 large eggs, beaten
> ¼ cup dehydrated corn kernels, soaked in boiling water to cover for 20 minutes, then drained
> ¼ cup half-and-half

1. Preheat the oven to 350°F. Spray a 10-inch round cake pan with cooking spray.
2. In a medium bowl, whisk the flour, cornmeal, crumbled peppers, baking soda, and salt together. Add the milk, beaten eggs, and rehydrated corn and mix until well combined.
3. Pour the batter into the cake pan. Pour the half-and-half over the top of the batter. Bake until golden brown and springs back the in middle when pushed down, about 30 minutes. Serve it right from the pan, cut into wedges.

Sweet Potato Corn Bread

Makes 8 squares

> ¼ cup powdered dehydrated sweet potatoes
> 1 cup boiling water
> 2 cups self-rising cornmeal mix
> ¼ cup sugar
> 1 teaspoon ground cinnamon
> 1 cup milk
> ¼ cup (½ stick) butter, softened
> 1 large egg, beaten

1. Preheat the oven to 350°F. Spray an 8-inch baking pan with cooking spray.
2. In a small heatproof bowl, whisk the sweet potato powder and boiling water together, cover, and let sit for 15 minutes to rehydrate into a thick puree (do not drain off extra water).
3. In large bowl, whisk the dry ingredients together. Add the milk, butter, and egg and whisk until well combined. Add the rehydrated sweet potato puree and whisk until well combined. Pour into the baking pan and bake until golden brown and the center springs back when pushed down, about 40 minutes. Let cool for 15 minutes before cutting into squares in the pan.

DEHYDRATING BREAD FOR STUFFING AND BREADCRUMBS

Whether it's your own homemade or store bought, once it's gone stale, don't throw it out, dry it out! You can either cut it up into cubes or throw whole slices onto dehydrator trays to totally dry them out. After that, throw them together with different flavoring ingredients to create your own custom croutons, stuffing mixes, or breadcrumbs. You can experiment with all different types of bread, including gluten free, if you or a loved one has a gluten sensitivity.

Dehydrating bread cubes/slices: Cut the bread of your choice into 1-inch cubes. Place the cubes or slices on dehydrator trays in a single layer and dehydrate at 135°F for 3 to 4 hours. When dehydrated, the bread should be hard, completely dry, and crumble easily. Follow any of the recipes that follow for flavoring the cubes or turning dehydrated bread into flavored crumbs.

Storing flavored bread cubes and breadcrumbs: The cubes can be stored in canning jars with an oxygen pack or in ziptop plastic bags with an oxygen pack double-bagged in Mylar in a cool, dark place; they should keep for a year or longer. Do not vacuum seal them, as the suction will crush the cubes. The breadcrumbs can be vacuum-sealed with an oxygen pack and double-bagged in Mylar, or stored in a glass jar with an oxygen pack in a cool, dark place. Both cubes and crumbs will keep for up to a year.

Italian-Style Tomato-Garlic Bread Cubes

Makes 6 cups

  6 cups dehydrated bread cubes (use Italian bread or white bread)
  2 tablespoons chopped dehydrated tomatoes
  1 tablespoon crushed dehydrated oregano
  1 teaspoon powdered or crushed dehydrated garlic

In a large bowl, whisk the ingredients together until well combined. Use or store as directed (see above).

Spiced Holiday Bread Cubes

Makes about 6 cups

> 6 cups dehydrated bread cubes
> 2 tablespoons ground nutmeg
> 1 tablespoon coarsely ground dehydrated ginger
> 1 tablespoon dehydrated parsley, crushed
> 1 tablespoon dehydrated thyme, crushed
> 1 tablespoon salt
> 1 tablespoon black pepper
> 1 teaspoon ground cinnamon

In a large bowl, whisk the ingredients together until well combined. Use or store as directed (page 154).

Spiced Croutons

Sprinkle these over your favorite fall salad or use them to garnish butternut squash soup!

> 1 recipe Spiced Holiday Bread Cubes (recipe above)
> ¼ cup olive oil

1. Preheat the oven to 300°F.
2. Toss the bread cubes with the oil until lightly and evenly coated. Arrange in a single layer on a baking sheet and bake until nicely toasted, about 35 minutes, stirring and turning them several times.

Jalapeño-Garlic-Parsley Breadcrumbs

Makes 1 cup

> 6 slices dehydrated sliced white bread
> 1 tablespoon dehydrated parsley
> ½ dehydrated jalapeño pepper

Place all the ingredients in a blender or food processor and blend on the coarse or fine setting (your choice). Use or store as directed (page 154).

Zesty Lemon and Parsley Breadcrumbs

These crumbs are really tasty sprinkled over cooked vegetables.

Makes 1 cup

> 6 slices dehydrated white bread
> 1 tablespoon dehydrated parsley
> 1 tablespoon dehydrated lemon zest

Process the bread and parsley together in a blender or food processor on the fine setting. Transfer to a bowl, add the lemon zest, and stir to combine. Store as directed (page 154).

Tarragon and Plum Tomato Breadcrumbs

Makes 1 cup

> 6 slices dehydrated whole wheat bread, broken into pieces
> 6 slices dehydrated plum tomatoes
> 1 tablespoon dehydrated tarragon

Process all the ingredients together in a blender or food processor on the fine setting. Use or store as directed (page 154).

Pineapple-Cranberry-Sage Breadcrumbs

Makes 1 cup

> 6 slices dehydrated white bread, broken into pieces
> 1 tablespoon powdered dehydrated raw pineapple
> ½ teaspoon powdered dehydrated sage
> 1 tablespoon dehydrated chopped cranberries

1. Process the dehydrated bread, pineapple, and sage together in a blender or food processor on the coarse setting. Transfer to a bowl.
2. Stir in the dehydrated cranberries. Use or store as directed (page 154).

Bell Pepper-Tomato-Oregano Breadcrumbs

Makes 1 cup

> 6 slices dehydrated white bread, broken into pieces
> 6 slices dehydrated tomatoes
> ¼ cup dehydrated mixed chopped red and green bell peppers
> 1 teaspoon dehydrated oregano

Process all the ingredients together in a blender or food processor on the fine or coarse setting (your choice). Use or store as directed (page 154).

Pumpkin Seeds and Allspice Breadcrumbs

These breadcrumbs are delicious sprinkled over butternut squash soup, baked sweet potatoes, or casseroles.

Makes 1 cup

> 6 slices dehydrated whole wheat bread
> 2 teaspoons powdered dehydrated pumpkin
> ½ teaspoon ground allspice
> ¼ cup shelled and roasted pumpkin seeds

1. Process the dehydrated bread and pumpkin and allspice together into a blender or food processor on the coarse setting.
2. Transfer to a bowl, add the pumpkin seeds, and stir to mix. Use or stored as directed (page 154).

Cinnamony Green Grape and Onion Breadcrumbs

These make a wonderfully crispy coating on pork chops.

Makes 1½ cups

> 8 slices dehydrated white bread
> ¼ cup dehydrated chopped onions
> ½ teaspoon ground cinnamon
> ¼ cup dehydrated green grapes

1. Process the dehydrated bread and onions and cinnamon together in a blender or food processor on the fine setting.
2. Add the dehydrated grapes and blend on the coarse setting. Use or stored as directed (page 154).

Garlic, Tomato, Oregano, and Parsley Breadcrumbs

Makes 2 cups

> 6 slices dehydrated white bread
> ½ cup dehydrated sliced tomatoes
> 1 tablespoon dehydrated parsley
> 1 teaspoon dehydrated oregano
> 4 slices dehydrated garlic, crushed

Process all the ingredients together in a blender or food processor on the coarse setting. Use or store as directed (page 154).

HOMEMADE CRACKERS FROM THE DEHYDRATOR

Buying crackers at the store can be crazy expensive, so why not make your own? With your dehydrator, it's incredibly simple and a lot healthier. I use a flaxseed base for my cracker recipes. Soaking flaxseeds in warm water for 1 to 2 hours creates a slick, gelatinous substance to which you then can add your choice of ingredients. That gets spread on drying sheets and, after a few hours in the dehydrator, voila—tasty homemade crackers!

All of the recipes that follow can be doubled. Store the crackers in large canning jars with an oxygen pack, out of the way of heat and light. Stored that way, they should keep for years. Do not vacuum seal crackers, as the suction will crush them.

Important Tip: Make sure not to spread your cracker mixture out too thin or you will end up with chips, not crackers. A rubber spatula works best for spreading and flattening the mixture, and a pizza cutter is the easiest way to cut it into squares.

REFRESH STALE CRACKERS IN THE DEHYDRATOR!

If you have crackers that have lost their crunch, don't toss them; dehydrate them back to crispiness! Place them in your dehydrator at 135°F for 1 to 2 hours and they will be fresh and crispy again! This also works for stale cereal.

Flaxseed Base

1 cup flaxseeds
2 cups warm water

In a medium bowl, soak the flax seed in the water until the mixture is thick and gelatinous, 1 to 2 hours.

Cucumber and Tomato Flax Crackers

Makes 25 (2-inch) square crackers

½ fresh tomato
½ fresh cucumber (do not peel)
2 tablespoons chopped fresh parsley
1 recipe Flaxseed Base (page recipe above)

1. Preheat the dehydrator to 125°F. Set a drying sheet in a dehydrator tray.
2. Puree the tomato, cucumber, and parsley together in a blender or food processor until smooth; pour into a medium bowl. Stir in the flaxseed base until well combined.
3. Spread the cracker mixture into a 10-inch square on the drying sheet, smoothing the surface with a rubber spatula and using a straight edge to get nice edges. Dehydrate for 3 hours.
4. Remove the tray from the dehydrator and use a pizza wheel or straight edge to cut the square into 2-inch square crackers. Place the tray back in the dehydrator for another 8 to 10 hours. When

the crackers have completely cooled, snap them apart along the perforated lines. Store as directed (page 159).

Apple, Sweet Potato, and Sesame Flax Crackers

Makes 50 (2-inch) square crackers

 1 fresh apple
 ¼ cup mashed cooked sweet potato
 ¼ cup sesame seeds
 1 recipe Flaxseed Base (page 159)

1. Preheat the dehydrator to 125°F. Set drying sheets in two dehydrator trays.
2. Core the apple, but leave the peel on. Cut into chunks and place in a blender with the sweet potato and sesame seeds and blend into a smooth puree. Pour into a medium bowl. Stir in the flaxseed base until well combined.
3. Spread half the cracker mixture into a 10-inch square on each of the drying sheets, smoothing the surface with a rubber spatula and using a straight edge to get nice edges. Dehydrate for 3 hours.
4. Remove the trays from the dehydrator and use a pizza wheel or straight edge to cut the squares into 2-inch square crackers. Place the trays back in the dehydrator for another 10 hours. When the crackers have completely cooled, snap them apart along the perforated lines. Store as directed (page 159).

Oatmeal-Raisin Flax Crackers

Makes 50 (2-inch) square crackers

 1 fresh apple
 1 recipe Flaxseed Base (page 159)
 ½ cup dehydrated grapes
 1 tablespoon apple pie spice
 1 cup rolled (old-fashioned) oats

1. Preheat the dehydrator to 125°F. Set drying sheets in two dehydrator trays.
2. Core the apple, but leave the peel on. Cut into chunks and puree in a blender until smooth. Pour into a medium bowl. Stir in the remaining ingredients until well combined.
3. Spread half the cracker mixture into a 10-inch square on each of the drying sheets, smoothing the surface with a rubber spatula and using a straight edge to get nice edges. Dehydrate for 3 hours.
4. Remove the trays from the dehydrator and use a pizza wheel or straight edge to cut the squares into 2-inch square crackers. Place the trays back in the dehydrator for another 10 hours. When the crackers have completely cooled, snap them apart along the perforated lines. Store as directed (page 159).

Seeds and More Seeds Flax Crackers

Makes 25 (2-inch) square crackers

> ¼ cup sunflower seeds
> ¼ cup sesame seeds
> ¼ cup shelled pumpkin seeds
> 1 recipe Flaxseed Base (page 159)

1. Preheat the dehydrator to 125°F. Set a drying sheet in a dehydrator tray.
2. Stir all the seeds into the flaxseed base until well combined.
3. Spread the cracker mixture into a 10-inch square on the drying sheet, smoothing the surface with a rubber spatula and using a straight edge to get nice edges. Dehydrate for 3 hours.
4. Remove the tray from the dehydrator and use a pizza wheel or straight edge to cut the square into 2-inch square crackers. Place the tray back in the dehydrator for another 8 to 10 hours. When the crackers have completely cooled, snap them apart along the perforated lines. Store as directed (page 159).

Soy and Ginger Flax Crackers

Makes 25 (2-inch) square crackers

> 1½ teaspoons soy sauce
> 1 teaspoon coarsely ground dehydrated ginger
> 1 recipe Flaxseed Base (page 159)

1. Preheat the dehydrator to 125°F. Set a drying sheet in a dehydrator tray.
2. Stir the soy sauce and ginger into the flaxseed base until well combined.
3. Spread the cracker mixture into a 10-inch square on the drying sheet, smoothing the surface with a rubber spatula and using a straight edge to get nice edges. Dehydrate for 2 hours.
4. Remove the tray from the dehydrator and use a pizza wheel or straight edge to cut the square into 2-inch square crackers. Place the tray back in the dehydrator for another 6 to 8 hours. When the crackers have completely cooled, snap them apart along the perforated lines. Store as directed (page 159).

Pineapple-Coconut Crackers

These crackers are light and flaky, like a pastry.

Makes 25 (2-inch) square crackers

> **1 cup pineapple juice, coconut juice, or water**
> **½ cup shredded fresh coconut or unsweetened flaked coconut**
> **½ cup chopped fresh pineapple, steamed over boiling water until bright yellow and tender, 3 to 5 minutes**

1. Preheat the dehydrator to 125°F. Set a drying sheet in a dehydrator tray.
2. Place the ingredients in a blender and blend until smooth.
3. Pour the cracker mixture onto the drying sheet. Pick up the dehydrator tray and slap on the counter a couple times to level the mixture. Spread the mixture into a 10-inch square on the drying sheet, smoothing the surface with a rubber spatula and using a straight edge to get nice edges. Dehydrate for 6 hours.
4. Remove the tray from the dehydrator and use a pizza wheel or straight edge to cut the square into 2-inch square crackers. Place the tray back in the dehydrator for another 6 hours. When the crackers have completely cooled, snap them apart along the perforated lines. Store as directed (page 159).

Strawberry-Coconut Crackers

Makes 25 (2-inch) square crackers

> **1 cup hulled ripe strawberries**
> **½ cup shredded fresh coconut or unsweetened flaked coconut**
> **½ cup coconut juice or water**
> **2 tablespoons lemon juice**

1. Preheat the dehydrator to 125°F. Set a drying sheet on a dehydrator tray.
2. Place the ingredients in a blender and blend until smooth.
3. Pour the cracker mixture onto the drying sheet. Pick up the dehydrator tray and slap on the counter a couple times to level the mixture. Spread the mixture into a 10-inch square on the drying sheet, smoothing the surface with a rubber spatula and using a straight edge to get nice edges. Dehydrate for 6 hours.
4. Remove the tray from the dehydrator and use a pizza wheel or straight edge to cut the square into 2-inch square crackers. Place the tray back in the dehydrator for another 6 hours. When the crackers have completely cooled, snap them apart along the perforated lines. Store as directed (page 159).

Top to bottom: Pineapple-Coconut Crackers (page 162), Strawberry-Coconut Crackers (page 162), dehydrated: chopped pineapple, sliced coconut, sliced strawberries, and banana chips.

Top to bottom: Veggie Spread (page 194) garnished with dehydrated summer squash, zucchini, and red pepper; Pineapple-Carrot Spread (page 193) garnished with dehydrated shredded pineapple and carrots; Strawberry Cream Cheese (page 194) garnished with dehydrated sliced strawberries; Blueberry Bread (page 147); Date-Nut Bread (page 148)

Top to bottom, left to right: Deep-Dish Apple Pie (page 320), Pumpkin Pie (page 321), dehydrated pumpkin, dehydrated apple slices, pumpkin pie slice, apple pie slice.

Top left, moving clockwise: Mixed Berry Gelatin (page 331) garnished with dehydrated dragon fruit; Cherry-Apple-Orange-Gelatin (page 333) garnished with dehydrated orange and apple; Green Kiwi Gelatin (page 333), garnished with dehydrated kiwi and cherries; Orange and Apple Gelatin (page 334) garnished with dehydrated orange and cherries; Lemon-Papaya-Pineapple Gelatin (page 335) garnished with dehydrated cherries

Top, moving clockwise: Pineapple-Coconut Yogurt Parfait (page 191) garnished with dehydrated pineapple and coconut; Cherry-Papaya Yogurt Parfait (page 192) garnished with dehydrated papaya and cherries; Peach-Raspberry Yogurt Parfait (page 192) garnished with dehydrated peach slice and raspberries; Kiwi-Strawberry Yogurt Parfait (page 193) garnished with dehydrated strawberry and kiwi slices

Top bowl, left to right: Dehydrated mushrooms, jalapenos, cabbage, pumpkin, sweet potato, beets, onions, zucchini, winter squash, summer squash, radishes.

Bottom platter, top to bottom, left to right: Dehydrated whole chile peppers, potato slices, eggplant slices, peas and carrots, shredded zucchini, whole red bell pepper, chopped celery, refried beans, okra, mixed bell peppers, whole red bell pepper, shredded carrots, broccoli, whole baby carrots, corn, shredded leeks, sliced black olives, snow peas, sliced cherry tomatoes, cauliflower, sliced green onions, Brussels sprouts, sliced onion.

Left bowl, left to right: Dehydrated sliced grapefruit, honeydew, cantaloupe, oranges, lemons, mango, kiwi, cooked chopped pineapple, dehydrated raw papaya, sliced coconut, figs, star fruit, dragon fruit.

Right bowl, top to bottom: Dehydrated: apple slices (with and without peels), sliced peaches, apricots, plums, banana chips, orange chunks and strawberries, raspberries, blackberries, chopped dates, Maraschino cherries, cranberries, blueberries.

Top to bottom, left to right: Spinach-Artichoke Dip (page 268), dehydrated artichokes and leeks, dehydrated spinach, dehydrated radishes, crumbled Hummus Leather (page 100), rehydrated Hummus Leather garnished with dehydrated roasted red pepper, Cheesy Microwave Refried Beans (page 269), Rehydrated Hummus, dehydrated refried beans, crumbled Fresh Salsa Leather (page 98), rehydrated Fresh Salsa Leather, dehydrated sliced tortillas.

Chicken Dumpling Stew (page 248)

Full of Beans Chili (page 211)

Focaccia, left to right: Black Olive and Tomato Focaccia (page 219), Pineapple and Bacon Focaccia (page 220); *Oils, left to right:* Shallot and Garlic Oil, Mum-Dill-Juniper Berry Oil, Rose Petal-Garlic-Jasmine Oil (small), Spicy Roasted Red Chile Pepper Oil (tall), Lemony Lemongrass Oil (page 170 for all).

Summer Soup (page 243)

Stuffed Eggplant Rolls (page 215)

The dehydrated ingredients for Summer Soup, left to right: Collard greens, sliced elephant garlic, cabbage, squash, zucchini, tomato, potato, carrots, summer squash, sliced onion, rosemary, mushrooms, red bell pepper.

Shredded Summer Casserole with Chicken (page 221)

Tuna Noodle Casserole (page 235)

Individual Peach Bread Puddings (left, page 329), Individual Raspberry-Apple Breakfast Puddings (right, page 197)

Roast chicken glazed with rehydrated Lemon Leather (page 93) and Spiced Apple Stuffing (page 296), garnished with dehydrated cranberries.

Top left, moving clockwise: Chocolate-Beet Bundt Cake (page 315), Hawaiian Cookies (page 304), Sweet Potato Brownies with Pumpkin Cream Cheese Frosting (page 312), Lemon Bars (page 307), Pumpkin Spice and Apple Zucchini cookies (page 305 and 300), Fast and Easy Tarts (strawberry and lemon pineapple; page 323).

Left to right: Peach-Mango Leather (page 95), Chocolate-Banana Leather (page 95), Strawberry Leather (page 89), Chocolate-Covered Orange Slices (page 179), Just-Add-Water Garden Vegetable Soup in a Jar (page 176), Homemade Potpourri (page 184), Dried Food Ornaments (page 184), White Chocolate with Dehydrated Fruits (page 180), Caramel Apple-Cherry Popcorn (page 178).

Edible Ornaments (page 183)

Chocolate-Covered Pretzel Sticks (page 181) garnished with (left, moving clockwise) dehydrated: grapes, strawberry slices, pineapple and coconut, banana and mango and cherry, orange zest.

11

Flavor Boosters, Snacks, & Instant Soup Mixes

This chapter explores the powerhouse of possibilities in your dehydrated pantry. With a rainbow range of dehydrated fruits, vegetables, and herbs at your command, you can make your own signature rubs and flavored salts, sugars, and oils for cooking, as well as dried fruit and veg snacks and healthful instant soups, with nary a pinch of salt or MSG in sight!

FLAVOR RUBS

Rubs can be used to spice up chicken, ribs, pork chops, roasts, steaks, hamburgers, turkey burgers, shrimp, fish, and just about anything else you can think of. With your pantry of dehydrated produce, along with some store-bought spices, you can create your own signature blends. To preserve freshness, vacuum pack your rubs or store them in canning jars with an oxygen pack. Either way, keep them away from direct light and heat.

To get you started, here are a few of our favorite combinations.

Jerk Rub

This works particularly well on chicken and steak. When we use it, we first marinate the meat for an hour in a mix of ½ cup red or white wine vinegar, 2 tablespoons olive oil, and 1 tablespoon soy sauce, then coat it with the rub and let sit in the refrigerator for 2 to 4 hours before cooking. Use about 1 tablespoon of rub per pound of meat.

Makes ⅔ cup

- 6 dehydrated habanero peppers
- 6 dehydrated scallions
- 2 tablespoons whole allspice
- 1 tablespoon coarse salt
- 2 teaspoons cayenne pepper
- 1½ teaspoons ground cinnamon
- 1 teaspoon ground coriander
- 1 teaspoon ground nutmeg
- 1 teaspoon black peppercorns

Combine the ingredients in a spice grinder or blender and process into a coarse powder.

Garden Herb Rub

This is a versatile rub; try it with chicken, pork, lamb, or any kind of seafood. To use this, coat the meat with a little olive oil, then apply 1 tablespoon of rub per pound of meat and let stand in the refrigerator for 4 hours before cooking.

Makes 1 cup

- 1 cup dehydrated parsley
- ½ cup dehydrated oregano
- ¼ cup dehydrated rosemary
- 2 tablespoons dehydrated tarragon
- 2 tablespoons dehydrated thyme
- 1 tablespoon coarse salt
- 1 teaspoon coarsely ground black pepper

Combine the ingredients in a spice grinder or blender and process into a coarse powder.

Lemon-Cumin Spice Rub

This works best with chicken and shrimp. My favorite way to use it is to brush or toss the chicken or shrimp with a mixture of 1 tablespoon brown sugar and 2 tablespoons water, then to apply 1 tablespoon of the rub per chicken breast or toss ¼ cup of the rub per pound of shrimp. Let sit in the refrigerator for 4 to 6 hours before cooking.

Makes ½ cup

> ¼ cup ground cumin
> 2 tablespoons dehydrated lemon zest
> 2 tablespoons paprika
> 2 tablespoons ground cardamom
> 2 tablespoons dehydrated oregano
> 1 tablespoon ground cinnamon
> 1 tablespoon coarsely ground black pepper
> 1 tablespoon cayenne pepper

Combine the ingredients in a spice grinder or blender and process into a coarse powder.

Spicy Orange-Ginger Rub

This is a tasty combination for chicken or seafood. It makes enough to rub into 1 pound of protein. Apply the rub and refrigerate for 1 to 2 hours. For a quick entrée, melt ¼ cup butter in a skillet over medium heat, then sear the seasoned chicken or seafood until golden brown on both sides. Add 2 cups orange juice and 2 tablespoons honey and let simmer until it thickens into a nice sauce.

Makes about ¼ cup

> 2 tablespoons dehydrated orange zest
> 2 tablespoons powdered dehydrated ginger root
> ½ teaspoon cayenne pepper

Combine the ingredients in a spice grinder or blender and process into a coarse powder.

Derek's Secret Dry Rub

This is an all-purpose rub that works equally well with meat, poultry, or seafood, and particularly well with brisket and ribs. Use 1 tablespoon of rub per pound; for meat and poultry, rub it in, then let it sit in the refrigerator overnight. When using it with seafood, don't let it sit for more than an hour before cooking.

Makes about 1¾ cups

- ¾ cup paprika
- ¼ cup sea salt
- ¼ cup granulated sugar
- 3 tablespoons chili powder
- 2 tablespoons powdered dehydrated garlic
- 2 tablespoons powdered dehydrated onion
- 5 teaspoons cayenne pepper

Combine the ingredients in a spice grinder or blender and process into a coarse powder.

KEEP IT FLOWING

Add a little bit of rice to your flavored salts to absorb excess moisture and avoid clumping. (1 tablespoon rice to 6 tablespoons powder).

FLAVORED SUGARS AND SALTS

Try using your favorite fruit and veggie combinations to season your salt and sugar. It's a simple 3:1 ratio—3 tablespoons coarsely ground dehydrated fruit or vegetable of your choice to 1 tablespoon sugar or salt. Blend into a fine powder in the blender or a spice grinder and try it on everything!!

For flavored salts, garlic, onion, and celery are obvious choices but on the following pages I've included some less obvious options, along with my favorite flavored sugar combinations.

3 MORE SWEET WAYS WITH YOUR DEHYDRATOR

- **Stevia** is a zero-calorie sugar derived from the herb of the same name, which is grown in the South as a perennial and in more northern climes as an annual. Stevia is also attractive to people on a sugar- or carb-controlled diet, as it does not affect blood glucose levels. Grow it at home and you can use the dehydrator to make your own sweetener. Dehydrate as directed on page 103 for leafy herbs (6 to 8 hours). Grind it into a powder, and there you are. Take note that stevia is very sweet, so only use a small amount at a time, and use less when substituting for regular sugar in recipes.

- **Honey sugar** is ground dehydrated honey, which makes a wonderfully crunchy topping for baked goods. To make it, spread honey on a drying sheet set in a dehydrator tray and dehydrate at 125°F for up to 24 hours. Flake off the honey and grind it into a fine or coarse sugar. Be aware that dehydrated honey quickly absorbs moisture from the air, so store it airtight and only sprinkle it on right before serving. Otherwise, if the dessert sits out for even a short period of time, that honey crunch you worked so hard for will turn into honey goo.

- **Date sugar** is a more nutritious substitute for regular white sugar. To make it, for every 3 cups dehydrated chopped dates, add ¼ cup cane sugar, and process in a food processor until a fine powder. Store in a canning jar, adding an oxygen pack, in a cool, dry place, where it will keep for five or more years.

Piña Colada Sugar

Sprinkle it on top of muffins, quick breads, or cakes before popping into the oven and as decorative touch on frosted cakes or cupcakes.

Makes ¼ cup

  2 tablespoons coarsely ground dehydrated pineapple
  1 tablespoon coarsely ground dehydrated coconut
  1 tablespoon granulated sugar

Blend into a fine powder in a blender or spice grinder.

Peach Sugar

Add it to pie or cobbler fillings, muffins, cakes, or your morning tea.

Makes ¼ cup

  3 tablespoons coarsely ground dehydrated peaches
  1 tablespoon granulated sugar

Blend into a fine powder in a blender or spice grinder.

Cranberry-Orange Sugar

Great for muffins and to add extra flavor to your tea.

Makes ¼ cup

2 tablespoons dehydrated chopped cranberries
1 tablespoon coarsely ground dehydrated sliced orange
1 tablespoon granulated sugar

Blend into a fine powder in a blender or spice grinder.

Cherry-Mango Sugar

Makes ¼ cup

2 tablespoons dehydrated coarsely ground mango
1 tablespoon dehydrated coarsely ground maraschino cherries
1 tablespoon granulated sugar

Blend into a fine powder in a blender or spice grinder.

Raspberry Sugar

Delicious added to cakes and sprinkled over frostings!

Makes ¼ cup

3 tablespoons coarsely ground dehydrated powdered raspberries
1 tablespoon granulated sugar

Blend into a fine powder in a blender or spice grinder.

Jalapeño Salt

Incredibly delicious sprinkled on corn on the cob, french fries, or popcorn!

Makes ¼ cup

3 tablespoons dehydrated thinly sliced jalapeños
1 tablespoon salt

Blend into a fine powder in a blender or spice grinder.

Orange Salt

An easy way to add a hint of orange flavor to chicken, rice, and vegetables.

Makes ¼ cup

3 tablespoons coarsely ground dehydrated sliced oranges
1 tablespoon salt

Blend into a fine powder in a blender or spice grinder.

Lemon Salt

This is nice on chicken, seafood, rice, or vegetables.

Makes ¼ cup

3 tablespoons coarsely ground dehydrated sliced lemon
1 tablespoon salt

Blend into a fine powder in a blender or spice grinder.

Hot Banana Salt

This is so good on popcorn!

Makes ¼ cup

3 tablespoons coarsely ground dehydrated sliced bananas
3 slices dehydrated jalapeño
1 teaspoon salt

Blend into a fine powder in a blender or spice grinder.

INFUSED WATER

Why pay $3 for an 8-ounce bottle of infused water, which may also have unwanted sugars added, when you can create the flavors you want using dehydrated fruits at home for pennies?

Put as much or as little fruit as you want—depending on how strong of a flavor you are trying to achieve—in a 1-quart glass canning jar and fill with cool water. Allow the fruit to infuse the water in the refrigerator overnight. Then, pour the water through a filter into another clean bottle and enjoy your water!

Here are some of my favorite combinations to get you started:

- Cucumber, mint, and lime
- Orange and mango
- Grapefruit, lime, and cranberry
- Strawberry and kiwi
- Pineapple and coconut

INFUSED OILS

With a pantry full of dehydrated herbs and fruits, making your own infused oils is a snap. They are wonderful for adding a punch of fresh flavor to any dish or to use as a dipping sauce for bread. Infused oils also make beautiful gifts!

Making infused oils with dehydrated herbs, fruits, and flowers is also the safe way to make them. Fresh produce contains water; water is conducive to bacterial growth. Add fresh herbs to oil and you open yourself up to the possibility of bad bacteria, including the bacteria responsible for botulism. Make your infused oils with dehydrated items and you remove water, thereby making an environment that doesn't support bacterial growth.

Part of the fun of making infused oils is experimenting. The dried items add flavor but the oils themselves also have flavors. Olive oil has a stronger taste while canola oil is milder, and therefore each will pair better with a different set of herbs.

Be sure to start with bottles that have been thoroughly cleaned and are completely dry. Pour the oil in, leaving room to add whatever dehydrated herbs, flowers, and other ingredients you choose. Cap the bottle tightly and store in a cool, dry place for 1 to 2 weeks to allow the flavor to develop. Once the oil is opened, it will last longer if refrigerated and is best if used within a few months.

Here are some of my favorite combinations:

- *Shallot and Garlic Oil:* Extra virgin olive oil and dehydrated shallot and garlic slices
- *Mum-Dill-Juniper Berry Oil:* Extra virgin olive oil and dehydrated chrysthanthemums, dill fronds, and juniper berries
- *Rose Petal-Garlic-Jasmine Oil:* Extra virgin olive oil and dehydrated rose petals, garlic slices, and jasmine flowers
- *Spicy Roasted Red Chile Pepper Oil:* Extra virgin olive oil and dehydrated chives and roasted red chile peppers sliced in half lengthwise
- *Lemony Lemongrass Oil:* Extra virgin olive oil and dehydrated lemongrass stalks, lemon slices, and olive leaves
- *Mediterranean Oil:* Extra virgin olive oil and dehydrated olive leaves, lemongrass stalks, dill fronds, cucumber spears, and garlic slices
- *Cilantro, Coconut, and Lime Oil:* Canola oil and dehydrated coconut slices and lime slices

DEHYDRATOR SNACK COMBOS

One of the beauties of dehydration is that you enjoy many of the items while still dehydrated. They make deliciously crispy snacks and are naturally sweet because the process of dehydration concentrates their sugars. You can divide these mixes into serving sizes to put into small ziptop bags for a quick grab-and-go snack and put it all in a bag and throw it in your backpack for an on-the-trail energy booster.

Finny's Favorite Trail Mix

Makes 2¼ cups

> ½ cup dehydrated apple slices
> ½ cup dehydrated grapes
> ½ cup dehydrated banana chips
> ½ cup dehydrated peach slices
> ¼ cup dehydrated coconut slices

Mix together in a small bowl.

Parker's Pack 'n' Go

Makes 2 cups

> ½ cup dehydrated pineapple chunks
> ½ cup dehydrated sliced mango, cut into small pieces with scissors
> ½ cup dehydrated apricot halves, cut into small pieces with scissors
> ½ cup mini pretzel sticks

Mix together in a small bowl.

Brayden's Brain Power Pack

Makes 2 cups

> ½ cup dehydrated refried beans broken into small pieces
> ½ cup dehydrated sliced sweet potatoes
> ½ cup dehydrated Brussels sprouts (salt the cooked sprouts before dehydration)
> ½ cup dehydrated snow peas (salt the cooked snow peas before dehydration)

Mix together in a small bowl.

HOMEMADE INSTANT SOUP MIXES

These soup mixes are great for camping trips, to have on hand for that busy student, or as a convenient quick lunch. Just add boiling water, wait 2 minutes, and enjoy!

In order for these mixes to be truly instant, meaning all the ingredients will be ready to eat just by adding boiling water and waiting a couple of minutes, the dehydrated produce that goes into them needs to have been cooked until fully tender before dehydration. The same goes for any produce powders (as is the case for using them to make instant baby food).

The reason for this is that the process of food dehydration does not cook your food, it simply creates a waterless version of it. If you fully cook peas until light green and tender and then dehydrate, they will rehydrate to a fully cooked pea. If the peas were quickly blanched before dehydration, when you rehydrate them, they will require further cooking to make them tender.

There are, of course, exceptions: mushrooms, tomato slices, spinach, green onions, and herbs do not require prior cooking to work in instant soups.

Note: Salt should only be added *after* the soup has been hydrated.

Instant Mushroom Soup

A snappy but hearty soup for the mushroom lover.

Makes 1 serving

- 2 tablespoons powdered dehydrated mushrooms
- 1 tablespoon store-bought powdered cream
- 1 tablespoon crushed dehydrated sliced mushrooms
- 1 teaspoon powdered beef bouillon cube or Vegetable Stock Powder (page 82)
- ½ teaspoon cornstarch

Combine all the ingredients. For short-term storage, place in a small ziptop plastic bag, pressing out all the air. For long-term storage (1 year or more), vacuum seal. To enjoy your soup, add 1 cup boiling water, stir, and let cool a bit.

Instant Cream of Tomato and Red Roasted Chile Pepper Soup

This soup is simply soothing and splendid. Seriously.

Makes 1 serving

> 2 tablespoons powdered dehydrated tomatoes
> 1 tablespoon store-bought powdered cream
> ½ teaspoon powdered dehydrated roasted red chile pepper
> Pinch of crumbled dehydrated stevia leaf or sugar

Combine all the ingredients. For short-term storage, place in a small ziptop plastic bag, pressing out all the air. For long-term storage (1 year or more), vacuum seal. To enjoy your soup, add 1 cup boiling water, stir, and let cool a bit.

Instant Tomato-Spinach-Rice Soup

Quick and easy soup when you want it!

Makes 1 to 2 servings

> ¼ cup dehydrated spinach or collard greens, crumbled
> ¼ cup minute rice
> 3 dehydrated tomato slices, crumbled
> 1 tablespoon Vegetable Stock Powder (page 82)
> Pinch of crushed dehydrated red chile pepper

1. Combine the ingredients. If you vacuum seal with an oxygen absorber, it will keep for 5 years or more. If stored in a ziptop plastic freezer bag, it will keep for 1 month.
2. **To prepare:** In a pot, bring to a boil with 2½ cups water. Reduce the heat to a simmer and cook for 3 minutes. Remove from the heat, cover, and let sit for 2 minutes.

Instant Potato and Carrot Soup

This soup is just too good to be instant.

Makes 1 serving

¼ cup dehydrated shredded cooked potatoes
1 tablespoon dehydrated shredded cooked carrots, crushed
1 teaspoon dehydrated shredded cooked green bell pepper, crushed
1 teaspoon powdered chicken bouillon cube or Vegetable Stock Powder (page 82)

Combine all the ingredients. For short-term storage, place in a small ziptop plastic bag, pressing out all the air. For long-term storage (1 year or more), vacuum seal. To enjoy your soup, add 1 cup boiling water, stir, and let cool a bit.

Instant Bean Soup

Quick, filling, and delicious—a must-try.

Makes 1 serving

¼ cup dehydrated refried beans
1 tablespoon dehydrated cooked shredded carrots, crumbled
1 slice dehydrated tomato, crumbled
1 teaspoon powdered chicken bouillon cube or 1 teaspoon Vegetable Stock Powder (page 82)

Combine all the ingredients. For short-term storage, place in a small ziptop plastic bag, pressing out all the air. For long-term storage (1 year or more), vacuum seal. To enjoy your soup, add 1 cup boiling water, stir, and let cool a bit.

12

Gifts from the Dehydrator

You have truly come a long way in the art of dehydrating since you first picked up this book. You have been lectured on the definitions and the science behind food dehydration, and we learned of its many benefits. We time traveled back to ancient Egypt to learn a little history, and then back to today to pick out your first dehydrator together. You've learned how to dehydrate a wide variety of fruits, vegetables, herbs, and meats, and then how to use those dehydrated ingredients in tasty recipes.

The best way to end a journey of discovery such as this is to begin a new journey: to teach others about food dehydration. In this chapter, we will learn how to make great gifts to show others your knowledge and excitement about the many benefits of food dehydration.

Tip

If the soup you choose includes bouillon cubes, those should be placed in a small ziptop plastic bag and set on top of the other ingredients in the jar, to prevent introducing any moisture to the dehydrated ingredients. Remember to tell your gift recipient to remove the bouillon cube bag and oxygen pack before cooking!

Just-Add-Water Garden Vegetable Soup in a Jar

Meals in a jar are a fun and easy way to give a great gift. Use my recipe below or design your own signature soup, and layer the dehydrated ingredients in a canning jar. Add an oxygen pack, attach a label or decorative tag with the cooking directions, and decorate with a bow.

Makes 10 servings

1 cup dehydrated sliced potatoes
¼ cup dehydrated sliced green onions
½ cup dehydrated sliced tomatoes
½ cup dehydrated sliced summer squash
½ cup dehydrated sliced carrots
½ cup dehydrated sliced zucchini
½ cup dehydrated shredded cabbage
¼ cup powdered dehydrated vegetable stock (page 82)

1. Layer the dehydrated ingredients in a 1-quart canning jar in the order listed. The jar should be filled to the top, and it's okay to push the ingredients down in order to fit them all.
2. Tie a gift card onto the neck of the jar, with the name of the soup and these directions: To make the soup, combine the soup mix with 16 cups water in a large pot, bring to a boil, reduce the heat to low, and simmer until the vegetables are tender and the soup thickened, about 3 hours. Or combine the soup mix and water in a slow cooker and cook on LOW for 6 hours.

Lollipops with Dehydrated Foods

What a way to make sure the kids get their fruits and vegetables—hide them in plain sight in a lollipop! These vibrant treats will keep everyone laughing, and they taste good too! Dehydrated herbs, flowers, veggies, and fruits can all be used in these lollipops.

Materials

Dehydrated chopped or sliced fruits and vegetables, herbs, flowers, and citrus zest of your choice
Round hard candies of your choice (sugar-free and transparent candies work best)
Nonstick saucepan
Teflon lollipop molds with stick holders
Lollipop sticks
Cellophane bags
Ribbons

1. Put the dehydrated items you intend to use in small bowls.

   Place the hard candies (in a layer about 1 inch deep) in a small nonstick saucepan over medium-low heat until melted (do this slow and low so the candies don't burn). It is important to watch the saucepan because the candies melt fast. After the candies have melted, turn burner to low.

2. Very carefully, pour a small amount of the liquid candy into a lollipop mold. Quickly place a dehydrated item on top, such as a slice of dehydrated cucumber—or you could put both a dehydrated banana and a strawberry slice. Insert the lollipop stick, then pour a small amount of liquid candy over the dehydrated item(s). Repeat with the remaining lollipop molds, returning the pan of melted candies to low heat whenever you're not using it to keep the sugar liquefied. Allow the candies to cool completely before removing from the mold. The lollipops should easily pop out by inverting the pan and applying a small amount of pressure.

3. Place each lollipop in a cellophane bag and tie with a ribbon. Stored in a cool, dry place, they should keep for a year or more. Once they become soft, they should be discarded.

Banana Split Popcorn

Are you looking for that special and unique party favor for your guests that will both look and taste amazing? Well, this one will make you a star!

Makes about 2 1/2 quarts

> 10 cups popped popcorn
> 1 1/2 cups chocolate melting wafers
> 5 tablespoons dehydrated halved maraschino cherries
> 2/3 cup dehydrated sliced bananas
> 5 tablespoons dehydrated cubed pineapple
> 1/2 cup mini marshmallows

1. Lay a large sheet of wax paper on the counter and spread the popcorn out evenly. Check for and discard unpopped kernels.

2. Melt the chocolate in a slow cooker on LOW, in the microwave, or in the top of double boiler set over simmering water (be sure not to let any water or steam get into the melting chocolate or it will seize or clump up). Pour the warm melted chocolate into a food-safe plastic squeeze bottle. Let the bottle sit in a bowl of hot water.

3. Evenly sprinkle the cherries, bananas, pineapple, and marshmallow over the popcorn, then drizzle the melted chocolate on top. Do not stir the mixture, but instead allow it to cool as is.

4. Once cool, place handfuls into individual cellophane bags and close with a bow. Stored in a cool, dry place, they should keep 3 to 4 weeks.

Caramel Apple-Cherry Popcorn

This is a blend of two of my favorite things: caramel apples and popcorn, with a little extra tangy flavor from the cherries.

Makes 10 servings

¼ cup (½ stick) unsalted butter

1 cup firmly packed brown sugar

¼ cup corn syrup

1½ teaspoons salt

1 teaspoon vanilla extract

¼ teaspoon cream of tartar

12 cups popped popcorn (remove any unpopped kernels)

2 cups dehydrated apple slices, each slice cut into 3 pieces

½ cup dehydrated Maraschino cherries

1. Preheat the oven to 200°F.
2. In a small, heavy saucepan, melt the butter, then add the brown sugar and corn syrup and bring to a boil. Reduce the heat to low and simmer for 5 minutes, then stir and cook until golden brown in color, about another 3 minutes. Remove from the heat and stir in the salt, vanilla, and cream of tartar.
3. Place the popcorn in a large bowl with plenty of room for mixing. Slowly pour the caramel over the popcorn, then mix until the popcorn is well coated. Spread the popcorn in a single layer on rimmed baking sheets and bake for 20 minutes.
4. Remove from the oven, sprinkle the apples and cherries over the hot popcorn, and transfer to wax paper to cool.
5. When the popcorn has cooled, break apart, place handfuls into individual cellophane bags, and close with a bow. It will keep in a cool, dry place for up to 2 months.

Candy Apple Slices

If you were to take a fresh slice of apple and dip it into candy apple coating, the coating would not stick to the wet sliced part of the apple. However, a dehydrated apple slice can be completely dipped and coated with ease, and will store ten times longer. This elegant, crunchy, delicious creation makes a brilliant addition to any gift box!

Materials

Dehydrated ¼-inch-thick apple slices with peel on
1 (5-ounce) candy apple coating kit, prepared according to package directions
Cookie sheet lined with waxed paper
Paper cup liners
Decorative gift box

1. Working with one slice at a time, dip the apples in the warm candy coating, then shake off as much of it as you can, so you get the thinnest possible coating. Set the apple slices on the lined cookie sheet until cool.
2. Fill your gift box, putting each candy apple slice in its own paper cup. Do not stack them on top of each other. Stored in a cool, dry place, they should keep for 2 weeks.

Variation: You can also use this recipe with caramel apple coating, and dip each slice in crushed nuts!

Chocolate-Covered Orange Slices

This is chocoholic nirvana. I have watched many faces light up as they took their first bite of one of my chocolate orange slices. No words needed to be spoken—I could tell by their expressions that they were in love.

Materials

Chocolate melting wafers (milk, dark, or white)
Small slow cooker or double boiler (optional)
Dehydrated ¼-inch-thick orange slices with the peel on
Cookie sheet lined with waxed paper
Paper cup liners
Decorative gift box

1. Melt the chocolate in a small slow cooker on LOW, in the microwave, or in the top of double boiler set over simmering water (be sure not to let any water or steam get into the melting chocolate or it will seize or clump up).
2. Dip the orange slices halfway in the melted chocolate. Set them on the lined cookie sheet and put in the freezer until the chocolate completely hardens.
3. Transfer each slice to its own paper cup and place in a pretty box. They will keep for weeks or months at room temperature, remaining incredibly delicious.

Box of Chocolates with Dehydrated Fruit

This makes a perfect holiday treat displayed in a festive gift box.

Materials

Chopped dehydrated fruits, herbs, edible flowers, chile pepper, and/or coconut

Nondehydrated items like mini marshmallows, semisweet cocoa powder, crisped rice cereal, caramels, and/or sea salt

Chocolate melting wafers (milk, dark, or white)

Small slow cooker or double boiler (optional)

Cupcake or muffin tin and liners or a chocolate mold tray

Paper candy cups

Decorative box(es)

1. Set out small dishes filled with your dehydrated and non-dehydrated ingredients.

2. Melt the chocolate in a small slow cooker, in the microwave, or in the top of double boiler set over simmering water (be sure not to let any water or steam get into the melting chocolate or it will seize or clump up).

3. For each chocolate you wish to make, place the dehydrated and companion ingredients in separate paper cup liners in a tin or in a chocolate mold. Only use enough so that a pinch ends up in each candy. Add one tablespoon of melted chocolate to each liner or mold and allow the chocolate to set and harden.

4. Once the chocolate has hardened, transfer the cups to a gift box. If using a chocolate mold, remove the chocolates from the mold and place in a candy cup before putting in the box. Stored in a cool, dry place, white- and milk chocolate-covered candies will keep for up to 6 months; those covered with dark chocolate will keep for up to 1 year.

MY FAVORITE BOX OF CHOCOLATE COMBINATIONS

- Dehydrated cherries and sliced bananas, and walnuts
- Dehydrated cherries and sliced pineapple and bananas
- Finely chopped dehydrated Gobi berries and sea salt—this is a must-try. If Gobi berries are not available, substitute chopped cranberries. Yum!
- Crushed dehydrated peppermint leaves and rice crisp cereal
- Finely chopped dehydrated apples, and caramel
- Dehydrated grapes, almonds, and marshmallows
- Chopped dehydrated chile pepper (my favorite!)
- Finely chopped dehydrated apples and cranberries
- Chopped dehydrated pineapple and bacon bits (yes, bacon bits)
- Chopped dehydrated maraschino cherries and almonds
- Coarsely ground dehydrated ginger, and chopped dehydrated orange slices
- Chopped dehydrated pineapple, sea salt, and white chocolate
- Chopped dehydrated strawberries and white chocolate

Chocolate-Covered Pretzel Sticks

Just looking at these salty, sweet, crunchy treats will make your mouth water. This is a gift that will make anyone, no matter how young or old, smile from ear to ear.

Materials

Cookie sheet
Chocolate melting wafers (milk, white, or dark)
Small slow cooker or double boiler (optional)
Pretzel sticks
Chopped dehydrated fruits
Chopped dehydrated citrus peels
Crushed fruit leathers (page 86—use leathers that are brittle and crunchy for this)
Cellophane bags
Ribbon

1. Place the cookie sheet in the freezer.
2. Melt the chocolate in a small slow cooker on LOW, in the microwave, or in the top of a double boiler set over simmering water (be sure not to let any water or steam get into the melting chocolate or it will seize or clump up).
3. Working with one pretzel stick at a time, hold it over the cooker and spoon chocolate over one end while twirling it to fully cover. Make sure to be consistent, covering the same amount of the stick with chocolate each time.
4. Lay the pretzel stick on the cold cookie sheet. Once you fill the sheet with chocolate-covered pretzels, place it back in the freezer. While they chill, line up your dehydrated items in little dishes so you can grab them quickly.

OTHER GREAT EDIBLE GIFTS FROM THE DEHYDRATOR

You'll find other wonderful gift ideas elsewhere in the book, including:

- Herbal teas (pages 106–13)
- Flavor rubs
- Flavored sugars and salts (put a selection of them in small individual glass jars with flip tops)
- Flavored oils

5. Remove the cookie sheet from the freezer. Working with one pretzel stick at a time, apply first a second coating of chocolate, then (quickly) the dehydrated items of your choice, onto the stick and place back on the chilled cookie sheet. Coat all of the pretzel sticks in this manner. When finished, return the cookie sheet to the freezer.

6. When the chocolate has hardened completely (it should only take a few minutes), place the chocolate-covered end of each stick in a cellophane bag and tie with a ribbon. Stored in a cool, dry place, they will keep for up to 6 months.

Dehydrated Cake Cube Chocolates

We are always looking for new great ways to reinvent our favorite treats, and who doesn't love cake?!

Materials:

Your favorite cake recipe baked in a sheet pan and cooled completely (or use a store-bought cake)
Cookie sheet
Chocolate melting wafers (milk, dark, or white)
Slow cooker or double boiler (optional)
Chopped or crushed dehydrated fruits, herbs, edible flowers, and/or coconut
Paper candy cups
Decorative box(es)

1. Cut the cake into 1-inch cubes. Spread them on a dehydrator tray and dehydrate at 125°F for 6 hours, until crunchy.
2. Put the cookie sheet in the freezer.
3. Melt the chocolate in a small slow cooker on LOW, in the microwave, or in the top of double boiler set over simmering water (be sure not to let any water or steam get into the melting chocolate or it will seize or clump up).
4. Using a skewer, dip each cake cube in the melted chocolate and place on the chilled cookie sheet. While the chocolate is still tacky, decorate them with your dehydrated items and/or sprinkles. Once the chocolate has completely hardened, place each cube in a paper candy liner and then into a decorative candy box. Stored in a cool, dry place, they will keep for up to 2 months.

Edible Ornaments

These ornaments are made from store-bought fondant. Fondant is a pliable icing that can be rolled out and is often used on wedding cakes. It's available in different colors, or you can buy white and color it yourself by kneading the food coloring of your choice into it until you achieve the shade you want. You can also customize the flavoring of the fondant in the same way, kneading the flavor extract of your choice into the fondant before rolling it out. I strongly recommend you do this, as store-bought fondant, straight out of the box, tastes kind of like sugary Play-Doh. Whatever flavor you prefer, try adding 1 teaspoon extract per 2 cups of fondant. I like to use almond extract. (**Note:** Never use flavor extracts designed for candy making; they will turn the fondant gelatinous and sticky.)

Materials

    Cooking spray or confectioners' sugar
    Fondant
    Rolling pin
    Cookie cutters
    Skewer
    Food-safe markers
    Food-safe paintbrushes
    Flavor extract
    Sprinkles, candies, and other edible decorations
    Cake decorating food coloring (don't use regular food coloring, it's too liquid)
    Ornament hangers or ribbon

1. Before you start, spray the work surface with cooking spray or sprinkle it with confectioners' sugar. Roll out the fondant ⅛ inch thick.
2. Use cookie cutters to cut out your desired shapes. With a skewer or pointed end of a paintbrush, make a hole at the top for a hanger or ribbon. You can use food-safe markers to write directly on the fondant. Dip a clean food-safe paintbrush in flavor extract, then brush it over the ornament to create a sticky surface you can use to attach sparkles, sprinkles, and/or candy decorations. Cake decorating food color and a paintbrush can be used to paint designs on the ornaments. Make sure to clean the brushes between colors and extracts.
3. Place the ornaments on dehydrator trays and dehydrate at 125°F and no higher, for 8 to 10 hours. At temperatures above 125°F, the fondant will discolor. Stored in an airtight container in a cool, dry place, they should keep for up to 2 years. To hang, insert a ribbon through the hole and tie in a bow, or use an ornament hanger.

Dried Food Ornaments

These ornaments are beautiful and precious. When I give them as gifts, the first question always is, "Oh wow! Where did you buy these?"

Materials:

Twine or thin ribbon (make sure the string is not so thin that it tangles or breaks easily)
Needle with a large eyelet
Small round Styrofoam balls
Glue gun and glue sticks
Dehydrated fruits, fruit peelings, herbs, and flowers of your choice
Can of fast-dry clear acrylic spray paint (high or low gloss)

1. Thread the needle with the twine or ribbon, then pull it through a Styrofoam ball to create a loop about 3 inches in diameter. Remove the needle, tie a good strong knot, and cut any extra string.
2. Using a glue gun, glue dehydrated fruits, peelings, herbs, and/or flowers to each Styrofoam ball, making sure to cover the ball so no Styrofoam is showing. Then, hold the string and lightly spray the entire ball with acrylic spray. Hang and let air-dry for 24 hours before placing in a gift box.

Homemade Potpourri

The fun thing about potpourri is that you can make your own personalized mix of scents and textures.

Materials

Small pine cones and tree bark
Dehydrated fruit peelings, berries, ginger, flowers, and/or herbs
Cinnamon sticks, nut shells, pine needles
Scented oils or perfumes (optional)
Transparent, breathable pull-string nylon, lace, or burlap pouches
Ribbon
Glue gun

1. If using, place pine cones and/or tree bark in a pot of boiling water for 15 minutes to kill any bugs or contaminants. Place on dehydrator trays and dehydrate at 135°F for 6 to 8 hours.
2. Gather your dehydrated items as well as others you might be using, like cinnamon sticks and other whole spices, nut shells, and pine needles.
3. If using scented oils, place each of your dehydrated items in separate paper bags and spray or sprinkle the oil in each bag. Close the bags with rubber bands and store in a closet away from food for 2 to 3 days. If the items are still moist after 3 days, spread on a dehydrator tray and dehydrate at 135°F for several hours.
4. Get creative and combine the scents and colors of your choice, add them to breathable nylon bags, and close with a drawstring or decorative bow. Try hot-gluing decorative flowers or cinnamon sticks to the bag for an attractive touch.

Dried Wreaths

If you have ever purchased a dried wreath from the store, you know how expensive they are. Well, crank up your dehydrator, because we have a solution for you! You can use flowers and herbs from your garden, as well as bark, twigs, and leaves collected from a walk in the woods. You can even use peelings from grapefruit, oranges, lemons, limes, and apples that would have otherwise been consigned to the compost heap.

Turn this project into a fun family activity to create something you will remember and that will last for years to come, or make something memorable for a cherished friend.

Materials

Small pine cones, tree bark, and/or twigs
Glue gun
Foam ring
Dehydrated fruit peelings, berries, ginger, flowers, and/or herbs
Nondehydrated items like cinnamon sticks, nut shells, and/or pine needles
Ribbon

1. If using, place pine cones, tree bark, and/or twigs in a pot of boiling water for 15 minutes to kill any bugs or contaminants. Place on dehydrator trays and dehydrate at 135°F for 6 to 8 hours.
2. Using the glue gun, get creative and decorate the foam ring with your choice of dehydrated and nondehydrated items. When you're finished, attach a ribbon for hanging.

All-Natural Soap

With a dehydrator, you can create your own personalized soaps at home, using items from your dehydrated pantry, at a fraction of the cost of store-bought natural soaps.

Materials

Melt-and-pour soap kit (all-natural soap kits are sold online and at national craft stores)
Crushed and chopped dehydrated fruits, herbs, vegetables, and/or edible flowers of your choice
Sharp knife
Tissue paper
Ribbon or stickers

1. Follow the directions on the package for the melt-and-pour kit, filling the mold halfway with melted soap, then adding your favorite dehydrated items. Finish filling the mold with melted soap and let it set as directed. If using a pan instead of a mold, you will need to use a warm, dry sharp knife to cut the soap into slices or blocks.
2. Wrap each block of soap in tissue paper and fasten with a pretty sticker or ribbon.

MY FAVORITE DEHYDRATED COMBINATIONS FOR MAKING NATURAL SOAP

- Coarsely chopped dehydrated lavender and lemongrass
- Dehydrated marigold petals and coarsely chopped dehydrated orange peel
- Crushed dehydrated peppermint leaves
- Rolled oats and finely chopped dehydrated green apple peels
- Finely chopped dehydrated grapefruit and orange peels
- Dehydrated rose petals and finely chopped dehydrated orange peels
- Dehydrated rosemary and basil leaves and dehydrated dragon fruit slices, cut into quarters
- Dehydrated chocolate mint leaves and chamomile flowers
- Dehydrated sliced cucumber and lime, finely chopped
- Dehydrated shredded coconut and chocolate mint leaves, crushed
- Finely chopped dehydrated mango and brown sugar (brown sugar is a natural exfoliant)
- Dehydrated honeysuckle flowers and chopped dehydrated pear peels
- Crushed cloves and finely chopped dehydrated pumpkin

Dehydrated Apple People

It's so much fun to make these little grandma and grandpa dolls. They're truly one-of-a-kind gifts for kids and grownups alike!

Materials

Apples

Apple peeler (optional)

Sharp paring knife to carve with

¼-inch wooden dowels

Lemon juice or ascorbic acid solution

Box of salt

1-gallon ziptop plastic bag

Cake decorating food coloring (don't use regular food coloring—it's too liquid)

Fine-tipped paintbrushes

Can of fast-dry clear acrylic spray paint

Glue gun and glue sticks

Yarn or doll hair

Beads for eyes

Thin wire, fashioned into eyeglasses

1. Peel the apples, but do not core them. Carve the nose first, making it larger than normal. Make the eyes large and deep, and the mouth very defined; and don't forget to make two large ears. Remember, once the apples are dehydrated, everything will shrink and become more size appropriate.
2. Push a dowel all the way through each apple, directly through the core. Remove the dowels, and set them aside; you will need them again when the apples are dehydrated.
3. Soak the apple heads in lemon juice or ascorbic acid for 15 minutes.
4. Pour 2 cups of salt into the plastic bag. One at a time, remove the apples from the liquid, place in the bag, seal, and shake the bag until the apple is completely covered with salt.
5. As you remove the apples from the bag, place them on a dehydrator tray, stem side up. Some of the trays will have to be removed from the dehydrator to allow space for the whole apple. When you have placed all of the apples on the tray, dehydrate at 125°F for 48 hours, until completely dried.
6. Remove the apples from the dehydrator, then paint the faces on with the food coloring.
7. Place the apples back on the tray and dehydrate at 125°F for another 2 to 4 hours to dry the food coloring.
8. Spray the heads with the acrylic spray. Let spray dry completely, then add a second coat if needed. This will protect the apple from absorbing moisture from the air and rotting.
9. Hot-glue on the hair, beads for eyes, and wire-frame glasses.
10. Place a dab of hot glue on the end of each dowel and push it back into the hole in the bottom of each apple. The stick can be glued onto a cloth doll body, or placed into a plastic bottle weighed down with sand, then decorated with fabric clothes.

13

Breakfast & Brunch

Use your dehydrated fruits and veggies in a combination of different breakfast recipes, including delicious smoothies. Also try your favorite dehydrated fruits in your yogurt, cereal, or oatmeal.

SMOOTHIES

Dehydrated fruits can be used to make fabulous quick and healthy smoothies and shakes! The easiest way to do this is to choose a selection of your favorite dehydrated fruits and grind them each into a fine powder using a blender or food processor (see page 81 for more on this).

When you wake in the morning, simply throw a scoop of this and a scoop of that into your blender along with yogurt and whatever else you like. Process for a minute or so and you have an instant breakfast drink or midafternoon pick-me-up. Use Greek yogurt if you want a thicker, more robust smoothie and an additional blast of protein!

Blueberry Smoothie

A sweet smoothie packed with antioxidants! Feel free to substitute in your favorite berry powder.

Makes 1 to 2 servings

> ½ cup plain yogurt
> ½ cup milk
> 5 ice cubes
> 1 tablespoon powdered dehydrated blueberries
> 1 tablespoon honey

Blend all the ingredients in a blender until smooth.

Blueberry-Apple Smoothie

This has such a beautiful, bright color, and even brighter flavor!

Makes 1 to 2 servings

> 1 cup vanilla yogurt
> ½ cup milk
> 5 ice cubes
> 3 tablespoons firmly packed brown sugar
> 2 teaspoons powdered dehydrated apple
> 2 teaspoons powdered dehydrated blueberries or other berries
> ½ teaspoon ground cinnamon

Blend all the ingredients in a blender until smooth.

Strawberry, Kiwi, and More Smoothie

A classic smoothie flavor, reinvented with dehydrated fruits!

Makes 1 to 2 servings

> ¾ cup water
> ½ cup vanilla yogurt
> 5 ice cubes
> 1 teaspoon powdered dehydrated banana
> 1 teaspoon powdered dehydrated strawberries
> 1 teaspoon powdered dehydrated kiwi
> 1 teaspoon powdered dehydrated pineapple

Blend all the ingredients in a blender until smooth.

Strawberry-Banana Smoothie

This classic smoothie will be a family favorite.

Makes 2 servings

> 2 cups milk
> ½ cup dehydrated banana chips
> ¼ cup dehydrated sliced strawberries
> ¼ cup plain yogurt
> 1 tablespoon sugar
> 5 ice cubes

Blend all the ingredients in a blender until smooth.

Chocolate-Banana Smoothie

A rich and heavenly treat you simply have to try.

Makes 1 to 2 servings

> ½ cup plain yogurt
> ½ cup milk
> 5 ice cubes
> 1½ tablespoons chocolate syrup
> 2 teaspoons powdered dehydrated sliced banana

Blend all the ingredients in a blender until smooth.

Orange Creamsicle Shake

All the flavor of a creamsicle, with none of the drippy mess!

Makes 1 to 2 servings

> ½ cup orange sherbet
> ½ cup vanilla yogurt
> ½ cup milk
> 2 teaspoons powdered dehydrated peeled orange slices

Blend all the ingredients in a blender until smooth.

Date Sugar Smoothie

This slightly sweet smoothie resonates with the distinct flavor of dates.

Makes 1 to 2 servings

½ cup plain yogurt
½ cup milk
5 ice cubes
1 tablespoon date sugar (page 167)

Blend all the ingredients in a blender until smooth.

Hot Tomato Smoothie

A spicy, smooth, and hearty smoothie!

Makes 1 to 2 servings

½ cup water
5 ice cubes
1 ½ teaspoons powdered dehydrated tomato
1 teaspoon sugar
¼ teaspoon powdered dehydrated habanero chile pepper

Blend all the ingredients in a blender until smooth.

PERFECT PARFAITS

These yogurt parfaits are as delicious as they are beautiful. Try any combination of fruit to make your favorite. These cold and creamy parfaits are great for breakfast, a midday snack or a healthy option for dessert.

Pineapple-Coconut Yogurt Parfait

Makes 1 serving

> 4 tablespoons plain yogurt
> 2 tablespoons dehydrated steamed chopped pineapple
> 1 tablespoon dehydrated shredded coconut
> 2 small pieces dehydrated steamed pineapple and shredded coconut for garnish

1. Place 1 tablespoon of yogurt in the bottom of a parfait glass. Top with 1 tablespoon of the pineapple, another tablespoon of yogurt, the coconut, another tablespoon of yogurt, the remaining tablespoon pineapple, and the final tablespoon of yogurt.
2. Garnish with the pineapple and coconut and enjoy!

Cherry-Papaya Yogurt Parfait

Makes 1 serving

> 4 tablespoons plain yogurt
> 2 tablespoons dehydrated chopped papaya
> 1 tablespoon dehydrated maraschino cherries
> 2 pieces dehydrated chopped papaya and 2 maraschino cherries for garnish.

1. Place 1 tablespoon of yogurt in the bottom of a parfait glass. Top with 1 tablespoon of the papaya, another tablespoon of yogurt, the cherries, another tablespoon of yogurt, the remaining tablespoon papaya, and the final tablespoon of yogurt.
2. Garnish with the papaya and cherries and enjoy!

Peach-Raspberry Yogurt Parfait

Makes 1 serving

> 4 tablespoons plain yogurt
> 2 tablespoons chopped dehydrated peaches
> 1 tablespoon dehydrated raspberries
> 2 pieces chopped dehydrated peaches and 2 dehydrated raspberries for garnish

1. Place 1 tablespoon of yogurt in the bottom of a parfait glass. Top with 1 tablespoon of the peaches, another tablespoon of yogurt, the raspberries, another tablespoon of yogurt, the remaining tablespoon peaches, and the final tablespoon of yogurt.
2. Garnish with the peaches and raspberries and enjoy!

Kiwi-Strawberry Yogurt Parfait

Makes 1 serving

4 tablespoons plain yogurt
2 tablespoons dehydrated sliced strawberries
1 tablespoon chopped dehydrated kiwi
2 pieces chopped kiwi and 2 dehydrated strawberry slices for garnish

1. Place 1 tablespoon of yogurt in the bottom of a parfait glass. Top with 1 tablespoon of the strawberries, another tablespoon of yogurt, the kiwi, another tablespoon of yogurt, the remaining tablespoon strawberries, and the final tablespoon of yogurt.
2. Garnish with the kiwi and strawberries and enjoy!

Toasted Coconut Breakfast Spread

This creamy, crunchy spread is great on bagels or English muffins and a healthy alternative to cream cheese.

Makes 16 servings

1 cup dehydrated shredded coconut (toasted coconut preferably; if yours isn't toasted, follow step 1)
1 (16-ounce) container low-fat cottage cheese
1 tablespoon honey
2 teaspoons vanilla extract
½ cup chopped macadamia nuts

1. Preheat the oven to 400°F. Spread the coconut evenly on a baking sheet and bake on the upper rack for 2 to 4 minutes. Do not take your eyes off the coconut; it can turn from white to black in a matter of seconds. Remove from the oven and let cool on the baking sheet.
2. Place the cottage cheese, honey, and vanilla in a food processor or blender and process until smooth. Add the cooled toasted coconut and nuts and pulse to combine.
3. Scoop the spread back into the cottage cheese container and refrigerate for up to 10 days.

Pineapple-Carrot Spread

Makes 1⅔ cups

¼ cup dehydrated steamed cubed pineapple, cut into small pieces with kitchen scissors
2 tablespoons dehydrated shredded carrots
2 cups boiling water
1 cup cream cheese, softened

1. In a small heatproof bowl, combine the dehydrated pineapples and carrots, pour the boiling water over, cover, and let sit 15 to 20 minutes to rehydrate. Drain off any remaining water (do not squeeze out or pat dry).
2. Add the cream cheese to the bowl and cream together. This will keep, tightly covered, in the refrigerator for up to 2 weeks.

Strawberry Cream Cheese

Add dehydrated fruit to your cream cheese to make this delicious flavored spread.

Makes 1½ cups

1 strawberry leather (page 89)
1 cup water
1 tablespoon dehydrated thinly sliced strawberries
1 cup cream cheese, softened

1. Place the leather in a small saucepan with the water, bring to a boil, reduce the heat to low, and simmer until the leather has dissolved and the liquid thickened. Remove from the heat and let cool completely.
2. Stir in the dehydrated strawberry slices, then add the cream cheese and cream together. This will keep, tightly covered, in the refrigerator for up to 2 weeks.

Veggie Spread

This is delicious spread on bread but also try a spoonful in the center of an omelet.

Makes 2 cups

2 tablespoons dehydrated shredded carrots
2 tablespoons dehydrated shredded zucchini
2 tablespoons dehydrated shredded summer squash
2 tablespoons dehydrated chopped mixed red and green bell peppers
2 cups boiling water
1 cup cream cheese, softened

1. In a small heatproof bowl, combine the dehydrated vegetables and boiling water, cover, and let sit for 15 minutes to rehydrate. Drain off any remaining water.
2. Add the cream cheese and cream together. This will keep, tightly covered, in the refrigerator for up to 2 weeks.

Pumpkin and Orange Marmalade

This is delicious on toast or spread over phyllo dough as a filling.

Makes 1½ cups

> 1 cup water
> 1 cup orange juice
> ⅔ cup sugar
> ¼ cup powdered dehydrated pumpkin
> ¼ cup dehydrated thinly sliced orange with the peel, cut into small pieces with kitchen scissors

1. In a medium saucepan, whisk all the ingredients together. Bring to a boil, reduce the heat to low, and simmer about 20 minutes, until it reaches the consistency you like.
2. Pour into a sterilized pint canning jar, cover, let cool to room temperature, then refrigerate. It will keep in the refrigerator up to 1 month.

Sweet Potato Pancakes

This truly is the breakfast of champions because sweet potato pancakes are much more filling and nutritious than regular pancakes—I like serving mine with pecan syrup.

Makes eight 6-inch pancakes

> 1 cup all-purpose flour
> 1 cup whole wheat flour
> 4 teaspoons baking powder
> 1 teaspoon ground cinnamon
> Pinch of ground nutmeg
> ½ cup dehydrated sliced sweet potatoes
> 1 cup boiling water
> 2 tablespoons brown sugar
> 2 large eggs
> 4 teaspoons butter, melted
> 2 cups milk

1. In a small bowl, whisk both flours, the baking powder, and the spices together.
2. In a large heatproof bowl, combine the dehydrated sweet potatoes and boiling water, cover, and let sit for 15 minutes to rehydrate. Stir until the mixture is smooth. Whisk in the brown sugar, then the eggs and melted butter, then the milk. Whisk in the flour mixture until a smooth consistency is reached.

3. Melt the butter in a large skillet or on a griddle over medium-high heat. Ladle in about ¼ cup of the batter per pancake and cook until bubbles form on the surface. Turn them over and cook until the other side is dark golden brown.

Zucchini and Feta Cheese Omelet

This omelet is a delicious way to eat your vegetables!

Makes 1 to 2 servings

½ cup dehydrated shredded zucchini
2 tablespoons dehydrated sliced onions
1 cup boiling water
6 large egg whites
¼ cup cubed feta cheese
Salt and black pepper

1. In a small heatproof bowl, combine the dehydrated zucchini and onions. Pour the boiling water over, cover, and let sit for 5 minutes to rehydrate. Drain off any remaining water.
2. In a medium bowl, whisk the egg whites, then beat in the rehydrated vegetables and feta.
3. Spray a small skillet with cooking spray. Place over medium-low heat for a minute. Pour in the egg mixture and cook until firm underneath. Loosen from the pan, flip over, and cook the other side. Season with salt and pepper to taste.

Apple Oven Pancake

This oven pancake is nothing short of spectacular in both taste and appearance.

Makes 6 servings

2 cups dehydrated sliced apples
½ cup dehydrated green grapes
1 cup boiling water
¼ cup firmly packed brown sugar
½ teaspoon ground cinnamon
3 tablespoons butter, melted
4 large eggs
1 cup milk
⅔ cup all-purpose flour
Confectioners' sugar
Dehydrated raspberries for garnish

1. Preheat the oven to 350°F.
2. In a medium heatproof bowl, combine the dehydrated apples and grapes. Pour the boiling water over, cover, and let sit for 15 minutes to rehydrate. Add the brown sugar, cinnamon, and 2 tablespoons of the butter, stir together until well combined, and then pour into a 9-inch pie plate.

Bake for 15 minutes. Remove from the oven. Increase the oven temperature to 425°F and let it fully reheat.

3. In a medium bowl, whisk the eggs, milk, flour, and the remaining 1 tablespoon butter together. Pour this mixture over the ingredients in the pie plate. Bake until the pancake puffs up and browns on the top, another 15 to 20 minutes.

4. Remove from the oven, sprinkle with confectioners' sugar, and garnish with dehydrated raspberries.

Individual Raspberry-Apple Breakfast Puddings

Try this as a sweet breakfast treat or as a dessert.

Makes 4 servings

> 4 croissants, cut into 1-inch cubes
> 1 cup dehydrated raspberries
> 1/4 cup dehydrated sliced green apples with peels, each cut in half
> 1 2/3 cups milk
> 1/2 cup maple syrup
> 2 large eggs
> 2 tablespoons butter, softened
> 1 teaspoon vanilla extract

1. Preheat the oven to 350°F. Set four 1 1/2-cup ceramic baking dishes on a cookie sheet.

2. In a large bowl, combine the croissant cubes and dehydrated raspberries and apples.

3. In a medium bowl, whisk the milk, 1/4 cup of the maple syrup, the eggs, butter, and vanilla together, then pour over the croissants and raspberries and lightly toss until evenly coated. Divide the mixture evenly between the baking dishes. Drizzle 1 tablespoon maple syrup over the top of each. Bake until the puddings puff up and turn golden brown on top, about 20 minutes.

Cheesy Hash Brown Breakfast Casserole

Eggs, sausage, and hash browns—an all-American breakfast in a quick and easy casserole.

Makes 6 servings

> 3 cups dehydrated shredded potatoes
> ½ cup dehydrated chopped tomatoes
> ½ cup dehydrated chopped green bell peppers
> ¼ cup dehydrated sliced mushrooms
> ¼ cup dehydrated chopped onions
> 6 cups boiling water
> 6 large eggs
> ½ cup half-and-half
> 2 tablespoons butter, melted
> 1 cup chopped cooked breakfast sausages
> 1 cup shredded mozzarella cheese
> 1 cup shredded cheddar cheese

1. In a large heatproof bowl, combine the dehydrated ingredients. Pour the boiling water over, cover, and let sit for 15 minutes to rehydrate. Drain off any remaining water.
2. Preheat the oven to 350°F. Spray a deep 10-inch square baking dish with cooking spray.
3. In another large bowl, beat the eggs, half-and-half, and melted butter together until smooth. Stir in the sausage, cheeses, and rehydrated ingredients until well combined. Pour into the baking dish and bake until cooked through and light golden on top, about 35 minutes.

Hash Brown and Spinach Casserole

Give yourself a nutritious boost by adding spinach to your morning hash browns.

Makes 4 servings

> 2 cups dehydrated spinach leaves
> 1½ cups dehydrated shredded potatoes
> ¼ cup dehydrated sliced mushrooms
> 1 teaspoon crushed dehydrated garlic
> ½ teaspoon crushed dehydrated dill
> 2½ cups boiling vegetable broth or water
> 6 large eggs
> ¼ cup milk
> ⅔ cup shredded mozzarella cheese

1. Preheat the oven to 350°F. Spray a 10-inch square baking dish with cooking spray.
2. In a medium bowl, combine the dehydrated spinach, potatoes, mushrooms, garlic, and dill. Pour the boiling broth over, cover, and let sit until the broth is absorbed, about 10 minutes. Transfer the mixture to the baking dish.

3. In a small bowl, beat the eggs and milk together and pour over the vegetables. Lightly fold everything together. Sprinkle with the mozzarella and bake until cooked through, the cheese is melted, and the top is a light golden color, 20 to 25 minutes.

Bagel, Broccoli, and Roasted Red Pepper Casserole

Loaded with veggies, this morning casserole will satisfy your hunger. Plus, it's a great way to use up those bagels that are starting to get stale.

Makes 8 servings

> ½ cup dehydrated broccoli florets
> ½ cup dehydrated sliced mushrooms
> ¼ cup dehydrated roasted red bell pepper strips
> ¼ cup dehydrated chopped onions
> 4 cups boiling water
> 6 large eggs
> 2½ cups milk
> ¼ cup (½ stick) butter, melted
> 2 cups shredded cheddar cheese
> 3 plain bagels, cut into 1-inch cubes

1. Preheat the oven to 350°F. Spray a 10 x 12-inch baking dish with cooking spray.
2. In a medium heatproof bowl, combine the dehydrated ingredients. Pour the boiling water over, cover, and let sit for 15 minutes to rehydrate. Drain off any remaining water.
3. In a large bowl, beat the eggs, milk, and butter together until smooth. Fold in the cheese, bagels, and rehydrated ingredients. Pour into the baking dish and bake until cooked through and the top turns golden, about 50 minutes.

Strawberry-Rhubarb Crumb Cake

A delicious summer crumb cake that you can make all year round with your dehydrated rhubarb and strawberries!

Makes one 10-inch cake, 8 servings

Filling

    1 cup dehydrated chopped rhubarb
    1 cup dehydrated sliced strawberries
    3 cups water
    2 tablespoons lemon juice
    ⅓ cup cornstarch

Cake

    3 cups all-purpose flour, sifted
    1 teaspoon baking powder
    1 teaspoon baking soda
    1 teaspoon salt
    1 cup (2 sticks) butter, softened
    1 cup sugar
    2 large eggs
    1 teaspoon vanilla extract
    1½ cups buttermilk

Topping

    ¾ cup firmly packed light brown sugar
    ¾ cup all-purpose flour
    ¼ cup (½ stick) butter, softened

1. In a medium saucepan, combine the dehydrated rhubarb and strawberries, water, and lemon juice. Bring to a boil, stir, cover, reduce the heat to a simmer, and cook until the rhubarb is tender, about 5 minutes, stirring occasionally.
2. Add the cornstarch and stir until the mixture thickens. Remove from the heat and set aside to cool.
3. Preheat the oven to 350°F. Spray a 10-inch deep-dish cake pan with baker's spray.
4. In a small bowl, whisk the flour, baking powder and soda, and salt together.
5. In a large bowl, beat the butter and sugar together until smooth. Add the eggs, one at a time, beating well after each. Beat in the vanilla. Whisk in the buttermilk. Add the flour mixture and stir until well combined.
6. Pour half of the batter into the cake. Spoon in the rhubarb-and-strawberry filling and spread it over the batter. Pour the rest of the batter over the filling.
7. In a small bowl, work the brown sugar, flour, and butter together with your fingertips until crumbly. Sprinkle evenly over the top of the batter. Bake until the top is golden brown and the center springs back when pushed down, 40 to 45 minutes. Let cool in the pan for 1 hour, then cut and serve straight from the pan.

Blueberry-Lemon Muffins

Chock-full of berries with an extra snap of flavor provided by the addition of lemon zest. And there's no need to rehydrate the blueberries—they go straight from your pantry into the batter!

Makes 12 muffins

> 2 large eggs
> ½ cup firmly packed brown sugar
> ¼ cup (½ stick) butter, melted
> 1 teaspoon vanilla extract
> ½ teaspoon dehydrated lemon zest
> 1½ cups milk
> 2¼ cups all-purpose flour
> 1 tablespoon baking powder
> ¼ cup dehydrated blueberries

1. Preheat the oven to 350°F. Put liners in a regular-size muffin pan.
2. In a large bowl, beat the eggs and brown sugar together, then add the butter, vanilla, and lemon zest and beat until smooth. Whisk in the milk. Add the flour and baking powder and mix just until combined (don't overmix or your muffins will be tough). Fold in the blueberries and let batter sit for 10 minutes.
3. Ladle the batter into the liners, filling them no more than three-quarters of the way full. Bake until the tops are golden brown and spring back when touched, about 20 minutes.

Raspberry-Peach Muffins

Sweet and moist muffins perfect for breakfast on the go or a great snack.

Makes 18 muffins

> ½ cup chopped dehydrated sliced peaches
> 1 cup boiling water
> 1 cup milk
> ½ cup (1 stick) butter, melted
> ½ cup firmly packed light brown sugar
> 1 large egg
> 2¼ cups all-purpose flour
> 1 tablespoon baking powder
> 1 cup dehydrated raspberries
> 2 tablespoons crushed walnuts

1. Preheat the oven to 350°F. Place liners in a regular-size muffin pan.
2. In a small heatproof bowl, combine the dehydrated peaches and boiling water, cover, and let sit for 10 minutes to rehydrate. Drain off any remaining water.
3. In large bowl, whisk the milk, butter, brown sugar, and egg together until smooth. Add the flour and baking powder and stir just until combined (don't overmix or your muffins will be tough).

Gently fold in the peaches, dehydrated raspberries, and walnuts and let the batter sit for 5 minutes.

4. Ladle the batter into the liners, filling them no more than three-quarters of the way full. Bake until the tops are golden brown and spring back when touched, about 20 minutes.

Raspberry-Lemon Muffins

Tart and tangy! The raspberries rehydrate right in the batter before going into the oven.

Makes 18 muffins

1 cup sugar
2 large eggs, beaten
½ cup neutral-flavored cooking oil of your choice
1 teaspoon lemon extract
1 cup half-and-half
½ cup water
2 cups all-purpose flour, sifted with 1 tablespoon baking powder and ½ teaspoon salt
1 cup dehydrated raspberries

1. In a large bowl, whisk the sugar, eggs, oil, lemon extract, half-and-half, and water together in that order. Add the flour mixture and mix just until combined (don't overmix or your muffins will be tough). Fold in the dehydrated raspberries and let the batter sit for 10 minutes.
2. Preheat the oven to 350°F. Place liners in a regular-size muffin pan.
3. Ladle the batter into the liners, filling them no more than three-quarters of the way full. Bake until the tops are golden brown and spring back when touched, about 20 minutes.

Sour Cream and Carrot Muffins

These spiced carrot muffins are moist and delicious.

Makes 12 muffins

½ cup dehydrated shredded carrots
2 cups boiling water
1¾ cups all-purpose flour
2 teaspoons baking powder
1½ teaspoons ground cinnamon
1 teaspoon baking soda
¼ teaspoon salt
1 cup sour cream
½ cup (1 stick) butter, melted
⅓ cup firmly packed brown sugar
1 large egg

1. In a medium heatproof bowl, combine the dehydrated carrots and boiling water, cover, and let sit for 15 minutes to rehydrate. Drain off any remaining water.
2. Preheat the oven to 350°F. Put liners in a regular-size muffin pan.
3. In a small bowl, whisk the flour, baking powder, cinnamon, baking soda, and salt together.
4. In a large bowl, whisk the sour cream, butter, brown sugar, and egg together until smooth. Add the flour mixture and mix just until combined (don't overmix or your muffins will be tough). Fold in the carrots. Ladle the batter into the liners, filling them no more than three-quarters of the way full. Bake until the tops are golden brown and spring back when touched, about 30 minutes.

Blender Orange-Coconut Muffins

Start your day with the tropical taste of coconut!

Makes 18 muffins

> ½ cup dehydrated sliced peeled oranges, cut into small pieces with kitchen scissors
> 2 cups boiling water
> ⅔ cup orange juice
> ½ cup (1 stick) butter, softened
> ¼ cup sugar
> 1 large egg
> 1½ cups all-purpose flour
> 2 teaspoons baking powder
> ½ teaspoon baking soda
> ½ teaspoon salt
> ½ cup dehydrated shredded coconut, finely chopped
> 2 tablespoons cold butter
> 1½ teaspoons dehydrated orange zest

1. In a small heatproof bowl, combine the dehydrated oranges and boiling water, cover, and let sit for 15 minutes to rehydrate. Drain off any remaining water (do not squeeze or pat dry the oranges).
2. Preheat the oven to 350°F. Put liners in a regular-size muffin pan.
3. In a blender, puree the orange juice, softened butter, sugar, egg, and rehydrated oranges together until smooth. Add the flour, baking powder and soda, and salt and process until smooth.
4. In a small bowl, work the coconut, cold butter, and orange zest together with your fingertips until in fine crumbles.
5. Pour the batter into the liners, filling them no more than three-quarters of the way full. Sprinkle the topping over each muffin, and bake until the tops are golden brown and spring back when touched, about 20 minutes.

Pumpkin-Chocolate Chip Granola Bars

Pumpkin and chocolate come together in this sweet spiced granola bar. A sweet and nutritious treat for when you're on the go.

Makes 10 to 12 bars

> **1 tablespoon powdered dehydrated pumpkin**
> **½ cup boiling water**
> **3 ¼ cups rolled (old-fashioned) oats**
> **½ teaspoon pumpkin pie spice**
> **½ teaspoon ground cinnamon**
> **¼ teaspoon ground nutmeg**
> **½ teaspoon salt**
> **¾ cup firmly packed brown sugar**
> **¼ cup applesauce**
> **¼ cup honey**
> **1 teaspoon vanilla extract**
> **1 cup chocolate chips**

1. Preheat the oven to 350°F. Spray an 8-inch square baking pan with cooking spray.
2. In a medium heatproof bowl, whisk the pumpkin powder and boiling water together, cover, and let sit for 15 minutes to rehydrate. Whisk until smooth.
3. In a large bowl, whisk the oats, spices, and salt together. Add the brown sugar, applesauce, honey, and vanilla to the rehydrated pumpkin and whisk until smooth. Pour over the oat mixture and stir until all of the oats are moistened. Stir in the chocolate chips.

   Evenly press the oat mixture into the baking pan. Bake until golden brown, 30 to 35 minutes. Remove from the oven and let cool on a wire rack for 5 minutes. Using a sharp knife, cut into bars. Remove from the pan and let cool completely.

14

Soups, Stews & Chili

Everyone loves a good soup, stew, or chili, and they're perfect preparations for using dehydrated ingredients, because they rehydrate as the soup simmers. For more soup and stew recipes, see the Slow Cooker chapter (page 239), or pages 172–74 for instant soup mixes made from dehydrated ingredients.

Asparagus and Red Pepper Soup

This is a wonderful springtime soup.

Makes 6 servings

2½ cups dehydrated 1-inch asparagus pieces
½ cup dehydrated diced potatoes
½ cup dehydrated thinly sliced leeks
½ cup dehydrated chopped red bell pepper
6 dehydrated garlic slices, crushed
Pinch of crushed dehydrated roasted red pepper
1 tablespoon dehydrated tarragon
1 tablespoon soy sauce
4 cups water
2 cups vegetable broth
2 cups half-and-half

1. Place all the ingredients, except the half-and-half, in a large saucepan, stir to combine, and bring to a boil. Reduce the heat to a simmer, cover, and cook for 1 hour.

2. Remove the saucepan from the heat. Using a strainer, remove 1 cup of solids from the soup and set aside. Stir the half-and-half into the remaining soup in the pan. Using an immersion blender, puree until smooth. Stir the reserved vegetables into the pureed soup and heat through before serving.

Cheesy Broccoli Soup

Cheese and broccoli make a wonderful combination and the addition of yogurt makes it even creamier. Feel free to swap out the broccoli for your favorite vegetable.

Makes 6 servings

> 1 cup dehydrated broccoli florets
> 2 cups boiling water
> ¼ cup dehydrated chopped carrots
> 2 tablespoons dehydrated diced onions
> 2 tablespoons dehydrated chopped celery
> 1 teaspoon dehydrated garlic, crushed
> ¼ teaspoon dehydrated thyme
> 4 cups chicken broth
> 2 cups shredded Swiss cheese
> 1 cup plain yogurt

1. Place the broccoli in a heatproof bowl and pour the boiling water over. Cover and let sit for 15 minutes to rehydrate.
2. Combine the carrots, onions, celery, garlic, thyme, and broth in a medium saucepan. Cover, bring to a boil, reduce the heat to a simmer, and cook for 20 minutes.
3. Remove the pan from the heat and gently stir in the cheese and yogurt until melted and well mixed. Add the broccoli with any remaining soaking water, stir lightly until mixed, cover, and simmer for another 20 minutes.

Broccoli and Carrot Soup

This is perfect antidote to a cold winter afternoon; the kids will love it.

Makes 8 servings

3 tablespoons butter
3 tablespoons all-purpose flour
4 cups chicken or vegetable broth
4 cups water
1 cup milk
1 cup dehydrated chopped carrots
1 cup dehydrated broccoli florets
½ cup dehydrated chopped onion
¼ cup dehydrated chopped celery
½ teaspoon crumbled dehydrated thyme
3 dehydrated garlic slices, crushed
2 cups shredded Swiss cheese

1. Melt the butter in a large saucepan over medium heat. Add the flour and whisk constantly until smooth. Slowly add the broth, whisking constantly, then stir in the water and milk. Do not allow the mixture to come to a boil.
2. Reduce the heat to a simmer, add all the dehydrated ingredients, cover, and cook for 40 to 45 minutes.
3. Remove the pan from the heat and very slowly stir in the cheese until melted. Heat through over low heat.

Cucumber and Parsley Soup

A taste of summer in the middle of winter! The parsley provides a healthy helping of vitamin C.

Makes 4 servings

1 cup dehydrated sliced cucumbers
½ cup dehydrated cubed potatoes
¼ cup dehydrated sliced green onions
¼ cup dehydrated parsley
Pinch of dehydrated rosemary
½ teaspoon mustard seeds
Black pepper
1 large chicken or vegetable bouillon cube
6½ cups boiling water

Place all the ingredients in a large saucepan, cover, and bring to a rolling boil. Reduce the heat to medium and simmer for 30 minutes.

Cream of Mushroom Soup

This smooth and satisfying soup flavored with thyme and garlic will be an instant classic in your home. Try using any leftovers in place of condensed cream of mushroom soup in casseroles.

Makes 6 servings

> 1¼ cups dehydrated sliced mushrooms
> 3 dehydrated garlic slices, crushed
> ½ teaspoon dehydrated thyme
> 3 cups boiling water
> 3 cups beef broth
> ½ cup half-and-half
> 1 tablespoon dehydrated parsley

1. Combine the mushrooms, garlic, thyme, water, and broth in a large saucepan over medium heat. Let simmer until the mushrooms are tender, about 30 minutes.
2. Puree the soup in the pan with an immersion blender until smooth. Reduce the heat to low and stir in the half-and-half; simmer until heated through.
3. Serve the soup sprinkled with the dehydrated parsley.

Chopped Red Potato Soup

A simple and easy meal, this soup is full of flavor.

Makes 6 servings

> 2 cups dehydrated cubed red potatoes (with skin on)
> 1 cup dehydrated sliced onion
> 1 teaspoon crumbled dehydrated dill
> 8 cups water or vegetable broth
> 1 cup milk
> 3 tablespoons all-purpose flour
> ¼ cup sour cream
> Shredded cheddar cheese and bacon bits for serving

1. Place the potatoes, onion, dill, and water in a large saucepan over medium heat. Cover and let simmer for 45 minutes.
2. In a small bowl, whisk the milk and flour together. Slowly pour this into the saucepan, stirring constantly. Let simmer until heated through and thickened, about another 5 to 10 minutes.
3. Remove from the heat and stir in the sour cream. Serve sprinkled with bacon bits and a little cheddar.

Spicy Pumpkin Soup

This richly flavored soup packs a punch with the addition of dehydrated jalapeños.

Makes 6 servings

1 tablespoon cooking oil of your choice
¼ cup dehydrated chopped onion
8 dehydrated garlic slices, crushed
1 dehydrated jalapeño pepper, crumbled
1½ tablespoons ground cumin
1½ tablespoons dehydrated oregano
1½ teaspoons salt, plus more for sprinkling
8 cups vegetable broth
¼ cup powdered dehydrated pumpkin
1 (15-ounce) can white beans, drained and rinsed
2 tablespoons red wine vinegar
2 tablespoons honey
1 cup French-fried onions
Cayenne pepper

1. Heat the oil in a large saucepan over medium-high heat. Add the onion, garlic, and jalapeño and cook, stirring, until softened, 3 to 5 minutes. Add the cumin, oregano, and salt and stir for another 2 minutes.
2. Add the broth, powdered pumpkin, and beans and stir to combine. Reduce the heat to medium and let simmer for 20 minutes, uncovered.
3. Preheat the oven to 400°F.
4. Stir the vinegar and honey into the soup and simmer another 3 to 5 minutes.
5. Spread the French-fried onions on a baking sheet, sprinkle with a dash or two of cayenne and a little salt, and bake until crispy, 3 to 4 minutes.
6. Using an immersion blender, puree the soup in the pot until smooth. Serve the soup warm, sprinkled with the onions.

Lemony Chicken and Rice Soup

Lemongrass is the secret to this wonderfully light-tasting soup.

Makes 6 servings

1 tablespoon olive oil
1 skinless, boneless chicken breast
½ cup dehydrated spinach leaves, crushed
¼ cup dehydrated sliced onion
1 tablespoon dehydrated 1-inch lemongrass pieces
⅓ cup lemon juice
⅔ cup uncooked long-grain rice
6 cups chicken broth
6 dehydrated lemon slices

1. Heat the oil in a small skillet over medium heat. Add the chicken breast and cook all the way through, turning several times. Remove from the heat. When cool enough to handle, cut into ½-inch cubes.
2. Place the spinach, onion, lemongrass, lemon juice, rice, broth, and chicken in a large saucepan, cover, and bring to boil. Reduce the heat to a simmer and cook for 30 minutes.
3. Ladle the soup into 6 bowls and float 1 dehydrated lemon slice on top of each as a garnish.

Beef, Eggplant, and Mushroom Stew

Packed with flavor and nutrients, this hardy stew is perfect for the family with a big appetite.

Makes 4 servings

1 cup dehydrated sliced eggplant (with skin on)
2 cups boiling water
4 tablespoons olive oil
1 pound boneless beef stew meat, trimmed of fat and cut into ½-inch cubes
1 cup dehydrated sliced mushrooms
½ cup dehydrated chopped onion
3 dehydrated garlic slices, crushed
1 (1-inch) piece dehydrated red roasted pepper, crumbled
1 tablespoon dehydrated lemon zest
4 cups beef broth
2 tablespoons cornstarch

1. Place the eggplant in a heatproof bowl and pour the boiling water over. Cover and let sit for 15 minutes to rehydrate. Drain off any remaining water and set the eggplant on paper towels; do not pat dry.
2. Heat 2 tablespoons of the oil in a large skillet over medium-high heat. Add the eggplant to the hot oil and brown well on both sides. Remove from the pan.

3. Heat the remaining 2 tablespoons oil in the same skillet. Add the beef cubes and sear until nicely browned on all sides. Remove the skillet from the heat.

4. Combine the beef, mushrooms, onion, garlic, pepper, lemon zest, and broth in a large saucepan, cover, and bring to boil. Reduce the heat to a simmer and cook for 20 minutes.

5. Add the cornstarch and stir until the broth thickens, then fold in the eggplant, cover, and simmer until the beef is tender, about another hour.

Full of Beans Chili

This chili is a snap to make and goes great with corn bread. Try it with my Double Corn Bread with Chile Peppers (page 152).

Makes 6 servings

1 pound ground beef
¼ cup dehydrated sliced onions
2 cups dehydrated sliced tomatoes
¼ cup dehydrated chopped green bell peppers
½ tablespoon crushed dehydrated chile peppers
1 (15-ounce) can pinto beans
1 (15-ounce) can red kidney beans
1 Tomato Puree Leather (page 99), broken into pieces
6 cups water

1. Brown the ground beef in medium skillet over high heat until no longer pink, breaking up any clumps with a wooden spoon. Drain off any fat.

2. Add the remaining ingredients and bring to a boil. Reduce the heat to a gentle simmer and cook until thick, stirring occasionally, 45 to 60 minutes.

15

Main Courses

These main course meals are easy to prepare and packed with flavor. Many of these are a flavorful variation on classic favorites. It is easy to get in a rut making the same dinners over and over, especially when your favorite fruits and veggies are out of season. By using dehydrated food you can use those fruits and veggies anytime. These main courses offer you simple and easy meal ideas to help you add something new to your dinner table. Also be sure to check out the Slow Cooker chapter for even more options!

Layered Vegetable Enchilada

This is a surefire way to get your kids to eat their veggies. With layers of roasted vegetables, cheese, and tortillas topped with a spicy enchilada sauce, this meal will be a family favorite.

Makes 4 servings

½ cup dehydrated chopped zucchini
½ cup dehydrated chopped summer squash
½ cup dehydrated sliced onion
1 dehydrated chile pepper, crumbled
1 dehydrated jalapeño pepper, crumbled
2 cups boiling water
1 tablespoon olive oil
Salt and pepper
1 (15-ounce) can black beans, drained and rinsed
¼ cup dehydrated cilantro, crumbled
4 dehydrated garlic slices, crushed
1 teaspoon ground cumin
1 teaspoon chili powder
2 cups red enchilada sauce
9 or 10 small corn tortillas
2 cups shredded Monterey Jack cheese

1. Place the zucchini, summer squash, onion, and chile and jalapeño peppers in a large heatproof bowl and pour the boiling water over. Let sit 15 to 20 minutes to rehydrate.
2. Preheat the oven to 400°F.
3. Drain off any remaining water. Add the oil and toss with the vegetables until they are coated, then arrange them in a single layer on a baking sheet. Roast until nicely browned, about 30 minutes, stirring occasionally. Remove from the oven, season with salt and pepper, and let cool.
4. Reduce the oven temperature to 350°F. Spray an 8-inch square baking pan with cooking spray.
5. Place the roasted vegetables, black beans, cilantro, garlic, cumin, and chili powder in a medium bowl, stir to combine, and season with salt and pepper.
6. Spread ¼ cup of enchilada sauce in the bottom of the baking pan. Add a layer of tortillas, to completely cover the bottom. (You might have to cut the tortillas to make them fit.) Top with one third of the vegetable/bean mixture and one third of the cheese. Make a second layer of tortillas, enchilada sauce (use half the remaining sauce), vegetables/beans, and cheese. Top with a layer of the remaining tortillas, enchilada sauce, vegetables/beans, and cheese.
7. Spray a sheet of aluminum foil with cooking spray and cover the pan. Bake the enchiladas for 20 minutes. Remove the foil and bake until the cheese melts and the enchiladas are bubbling, about another 10 minutes. Remove from the oven and let cool for 10 minutes. Cut into squares and serve warm.

Variation: You can add a layer of cooked ground beef or turkey to make this even more substantial.

Broccoli and Cheddar Strata Sandwiches

A rich and satisfying sandwich that has to be eaten with a fork. What a delicious way to eat your broccoli!

Makes 2 sandwiches

> 1 cup dehydrated broccoli florets
> 1 tablespoon butter, softened
> 4 slices hearty whole-grain bread, crusts removed
> 1 cup shredded cheddar cheese
> 2 cups milk
> 2 large egg whites
> ½ teaspoon hot sauce

1. Place the broccoli in a medium saucepan, cover with water, and bring to a boil. Cover, reduce the heat to medium-low, and simmer for 15 minutes; do not stir. Drain off the water; drain the florets on paper towels (but do not squeeze or pat them dry).
2. Preheat the oven to 350°F.
3. Butter one side of each slice of bread and place two slices buttered side down in an 8-inch square baking pan. Arrange the broccoli over the bread, then sprinkle the cheese over the broccoli. Top with the remaining two slices bread, buttered side up.
4. In a medium bowl, whisk the milk, egg whites, and hot sauce together, then pour evenly over the bread. Bake until it puffs up and is lightly browned on top, about 35 minutes.

Eggplant Parmesan Casserole

Eggplant Parmesan is a family favorite but let's face it, it is time-consuming to make. This casserole has all the flavor you love without all the effort.

Makes 6 servings

> 3 cups dehydrated sliced eggplant
> 4 cups boiling water
> 4 cups dehydrated sliced tomatoes
> ¼ cup dehydrated chopped onions
> 4 dehydrated garlic slices, crumbled
> ¼ cup dehydrated basil, crumbled
> 1½ tablespoons dehydrated thyme, crumbled
> 1 tablespoon dehydrated finely grated carrot
> 1 teaspoon sugar
> 6 cups water
> ½ cup (or more) grated Parmesan cheese
> ¼ cup fresh breadcrumbs
> ¼ cup olive oil
> 1 pound mozzarella cheese, sliced ⅛ inch thick

1. Place the eggplant in a large heatproof bowl, pour the boiling water over, cover, and let sit for 15 to 20 minutes to rehydrate.
2. Place the tomatoes, onions, garlic, basil, thyme, carrots, and sugar in a large saucepan, add the 6 cups water, stir to combine, and bring to a boil. Reduce the heat to a simmer, cover, and cook for 40 minutes. Remove from the heat. Puree using an immersion blender, leaving the mixture a little chunky.
3. Preheat the oven to 350°F.
4. Drain the eggplant. On a plate, mix the Parmesan and breadcrumbs together. Dredge the eggplant slices on both sides in the crumbs.
5. Heat the oil in a large skillet over medium-high heat. Add the eggplant and brown well on each side.
6. Arrange the browned eggplant slices in a single layer in a 9 x 13-inch baking dish, pour the sauce over, and arrange the mozzarella slices on top. Bake until the cheese melts and the sauce is bubbling, about 20 minutes.

Stuffed Eggplant Rolls

Instead of eggplant Parmesan, try these easy-to-make stuffed eggplant rolls. Not only flavorful, they also make a beautiful presentation, perfect for your next dinner party.

Makes 6 servings

> 6 dehydrated eggplant slices, cut lengthwise
> 6 to 8 cups boiling water
> 1 cup ricotta cheese
> 1 large egg
> ¼ cup dehydrated sliced tomatoes, crumbled
> 1 teaspoon crumbled dehydrated chile pepper
> 2 tablespoons olive oil
> 1 recipe Bell Pepper-Tomato-Oregano Breadcrumbs (page 157)
> ½ cup tomato sauce

1. Place the eggplant slices in a 10-inch square baking dish, pour the boiling water over until the slices are completely covered, cover, and let sit for 20 minutes to rehydrate.
2. Preheat the oven to 350°F. Spray a 10-inch square baking dish with cooking spray.
3. In a medium bowl, mix the ricotta, egg, tomatoes, and chile pepper together. Refrigerate until ready to use.
4. Heat the oil in a large skillet over medium-high heat. Remove one slice of eggplant at a time from the soaking water (do not pat dry) and dredge on both sides in the bread crumbs, pressing down a little on the eggplant to make the crumbs stick. Place in the hot skillet, reduce the heat to medium, and cook until browned on both sides. Drain on paper towels. Repeat with the remaining eggplant slices.
5. Take a heaping spoonful of the ricotta mixture and place it at one end of each eggplant slice. Roll up the eggplant and place in the baking dish. When all the eggplant slices have been stuffed, bake until heated through, 20 to 25 minutes.
6. Serve with a spoonful of tomato sauce drizzled over the top.

Quinoa, Squash, and Tomato Casserole

This well-seasoned casserole is tasty and healthy.

Makes 6 to 8 servings

> 1½ cups cooked quinoa
> 1 dehydrated roasted red chile pepper, cut into ½-inch pieces with kitchen scissors
> 2 cups dehydrated sliced (¼-inch) summer squash
> 10 dehydrated tomato slices
> 2 dehydrated garlic slices, crushed
> 1 tablespoon dehydrated basil, crumbled
> 3 cups chicken or vegetable broth, brought to a boil
> 1 cup fat-free milk
> 3 large eggs
> 2 tablespoons butter, melted
> 1 cup grated cheese of your choice
> 1 cup cubed (½ inch or smaller) bread

1. Preheat the oven to 375°F.
2. Spread the cooked quinoa over the bottom of an oiled 10-inch-square deep-dish casserole. Arrange the chile pieces over the quinoa, then the squash, then the tomatoes. Sprinkle crushed garlic and basil over the top of vegetables. Pour the boiling broth over, cover, and let sit to rehydrate for 10 minutes.
3. In a small bowl, whisk together the milk, eggs, and butter and pour evenly over the quinoa and vegetables. Cover and bake for 20 minutes.
4. Remove from the oven, top with the cubed bread and cheese, and bake until the casserole is bubbling and the cheese has melted, about another 20 minutes.

Spinach and Ricotta Stuffed Shells

These pasta shells are bursting with a cheesy spinach filling. Spinach is the perfect way to add extra nutrients to a yummy pasta dish.

Makes 6 servings

> 1 teaspoon olive oil
> 1 (16-ounce) package jumbo pasta shells
> 1 (15-ounce) container ricotta cheese
> 1½ cups dehydrated spinach
> 1 large egg
> 1 tablespoon fresh lemon juice
> 2 dehydrated garlic slices, crumbled
> 1 tablespoon sugar
> 1 jar (16-ounce) marinara sauce
> ½ cup grated Parmesan cheese
> ½ cup shredded mozzarella cheese

1. Preheat the oven to 350°F. Grease a 9 x 12-inch baking dish with the oil.
2. Cook the pasta according to the package directions. Drain and set aside to cool.
3. In a large bowl, mix the ricotta, spinach, egg, lemon juice, garlic, and sugar. Fill the shells with the mixture, placing them in the casserole dish. Pour the marinara sauce over shells, top evenly with the cheeses, cover with aluminum foil, and bake until the sauce bubbles and the cheese melts, about 45 minutes.

Pasta Primavera

Spring vegetables make this dinner entrée delicious and healthy.

Makes 6 servings

½ cup dehydrated chopped onions
2 cups warm water
½ cup dehydrated broccoli florets
¼ cup dehydrated shredded carrots
1 cup dehydrated mixed red and green bell pepper strips
3 cups boiling water
1 (8-ounce) package refrigerated linguine
2 tablespoons olive oil
2 dehydrated garlic slices
1 cup dehydrated sliced mushrooms
2 teaspoons dehydrated basil, crumbled
1 teaspoon dehydrated red chile peppers, crumbled
¼ cup whole wheat flour
Salt and pepper
½ cup store-bought powdered milk
1 cup sour cream
1 cup grated Parmesan cheese
2 teaspoons dehydrated parsley, crumbled

1. Place the onions in a small bowl, pour 1 cup of the warm water over, cover, and let sit for 15 minutes to rehydrate; drain off any remaining water.
2. In a heatproof medium bowl, combine the broccoli, carrots, and peppers and pour the boiling water over. Cover and let sit for 20 minutes to rehydrate; drain off any remaining water.
3. Bring a large pot of salted water to a boil and cook the linguine according to package directions.
4. Meanwhile, heat the oil in a large skillet over high heat. Add the onions and garlic and cook, stirring, for 1 minute. Add the broccoli, carrots, bell peppers, mushrooms, basil, and chile pepper flakes and stir to combine. Reduce the heat to medium. Sprinkle over the flour and stir to combine. Season with salt and pepper to taste.
5. In a medium bowl, whisk together the powdered milk, sour cream, and remaining 1 cup warm water until smooth. Stir into the vegetable mixture. You can adjust the consistency of the sauce by adding water a tablespoon or two at a time.
6. Pour the vegetable mixture over the drained linguine and sprinkle with the Parmesan and parsley.

Variation: Try adding peeled and deveined shrimp to this light and delicious meal.

Zucchini and Mushroom Lasagna

Saucy lasagna layered with veggies to make a hearty vegetarian meal.

Makes 6 servings

3 cups dehydrated sliced zucchini

1 cup dehydrated sliced onions

1 cup dehydrated sliced mushrooms

2 dehydrated garlic slices, crumbled

5 cups boiling water

1 (15-ounce) container ricotta cheese

2 large eggs

1 tablespoon dehydrated parsley, crumbled

1 tablespoon sugar

2 (6-ounce) cans tomato paste

3½ cups water

1 teaspoon dehydrated thyme, crumbled

1 teaspoon dehydrated oregano, crumbled

1 teaspoon dehydrated basil, crumbled

9 lasagna noodles, cooked according to package directions, drained, and rinsed with cold water

2½ cups shredded mozzarella cheese

¼ cup grated Parmesan cheese

1. Preheat the oven to 350°F. Coat a 9 x 12-inch deep baking dish with cooking spray.
2. Place the dehydrated zucchini, onions, mushrooms, and garlic in a large heatproof bowl, pour the boiling water over, cover, and rehydrate for 15 minutes, then drain.
3. In a medium bowl, whisk together the ricotta, eggs, parsley, and sugar.
4. Combine the tomato paste, 3½ cups water, thyme, oregano, and basil in a medium saucepan and heat to a simmer over medium heat.
5. Make the following layers in the casserole dish:
   2 cups tomato sauce
   Half the zucchini, onion, and mushroom mixture
   Noodles
   All of the ricotta mixture
   Noodles
   Remaining zucchini, onion, and mushroom mixture
   Noodles
   Remaining sauce
   All of the mozzarella and Parmesan
6. Bake until bubbling and the cheese is melted, about 40 minutes. Remove from the oven and let sit for 10 minutes before cutting.

Black Olive and Tomato Focaccia

These focaccia and pizza recipes are nice opportunities to use your infused olive oils (page 170).

Makes 1 pizza; 4 servings

1 pound refrigerated pizza dough
3 tablespoons olive oil
10 dehydrated tomato slices
½ cup dehydrated sliced onions
¼ cup dehydrated sliced black olives
¼ cup dehydrated sliced mushrooms
3 cups boiling water
1 tablespoon powdered dehydrated tomatoes
½ teaspoon powdered dehydrated chile peppers
1 cup shredded mozzarella cheese

1. On a lightly floured work surface, roll the dough out to a 9-inch circle.
2. Grease a 9-inch-round deep-dish oven pan with 1 tablespoon of the olive oil (use the entire tablespoon in the bottom of the pan), press the dough into the dish, and let rest while you prepare the toppings.
3. Preheat the oven to 350°F.
4. In a medium bowl, combine the dehydrated tomatoes, onions, black olives, and mushrooms, pour the boiling water over, cover, and let sit 15 minutes to rehydrate. Drain any remaining water and set the vegetables on paper towels to drain further (but do not pat dry).
5. Brush the top of the dough with 1 tablespoon olive oil. Sprinkle with the powdered tomatoes and chile peppers. Layer the rehydrated tomato slices, onions, olives, and mushrooms on top of the dough. Drizzle the remaining 1 tablespoon olive oil over the top and sprinkle with the mozzarella. Bake until heated through and the cheese is nicely bubbly, about 45 minutes. Wait a minute or two before slicing.

Pineapple and Bacon Focaccia

Makes 1 pizza; 4 servings

> 1 pound refrigerated pizza dough
> 3 tablespoons olive oil
> 1 cup dehydrated shredded pineapple
> ½ cup dehydrated chopped green bell peppers
> 3 cups boiling water
> 1 tablespoon chopped dehydrated lemongrass
> ½ cup chopped cooked bacon
> 1 cup crumbled feta cheese

1. On a lightly floured work surface, roll the dough out to a 9-inch circle.
2. Grease a 9-inch round deep-dish oven pan with 1 tablespoon of the olive oil (use the entire tablespoon in the bottom of the pan), press the dough into the dish, and let rest while you prepare the toppings.
3. Preheat the oven to 350°F.
4. In a medium bowl, combine the dehydrated pineapple and bell peppers, pour the boiling water over, cover, and let sit 15 minutes to rehydrate. Drain any remaining water and set the vegetables on paper towels to drain further (but do not pat dry).
5. Brush the top of the dough with 1 tablespoon olive oil. Sprinkle with the lemongrass. Layer the rehydrated pineapple and bell peppers on top of the dough. Drizzle the remaining 1 tablespoon olive oil over the top and sprinkle with the bacon and feta. Bake until heated through and the cheese is nicely bubbly, about 45 minutes. Wait a few minutes before slicing.

Dried Veggie Pizza Pie

Makes 1 pizza; 4 servings

> 1 pound refrigerated pizza dough, at room temperature
> 2 tablespoons olive oil
> ¾ cup dehydrated shredded zucchini
> ½ cup dehydrated sliced tomatoes
> ¼ cup dehydrated sliced onions
> ¼ cup dehydrated banana peppers sliced across into rings
> ¼ cup dehydrated mushrooms
> ¼ cup dehydrated black olives
> 3 cups boiling water
> 1½ cups tomato sauce of your choice
> ¼ teaspoon powdered dehydrated roasted red peppers
> ½ cup shredded mozzarella cheese

1. On a lightly floured work surface, roll the dough out to a 9-inch circle. Place on a pizza pan and brush with 1 tablespoon of the olive oil. Let it rest while you prepare the toppings.

2. Preheat the oven to 350°F.
3. In a medium bowl, combine the dehydrated zucchini, tomatoes, onions, banana peppers, mushrooms, and olives, pour the boiling water over, cover, and let sit for 15 minutes to rehydrate. Drain any remaining water and set the vegetables on paper towels to drain further (but do not pat dry).
4. In a small bowl, combine the sauce and roasted red pepper powder. Spread over the pizza dough.
5. Toss the rehydrated vegetables with the remaining 1 tablespoon olive oil until they are coated. Layer the vegetables over the sauce. Sprinkle with the cheese, and bake until golden brown and the cheese is nicely bubbly, 40 to 45 minutes. Wait a few minutes before slicing.

Shredded Summer Casserole with Chicken

Keep those garden squash coming! You'll want to have plenty of dehydrated shredded squash on hand to make this family favorite.

Makes 6 servings

2 cups dehydrated shredded summer squash

2 cups dehydrated shredded zucchini

1 cup dehydrated shredded carrots

1 cup dehydrated sliced onions

6 cups boiling water

1 tablespoon butter

½ teaspoon dehydrated rosemary, crumbled

4 cups half-cooked spaghetti, still warm

1 cup chicken broth

1 cup shredded mozzarella cheese

1 cup shredded cheddar cheese

2 cups chopped cooked chicken

1. Preheat the oven to 350°F. Spray a deep 9 x 12-inch baking dish with cooking spray.
2. In a large heatproof bowl, combine the squash, zucchini, carrots, and onions. Pour the boiling water over, cover, and let sit for 15 minutes to rehydrate; do not drain.
3. Add the butter and rosemary to the cooked spaghetti and toss to evenly coat the noodles. Add the spaghetti to the bowl with the vegetables along with the broth, both cheeses, and chicken. Toss to combine, then pour into casserole dish. Bake until bubbling and the cheese has melted, 50 to 60 minutes.

Chicken Couscous with Raisins and Lime

This savory dish bursts with the chewy richness of raisins, with just a hint of lime.

Makes 4 servings

> 1 tablespoon olive oil
> 1 teaspoon dehydrated sliced garlic, crumbled
> 1 cup dehydrated chopped tomatoes
> 1½ pounds skinless, boneless chicken breasts, cut into chunks, or 2 (15-ounce) cans chicken with juice
> 1½ cups water
> 2 chicken bouillon cubes
> ½ cup raisins
> 1½ cups couscous
> 2 tablespoons dehydrated parsley, crumbled
> 1 tablespoon dehydrated sliced limes, crushed
> Salt and pepper

1. Heat the oil in a large skillet over medium heat. Add the garlic and tomatoes and cook, stirring, until heated through. Add the chicken, water, bouillon, and raisins and bring to a boil. Reduce the heat to medium-low and simmer until the chicken is cooked through.
2. Stir in the couscous and cover. Remove the pan from the heat and let sit 5 minutes. Add the parsley, limes, and salt and pepper to taste and toss gently to combine.

Variation: Omit the chicken for a delicious side dish.

Chicken and Asparagus Casserole

A delicious and colorful dish.

Makes 6 servings

> 1 cup dehydrated asparagus pieces
> ¼ cup dehydrated chopped onions
> ½ cup dehydrated mixed chopped red and green bell peppers
> 3 cups boiling water
> 1 (16-ounce) bag egg noodles
> 2 cups chopped cooked chicken
> 2 teaspoons dehydrated sliced garlic, crumbled
> 1 (10.5-ounce) can condensed cream of asparagus soup
> 1 soup can water
> 2 large eggs, beaten
> 1 cup ricotta cheese
> 2 cups shredded white cheddar cheese

1. Preheat the oven to 350°F. Spray a 9 x 13-inch baking dish with cooking spray.
2. In a large heatproof bowl, combine the asparagus, onions, and peppers. Pour the boiling water over, cover, and let sit for 20 minutes to rehydrate. Drain off any remaining water.
3. Meanwhile, cook the egg noodles according to the package directions.
4. Stir the chicken, garlic, condensed soup, soup can of water, eggs, ricotta, 1 cup of the shredded cheese, and the cooked egg noodles into the rehydrated vegetables until well mixed. Pour the mixture into the baking dish, sprinkle evenly with the remaining 1 cup cheese, and bake until bubbling and the cheese is melted, about 35 minutes.

Chicken Pot Pie

This family favorite is the ultimate in comfort food, with its flaky crust and warm, creamy filling chock-full of your favorite veggies.

Makes 8 servings

> 1 cup dehydrated cubed or sliced potatoes
> ½ cup dehydrated peas
> ½ cup dehydrated sliced carrots
> ¼ cup dehydrated chopped celery
> ¼ cup dehydrated sliced onions
> 3 chicken bouillon cubes, crushed
> 2 tablespoons all-purpose flour
> 6 cups water
> 2 cups cubed cooked chicken
> 2 frozen 9-inch deep-dish pie crusts, defrosted
> 1 large egg, lightly beaten

1. Preheat the oven to 400°F.
2. In a large saucepan, combine the dehydrated ingredients, sprinkle over the crushed bouillon cubes and flour, and pour in the water. Cover and let simmer over medium heat, stirring occasionally, until thickened, about 45 minutes. During the last 10 minutes or so of cooking, stir in the chicken to heat through.
3. While the filling cooks, fit one of the crusts into a 9-inch deep-dish pie plate. When the filling is ready, pour it into the crust. Place the other crust over it, trim the edges, and then seal them together, making a fluted edge. Cut several steam vents into the top crust and brush with the beaten egg. Bake until the crust is golden, about 40 minutes. (If the pie edge begins to brown too quickly, cover it with aluminum foil). Remove from the oven and let sit for 10 minutes before serving.

Roasted Chicken Breasts with Cheesy Zucchini Stuffing

Add something extra to ordinary chicken and stuffing with cheese and zucchini.

Makes 6 servings

>   2 cups dehydrated shredded zucchini
>   2 tablespoons dehydrated chopped onions
>   1 tablespoon dehydrated parsley, crumbled
>   3 cups boiling water
>   ¼ cup (½ stick) butter
>   2 cups dehydrated ½-inch bread cubes
>   1 large egg, beaten
>   ¾ cup shredded Swiss cheese
>   ⅛ teaspoon black pepper, plus more to taste
>   6 skin-on, bone-in chicken breast halves
>   Olive oil
>   Salt

1. Preheat the oven to 350°F.
2. In a large heatproof bowl, combine the zucchini, onions, and parsley. Pour the boiling water over, cover, and let sit for 15 minutes to rehydrate. Drain off any remaining water.
3. Melt the butter in a medium skillet over low heat. Add the zucchini, onion, and parsley and stir to combine and coat with the butter. Cover and cook for 5 minutes. Remove from the heat and stir in the bread cubes, beaten egg, cheese, and pepper.
4. Wash the chicken breasts and pat dry. Very carefully pry the skin away from the chicken on each breast to make a pocket. Fill the pockets with as much of the zucchini mixture as possible. Rub olive oil on the skin of the chicken, season with salt and pepper (optional), and place in a baking dish large enough that they fit in a single layer. Mound any extra stuffing on top of the chicken. Bake until cooked through, about 1 hour.

Crispy Tomato-Garlic Chicken Cutlets

These cutlets would make a delicious foundation for chicken Parmesan.

Makes 8 servings

>   1½ cups Italian-Style Tomato-Garlic Bread Cubes (page 154)
>   ¾ cup mayonnaise
>   ½ teaspoon powdered dehydrated tomatoes or tomato puree
>   8 boneless, skinless chicken breast halves

1. Preheat the oven to 400°F. Spray a 9 x 12-inch baking dish with cooking spray.
2. In a blender, grind the bread cubes into crumbs.
3. Place the crumbs on a large plate. In a large shallow bowl, whisk the mayonnaise and tomato powder together.

4. Place the chicken in the bowl with the mayonnaise and turn to coat the pieces evenly. Take each piece of chicken and dredge it evenly in the crumbs. Place the chicken in a single layer in the baking dish. Bake until the juice runs clear at the thickest part of each piece of chicken, 35 to 40 minutes.

Variation: This recipe also works very nicely when made with fish fillets instead of chicken. Adjust the cooking time, which should be shorter for the fillets.

Savory Chicken and Rice

Chicken and rice is a "go-to" recipe for our family. This version adds a little spicy pizzazz with ginger, cinnamon, and cayenne.

Makes 8 servings

Chicken

 1½ teaspoons coarsely ground dehydrated ginger
 ½ teaspoon ground cinnamon
 ¼ teaspoon cayenne pepper
 4 boneless, skinless chicken breast halves, cut into 1-inch cubes (about 4 cups)
 2 tablespoons olive oil

Sauce

 3 tablespoons butter
 ¼ cup dehydrated chopped onions
 2 teaspoons crushed dehydrated garlic
 2 cups tomato sauce
 1 tablespoon tomato paste
 2½ cups water
 1 cup dehydrated chopped tomatoes
 ¼ cup dehydrated peas
 ⅓ cup heavy cream
 6 cups cooked long-grain rice

1. Mix the ginger, cinnamon, and cayenne together, then sprinkle evenly over the chicken cubes.
2. Heat the oil in a large skillet over medium-high heat. Add the chicken cubes and cook until cooked all the way through. Keep warm.
3. Melt the butter in a medium saucepan over medium heat. Add the onions and garlic and cook, stirring, until golden, about 1 minute. Stir in tomato sauce, tomato paste, water, and dehydrated tomatoes and peas; cover and simmer until the peas are tender, about 45 minutes.
4. Stir in the cream for 1 minute, then remove from stove.
5. On a platter, arrange the chicken on top of the rice, then pour the sauce over the chicken.

Cranberry BBQ Chicken

Tart cranberries and zesty barbecue sauce create a tangy zing for chicken.

Makes 4 to 6 servings

1 cup dehydrated chopped cranberries
¼ cup dehydrated chopped celery
¼ cup dehydrated chopped onions
4 cups water
3 tablespoons butter
1 cup barbecue sauce
1 teaspoon hot sauce
1 tablespoon olive oil
1 (4-pound) chicken, cut into 8 to 10 serving pieces

1. Place the cranberries, celery, onions, water, butter, barbecue sauce, and hot sauce in a large saucepan and stir to combine. Bring to a boil, reduce the heat to low, and simmer until thick, about 40 minutes.
2. Preheat the oven to 350°F.
3. Heat the oil in a large skillet over high heat. Add the chicken and brown on all sides. Transfer to a 9 x 13-inch baking dish and pour the barbecue sauce over. Bake until the chicken is completely cooked through, 45 minutes.

Cranberry and Maple Turkey

A delicious sweet and tangy holiday sauce to complement your turkey.

Makes 4 servings

1 cup water
½ cup maple syrup
¼ cup dehydrated chopped cranberries
1 tablespoon sugar
1 tablespoon butter
1 teaspoon powdered dehydrated oranges
1 tablespoon olive oil
1 pound turkey breast cutlets

1. In a medium saucepan, combine the water, maple syrup, cranberries, sugar, butter, and orange powder and bring to a boil. Reduce the heat to low and simmer until thickened, about 20 minutes.
2. Meanwhile, in a large skillet, heat the oil over medium-high heat, then brown the turkey cutlets on both sides until golden and cooked through. Pour the sauce over the cooked turkey and serve.

Pan-Seared Turkey Cutlets with Curried Fruit

Add the warmth of curry to sweet fruit for a wonderfully flavorful dish.

Makes 4 servings

> ¼ cup dehydrated apricot halves, cut into strips with kitchen scissors
> ¼ cup dehydrated grapes
> ¼ cup dehydrated chopped mango
> ¼ cup dehydrated chopped onions
> 4 cups water
> ½ cup mayonnaise
> 1 teaspoon curry powder
> 1 tablespoon cooking oil of your choice
> 4 turkey breast cutlets

1. Place the apricots, grapes, mango, onions, and water in a large saucepan. Bring to a boil, reduce the heat to a simmer, cover, and cook until tender, about 20 minutes.
2. Drain off any excess water. Stir in the mayonnaise and curry. Bring to a simmer over medium heat and cook until thickened, stirring constantly. Remove from the heat and cover.
3. Heat the oil in a large skillet over high heat. Add the cutlets and cook until golden brown on each side and cooked through.
4. Place a cutlet on each plate, top with ¼ cup of the mixed fruit, and serve.

Breaded Pineapple-Cranberry-Sage Turkey Cutlets

These cutlets marry the holiday flavors of sage and cranberry with the unexpected tangy sweetness of pineapple.

Makes 4 servings

> 1 recipe Pineapple-Cranberry-Sage Breadcrumbs (page 156)
> 2 tablespoons olive oil
> 4 turkey breast cutlets

1. Place the breadcrumbs in a large shallow bowl.
2. Rub a little of the oil onto both sides of each cutlet, then coat the cutlets completely with the breadcrumbs.
3. In a large skillet over medium-high heat, heat the remaining oil until hot. Add the cutlets to the hot oil and cook until golden brown and cooked through, 2 to 3 minutes per side.

Turkey and Spinach Meat Loaf

This meat loaf is a healthier version of mom's. Not only is it made with lean ground turkey, we also snuck in some spinach.

Makes 4 servings

½ cup milk
1 large egg
1 tablespoon Worcestershire sauce
1 pound lean ground turkey
½ cup dehydrated whole wheat breadcrumbs
½ cup dehydrated spinach, crushed
¼ cup dehydrated chopped onions
½ tablespoon powdered dehydrated tomato
4 dehydrated garlic slices, crushed
¼ teaspoon black pepper
½ cup boiling water
½ cup chile sauce

1. Preheat the oven to 350°F.
2. In a small bowl, whisk the milk, egg, and Worcestershire sauce together.
3. In a large bowl, combine the turkey, breadcrumbs, spinach, onions, tomato powder, garlic, and black pepper. Knead it together until thoroughly mixed. Stir in the milk mixture until well combined. Form into a loaf and place in a 9 x 5-inch loaf pan.
4. In a small heatproof bowl, pour the boiling water over the chile leather. Let sit for 10 minutes, then stir to create a chile sauce. Spread the chile sauce over the meat loaf. Bake until an instant-read thermometer inserted in the center registers 160°F, about 1 hour.

Jerky and Tomato Mac and Cheese

Elevate the flavors of everyday mac and cheese by adding jerky and tomatoes.

Makes 6 to 8 servings

½ cup dehydrated diced tomatoes
½ cup shredded or chopped jerky
4 cups water
2 cups uncooked elbow macaroni
3 tablespoons butter
¼ cup all-purpose flour
¼ teaspoon cayenne pepper
1 cup milk
1 cup half-and-half
½ cup low-sodium chicken broth
3 cups shredded sharp cheddar cheese

1. Place the tomatoes and jerky in a medium skillet and pour in the water. Bring to a boil, then reduce the heat to low and simmer for 25 minutes, adding a little more water if it all evaporates.
2. Meanwhile, preheat the oven to 400°F. Spray a 9 x 13-inch baking dish with cooking spray.
3. Cook the macaroni according to the package directions. Drain and return to the pot. When the jerky and tomatoes have finished simmering, add them to the pot with the macaroni and stir to combine. Cook over medium heat for 5 minutes, stirring a few times. Pour the macaroni mixture into the baking dish.
4. In the skillet that held the tomatoes and jerky, melt the butter over medium heat, then stir in the flour and cayenne to create a paste. Don't let the flour brown. Very slowly, whisking constantly, add the milk, then the half-and-half and broth. Bring the mixture to a boil. Remove from the heat and gently stir in the cheese until melted.
5. Pour the cheese sauce evenly over the macaroni and stir a few times to combine. Bake until bubbling, about 20 minutes. Remove from the oven and let sit for 10 minutes before serving.

So-Easy Meat Loaf

Mix up this meatloaf in a flash! It's all done in one bowl, with no separate rehydration needed for any of the ingredients. Quick and easy with virtually no cleanup. It's delicious served with a little beef gravy.

Makes 6 servings

> 1 pound ground beef or ground turkey
> 1 large egg
> ¼ cup dehydrated mixed chopped green and red bell peppers
> ¼ cup dehydrated chopped onions
> ¼ cup dehydrated chopped tomatoes
> ½ cup plain dehydrated breadcrumbs
> ½ cup water
> 2 tablespoons half-and-half

1. Preheat the oven to 350°F. Spray a 9 x 5-inch loaf pan with cooking spray.
2. Place all the ingredients in a large bowl and mix together well. Form into a loaf that will fit into the pan. Bake until cooked all the way through, about 35 minutes. Remove from the oven and let sit for 10 minutes before slicing.

Ashley's Famous Cabbage Bake

Amazingly good!

Makes 8 servings

> 6 cups dehydrated shredded cabbage
> ½ cup dehydrated sliced onions
> 1 tablespoon olive oil (optional)
> 1 pound ground beef or turkey
> 1 cup uncooked long-grain rice
> ¼ cup (½ stick) butter
> 1 (10.5-ounce) can condensed tomato soup
> 6½ cups boiling water
> 1 cup shredded cheddar cheese

1. Layer the dehydrated cabbage and onions in a 9 x 13-inch baking dish that has been sprayed with cooking spray.
2. Combine the meat and rice in a medium skillet and cook over medium-high heat, breaking up any clumps of meat, until the meat is no longer pink and the rice has browned. (If using lean ground turkey, first heat the olive oil in the pan, then add the turkey and rice.) Remove from the heat and layer over the cabbage and onions.
3. In a heatproof medium bowl, combine the butter, tomato soup, and boiling water. Stir until the butter melts and everything is well combined, then pour the contents of the baking dish over, cover, and let sit for 20 minutes to allow the vegetables to rehydrate; do not pour off any remaining liquid.
4. Preheat the oven to 350°F.
5. Sprinkle the cheese evenly over the top of the casserole and bake until bubbling and the cheese is melted and golden brown, about 1½ hours. Let sit for 5 minutes before serving.

Beef, Spinach, and Potato Casserole

This dish is easy to make, packed with flavor, and budget-friendly.

Makes 6 to 8 servings

> 3 cups dehydrated sliced potatoes
> ½ cup dehydrated sliced mushrooms
> 6 cups boiling water
> 2 tablespoons butter
> 2 pounds ground beef
> ¼ cup dehydrated chopped onions
> 1 cup beef broth
> 3 cups dehydrated spinach
> 1½ cups shredded mozzarella cheese

1. Preheat the oven to 350°F.
2. In a large heatproof bowl, combine the potatoes and mushrooms. Pour the boiling water over, cover, and let sit for 20 minutes to rehydrate. Drain off any remaining water. Add the butter to the mixture and stir until melted and mixed in.
3. Brown the ground beef in a large skillet with the onion until no longer pink, breaking up any clumps with a wooden spoon. Drain off the fat and transfer the beef to a 9 x 13-inch baking dish, covering the bottom. Pour the broth over. Arrange the dehydrated spinach on top of the beef. Sprinkle evenly with 1 cup of the cheese over spinach. Arrange the potato and mushroom mixture over the cheese and cover. Bake for 40 minutes.
4. Sprinkle the remaining ½ cup cheese over the top and bake, uncovered, until the cheese melts, another 10 to 15 minutes.

Sloppy Joes

Bring out your inner child with this tangy and sweet childhood favorite.

Makes up to 10 servings (we love to pile it on, so we usually get about 6 servings)

> 2 tablespoons butter
> 2½ pounds ground beef
> ¼ cup dehydrated chopped green bell peppers
> 2 tablespoons dehydrated chopped onions
> 5 dehydrated garlic slices, crushed
> 1½ cups water
> 1½ cups ketchup
> 2 tablespoons brown sugar
> 2 teaspoons chili powder
> 1 teaspoon dry mustard (like Colman's)
> ½ teaspoon dehydrated red chile peppers, crumbled
> 2 tablespoons tomato paste (optional)
> 1½ teaspoons Worcestershire sauce
> Salt and black pepper
> Kaiser rolls
> Grated sharp cheddar cheese (optional)

1. Melt the butter in a large skillet over medium-high heat. Add the ground beef and brown until no longer pink, breaking up any clumps with a wooden spoon. Drain off most of the fat.
2. Add the bell peppers, onions, garlic, and water to the ground beef. Cook until the vegetables begin to soften, which will take a few minutes. Add the ketchup, brown sugar, chili powder, mustard, and chile peppers and stir to combine. Let simmer for 15 minutes, then stir in the tomato paste (if using) and Worcestershire sauce and season to taste with salt and pepper.
3. For each sloppy Joe, split open a Kaiser roll, spread the cut sides with a little butter, and brown on a griddle or skillet over medium heat. Ladle the meat mixture over the bottom roll, sprinkle with cheese if you like, top with the other half of the roll, and enjoy.

Summer Taco Casserole

The perfect way to spice up a family dinner. This casserole has all the flavor of tacos, packed with nutritious vegetables.

Makes 8 servings

2 cups dehydrated cubed potatoes
2 cups dehydrated sliced (¼-inch) zucchini
½ cup dehydrated chopped tomatoes
¼ cup dehydrated chopped onions
5 cups boiling water
2 pounds ground beef
1 (1-ounce) package taco seasoning mix
1 tablespoon olive oil
2 cups shredded Mexican cheese

1. Preheat the oven to 350°F.
2. In a large bowl, combine the dehydrated ingredients. Pour the boiling water over, cover, and let sit 20 to 25 minutes to rehydrate. Drain off any remaining water.
3. Brown the beef in a large skillet over high heat until no longer pink, breaking up any clumps with a wooden spoon. Drain off any fat and stir in the taco seasoning. Transfer the beef to a 9 x 13-inch baking dish and spread over the bottom.
4. Add the olive oil to the vegetables and toss to coat. Spread the vegetables over the beef. Sprinkle the cheese evenly over the vegetables. Bake until bubbling and cheese is melted, about 30 minutes.

Pork Fried Rice

You can serve this Asian-inspired rice dish as a side or make it the main event.

Makes 8 servings

5 cups water
2 cups uncooked long-grain rice
¼ cup dehydrated peas
¼ cup dehydrated shredded carrots
1¼ tablespoons cooking oil of your choice
2 dehydrated garlic slices, crushed
1 pound cubed (½-inch) cooked pork
4 large eggs, beaten
⅓ cup soy sauce

1. In a medium saucepan, combine the water, rice, and dehydrated peas and carrots, bring to a boil, reduce the heat to low, cover, and cook until the rice is tender, 15 to 20 minutes. (At this point, you can let the rice cool completely and refrigerate overnight. You have better results cooking fried rice with cold rice.)

2. In a large skillet over medium heat, heat 1 tablespoon of the oil, then add the garlic and cooked pork and stir to coat with the oil. Increase the heat to medium-high, add cooked rice, carrots, and peas, and stir-fry until the rice turns light brown and get crunchy in places. Push the rice mixture to the side of pan, add the remaining ¼ tablespoon oil, add the eggs, and scramble. Mix into the rice mixture, pour the soy sauce over, and stir until everything is evenly coated. Taste and add more soy sauce, if necessary.

Pork and Beef Meatballs

Simmer these in tomato sauce, then serve over spaghetti or as a meatball wedge, with cheese melted over.

Makes 10 meatballs

> ½ pound ground pork
> ½ pound ground beef
> 1 recipe Garlic, Tomato, Oregano, and Parsley Breadcrumbs (page 158)
> ¼ cup dehydrated chopped green bell peppers
> ¼ cup half-and-half
> 2 tablespoons dehydrated chopped onions
> 1 large egg, beaten
> ½ tablespoon cooking oil of your choice

1. In a large bowl, combine all the ingredients except the oil and knead together until thoroughly mixed. Divide the mixture into 10 equal pieces, and form into round meatballs.
2. In a large skillet over medium heat, heat the oil. Place the meatballs in the hot oil and cook until browned on all sides and cooked through, about 30 minutes.

Stromboli

Bring this to your next potluck.

Makes 8 servings

¼ cup dehydrated chopped bell peppers
2 tablespoons dehydrated sliced black olives
1 tablespoon dehydrated minced onion
½ tablespoon crushed dehydrated garlic
½ cup pizza sauce
½ cup water
1 pound pizza dough
¼ pound salami slices
¼ pound pepperoni slices
2 cups shredded mozzarella cheese
1 cup grated Parmesan cheese
1 tablespoon butter, melted
Cracked black peppercorns

1. Preheat the oven to 400°F.
2. In a small saucepan, combine the bell peppers, olives, onion, garlic, pizza sauce, and water. Bring to a boil, then remove from the heat and let cool.
3. Roll out the pizza dough on a piece of parchment paper into an 11 x 15-inch rectangle. Spread the pizza sauce mixture over the dough, leaving a 2-inch border around all the sides. In layers, arrange the salami, pepperoni, and cheeses on top of the sauce.
4. Lifting the parchment paper, gently roll one short end of the dough toward the other short end, creating a log, with the seam facing down.
5. Brush the loaf with the melted butter, sprinkle with pepper, and bake until golden brown, 25 to 30 minutes. Remove from the oven and let sit for 10 minutes before slicing.

Zesty Lemon and Parsley Breaded Haddock

Fresh tasting, with a light crunch.

Makes 3 servings

1 recipe Zesty Lemon and Parsley Breadcrumbs (page 156)
3 haddock fillets (each about 4 inches square)
2 tablespoons olive oil

1. Place the crumbs in a large shallow bowl, then press each haddock fillet in them, coating the fillets completely.
2. In a large skillet over medium-high heat, heat the oil until hot. Place the haddock in the hot oil and cook until golden brown and cooked through, about 7 minutes per side.

Creamy Hawaiian Tuna

Add a little South Pacific flavor to dinner tonight. This is delicious served over biscuits or pasta.

Makes 6 servings

> ½ cup dehydrated peas
> ½ cup dehydrated steamed cubed pineapple
> ½ teaspoon dehydrated tarragon, crumbled
> 3 cups water
> 1 cup milk
> ½ tablespoon cornstarch
> 2 (6-ounce) cans solid white tuna

1. Stir the peas, pineapple, tarragon, water, and milk together in a medium saucepan over medium heat, cover, and simmer until the peas and pineapple are tender, about 20 minutes.
2. Stir in the cornstarch until it thickens, then fold in the tuna. Let heat through and serve.

Tuna Noodle Casserole

In this recipe, rehydration is a snap—the vegetables get thrown into the boiling water along with the pasta.

Makes 8 to 10 servings

> ¾ cup dehydrated sliced mushrooms
> ½ cup dehydrated peas
> ½ cup dehydrated chopped carrots
> 1 (16-ounce) bag egg yolk noodles
> 1 (10.5-ounce) can condensed cream of mushroom soup
> ½ cup sour cream
> ¼ cup milk
> 2 (6-ounce) cans solid-pack tuna, drained
> ½ cup dehydrated breadcrumbs of your choice (pages 155–58)

1. Preheat the oven to 375°F. Lightly coat a 9 x 13-inch baking dish with cooking spray.
2. Place all the dehydrated vegetables in a large pot with water and bring to a boil. Add the noodles and cook until al dente. Drain and return to the pot. Stir in the soup, sour cream, milk, and tuna. Pour into the baking dish. Evenly sprinkle the breadcrumbs over the top. Bake until bubbling, 35 to 40 minutes.

Salmon with Dill and Almonds

Refreshing dill and lemon create a beautifully flavored salmon dish with just the right amount of crunch.

Makes 4 servings

> 8 dehydrated lemon slices
> 2 tablespoons dehydrated dill, crumbled
> 4 (6-ounce) salmon fillets
> 1 tablespoon olive oil
> 1 cup sliced almonds
> 1 cup water

1. Preheat the oven to 350°F.
2. Spray the bottom of a 9 x 13-inch deep-dish baking dish with cooking spray, and then arrange the lemon slices over the bottom. Sprinkle the lemons with 1 tablespoon of the dehydrated dill.
3. Rub down the fish with the olive oil and sprinkle on the remaining 1 tablespoon dill. Set the fillets in a single layer in the dish, then sprinkle ¼ cup almonds over each fillet. Lightly spray the almonds with cooking spray. Pour the water in the dish. Cover the dish with aluminum foil and bake for 20 minutes.
4. Remove the foil and put the dish back into the oven on a low broil until the almonds are golden brown, about 5 minutes.

Salmon and Noodle Casserole

A simple, delicious meal that uses canned salmon. It's also a tasty way to use up any leftovers you might have from Salmon with Dill and Almonds.

Makes 6 servings

> ¼ cup dehydrated chopped onions
> ¼ cup dehydrated thinly sliced carrots
> 2 tablespoons dehydrated chopped celery
> 2 teaspoons dehydrated dill, crumbled
> Boiling water
> 6 ounces uncooked wide egg noodles
> 1 teaspoon olive oil
> 1 (15-ounce) can salmon, drained and skin and bones removed
> 1 (10-ounce) can of condensed cream of celery soup
> ¾ cup milk
> ½ cup sour cream
> 1 cup shredded cheddar cheese

1. Preheat the oven to 325°F. Spray a deep-dish 2-quart baking dish with cooking spray.
2. In a small heatproof bowl, combine the dehydrated onions, carrots, celery, and dill. Pour enough boiling water over to submerge everything, cover, and let sit for 15 minutes to dehydrate; drain off any remaining water.
3. Cook the noodles according to the package directions until they are about halfway cooked. Drain, transfer to the baking dish, and toss with the oil. Add the rehydrated vegetables and remaining ingredients and stir to combine well. Bake until bubbling, about 35 minutes.

Salmon Pie

Simple and delicious.

Makes 8 servings

> ½ cup cottage cheese
> 1 tablespoon lemon juice
> 2 cups milk
> 4 large eggs
> ¾ cup Bisquick
> 1 teaspoon dehydrated dill, crumbled
> 7 ounces cooked salmon (if using canned, drain and remove the skin and bones)
> ½ cup grated Parmesan cheese
> ¼ cup dehydrated sliced green onions
> ¼ cup dehydrated shredded carrots
> ¼ teaspoon paprika
> ¼ teaspoon salt

1. Preheat the oven to 350°F. Spray a 9-inch pie plate with cooking spray.
2. Place the cottage cheese and lemon juice in a blender and process until smooth. Add the milk, eggs, Bisquick, and dill; blend again until smooth.
3. Place the salmon, Parmesan, green onions, and carrots in the pie plate and toss to combine well.
4. Pour the Bisquick mixture evenly over the salmon mixture, covering it. Sprinkle the paprika and salt over the top, and bake until golden brown, and the center of the pie springs back when touched, about 40 minutes.

Pesto Crab Lasagna

This deep-dish lasagna is packed with flavor and perfect for feeding a crowd.

Makes 12 servings

1 (8-ounce) container ricotta cheese
4 ounces small-curd cottage cheese
½ cup grated Parmesan cheese
1 large egg
2 tablespoons dehydrated sliced green onions
1 cup dehydrated broccoli florets
½ cup dehydrated shredded carrots
½ cup dehydrated mixed green, yellow, and red bell pepper strips
¼ cup dehydrated chopped tomatoes
4 cups boiling water
1 cup pesto
1 (8-ounce) can crab meat, drained and picked over for shells and cartilage
3 tablespoons butter or margarine
4 dehydrated garlic slices, crushed
3 tablespoons all-purpose flour
2 cups milk
20 no-boil lasagna noodles
2 cups shredded mozzarella cheese

1. Preheat the oven to 350°F. Spray a deep 9 x 13-inch baking dish with cooking spray.
2. In a medium bowl, combine the ricotta, cottage cheese, Parmesan, and egg until well mixed. Stir in the dehydrated green onions.
3. In a large heatproof bowl, combine the broccoli, carrots, bell peppers, and tomatoes. Pour the boiling water over, cover, and let sit for 15 minutes to rehydrate. Drain off any remaining water (do not press or squeeze out water). Stir in the pesto and crab meat.
4. In a small saucepan, melt the butter over medium heat, then add the garlic and stir for 1 minute. Add the flour and stir until smooth. Remove from the heat and slowly whisk in 1¾ cups of the milk. Return the pan to the heat and cook, stirring constantly, until bubbling, about 1 minute.
5. Pour the remaining ¼ cup milk into the bottom of the baking dish. Cover the bottom with four of the lasagna noodles. Spread half of the ricotta mixture over the noodles, then cover the ricotta with another 4 noodles. Arrange half of the crab mixture over the noodles, then sprinkle with ¾ cup of the mozzarella.
7. Repeat the noodle, ricotta, noodle, and crab layers, and end with the last 4 lasagna noodles. Pour the butter and garlic sauce over the top, then sprinkle with the remaining mozzarella. Bake until the cheese is melted and the sauce is bubbling around the sides, about 45 minutes. Remove from the oven and let sit for 10 minutes before slicing.

16

Slow Cooker Recipes

Slow cookers and dehydrated foods make great friends, so much so that we've dedicated an entire chapter to slow cooker recipes that make use of dehydrated ingredients. The slow cooker is a wonderful time saver because it allows you to "set it and forget it"— prep your ingredients, toss them in the crock, cover, turn on, and go. When you pair the slow cooker with dehydrated ingredients, you save even more time. In the case of dehydrated prepared foods (like chili), just empty it from its storage container, add the appropriate liquid, cover, set, and go, leaving the slow cooker to rehydrate and heat up at the same time. Using dehydrated ingredients that have been already prepped (like chopped onions, sliced bell peppers, or chunks of potatoes) also saves you valuable time in the kitchen. Either way, you'll end up with a delicious meal prepared with little or no effort. Slow cookers are especially great for soups and stews.

Bean and Bowtie Soup

This bean and noodle soup is simple and satisfying.

Makes 8 servings

1 (15.5-ounce) can white kidney (cannellini) beans, drained and rinsed
½ cup quartered dehydrated tomato slices (cut them with kitchen scissors)
¼ cup dehydrated shredded carrots
¼ cup dehydrated sliced onion
1 teaspoon dehydrated parsley
1 teaspoon dehydrated marjoram
1 teaspoon dehydrated oregano
1 teaspoon dehydrated thyme
8 cups water
1 cup uncooked bowtie pasta

1. Place the beans, dehydrated vegetables and herbs, and water in a 6-quart slow cooker and stir to combine. Cover and cook on LOW for 4 hours.
2. Add the bowties, stir to combine, cover, and cook on HIGH until the pasta is just tender, about 30 minutes.

White Bean and Black Olive Stew

Looking for something different? This quick and easy stew marries the delightful flavors of citrus with the earthy flavors of olives. It is a beautiful stew of contrasting colors, great for your next dinner party.

Makes 10 servings

4 cups cooked white beans, drained and rinsed
1 cup dehydrated halved grape tomatoes
1 cup dehydrated chopped zucchini
½ cup dehydrated sliced black olives
½ cup dehydrated sliced onions
¼ cup dehydrated chopped celery
¼ cup dehydrated parsley
2 tablespoons olive oil
2 tablespoons dehydrated sage, crumbled
1 teaspoon dehydrated lemon zest
1 teaspoon dehydrated sliced garlic, crushed
7 cups water

Place all the ingredients in a 6-quart slow cooker, stir to combine, and cover. Cook on LOW for 4 hours.

Spicy Black Bean Soup

This uses chile peppers to turn up the heat. Perfect to warm you up on a cold winter day.

Makes 8 servings

2 (15-ounce) cans black beans, drained and rinsed
1½ cups dehydrated sliced tomatoes
1 cups uncooked long-grain rice
½ cup dehydrated chopped onions
¼ cup dehydrated roasted red pepper strips
2 tablespoons dehydrated chopped celery
1 dehydrated chile pepper, crumbled
8 cups water

Place all the ingredients in a 6-quart slow cooker, stir to combine, and cover. Cook on LOW for 4 hours.

Bean Ragout with Cornmeal Dumplings

A robust bean stew with cherry tomatoes that burst with flavor.

Makes 6 servings

Bean Ragout
1 can (15-ounce) black beans, drained and rinsed
1 can (15-ounce) pinto beans, drained and rinsed
1 cup dehydrated halved cherry tomatoes
1 cup dehydrated sliced zucchini
⅔ cup dehydrated chopped bell peppers
¼ cup dehydrated chopped celery
2 tablespoons chili powder
2 teaspoons ground cumin
1 teaspoon dehydrated oregano
4 dehydrated garlic slices, crushed
1 dehydrated chile pepper, crumbled
7 cups water

Cornmeal Dumplings
¼ cup all-purpose flour
¼ cup cornmeal
1 tablespoon dehydrated parsley
½ teaspoon baking powder
¼ teaspoon salt
¼ cup milk
1 tablespoon vegetable shortening
1 tablespoon shredded cheddar cheese

1. Place all the ragout ingredients in a 6-quart slow cooker, stir to combine, and cover. Cook on low for 5 hours.
2. After the ragout has been cooking for at least 5 hours, and one hour before you want to serve the ragout, mix the flour, cornmeal, parsley, baking powder, and salt together in a small bowl, then stir in the milk, shortening, and cheese until the mixture has the consistency of drop cookie dough. Drop the dough by tablespoons on top of the simmering ragout, cover, and cook until the dumplings are risen and cooked through, about 45 minutes.

Beet Green Soup

This rich soup tastes wonderful served with a sprinkling of your favorite grated cheese.

Makes 5 to 6 servings

1 cup dried navy or Great Northern beans, rinsed and picked over
1 cup dehydrated beet greens
½ cup dehydrated sliced onions
¼ cup dehydrated sliced carrots
1 tablespoon white wine vinegar
2 teaspoons sugar
2 dehydrated garlic slices, crushed
Pinch of crushed dehydrated red chile pepper
Pinch of dehydrated thyme
4 cups vegetable or chicken broth
4 cups water

Place all the ingredients in a 6-quart slow cooker, stir to combine, and cover. Cook on LOW for 6 hours.

Vegetable Soup with Ginger

Dehydrated ginger adds flavor and flair to this vegetable soup.

Makes 6 to 7 servings

    1 cup dehydrated sliced tomatoes
    1 cup dehydrated corn kernels
    ½ cup dehydrated sliced zucchini, rounds cut in half with kitchen scissors
    ½ cup dehydrated cubed potatoes
    ½ cup dehydrated bell pepper strips
    ½ cup dehydrated sliced onion
    ¼ cup dehydrated chopped celery
    2 teaspoons coarsely ground dehydrated ginger
    1 teaspoon paprika
    1 teaspoon crushed dehydrated basil
    ½ teaspoon dehydrated sliced garlic, crushed
    8 cups water
    2 cups vegetable or chicken broth

Place all the ingredients in a 6-quart slow cooker, stir to combine, and cover. Cook on LOW for 5 hours.

Summer Soup

Summer vegetables make a delicious and hearty soup all year round!

Makes 10 servings

    ½ cup dehydrated sliced white potatoes
    ½ cup dehydrated sliced zucchini
    ½ cup dehydrated sliced summer squash
    ¼ cup dehydrated sliced carrots
    ¼ cup dehydrated sliced Roma tomatoes
    ¼ cup dehydrated sliced mushrooms
    ¼ cup dehydrated sliced onions
    ¼ cup dehydrated mixed green and red bell pepper strips
    2 whole dehydrated collard green leaves, broken into 2-inch pieces
    2 teaspoons dehydrated thyme
    1 teaspoon dehydrated rosemary
    6 vegetable or chicken bouillon cubes
    8 cups water

Combine all the ingredients in a 6-quart slow cooker, cover, and cook on LOW for 6 hours.

Barley Vegetable Soup

Quick, easy, and hearty.

Makes 8 servings

- ⅔ cup uncooked barley
- ½ cup dehydrated broccoli florets
- ½ cup dehydrated cauliflower florets
- ½ cup dehydrated chopped carrots
- ½ cup dehydrated sliced mushrooms
- ½ cup dehydrated sliced onions
- 4 cups water
- 3 cups vegetable or chicken broth

Place all the ingredients in a 6-quart slow cooker, stir to combine, and cover. Cook on LOW for 4 hours.

Sweet Potato and Bean Stew

This sweet and savory stew is hearty enough to satisfy the biggest of appetites.

Makes 4 servings

- 1 (15-ounce) can black beans, drained and rinsed
- 1½ cups dehydrated sliced sweet potatoes, each round cut in half with kitchen scissors
- 1 cup dehydrated cut green beans
- ¼ cup dehydrated chopped onions
- 2 teaspoons Caribbean jerk seasoning
- ½ teaspoon dehydrated thyme
- ¼ teaspoon ground cinnamon
- 6 cups water
- 1 (15-ounce) can vegetable broth

Place all the ingredients in a 6-quart slow cooker, stir to combine, and cover. Cook on LOW for 5 to 6 hours.

Pantry Broccoli and Cheese Soup

Kids and adults alike love this creamy, cheesy soup. Feel free to swap out the broccoli for your favorite vegetable.

Makes 10 servings

> 1 cup store-bought dehydrated cheese powder
> 6 cups water
> 2 cups vegetable or chicken broth
> 1 cup dehydrated broccoli florets
> 1/4 cup dehydrated chopped onions
> 1 tablespoon dehydrated parsley

In a 6-quart slow cooker, stir the dehydrated cheese with the water to combine. Add the remaining ingredients, stir, cover, and cook on LOW for 4 hours.

Guacamole Soup

Spice up your Taco Night with this wonderful soup. It combines fresh avocados (which, unfortunately, you can't dehydrate because of their high oil content) with dehydrated veggies and spices to liven up your taste buds.

Makes 6 servings

> 4 cups vegetable broth
> 1 cup water
> 3 ripe avocados, peeled, pitted, and mashed
> 1/4 cup dehydrated chopped onion
> 1/2 tablespoon dehydrated sliced garlic, crushed
> 1/4 of a dehydrated habanero chile pepper, crushed
> 1 tablespoon ground cumin
> 1 teaspoon dehydrated oregano
> 1 dehydrated bay leaf
> Salt and pepper
> 1 to 2 teaspoons honey
> 1 tablespoon fresh lime juice
> Sour cream, hot sauce, and tortilla chips for serving

1. Place the broth, water, mashed avocados, onion, garlic, habanero, cumin, oregano, bay leaf, and 1/2 teaspoon salt in a 6-quart slow cooker, stir to combine, and cover. Cook on LOW for 6 to 8 hours or HIGH for 3 to 4 hours.
2. Remove the bay leaf and use an immersion blender to puree the hot soup. Stir in the honey to taste and lime juice (if desired) and salt and pepper for taste.
3. Serve warm with sour cream, hot sauce, and tortilla chips.

Shredded Potato Soup

This savory soup has all the delicious flavors of a loaded baked potato. And if you have jerky in your pantry, cut it into small pieces with kitchen scissors and use it instead of the bacon.

Makes 6 servings

4 (14-ounce) cans chicken broth
3 cups water
2 cups dehydrated shredded potatoes
2 tablespoons bacon bits or crumbled bacon
2 tablespoons dehydrated sliced green onions
¼ teaspoon black pepper
¼ cup sour cream
¼ cup shredded cheddar cheese

1. Place the broth, water, potatoes, bacon, green onions, and pepper in a 6-quart slow cooker, stir to combine, and cover. Cook on HIGH for 2 hours or LOW for 4 hours.
2. Fold in the sour cream and cheese, cover, and let continue to cook just long enough to heat through and melt the cheese.

Apple-Butternut Soup

Naturally sweet, with all the flavors and aromas of a beautiful fall day—and no dairy.

Makes 8 to 10 servings

1 cup dehydrated shredded apples
1 cup dehydrated cubed butternut squash
1 cup dehydrated chopped potatoes
½ cup dehydrated sliced green onions
½ cup dehydrated sliced carrots
2 tablespoons dehydrated chopped celery
1 tablespoon dehydrated parsley
2 dehydrated garlic slices, crushed
2 whole cloves
7 cups vegetable broth

Place all ingredients in a 6-quart slow cooker, stir to combine, and cover. Cook on LOW for 6 hours.

Creamy Butternut Squash and Apple Soup

Sweet and creamy!

Makes 8 servings

¼ cup powdered dehydrated butternut squash

1 applesauce leather (page 86; dehydrated from 1 cup applesauce), broken into pieces

½ cup dehydrated chopped apples

1 tablespoon dehydrated chopped onion

1 tablespoon brown sugar

½ teaspoon ground sage

½ teaspoon coarsely ground dehydrated ginger

3 whole cloves

6 cups water

2 (14-ounce) cans chicken broth (or substitute vegetable broth to make this vegetarian)

½ cup heavy cream or half-and-half

1. Place all the ingredients except the cream in a 6-quart slow cooker, stir to combine, and cover. Cook on LOW for 6 hours.
2. Puree the soup with an immersion blender. Stir in the cream just before serving.

Chicken Minestrone Soup

A filling, nutritious dinner.

Makes 8 servings

1 tablespoon cooking oil of your choice

1 skinless, boneless chicken breast half

1 (16-ounce) can kidney beans, drained and rinsed

½ cup dehydrated halved grape tomatoes

¼ cup dehydrated chopped carrots

¼ cup dehydrated cut green beans

¼ cup dehydrated chopped summer squash

¼ cup dehydrated spinach leaves

½ cup grated Parmesan cheese

2 tablespoons dehydrated diced onion

4 cups chicken broth

4 cups water

1 cup uncooked elbow macaroni

1. Heat the oil in a medium skillet over medium-high heat. Add the chicken breast and cook until golden brown on both sides and cooked through. Remove from the heat. When cool enough to handle, cut into ½-inch cubes.

2. Place the chicken and remaining ingredients except the elbow macaroni in a 6-quart slow cooker, stir to combine, and cover. Cook on LOW for 3 hours.
3. Stir the macaroni into the soup, cover, and cook until tender, about 1 more hour.

Chicken Dumpling Stew

The ultimate comfort food! This hearty stew is rich and creamy, served over moist and delicious dumplings.

Makes 8 servings

Stew

2/3 cup all-purpose flour
1/4 cup store-bought powdered milk
10 cups water
2 cups chicken broth
2 whole skinless, boneless chicken breasts, cut into 1/2-inch cubes
1/2 cup dehydrated cubed potatoes (if using dehydrated sliced potatoes, increase to 1 cup)
1/2 cup mixed dehydrated bell pepper strips (red, yellow, green)
1/2 cup dehydrated sliced carrots
1/2 cup dehydrated peas
1/2 cup dehydrated sliced mushrooms
1/4 cup dehydrated sliced green onions
1/4 cup dehydrated chopped celery
3/4 teaspoon dehydrated rosemary
1/2 teaspoon dehydrated tarragon

Dumplings

2 cups Bisquick
1 cup water

1. Whisk the flour and powdered milk together in a 6-quart slow cooker to combine. Slowly pour in the water, whisking constantly so there are no lumps. Add the rest of the stew ingredients, stir to combine, and cover. Cook on HIGH for 5 1/2 hours.
2. To make the dumplings, mix the Bisquick and water together in a medium bowl. Thirty minutes before you're ready to serve dinner, dollop the biscuit dough 1 tablespoon at a time on top of the simmering stew. Cover and cook until the dumplings are risen and cooked through.

Chicken and Vegetable Soup

This quick, easy, and comforting orzo soup is packed with chicken and flavorful veggies.

Makes 5 to 6 servings

1½ cups chopped cooked chicken
½ cup dehydrated sliced carrots
½ cup dehydrated cut green beans
¼ cup dehydrated chopped onions
6 dehydrated tomato slices
2 dehydrated garlic slices, crushed
Pinch of crumbled dehydrated red chile pepper (optional)
Pinch of dehydrated thyme
6 cups water
4 cups chicken broth
⅔ cup uncooked orzo (rice-shaped pasta)

1. Place all the ingredients except the orzo in a 6-quart slow cooker, stir to combine, and cover. Cook on LOW for 4 to 5 hours.
2. Stir in the orzo, cover, and cook until tender, 20 to 30 minutes.

Chicken and Rice Soup with Okra

Classic chicken and rice soup packed with veggies and okra. If you're not a fan of okra, it's fine to leave it out.

Makes 6 servings

2½ cups chopped cooked chicken
1½ cups uncooked long-grain rice
1 cup dehydrated sliced okra
½ cup dehydrated sliced onions
¼ cup dehydrated green bell pepper strips
1 tablespoon dehydrated chopped celery
½ teaspoon Cajun seasoning
Pinch of crumbled dehydrated red chile pepper
2 dehydrated garlic slices, crushed
1 dehydrated bay leaf
4 cups chicken broth
4 cups water
3 tablespoons all-purpose flour
Salt

1. Place all the ingredients except the salt in a 6-quart slow cooker, stir to combine, and cover. Cook on LOW for 4 to 5 hours.
2. Add salt to taste prior to serving.

Lemongrass Chicken Soup

The fresh taste of lemongrass (even when it's dehydrated!) raises chicken soup to a new level. A great summertime soup.

Makes 5 to 6 servings

4 cups chicken broth
4 cups water
2 cups cubed cooked chicken
1 tablespoon dehydrated 1-inch lemongrass pieces
1 tablespoon dehydrated sliced green onions
1 tablespoon dehydrated parsley
2 dehydrated basil leaves
2 dehydrated garlic slices, crushed
1 teaspoon coarsely ground dehydrated ginger
Pinch of crumbled dehydrated red chile pepper
2 cups uncooked egg noodles
Salt

1. Place all the ingredients except the egg noodles and salt in a 6-quart slow cooker, stir to combine, and cover. Cook on LOW for 4 hours.
2. Stir in the egg noodles, cover, and cook until they are tender, 15 to 20 minutes. Taste for salt and serve.

Beef Barley Soup

This soup is bursting with big chunks of beef, hearty barley, and delicious vegetables.

Makes 8 servings

4 cups 1-inch cubes cooked beef
2/3 cup barley
1/2 cup dehydrated sliced carrots
1/4 cup dehydrated sliced mushrooms
1/4 cup dehydrated chopped onion
1/4 cup dehydrated chopped celery
1 dehydrated bay leaf
8 cups water
2 cups beef broth
Salt and pepper

1. Place all the ingredients except the salt and pepper in a 6-quart slow cooker, stir to combine, and cover. Cook on LOW for 5 to 6 hours.
2. Season with salt and pepper to taste.

Beef, Lentil, and Cabbage Soup

A scrumptious, filling soup.

Makes 10 servings

1 pound ground beef
2 cups dehydrated chopped cabbage
1 cup chopped dehydrated collard greens
1 cup dried lentils
½ cup dehydrated sliced carrots
½ cup dehydrated sliced onions
¼ cup dehydrated chopped celery
¼ cup dehydrated chopped green bell peppers
1 teaspoon dehydrated thyme, crumbled
1 dehydrated bay leaf
6 cups tomato juice
4 cups water
2 cups beef broth

1. Brown the ground beef in a medium skillet over high heat until there is no more pink, breaking up any clumps of meat with a wooden spoon. Drain off all the fat, then transfer the beef to a 6-quart slow cooker.
2. Add the remaining ingredients, stir to combine, and cover. Cook on LOW for 6 to 7 hours.

Hamburger Stew

So simple to make, and budget-friendly too!

Makes 8 servings

2 pounds ground beef
1 cup dehydrated corn kernels
1 cup dehydrated cut green beans
½ cup dehydrated sliced onions
½ cup dehydrated sliced carrots
1 tablespoon cornstarch
½ teaspoon dehydrated tarragon
6 small or 3 large beef bouillon cubes, crushed
10 cups water

1. Brown the ground beef in a medium skillet over high heat until there is no more pink, breaking up any clumps of meat with a wooden spoon. Drain off all the fat, then transfer the beef to a 6-quart slow cooker.
2. Add the remaining ingredients, stir to combine, and cover. Cook on LOW for 6 hours.

Beef Jerky Pea Soup

Traditionally, pea soup is paired with ham or a ham bone. Substituting jerky adds an interesting smoky flavor. Try Classic Jerky (page 117) or get creative with Smoky Salmon Jerky (page 119).

Makes 8 servings

2 cups dehydrated peas
½ cup finely shredded or chopped jerky
¼ cup dehydrated sliced onions
¼ cup dehydrated chopped carrots
¼ cup dehydrated chopped celery
1 teaspoon black pepper
1 teaspoon powdered dehydrated garlic
6½ cups water
4 cups chicken or vegetable broth

Process the peas in a blender until they are partially powdered. Place all the ingredients in a 6-quart slow cooker, stir to combine, and cover. Cook on LOW for 7 to 8 hours.

Sausage and Pasta Soup

Chock-full of vegetables and deliciously thickened by the addition of refried beans.

Makes 10 servings

1 pound bulk Italian pork sausage
2 cups crumbled dehydrated refried pinto beans
1 cup dehydrated sliced tomatoes, each cut into quarters with kitchen scissors
½ cup dehydrated sliced carrots
½ cup dehydrated whole green beans, cut into 2-inch pieces with kitchen scissors
¼ cup dehydrated chopped red bell peppers
¼ cup dehydrated sliced onions
1 tablespoon dehydrated chopped celery
1 tablespoon dehydrated parsley
1 teaspoon dehydrated oregano
4 dehydrated garlic slices, crushed
4 cups beef broth
6 to 7 cups water
2 cups orzo

1. Place the sausage in a medium skillet and cook over medium-high until no longer pink, breaking it up into small pieces. Drain any fat from the pan. Transfer the sausage to a 6-quart slow cooker.
2. Add the remaining ingredients except the pasta, stir, cover, and cook on HIGH for 3½ hours.
3. Remove cover, stir in the pasta, cover, and cook until the pasta is just tender, about another 30 minutes.

Classic Pea Soup

Just the way you like it, with savory bits of ham.

Makes 10 servings

2 cups dehydrated peas
¼ cup dehydrated sliced onion
¼ cup dehydrated chopped carrots
¼ cup dehydrated chopped potatoes
¼ cup chopped dehydrated collard greens
½ cup chopped ham
½ teaspoon ground allspice
6 cups water
4 cups chicken or vegetable broth

Place all the ingredients in a 6-quart slow cooker, stir to combine, and cover. Cook on LOW for 6 hours.

Harvest Pork Stew

Dehydrated sweet potatoes and pineapples give this stew a tangy, robust flavor.

Makes 6 servings

1 tablespoon cooking oil of your choice
1 pound pork tenderloin, cut into 1-inch cubes
1 cup dehydrated chopped potatoes
1 cup dehydrated sliced sweet potatoes, cut in half with kitchen scissors
½ cup dehydrated chopped carrots
½ cup dehydrated corn kernels
¼ cup dehydrated chopped or sliced red bell pepper
¼ cup dehydrated cubed pineapple
1 tablespoon dehydrated parsley, crumbled
¼ teaspoon dehydrated thyme
3 tablespoons cornstarch
4 cups chicken broth
4 cups water

1. Heat the oil in a large skillet over high heat. Add the pork cubes and sear on all sides until nicely browned. Transfer to a 6-quart slow cooker.
2. Add the remaining ingredients to the slow cooker, stir to combine, and cover. Cook on LOW for 6 hours.

Taco Chili

Serve this with your favorite taco toppings.

Makes 8 to 10 servings

   1 pound ground beef
   1 (15.5-ounce) can light red kidney beans
   1 (15.5-ounce) can dark red kidney beans
   1 (15.5-ounce) can pinto beans
   2 cups dehydrated sliced tomatoes
   ½ cup dehydrated sliced mushrooms
   ¼ cup dehydrated chopped onions
   ¼ cup dehydrated chopped green bell peppers
   ¼ cup dehydrated chopped red bell peppers
   2 dehydrated garlic slices, crushed
   1 (1.25-ounce) package taco seasoning
   7 cups water
   Tortilla chips

1. Brown the ground beef in a medium skillet over high heat until no longer pink, breaking up any clumps with a wooden spoon. Pour off any fat, then transfer the beef to a 6-quart slow cooker.
2. Add the remaining ingredients except the tortilla chips to the slow cooker, stir to combine, and cover. Cook on LOW for 4 hours.
3. Serve topped with tortilla chips.

Fiesta Chili

Wonderfully filling with or without the meat.

Makes 6 servings

   ½ teaspoon olive oil
   1 pound ground beef, turkey, or venison (optional)
   2 tablespoons red wine
   1 cup dehydrated Roma tomato slices
   ½ cup dehydrated corn kernels
   2 tablespoons dehydrated chopped onion
   2 tablespoons dehydrated chopped green bell pepper
   2 tablespoons dehydrated chopped red bell pepper
   1 tablespoon dehydrated garlic slices, crushed
   1 tablespoon dehydrated chopped celery
   1 teaspoon chili powder
   1 teaspoon powdered dehydrated tomatoes

½ teaspoon black pepper

½ teaspoon crushed dehydrated red chile pepper

¼ teaspoon ground cumin

¼ teaspoon ground coriander

2 beef or vegetable bouillon cubes

1 (15-ounce) can red kidney beans (don't drain)

1 (15-ounce) can black beans (don't drain)

4 cups water

1. If including the meat, heat the oil in a large skillet and cook the meat until no longer pink, breaking up any clumps. Stir in the wine.
2. Combine the remaining ingredients in a 6-quart slow cooker. Add the browned meat and stir to combine. Cover and cook on LOW 6 to 8 hours or HIGH for 4 hours.

Buffalo Chicken Chili

Buffalo, New York, my hometown, is the home of hot wings! Try combining the heat of authentic Buffalo hot wings with the hearty flavors of chili. This is a fun new take on the chicken wing.

Makes 4 servings

2 tablespoons butter

1½ pounds boneless, skinless chicken, cut into 1-inch cubes

1 cup dehydrated sliced tomatoes, crushed

2 tablespoons dehydrated chopped onion

1 tablespoon dehydrated chopped red bell pepper

1 tablespoon dehydrated chopped yellow bell pepper

1 tablespoon dehydrated chopped celery

1 tablespoon chili powder

1½ teaspoons powdered dehydrated tomato

½ teaspoon cayenne pepper

½ teaspoon crushed dehydrated red chile pepper

1 chicken bouillon cube

2 (15-ounce) cans pinto beans, drained and rinsed

4 cups water

½ cup crumbled blue cheese

1. Melt the butter in a medium skillet over medium-high heat. Add the chicken and cook until it no longer looks raw.
2. Combine the remaining ingredients except the blue cheese in a 6-quart slow cooker. Add the chicken and stir to combine. Cover and cook on LOW 6 to 8 hours or HIGH for 4 hours.
3. Serve in bowls, topped with a sprinkling of blue cheese.

White Chicken Chili

This is a lighter-style chili with fresh flavors that is great to serve all year round.

Makes 6 servings

    1 tablespoon vegetable oil
    2 pounds boneless, skinless chicken breasts, cut into 1-inch cubes
    ½ cup dehydrated corn kernels
    ¼ cup dehydrated sliced onions
    4 slices dehydrated garlic, crushed
    2 dehydrated lime slices (with peel on), crushed
    1 tablespoon dehydrated cilantro, crumbled
    1 teaspoon ground cumin
    4 chicken bouillon cubes
    1 (15-ounce) can Great Northern beans (don't drain)
    1 (15-ounce) can butter beans (don't drain)
    4 cups water

1. Heat the oil in a medium skillet over medium-high heat, then add the chicken and cook until no longer raw looking.
2. Combine the chicken and remaining ingredients in a 6-quart slow cooker. Cover and cook on LOW 6 to 8 hours or HIGH for 4 hours.

Creamy White Chicken Chili

This flavorful chili will comfort you on the coldest winter days.

Makes 6 servings

    1 tablespoon cooking oil of your choice
    1½ pounds boneless, skinless chicken breasts, cut into 1-inch cubes
    ¼ cup dehydrated sliced onions
    1 tablespoon crumbled dehydrated red chile peppers
    1 teaspoon ground cumin
    1 teaspoon dehydrated oregano
    1 teaspoon black pepper
    ½ teaspoon cayenne pepper
    2 dehydrated garlic slices, crushed
    2 chicken bouillon cubes
    2 (15-ounce) cans Great Northern beans (don't rinse)
    4 cups water
    1 cup sour cream
    ½ cup heavy cream

1. Heat the oil in a medium skillet over medium-high heat, then add the chicken and cook until no longer raw looking.
2. Combine the chicken and remaining ingredients except the sour cream and heavy cream in a 6-quart slow cooker. Cover and cook on LOW 6 to 8 hours or HIGH for 4 hours.
3. Stir in the sour cream and heavy cream and let heat through a few minutes before serving.

Vegetable Chili

This is a great chili for the vegetable lover. It will satisfy the heartiest of appetites.

Makes 8 servings

> 2 cups dehydrated shredded potatoes
> 1 cup dehydrated tomato slices, cut in half with kitchen scissors
> 1 cup dehydrated shredded zucchini
> ¼ cup dehydrated sliced onions
> ¼ cup dehydrated sliced yellow and green bell peppers
> 3 tablespoons powdered dehydrated sliced tomato
> 2 teaspoons chili powder
> 1 teaspoon ground cumin
> ½ of a dehydrated chile pepper, crumbled
> 1 (15-ounce) can garbanzo beans (don't rinse)
> 1 (15-ounce) kidney beans (don't rinse)
> 7 cups water

Combine all the ingredients in a 6-quart slow cooker. Cover and cook on LOW for 6 hours or HIGH for 4 hours.

Ziti Ratatouille

Chunky vegetables and chunky marinara create this easy and colorful pasta dish.

Makes 6 servings

> 1½ cups dehydrated sliced zucchini, each piece cut into quarters with kitchen scissors
> 1 cup dehydrated sliced eggplant (with skin on), each slice cut into 3 to 4 pieces with kitchen scissors
> 1 cup dehydrated sliced plum tomatoes, each piece cut in half with kitchen scissors
> ½ cup dehydrated chopped green bell pepper
> ¼ cup dehydrated chopped onion
> ¼ cup dehydrated sliced olives
> 8 dehydrated garlic slices, crushed
> 1 (24-ounce) jar marinara sauce
> ½ cup shredded Parmesan cheese
> 4 cups water
> 1 (16-ounce) box ziti

1. Place all the ingredients except the pasta in a 6-quart slow cooker, stir to combine, and cover. Cook on LOW for 4 to 5 hours.
2. When ready to serve, bring a large pot of salted water to a boil. Add the ziti and cook just until tender. Serve the ratatouille ladled over the drained pasta.

Artichoke Chicken

This easy recipe combines chicken and artichokes for a flavorful and delicious meal.

Makes 6 to 8 servings

   2 tablespoons cooking oil of your choice
   2 pounds skinless, boneless chicken breast, cut into 1-inch pieces
   1 cup dehydrated sliced tomatoes
   1 cup dehydrated sliced artichoke hearts
   ¼ cup dehydrated chopped onion
   ¼ cup dehydrated sliced black olives
   3 tablespoons quick-cooking tapioca
   2 teaspoons curry powder
   1 tablespoon dehydrated parsley
   1 teaspoon dehydrated basil
   4 cups water
   2 cups chicken broth

1. Heat the oil in a large skillet over high heat. Add the chicken and sear until nicely browned on all sides. Transfer to a 6-quart slow cooker.
2. Add the remaining ingredients to the slow cooker, stir to combine, and cover. Cook on LOW for 6 hours.

Chicken Gumbo with Rice

A traditional gumbo with savory chicken and spicy sausage.

Makes 6 servings

   2 tablespoons cooking oil of your choice
   1 pound skinless, boneless chicken breasts, cut into 1-inch pieces
   ½ pound hot Italian sausage, cut into ¼-inch-thick slices
   ¾ cup dehydrated sliced okra
   ½ cup white wine
   ½ cup dehydrated chopped green bell peppers
   ½ cup dehydrated chopped onions

¼ cup dehydrated chopped celery

2 tablespoons dehydrated chile peppers, crumbled

1 teaspoon paprika

¼ cup all-purpose flour

5 cups water

1 cup chicken broth

4 cups cooked rice for serving

1. Heat the oil in a large skillet over high heat. Add the chicken and sausage and sear on all sides until nicely browned. Transfer to a 6-quart slow cooker.
2. Add the remaining ingredients except the rice to the slow cooker, stir to combine, and cover. Cook on LOW for 6 to 8 hours.
3. Serve ladled over hot rice.

Chicken and Rice

Flavorful and satisfying, this makes a great family meal.

Makes 4 servings

1 tablespoon cooking oil of your choice

1 pound skinless, boneless chicken breast, cut into 1-inch pieces

½ cup uncooked long-grain rice

¼ cup dehydrated chopped red bell pepper

¼ cup dehydrated sliced green onions

2 tablespoons dehydrated chopped celery

2 dehydrated garlic slices, crushed

2 cups chicken broth

1 cup water

¼ cup grated Parmesan cheese

1. Heat the oil in a medium skillet over high heat. Add the chicken and sear until nicely browned on all sides. Transfer to a 6-quart slow cooker.
2. Add the remaining ingredients except the Parmesan to the slow cooker, stir to combine, and cover. Cook on LOW for 4 hours.
3. Stir in the Parmesan and serve.

Beef with Mushroom, Zucchini, and Carrots

This one is a real keeper!

Makes 6 to 8 servings

1 pound ground beef, cooked in a skillet until no longer pink
1 cup dehydrated sliced mushrooms
1 cup dehydrated shredded carrots
1 cup dehydrated shredded zucchini
½ cup dehydrated sliced onions
2 tablespoons powdered beef bouillon
1 tablespoon cornstarch
4 dehydrated garlic slices, crushed
1 (15-ounce) can black-eyed peas (don't drain)
7 cups water

Combine all the ingredients in a 6-quart slow cooker, cover, and cook on HIGH for 4 hours.

Corned Beef and Cabbage with Potatoes and Carrots

This traditional Irish meal is perfect for a hearty appetite.

Makes 8 servings

1 corned beef (2 pounds)
4 cups dehydrated sliced cabbage
1 cup dehydrated sliced potatoes
1 cup dehydrated sliced onions
½ cup dehydrated whole baby carrots
1 teaspoon crushed dehydrated garlic
1 teaspoon yellow mustard
2 dehydrated bay leaves
¼ cup orange juice
8 cups water

Place the corned beef in a 6-quart slow cooker, and layer on the other ingredients, pouring over the orange juice and water last. Cover and cook on LOW for 6 hours or until the corned beef is fork-tender.

Pork Loin Roast Stuffed with Mixed Dried Fruit

This fruit-stuffed pork serves up flavor as well as visual appeal.

Makes 8 to 10 servings

> 3 tablespoons olive oil
> 1 pork loin roast (4 to 5 pounds)
> ½ cup dehydrated sliced peaches, cut into small pieces with kitchen scissors
> ½ cup dehydrated plum halves, cut into small pieces with kitchen scissors
> ½ cup dehydrated apricot halves, cut into small pieces with kitchen scissors
> ¼ cup dehydrated chopped onions
> ¼ teaspoon dehydrated tarragon
> 4 dehydrated garlic slices, crushed
> 2 cups sherry

1. Heat 2 tablespoons of the oil in a large skillet over high heat. Add the roast and sear until nicely browned on all sides. Transfer the roast to a cutting board and let cool until it can be handled. Slice it in half lengthwise, but not all the way through, then open it, like a book.
2. Add the remaining 1 tablespoon oil to the skillet, along with the dehydrated fruit, onions, tarragon, garlic, and sherry. Cook over medium heat until the liquid is reduced by half. Remove from the heat and let cool for 5 to 10 minutes.
3. Layer the fruit and onions over half the butterflied pork, then fold the other half back over. Transfer to a 6-quart slow cooker and pour any remaining liquid from the skillet over the roast. Cover and cook on HIGH for 3 hours or LOW for 6 hours.
4. To serve, cut into ½-inch-thick slices.

Cabbage and Sausage

This flavorful combination is not only a crowd pleaser, it's budget-friendly too.

Makes 10 servings

> 1 tablespoon cooking oil
> 2 pounds sausage of your choice, cut into 1-inch pieces
> 4 cups dehydrated shredded cabbage
> 3 cups dehydrated sliced potatoes
> 1 cup dehydrated sliced onions
> ½ cup dehydrated chopped red bell pepper
> ½ cup firmly packed light brown sugar
> ½ cup dehydrated sliced carrots
> 4 dehydrated garlic slices, crushed
> 12 cups water

1. Heat the oil in a large skillet over high heat. Add the sausage and brown nicely on all sides. Transfer to a 6-quart slow cooker.

2. Add the remaining ingredients to the slow cooker, stir to combine, and cover. Cook on LOW for 6 hours.

Ham with Fruit Sauce

Dehydrated fruit added to old-fashioned ham creates a sweet and savory dinner.

Makes 10 servings

½ cup dehydrated cherries
½ cup dehydrated grapes
¾ cup firmly packed brown sugar
1 cup apple juice
¼ cup cornstarch
1 teaspoon ground cinnamon
½ teaspoon crumbled dehydrated chile pepper
1 fully cooked ham (6 pounds)

1. Mix the cherries, grapes, brown sugar, apple juice, cornstarch, cinnamon, and chile pepper in a medium bowl until the sugar and cornstarch dissolve.
2. Place the ham in a 6-quart slow cooker and pour in the fruit and juice mixture. Cover and cook on LOW for 6 hours.
3. Remove ham, place on a cutting board, and cover with aluminum foil until ready to cut. Meanwhile, uncover the slow cooker, turn the setting to HIGH, and cook until the mixture is thick, about 30 minutes.
4. Slice the ham, transfer to a platter, and ladle over the fruit sauce.

Turn On and Go Ham with Potatoes, Cabbage, Collards, and Carrots

Perfect for a busy lifestyle—throw this healthy meal in the slow cooker and come back when it's done.

Makes 6 to 8 servings

6 cups dehydrated shredded cabbage
2 dehydrated whole collard green leaves
4 cups dehydrated sliced potatoes
1 cup dehydrated sliced carrots
6 to 8 (½ inch thick) ham slices
10 cups water

In a 6-quart slow cooker, layer in the cabbage, then the collard greens, potatoes, and carrots. Place the ham slices on top of the carrots. Pour the water over everything. Cover and cook on LOW for 6 hours.

Sweet and Sour Cabbage and Apples

This warm and bubbly recipe is the perfect combination of sweet meets sour.

Makes 6 servings

>   4 cups dehydrated shredded cabbage
>   1 cup dehydrated sliced apples
>   ½ cup dehydrated grapes
>   ¼ cup firmly packed brown sugar
>   ¼ cup (½ stick) butter
>   5 ½ cups apple cider or apple juice
>   3 tablespoons cider vinegar

Place all the ingredients in a 6-quart slow cooker, stir to combine, and cover. Cook on LOW for 3 hours.

Shredded Beets

This sweet and colorful side is packed with nutrients.

Makes 8 servings

>   ½ cup dehydrated shredded beets
>   ½ cup dehydrated shredded apples
>   ½ cup dehydrated shredded potatoes
>   ½ cup dehydrated sliced onions
>   ¼ cup firmly packed brown sugar
>   1 tablespoon cider vinegar
>   ¼ teaspoon celery seeds
>   ¼ teaspoon ground cloves
>   6 cups water

Place all the ingredients in a 6-quart slow cooker, stir to combine, and cover. Cook on LOW for 4 hours.

Curried Potatoes, Cauliflower, and Peas

Curry makes these vegetables warm in flavor. Serve as a side dish or turn it into a main course by serving it over rice or egg noodles.

Makes 6 servings

> 2 cups dehydrated sliced red potatoes (with skins on)
> 1 cup dehydrated cauliflower florets
> 1 cup dehydrated cherry tomato halves
> ½ cup dehydrated peas
> ¼ cup dehydrated chopped onions
> 1 tablespoon coarsely ground dehydrated ginger or 1 teaspoon store-bought ground ginger
> ½ teaspoon ground cumin
> ½ teaspoon coriander seeds
> 4 dehydrated garlic slices, crushed
> 4 cups vegetable broth
> 4 cups water

Place all the ingredients in a 6-quart slow cooker, stir to combine, and cover. Cook on LOW for 5 to 6 hours.

Wild Rice, Fruit, and Nuts

This is the perfect side for your holiday turkey.

Makes 8 servings

> 2 cups uncooked wild rice, rinsed until the water runs clear
> ½ cup dehydrated chopped apples
> ½ cup dehydrated cranberries
> ½ cup dehydrated grapes
> ½ cup dehydrated apricot halves, cut into strips with kitchen scissors
> ½ cup slivered almonds, toasted
> ¼ cup dehydrated sliced green onions
> 2 tablespoons butter
> 2 tablespoons dehydrated parsley, crumbled
> 1 teaspoon ground cumin
> 6 cups chicken broth
> 1 cup orange juice

Place all the ingredients in a 6-quart slow cooker, stir to combine, and cover. Cook on LOW 5 to 6 hours.

Spicy Cheesy Wild Rice

A delicious side but so satisfying you could enjoy it on its own.

Makes 8 servings

1½ cups uncooked long-grain white rice
1 cup dehydrated corn kernels
1 cup dehydrated sliced tomatoes
¼ cup dehydrated mixed chopped red and green bell peppers
2 tablespoons dehydrated sliced green onions
2 dehydrated garlic slices, crushed
1 teaspoon ground cumin
4 cups chicken broth
2½ cups water
1 cup shredded cheese of your choice

1. Combine all the ingredients except the cheese in a 6-quart slow cooker, cover, and cook on HIGH for 3 hours.
2. Remove lid, stir in the cheese, cover, and cook until the cheese is melted and bubbling, about another 30 minutes.

17

Sides, Stuffings, Pickles & Salsas

MIX-AND-MATCH FRUIT SALADS

You can mix fresh fruits and dehydrated fruits together to make a wonderful healthy sweet treat. Fresh fruit is sweet, but dehydrated fruit is sweeter. By removing the water from your fruit you have concentrated the sweetness. By adding dehydrated fruit to a cup of fresh fruit you can turn an ordinary bowl of fruit into an interesting and healthy fruit dessert filled with texture! Dehydrated coconut is also always a great crunchy topper.

Making meals from dehydrated food entails more than just soups and stews! You can easily make side dishes and snacks from your dehydrated fruits and veggies. In this chapter, we will share our recipes for fruit salads, veggies, stuffings, and more.

Easy Tropical Salad

Make this beautiful fruit salad all year round using dehydrated tropical fruits.

Makes 4 servings

¼ cup dehydrated cubed (½-inch) pineapple
¼ cup dehydrated cubed (½-inch) papaya
¼ cup dehydrated sliced kiwi
¼ cup dehydrated peeled orange chunks
¼ cup dehydrated maraschino cherries
¼ cup dehydrated white grapes
½ cup dehydrated shredded coconut

1. Place the dehydrated fruit in a 1-quart canning jar with a lid, add lukewarm water to cover, cover, and refrigerate for 24 hours.
2. One hour prior to serving, drain off the extra water, place the rehydrated fruit in a large bowl, toss with the coconut for a delicious crunch, and serve.

Shredded Fruits and Vegetable Salad

This wonderful fruit salad marries the sweetness of fruit with the crunch and nutrition of veggies.

Makes 8 servings

½ cup dehydrated shredded carrots
½ cup dehydrated cubed pineapple
½ cup dehydrated shredded apples
½ cup dehydrated shredded zucchini
½ cup dehydrated grapes
¼ cup dehydrated shredded coconut
4 cups boiling water
2 cups heavy cream
2 tablespoons confectioners' sugar
2 teaspoons vanilla extract

1. In a large heatproof bowl, combine the dehydrated ingredients, then pour the boiling water over, cover, and let sit for 15 minutes to rehydrate.
2. In a medium bowl, using an electric mixer, whip the cream, confectioners' sugar, and vanilla together until soft peaks form. Set aside.
3. Drain the rehydrated ingredients in a colander. Dry the bowl and return the rehydrated items to it. Mix in the whipped cream, then transfer to an airtight container. Refrigerate for 6 hours and serve.

Pineapple and Shredded Carrot Gelatin

Sweet pineapple combined with the delicious light crunch of carrots. One of my favorites!

Makes 4 servings

1 (3-ounce) box pineapple or lemon gelatin
2 cups boiling water
2 tablespoons dehydrated steamed cubed pineapple (pineapple must be cooked before dehydration for the gelatin to set)
2 tablespoons dehydrated shredded carrots

In a medium bowl, mix the ingredients and let sit outside of the refrigerator for 30 minutes. Pour into a mold if you like, then refrigerate until firm, about 6 hours.

Cranberry Sauce

You'll never buy canned again!

Makes 4 servings

> ½ cup dehydrated chopped cranberries
> 1½ cups water
> ¾ cup sugar

1. In a small saucepan, combine the ingredients and bring to a rolling boil, whisking until the sugar is dissolved. Reduce the heat to medium and simmer until thickened, about 30 minutes.
2. Remove from the heat and let cool, then chill completely before serving.

Spinach-Artichoke Dip

The dehydrated radishes add a nice bit of peppery heat to this.

Makes about 2½ cups

> ¼ cup dehydrated sliced artichoke hearts, chopped
> ¼ cup dehydrated spinach, crumbled
> 2 tablespoons dehydrated sliced radishes, chopped
> 2 cups boiling water
> 1 cup grated Parmesan cheese
> ½ cup mayonnaise
> ½ cup sour cream
> 1 teaspoon powdered dehydrated garlic

1. Preheat the oven to 350°F.
2. In a medium bowl combine the dehydrated artichokes, spinach, and radishes, pour the boiling water over, cover, and let sit for 15 minutes to rehydrate. Drain any remaining water.
3. Add the remaining ingredients and mix well. Transfer to a small ovenproof crock and bake until bubbly, about 25 minutes. Serve with your favorite dippers.

Asparagus and Almonds

A quick and easy side dish with a nutty crunch.

Makes 4 servings

>   1 cup dehydrated 3-inch asparagus pieces
>   4 cups water
>   ¼ cup dehydrated mixed chopped green and red bell peppers
>   2 tablespoons butter
>   1 tablespoon lemon juice
>   ¼ cup sliced almonds

1. Combine the dehydrated asparagus and water in a medium saucepan, bring to a boil, cover, reduce the heat to medium-low, and simmer for 35 minutes.
2. Add the dehydrated peppers and simmer for another 10 minutes.
3. Drain off the water and stir in the butter, lemon juice, and almonds until well combined and the butter is melted.

Cheesy Microwave Refried Beans

This is a great side dish for any kind of Mexican entree. It can also do double duty as an easy-to-put-together bean dip to serve with tortilla chips.

Makes 10 to 12 servings

>   2 cups dehydrated refried beans
>   ¼ cup dehydrated chopped green chile or bell peppers
>   2 tablespoons dehydrated chopped tomatoes
>   1 tablespoon dehydrated chopped onion
>   ½ teaspoon crushed dehydrated jalapeño (optional)
>   2⅔ cups boiling water
>   ½ cup shredded mozzarella cheese

1. In a large bowl, toss the dehydrated ingredients together, pour the boiling water over, stir, cover, and let sit for 20 minutes to rehydrate.
2. Stir again. At this point you can cover and refrigerate for at least 30 minutes (it will thicken more in the refrigerator).
3. Pour the mixture into a microwave-safe baking dish, sprinkle with the mozzarella, and microwave on HIGH until hot all the way through and the cheese has melted, 1 to 2 minutes.

Red Beans and Rice

This Louisiana-style dish is spicy and satisfying.

Makes 6 servings

> 1 (16-ounce) bag dried small red beans (or use your own dehydrated shelled beans)
> 10 cups water
> ½ cup dehydrated chopped onions
> ½ cup dehydrated chopped celery
> ¼ cup dehydrated chopped green bell peppers
> 1 tablespoon crushed dehydrated parsley
> 1 tablespoon dehydrated sliced garlic, crushed
> 2 bay leaves
> 2 tablespoons olive oil
> 1 tablespoon Worcestershire sauce
> 1 tablespoon Tabasco sauce (optional)
> 1 teaspoon salt
> 1 teaspoon cracked black peppercorns
> 4 cups hot cooked long-grain rice

1. In a large bowl, soak the beans in the 10 cups water for 12 hours or overnight.
2. Three hours before dinner, drain the beans and place them in a large pot. Add the onions, celery, bell pepper, parsley, garlic, bay leaves, garlic, and enough water to cover the contents (about 4 cups). Bring to a boil, reduce the heat to medium, and simmer, uncovered, for 2 hours, adding more water if necessary to keep the mixture from sticking to the bottom.
3. Stir in the oil, Worcestershire, Tabasco if using, salt, and pepper and stir to combine. Reduce the heat to low, cover the pot, and let cook, stirring occasionally, until the beans are tender and vegetables are fully rehydrated, about 1 hour.
4. Serve ladled over the cooked rice.

Green Beans and Roasted Peppers

Use your refrigerator to rehydrate these green beans while they marinate with dehydrated roasted bell peppers. When it comes time to eat, just heat and serve.

Makes 6 servings

> 2 cups dehydrated cut green beans
> ½ cup dehydrated sliced onions
> 4 dehydrated roasted red bell pepper halves, cut into strips lengthwise with kitchen scissors
> Boiling water
> ½ teaspoon canning salt

1. Place the dehydrated ingredients in a 1-quart canning jar with a lid. Fill the jar with boiling water, put the lid on, and let cool, then refrigerate for 24 hours.
2. Add the salt and shake to combine. Empty the contents of the jar into a saucepan, heat up to a simmer, and serve.

Green Bean and Mushroom Bake

This is a holiday favorite at our house.

Makes 6 to 8 servings

> 3 cups dehydrated French-cut green beans
> 1 cup dehydrated sliced mushrooms
> ¼ cup dehydrated sliced onions
> ¼ cup dehydrated chopped red bell pepper
> 8 cups water
> 2 (10 ¾-ounce) cans condensed cream of mushroom soup
> 1 cup milk
> ½ cup sour cream
> 1 recipe Tarragon and Plum Tomato Breadcrumbs (page 156)

1. Preheat the oven to 350°F. Spray a 9 x 13-inch baking dish with cooking spray.
2. Combine the dehydrated green beans, mushrooms, onions, and peppers and water in a large saucepan, bring to a boil, cover, reduce the heat to a simmer, and cook until tender, about 30 minutes.
3. Drain water, then pour the vegetables into the baking dish.
4. Reusing the saucepan, whisk the cream of mushroom soup, milk, and sour cream together, then bring to a boil. Pour the hot mixture over the vegetables. Sprinkle the breadcrumbs evenly over the top. Bake until breadcrumbs are golden brown and the sauce is bubbling, 45 to 50 minutes.

Shredded Beets, Carrots, Cabbage, and Apples

This is a delicious and pretty side dish that's sweet, crunchy, and full of flavor.

Makes 8 servings

> **5 cups water**
> **¼ cup distilled white vinegar**
> **¼ cup sugar**
> **½ inch of dehydrated chile pepper, crumbled**
> **1 whole clove, crushed**
> **1 teaspoon cornstarch**
> **½ cup dehydrated shredded beets**
> **½ cup dehydrated shredded carrots**
> **½ cup dehydrated shredded apples**
> **½ cup dehydrated shredded cabbage**

1. In a large saucepan, combine the water, vinegar, sugar, and crushed chile and clove, stirring until well blended.
2. Fold in the remaining ingredients, cover, bring to a boil, reduce the heat to low, and simmer for 2 hours.

Crunchy Beet Fries

These are wonderful served with a flavored mayonnaise, like chipotle or pesto.

Makes 6 servings

> **2 cups dehydrated French fry-sliced beets (if you have it, use the French fry option on your food processor)**
> **Boiling water**
> **1½ cups cornstarch**
> **1 tablespoon salt**
> **1 tablespoon black pepper**
> **½ cup vegetable oil**

1. Place the beets in a 1-quart canning jar and fill with boiling water. Cover with the lid and let cool, then refrigerate for 24 hours.
2. Drain off any remaining water and lightly pat dry the beets with paper towels. In a medium bowl, whisk the cornstarch, salt, and pepper together. Toss the beets in the cornstarch mixture to coat completely; tap off any excess.
3. In a large skillet, heat the oil over medium-high heat. Fry the beets in batches without crowding them until golden and crispy on both sides. Transfer the fried beets to paper towels to drain, then serve.

Stuffed Banana Peppers

Serve these as a side or a hot and spicy appetizer to get your party going!

Makes 8 servings

> 8 dehydrated whole large banana peppers
> 1 recipe Jalapeño-Garlic-Parsley Breadcrumbs (page 155)
> 2 tablespoons grated Parmesan cheese
> 2 tablespoons olive oil
> 1 tablespoon water

1. Soak the dehydrated whole peppers in boiling water to cover until fully rehydrated, about 20 minutes, then pat dry.
2. Preheat the oven to 350°F.
3. In a small bowl, mix the remaining ingredients together thoroughly.
4. Slice each banana pepper lengthwise down the center on one side, open, and lay each on a 12-inch square of aluminum foil. Place 2 tablespoons of stuffing on one side of each pepper, fold the pepper closed, then roll up in the foil. Bake until thoroughly heated through, about 35 minutes.

Shredded Bell Pepper Bake

A hearty and wholesome casserole.

Makes 10 servings

> 4 cups cooked long-grain rice, cooled
> 2 cups dehydrated mixed shredded red and green bell peppers
> 1 cup dehydrated sliced tomatoes
> 1 (16-ounce) can kidney beans (do not drain)
> 1 (16-ounce) can tomato sauce
> 1 large egg
> 1 teaspoon chili powder
> 3 cups boiling water

1. Preheat the oven to 350°F. Spray a 9 x 13-inch baking pan with cooking spray.
2. In a large bowl, combine all the ingredients until well mixed. Pour into the baking pan and bake until golden brown, about 45 minutes.

Roasted Sesame Broccoli and Cauliflower

Add flavor to your veggies by roasting them with crunchy sesame seeds.

Makes 4 to 5 servings

1 cup dehydrated broccoli florets
1 cup dehydrated cauliflower florets
2 cups boiling water
¼ cup olive oil
1 tablespoon crumbled dehydrated thyme
1 tablespoon sea salt
2 tablespoons sesame seeds

1. Preheat the oven to 425°F.
2. In a large bowl, combine the broccoli and cauliflower, pour the boiling water over, cover, and let sit for 15 minutes to rehydrate.
3. Drain off any remaining water; do not pat the vegetables dry. Arrange them in a single layer on a baking sheet, drizzle with the oil, then sprinkle with the thyme, salt, and sesame seeds in that order. Roast until golden brown, with the edges starting to crisp up, 15 to 20 minutes.

Broccoli Rice

The perfect partner for any chicken or fish dish.

Makes 6 servings

6 cups water
3 cups uncooked long-grain rice
1 cup dehydrated broccoli florets
1 cup boiling water

1. Put the 6 cups water and rice in a rice cooker.
2. In a heatproof medium bowl, combine the dehydrated broccoli and boiling water, cover, and let sit for a few minutes to partially rehydrate the broccoli. Drain off any remaining water.
3. Add the broccoli to the rice cooker, shut the lid, and cook according to the manufacturer's directions to the desired consistency.

Maple-Glazed Brussels Sprouts with Bacon

Sweet and smoky meets nutty in this flavorful side dish.

Makes 4 servings

2 cups dehydrated Brussels sprout halves
¼ cup dehydrated chopped onions
4 cups water
¼ cup (½ stick) butter
¼ cup maple syrup or honey
4 slices bacon, cooked until crispy and crumbled

1. In a medium saucepan, combine the dehydrated Brussels sprouts and onions with the water, bring to a boil, reduce the heat to low, and cook until tender, about 35 minutes.
2. Drain off the water and stir in the butter, maple syrup, and bacon.

Brown Sugar Carrots with Pineapple and Raisins

A sweet and simple side dish.

Makes 4 servings

1 cup dehydrated shredded carrots
½ cup dehydrated cubed pineapple
¼ cup dehydrated grapes
4 cups water
2 tablespoons brown sugar
1 tablespoon butter

1. Combine the dehydrated carrots, pineapple, and grapes and water in a large saucepan, bring to boil, cover, reduce the heat to a simmer, and cook for 25 minutes.
2. Drain off the water, add the brown sugar and butter, and stir until mixed and melted.

Orange-Maple Glazed Carrots

These tender carrots are covered in a warm maple-citrus sauce.

Makes 6 servings

> 1 cup dehydrated sliced carrots
> 5 cups water
> ½ cup orange juice
> 1 tablespoon dehydrated orange zest
> ¼ cup maple syrup
> 3 tablespoons butter
> 1 teaspoon ground nutmeg

1. Combine the dehydrated carrots and water in a large saucepan, bring to a boil, cover, reduce the heat to medium-low, and simmer for 1 hour.
2. Drain off any remaining water. Add the orange juice and zest, maple syrup, butter, and nutmeg to the pan, stir to combine, cover, and simmer for 30 minutes.

Double Corn Pudding

This sweet cake-like recipe is a perfect accompaniment for a holiday meal.

Makes 8 servings

> 1 cup dehydrated corn kernels
> 4 cups water
> ¼ cup dehydrated minced onions
> 2 tablespoons dehydrated chopped chile peppers
> 2 tablespoons butter
> 1 tablespoon all-purpose flour
> 2 cups half-and-half
> 1 cup milk
> ¼ cup quick-cooking grits
> 4 large eggs

1. In a medium saucepan, combine the dehydrated corn and water, bring to a boil, cover, reduce the heat to medium, and cook until tender, 15 to 20 minutes. Remove from the heat and let cool completely in the water.
2. Preheat the oven to 325°F. Spray a 9 x 13-inch baking pan with cooking spray.
3. Drain the water from the corn. Add the dehydrated onions and chiles, butter, and flour and stir until well blended over medium heat. Slowly stir in the half-and-half and milk; bring to a boil. Stir in the grits, reduce the heat to low, and cook, stirring, until thick, about 10 minutes. Remove from the heat and stir in the eggs.
4. Pour the mixture into the baking pan and bake until it puffs up and the top turns golden brown, about 1 hour.

Chilled Cucumbers in Dill Sauce

There is nothing more refreshing than cold cucumbers in a creamy dill sauce.

Makes 6 servings

    4 cups dehydrated sliced cucumbers
    ½ cup dehydrated chopped onions
    2 cups cool water
    2 cups sour cream
    ½ cup mayonnaise
    ¼ cup lemon juice
    1 tablespoon crushed dehydrated dill
    2 teaspoons sugar
    1 teaspoon black pepper

1. In a large bowl, combine the dehydrated cucumbers and onions, pour the water over, cover, and let soak for 2 to 3 minutes to rehydrate. Drain off any remaining water.
2. In a medium bowl, whisk the remaining ingredients together until smooth. Add to the cucumbers and toss lightly to coat. Transfer to an airtight container and refrigerate for 8 hours before serving.

Cucumber-Lime Gelatin

A cool, fresh, and invigorating flavor.

Makes 4 servings

    1 (3-ounce) box lime gelatin
    2 cups boiling water
    ¼ cup dehydrated shredded cucumbers

In a medium bowl, mix the ingredients and let sit outside of the refrigerator for 30 minutes. Pour into a mold if you like, then refrigerate until firm, about 6 hours.

Grilled Portabella Mushroom Caps

Serve these on the side with a nice grilled steak or make them the main event, popped on a bun and served as a veggie burger.

Makes 6 servings

> 6 dehydrated whole portabella mushroom caps
> 1 cup ginger ale
> 2 tablespoons firmly packed brown sugar
> 1 tablespoon salt
> 2 teaspoons dry mustard (like Colman's)
> 1 teaspoon liquid smoke
> 1 teaspoon cayenne pepper
> Olive oil

1. Place the dehydrated whole mushroom caps in a large ziptop plastic bag.
2. In a small bowl, whisk the remaining ingredients except the olive oil together, then carefully pour over the mushrooms in the bag. Squish everything around to coat, then seal the bag and refrigerate overnight.
3. Remove the caps from the marinade and coat each with olive oil.
4. Grill the caps over low heat until tender and they have nice grill marks, 4 to 5 minutes per side.

Fried Mushrooms and Onions

Add instant flavor to any meal with this simple side dish. Spoon over chicken or steak or use as a side dish to complement your meal.

Makes 6 servings

> 1 cup dehydrated sliced mushrooms
> 1 cup dehydrated sliced onions
> 5 cups boiling water
> 3 tablespoons olive oil
> 1 teaspoon coarse-grain mustard
> 1 teaspoon paprika

1. In a large heatproof bowl, combine the mushrooms and onions, pour the boiling water over, cover, and let sit for 15 minutes to rehydrate. Drain off any remaining water, then drain the mushrooms and onions on paper towels (do not squeeze or pat them dry).
2. In a large skillet, heat the oil over high heat until good and hot. Add the mushrooms and onions and cook, stirring occasionally, until nicely brown. Add the mustard and paprika, cook for another minute, and serve.

Breaded Stuffed Mushrooms

Change this recipe up by using other flavor combinations of breadcrumbs or types of sausage.

Makes 8 servings

>1 recipe Bell Pepper-Tomato-Oregano Breadcrumbs (page 157)
>1 pound mild bulk pork sausage
>2 pounds large fresh white button mushrooms, wiped clean and stems removed

1. Preheat the oven to 400°F.
2. In a medium bowl, mix the breadcrumbs and raw sausage together, then place a heaping spoonful in the center of each mushroom cap. Set the stuffed caps on top of a broiler pan, add ¼ inch water to the bottom of the pan, and cover with aluminum foil. Bake for 40 minutes.
3. Uncover the pan and bake until the sausage is completely cooked through and the mushrooms are tender, another 10 minutes.

Fried Okra

If you think you don't like okra, you owe it to yourself to give this recipe a try. You will love it.

Makes 6 to 8 servings

>3 cups dehydrated 1-inch okra slices
>4 cups boiling water
>1 cup milk
>1 large egg
>½ cup cornmeal
>½ cup all-purpose flour
>2 tablespoons Creole seasoning
>1 teaspoon salt
>2 cups cooking oil of your choice

1. Place the okra in a heatproof medium bowl, add the boiling water, cover, and let sit for 10 minutes to rehydrate or until soft but not mushy. Drain off any remaining water, then drain the okra on paper towels, but do not pat dry.
2. In a medium bowl, whisk the milk and egg together.
3. In another medium bowl, combine the cornmeal, flour, Creole seasoning, and salt until blended.
4. Heat the oil in a large heavy skillet until hot. The oil should bubble when a piece of okra is dropped in it.
5. Dip the okra in the milk mixture, then transfer it to the flour mixture and gently mix until all the pieces are completely covered. Without crowding the okra in the skillet (you may have to fry it in two batches), fry it in the hot oil until golden brown on all sides, 4 to 5 minutes. Let drain on paper towels and serve.

Onions and Collard Greens with Sweet-and-Sour Bacon Glaze

Collard greens smothered in a tangy glaze.

Makes 6 servings

6¼ cups water
1 cup dehydrated sliced onions
6 large dehydrated collard greens
¼ cup sugar
2 tablespoons cider vinegar
½ tablespoon cornstarch
Pinch of crushed dehydrated chile pepper
4 slices bacon, cooked until crispy

1. In a large saucepan, bring 6 cups of the water to a boil, then add the dehydrated onions and collards. Cover the pan, reduce the heat to medium-low, and simmer until tender, about 20 minutes. Drain and transfer to a warm serving dish.
2. While the collards and onions simmer, combine the sugar, remaining ¼ cup water, vinegar, cornstarch, chile pepper, and crumbled bacon in a small saucepan. Whisk over low heat until the sugar and cornstarch are dissolved and the mixture thickens. Drizzle over the collard greens and onions and serve.

Buttery Peas and Onions with Bacon

Bacon is the star of this dish, adding a chewy saltiness to the buttered peas and onions.

Makes 6 servings

1 cup dehydrated peas
½ cup dehydrated sliced onions
5 cups water
2 tablespoons butter
4 slices bacon, cooked until crispy and crumbled

1. Combine the peas, onions, and water in a medium saucepan, bring to a boil, cover, reduce the heat to medium-low, and simmer for 40 minutes.
2. Drain off the water, stir in the butter until mixed and melted, and sprinkle with the bacon.

Peas and Spinach with Tarragon and Leeks

A creative side dish that is both flavorful and nutritious.

Makes 4 to 5 servings

> 1½ cups dehydrated peas
> 1 cup dehydrated spinach
> ⅔ cup dehydrated sliced leeks
> 3 tablespoons dehydrated tarragon, crumbled
> 4 cups vegetable broth
> 1 tablespoon butter
> 1 tablespoon olive oil
> 1 tablespoon all-purpose flour
> 1 tablespoon lemon juice

1. In a large saucepan, combine the peas, spinach, leeks, tarragon, broth, butter, and oil, bring to boil, reduce the heat to medium-low, and simmer until the peas and leeks are tender, 20 to 30 minutes.
2. Remove from the heat and stir in the flour. Serve with the lemon juice sprinkled on top.

Scalloped Potatoes

This warm and creamy potato dish is comforting and satisfying.

Makes 6 to 8 servings

> 6 cups dehydrated sliced potatoes
> 6 cups boiling water
> 1 cup cubed ham (optional)
> 2 cups milk
> 3 tablespoons all-purpose flour
> ½ cup dehydrated sliced onions or scallions

1. In a large heatproof bowl, combine the dehydrated potatoes and boiling water, cover, and let sit for 20 minutes to rehydrate; don't drain off any remaining water.
2. Preheat the oven to 350°F.
3. Arrange the potatoes in a 9 x 13-inch baking dish. Sprinkle the ham over the potatoes, if using.
4. In a medium bowl, whisk the milk, flour, and dehydrated onions together, then pour over the potatoes. Cover and bake for 45 minutes, then uncover and bake until golden brown on top, about another 15 minutes.

Potato-Apple Hash

This sweet and hearty hash is delicious for dinner or breakfast.

Makes 8 servings

2 cups dehydrated shredded apples
2 cups dehydrated shredded potatoes
½ cup dehydrated chopped onions
1 tablespoon dehydrated parsley
½ teaspoon dehydrated thyme
2 cups shredded cheese of your choice
1 tablespoon butter, melted
4 cups chicken or vegetable broth
1 cup water
6 slices bacon, cooked until crispy and crumbled

1. Preheat the oven to 350°F.
2. Combine the dehydrated apples, potatoes, onions, and herbs, cheese, and butter in a 10-inch square baking dish. Pour the broth and water over the mixture and sprinkle the crumbled bacon evenly over the top. Cover with aluminum foil and bake for 30 minutes.
3. Remove the foil and bake until browned on top, about another 15 minutes.

Spinach, Cheddar, and Rice Bake

A cheesy rice dish packed with flavor and nutrients.

Makes 8 servings

¼ cup dehydrated sliced onions
2 cups cooked long-grain rice
2 cups shredded cheddar cheese
4 large eggs, beaten
1¼ cups milk
1 teaspoon Worcestershire sauce
1 teaspoon crushed dehydrated thyme
2½ cups dehydrated spinach

1. Preheat the oven to 350°F. Spray a 9 x 13-inch baking dish with cooking spray.
2. In a large bowl, combine all the ingredients, folding in the spinach last. Pour the mixture into the baking dish and bake until bubbling and browned on top, about 25 minutes.

Au Gratin Squash Casserole

Save yourself the carbs by substituting squash for potatoes.

Makes 6 servings

> 2 cups milk
> 2 cups water
> ¼ cup (½ stick) butter
> 2 tablespoons all-purpose flour
> 3 cups dehydrated sliced (¼ to ⅜ inch thick) yellow summer squash
> 1 cup dehydrated sliced onions
> 2 cups shredded white cheddar cheese

1. Preheat the oven to 350°F. Spray a 9 x 13-inch baking dish with cooking spray.
2. In a medium saucepan, bring the milk, water, butter, and flour to a boil, whisking to combine. Remove from the heat.
3. Arrange the dehydrated squash slices in the baking dish and top with the dehydrated onions. Sprinkle over half of the cheese. Pour the white sauce over everything, then top with the remaining cheese. Bake until bubbling and golden brown on top, about 40 minutes. Remove from the oven and let sit for 10 minutes to firm up before serving.

Cheesy Fried Zucchini Planks

These make a tasty and nutritious appetizer as well as side dish.

Makes 6 servings

> 6 dehydrated lengthwise zucchini slices, ⅜ inch thick
> Boiling water
> 2 teaspoons crushed dehydrated oregano
> 1 dehydrated chile pepper, crushed
> 3 tablespoons olive oil
> ½ cup shredded mozzarella cheese

1. Arrange the zucchini slices in a single layer in a heatproof baking dish and pour in about 1 inch of boiling water. Cover and let soak for about 15 minutes.
2. Preheat the oven to 350°F.
3. Remove the zucchini slices from the water, set on paper towels to drain, and sprinkle both sides with the oregano and crushed chile. In a large skillet, heat the oil over medium-high heat. Brown the zucchini slices until golden brown in the hot oil.
4. Transfer the browned zucchini to a cookie sheet, sprinkle with the mozzarella, and bake until the cheese is melted and bubbling, 15 to 20 minutes.

Fried Zucchini and Summer Squash with Italian Spice

A healthy side dish to complement any meal.

Makes 6 servings

⅔ cup dehydrated sliced zucchini
⅔ cup dehydrated sliced summer squash
1 (0.6-ounce) package Italian dressing seasonings
¼ cup distilled white or cider vinegar
3 tablespoons olive oil

1. Place all the ingredients except the oil in a 1-quart canning jar with a lid and fill with hot water. Put the lid on and refrigerate for 24 hours.
2. Drain off the water, then place the squash and zucchini on paper towels (do not pat or squeeze dry).
3. In a large skillet, heat the oil over medium-high heat. Add the squash and fry until tender and golden brown on both sides.

Zucchini Gratin

Trade out the potatoes for squash in this classic cheesy casserole dish.

Makes 6 servings

4 cups dehydrated sliced zucchini
1 cup dehydrated sliced onions
6 cups boiling water
1 cup shredded mozzarella cheese
3 large eggs
¼ cup milk

1. Preheat the oven to 350°F.
2. In a large bowl, combine the zucchini and onions. Pour the boiling water over and let soak for 10 minutes.
3. Drain off any remaining water and pour the zucchini and onions into a 10-inch square baking dish. Sprinkle over the cheese and lightly toss with the vegetables.
4. In a small bowl, beat the eggs and milk together. Pour over the vegetables and bake until golden brown on top, about 45 minutes.

Zucchini and Feta Casserole

Give your zucchini a taste of the Mediterranean with this casserole.

Makes 8 servings

> 5 cups boiling water
> 3 cups dehydrated shredded zucchini
> 1 cup milk
> ½ cup grated Parmesan cheese
> 2 tablespoons butter, melted
> 2 large eggs
> 2 tablespoons crushed dehydrated parsley
> 1 tablespoon all-purpose flour
> 1 tablespoon crumbled dehydrated red chile pepper
> 2 teaspoons crushed dehydrated marjoram
> ½ cup crumbled feta cheese

1. Preheat the oven to 350°F. Spray a 10-inch baking dish with cooking spray.
2. In a large heatproof bowl, pour the boiling water over the zucchini, cover, and let sit for 15 minutes to rehydrate. Drain off any extra water (but do not press or squeeze the zucchini).
3. Arrange the zucchini in the baking dish.
4. In a medium bowl, whisk the milk, Parmesan, butter, eggs, parsley, flour, red pepper, and marjoram together until smooth and pour over the zucchini. Sprinkle the feta on top and bake until golden brown on top, 35 to 40 minutes.

Breaded Tarragon and Plum Tomato Zucchini

A must-try!

Makes 4 servings

> 2 cups dehydrated sliced zucchini
> 4 cups boiling water
> 2 tablespoons olive oil
> 1 recipe Tarragon and Plum Tomato Breadcrumbs (page 156)

1. Place the zucchini in a large bowl and pour the boiling water over. Cover and let sit 15 to 20 minutes to rehydrate. Drain off any remaining water and set the zucchini on paper towels.
2. Preheat the oven to 350°F. Spray a cookie sheet with cooking oil.
3. Working with one slice of zucchini at a time, lightly rub the oil on both sides, dip into the breadcrumbs, coating completely, and set on the cookie sheet. Don't overlap the slices.
4. Bake until golden brown, about 30 minutes. If you'd like them extra crisp, put them under a low broiler for the last 5 to 7 minutes of cooking time.

Instant Sweet Potatoes for One

Easy mashed sweet potatoes in no time! You can double the recipe.

Makes 1 serving

> 1 cup dehydrated mashed sweet potatoes
> 1 cup boiling water
> Butter to taste
> Salt and black pepper to taste

1. In a microwave-safe bowl, combine the dehydrated sweet potatoes and boiling water, cover, and let sit for 15 minutes to rehydrate.
2. Stir the potatoes, then microwave on HIGH until hot, about 2 minutes. Add butter, salt, and pepper and enjoy!

Sweet Potato, Apple, and Walnut Bake

Crunchy sweet potatoes so good they could be a dessert.

Makes 4 servings

> 1 cup dehydrated sliced sweet potatoes
> 1 cup dehydrated chopped apples
> 1 tablespoon dehydrated chopped dates
> 3 cups boiling water
> ½ cup firmly packed brown sugar
> ½ cup ground walnuts (do this in a food processor, not a blender)
> 2 tablespoons butter

1. In a large heatproof bowl, combine the dehydrated sweet potatoes, apples, and dates and pour the boiling water over. Cover and let sit until the water has cooled. Do not drain.
2. Preheat the oven to 350° F. Spray an 8-inch square baking dish with cooking spray.
3. Add the brown sugar, walnuts, and butter to the rehydrated fruit and stir until well combined. Pour into the baking dish and bake until golden brown, about 50 minutes.

Spiced Sweet Potato-Orange Bake

Spicy and sweet make this dish both naughty and nice.

Makes 10 servings

> 6 cups dehydrated sliced sweet potatoes
> ½ cup firmly packed brown sugar
> 1 quart (4 cups) orange juice
> 3 cups water
> 2 tablespoons ground cinnamon
> ½ teaspoon ground nutmeg
> ½ cup (1 stick) unsalted butter

1. Preheat the oven to 350°F.
2. Combine all the ingredients in a large saucepan and bring to a boil, stirring to combine well. Remove the pan from heat and let sit for 10 minutes. Stir, then pour the contents into a 10-inch square deep-dish baking dish, cover, and bake for 50 minutes.
3. Uncover and bake for another 10 minutes to brown the top.

Crispy Vegetable Cakes

These crunchy veggie cakes are a great side dish but you can also serve them as an appetizer, topped with a dollop of cold sour cream.

Makes 6 servings

> ½ cup dehydrated shredded potatoes
> ½ cup dehydrated shredded zucchini
> 2 cups boiling water
> 2 cups dry Italian-seasoned breadcrumbs
> 1 large egg, beaten
> 2 tablespoons milk
> ¼ cup olive oil

1. In a medium heatproof bowl, combine the dehydrated potatoes and zucchini and pour the boiling water over. Cover and let soak for 15 minutes. Drain off any remaining water.
2. Add the breadcrumbs, egg, and milk and stir until well combined.
3. In a large skillet, heat the oil over medium-high heat. Using a tablespoon, drop the mixture into the hot oil and press down with a metal spatula to flatten. Cook until the bottom is golden brown and crispy, then flip and cook the other side.

Garden Tabbouleh

A tasty way to make use of your dehydrated garden harvest.

Makes 8 servings

½ cup dehydrated chopped tomatoes
¼ cup dehydrated chopped onions
¼ cup dehydrated chopped green bell pepper
¼ cup dehydrated chopped yellow bell pepper
¼ cup dehydrated chopped parsley
1¼ cups bulgur
¼ cup lemon juice
3 tablespoons olive oil
4½ cups boiling water
1 (16-ounce) can red kidney beans (drained and rinsed)
1 cup small cubes feta cheese (optional)
½ cup pine nuts

1. In a large heatproof bowl, combine the dehydrated ingredients, bulgur, lemon juice, and oil. Pour the boiling water over and cover. Let cool to room temperature, then refrigerate overnight.
2. Stir in the beans, feta (if using), and pine nuts just before serving.

Ready-to-Make Classic Bread Stuffing

With this stuffing base in your pantry, you can cook up a tasty dressing any time! Just toss with the wet ingredients, pour into a baking dish, and into the oven it goes!

Makes 12 servings

Stuffing Base

9 cups dehydrated bread cubes
¼ cup dehydrated chopped celery
¼ cup dehydrated chopped onions
2 tablespoons poultry seasoning
2 tablespoons dehydrated parsley
1 tablespoon dehydrated sage
1 tablespoon dehydrated thyme
1 tablespoon salt
1 tablespoon black pepper

To Finish

½ cup (1 stick) butter, melted
2 large eggs, beaten
4 cups chicken broth

1. In a large bowl, toss the dry ingredients together until well combined. At this point, you can place it in a ziptop plastic bag with an oxygen pack.
2. When ready to prepare, preheat the oven to 375°F.
3. Add the melted butter to the stuffing mixture and toss to evenly coat, then add the eggs and toss to coat again. Stir in the broth. Pour the mixture into a 9 x 13-inch deep-dish casserole pan and bake until an instant-read thermometer inserted in the center registers 165°F.

Rosemary Apple Stuffing with Grapes and Walnuts

A sweet and savory stuffing that's perfect served with chicken or pork.

Makes 10 servings

> 4 cups chicken broth
> 2 cups water
> 2 cups dehydrated chopped apples
> ½ cup dehydrated grapes
> ¼ cup dehydrated chopped celery
> 1 teaspoon dehydrated rosemary, crushed
> 1 teaspoon dehydrated lemon zest
> 3 tablespoons butter, melted
> 8 cups dehydrated cubed white bread
> ¼ cup finely chopped walnuts

1. Preheat the oven to 350°F. Spray a 9 x 13-inch baking dish with cooking spray.
2. In a large pot, bring the broth and water to a boil. Remove from the heat, add the dehydrated apples, grapes, celery, rosemary, and lemon zest, stir to combine, cover, and let sit for 15 to 20 minutes to rehydrate.
3. Stir in the butter. Add the bread cubes and walnuts and toss until everything is thoroughly combined.
4. Pour into the baking dish and bake until the top is golden brown, about 1 hour.

Spiced Apple Stuffing

Makes 8 servings

> 1 recipe Spiced Holiday Bread Cubes (page 155)
> ½ cup (1 stick) butter, melted
> 2 large eggs
> 2 cups vegetable or chicken broth
> 1 cup water
> 2 cups dehydrated sliced green apples with peels, each cut in half

1. Preheat the oven to 375°F.
2. In a large bowl, toss the bread cubes and melted butter together until well combined. Add the eggs and toss again to combine. Add the broth and water and stir until well mixed. Stir in the dehydrated apples.
3. Pour into a 10-inch square baking dish and bake until an instant-read thermometer inserted in the center registers 165°F, 45 to 55 minutes.

Tomato-Garlic Stuffing

Makes 8 servings

> 1 recipe Italian-Style Tomato-Garlic Bread Cubes (page 154)
> ½ cup (1 stick) butter, melted
> 2 large eggs, beaten
> 3 cups vegetable or chicken broth

1. Preheat the oven to 375°F.
2. In a large bowl, toss the bread cubes and melted butter together until well combined. Add the eggs and toss again to combine. Add the broth and stir until well mixed.
3. Pour into a 10-inch square baking dish and bake until an instant-read thermometer inserted in the center registers 165°F, about 45 minutes.

Zucchini Bread Stuffing

The dehydrator is a great way to make the best use of a glut of zucchini from the garden. Make sure to dehydrate shredded as well as sliced zucchini—then making this delicious stuffing will be a snap!

Makes 6 servings

> 4 cups chicken or vegetable broth
> 3 cups water
> 2 cups dehydrated shredded zucchini
> ¼ cup dehydrated chopped onions
> 2 tablespoons dehydrated parsley
> 3 tablespoons butter
> 6 cups dehydrated bread cubes
> 1 large egg, beaten

1. In a large saucepan, bring the broth and water to a boil. Stir in the dehydrated zucchini, onions, and parsley and the butter. Cover and let soak for 15 to 20 minutes.
2. Preheat the oven to 350°F. Spray a 10-inch square baking dish with cooking spray.
3. Stir in the bread cubes and egg until well combined. Transfer the mixture to the baking dish and bake until golden brown on top, 35 to 40 minutes.

Spicy Pickles and Spicy Pickled Beets

Crunchy, spicy, and absolutely delicious!

Makes 2 quarts

> 5 cups water
> 2 cups distilled white vinegar
> 1 cup sugar
> 1 large dehydrated garlic slice
> ½ of a dehydrated chile pepper
> 6 black peppercorns
> 2 bay leaves
> 1½ teaspoons pickling salt
> 1½ cups dehydrated sliced cucumbers
> 1½ cups dehydrated sliced beets

1. In a large saucepan, combine the water, vinegar, and sugar. Break up the garlic and chile pepper and add to the pot, along with the peppercorns, bay leaves, and pickling salt. Bring to a rolling boil, stirring until the sugar dissolves. Reduce the heat to a simmer and cook for 5 minutes.
2. Put the dehydrated cucumbers in a sterilized 1-quart canning jar, the dehydrated beets in another (the cucumbers and beets should

CANNING SALT

Canning salt or pickling salt is similar to table salt, but does not have the additives that turn pickles dark. If you can't find canning salt, it's fine to use table salt; the pickles will taste the same but they may not look as appetizing. Look for it in the supermarket where other canning goods are sold.

each only come about one third of the way up the jar). Pour the boiling brine into the jars, making sure to get some garlic, bay leaf, and peppercorns in each jar. Put the lids on, let cool, and then put in the refrigerator. The next morning the beets will be tender and the cucumbers crunchy. They will keep in the refrigerator for up to 2 years.

Bread and Butter Pickles

Sweet and tangy—the perfect sandwich pickle!

Makes 1 quart

1½ cups water
½ cup distilled white vinegar
½ cup sugar
½ teaspoon celery seeds
½ teaspoon mustard seed
¼ teaspoon turmeric
2 cups dehydrated sliced (¼ inch) cucumbers
2 tablespoons dehydrated chopped onions
2 tablespoons dehydrated chopped green bell peppers

1. In a small saucepan, combine the water, vinegar, sugar, celery and mustard seeds, and turmeric and bring to a rolling boil, stirring until the sugar dissolves.
2. Place the dehydrated cucumbers, onion, and bell pepper in a sterilized 1-quart canning jar. Pour the boiling brine over the top of the cucumbers until the jar is three quarters full. Put the lid on, let cool, and refrigerate overnight. In the morning, you'll have pickles. They will keep in the refrigerator for up to 2 years.

Dill Pickle Slices

These dill slices are the perfect crunchy addition to a sandwich or burger.

Makes 1 quart

1½ cups water
½ cup distilled white vinegar
2 tablespoons sugar
⅛ teaspoon pickling spice
1 dehydrated dill branch with seeds on it
2 dehydrated garlic slices, chopped
18 dehydrated lengthwise cucumber slices
¼ cup canning salt

1. In a small saucepan, combine the water, vinegar, sugar, pickling spice, dill, and garlic and bring to a rolling boil, stirring until the sugar dissolves.

2. Arrange the dehydrated cucumber slices in a sterilized 1-quart canning jar. Pour the boiling brine over the cucumbers. Put the lid on, let cool, and refrigerate for 24 hours.

3. Add the canning salt, shake the jar, and refrigerate for another hour before enjoying. They will keep in the refrigerator for up to 2 years.

Corn Relish

This is delicious served alongside any kind of grilled meat, or you can use it as a dip with tortilla chips.

Makes 4 cups

> 1 3/4 cups water
> 1/4 cup distilled white vinegar
> 1/2 cup sugar
> 3/4 cup dehydrated corn kernels
> 1/2 teaspoon celery seeds
> 1/2 teaspoon mustard seeds
> 1/2 teaspoon turmeric
> 1/4 cup dehydrated shredded cabbage
> 1/4 cup dehydrated chopped tomatoes
> 1/4 cup dehydrated sliced cucumbers, cut into small pieces with kitchen scissors
> 2 tablespoons dehydrated chopped onions
> 2 tablespoons dehydrated mixed chopped red and green bell peppers
> 1 teaspoon crushed dehydrated chile pepper

1. In a small saucepan, combine the water, vinegar, sugar, dehydrated corn, celery and mustard seeds, and turmeric and bring to a boil. Reduce the heat to low and simmer for 10 minutes.

2. Put the dehydrated cabbage, tomatoes, cucumbers, onions, bell peppers, and chile pepper in a sterilized 1-quart canning jar. Transfer the corn from the pan to the jar using a slotted spoon, then pour in the brine until the jar is three quarters of the way full. Put the lid on, let cool, and refrigerate for 24 hours. This will keep refrigerated for up to 1 month.

Corn and Bean Salad

This is delicious served as a side dish or offered as an appetizer with tortilla chips.

Makes 8 to 10 servings

> 2¼ cups water
> ½ cup distilled white vinegar
> ¼ cup sugar
> ½ cup dehydrated corn kernels
> ¼ cup dehydrated chopped celery
> ¼ cup dehydrated sliced onions
> ¼ cup dehydrated mixed chopped green and red bell peppers
> Pinch of crumbled dehydrated red chile pepper
> ¼ cup cooked black-eyed peas
> ¼ cup cooked black beans
> ¼ cup olive oil

1. In a small saucepan, bring the water, vinegar, and sugar to a rolling boil, stirring until the sugar is dissolved.
2. Place all the dehydrated ingredients in a sterilized 1-quart canning jar with a lid. Pour in the boiling vinegar mixture until the jar is three quarters of the way full. Put on the lid, let cool to room temperature, then refrigerate overnight.
3. Drain off the water, add the peas, beans, and oil, toss to combine, and serve. This salad will keep, tightly covered, in the refrigerator for up to 3 months.

Tomato Chutney

This is delicious spread on a grilled cheese sandwich, or enjoy it on the side with meatballs or a roast.

Makes 1 quart

> 1¾ cups water
> ¼ cup cider vinegar
> ⅓ cup firmly packed light brown sugar
> ⅛ teaspoon ground cloves
> ⅛ teaspoon ground cinnamon
> ⅛ teaspoon mustard seeds
> ⅛ teaspoon cayenne pepper
> ⅛ teaspoon ground allspice
> ⅛ teaspoon coarsely ground dehydrated ginger
> 1 cup dehydrated chopped tomatoes
> ½ cup dehydrated chopped apples
> ½ cup dehydrated grapes
> 2 tablespoons dehydrated chopped onions

1. In a small saucepan, combine the water, vinegar, brown sugar, and spices and bring to a rolling boil, stirring until the sugar dissolves.
2. Put the dehydrated tomatoes, apples, grapes, and onions in a sterilized 1-quart canning jar. Pour in the boiling brine until the jar is three quarters of the way full. Put on the lid, let cool, and refrigerate for 24 hours. The chutney will keep in the refrigerator for up to 2 weeks.

Cherry Salsa

Add pizzazz to chicken or pork with this sweet and sassy salsa.

Makes 2 ½ cups

> ½ cup dehydrated cherry halves
> ¼ cup dehydrated chopped yellow bell peppers
> 2 tablespoons dehydrated chopped onion
> 1 teaspoon coarsely ground dehydrated ginger
> 2 tablespoons distilled white vinegar
> 1 teaspoon sugar
> 2 cups boiling water

1. Put the dehydrated ingredients in a sterilized 1-quart canning jar. Add the vinegar and sugar, then pour in the boiling water. Stir, then put the lid on and let cool.
2. Shake the jar and refrigerate for 24 hours. The salsa will keep in the refrigerator for up to 2 weeks.

Basil-Balsamic Plum Salsa

A sweet salsa with a deep, rich flavor. Try it with chicken or duck.

Makes 2 ½ cups

> 1 cup dehydrated plum halves
> ¼ cup dehydrated chopped green onions
> 1 ½ teaspoons crushed dehydrated basil
> ¼ cup balsamic vinegar
> 2 cups boiling water

1. With kitchen scissors, cut the dehydrated plum halves into small pieces and put in a sterilized 1-quart canning jar along with the dehydrated green onions, basil, and vinegar. Pour in the boiling water, put the lid on, and let cool.
2. Shake the jar and refrigerate for 24 hours. The salsa will keep in the refrigerator for up to 2 weeks.

Minted Peach Salsa

This refreshing salsa is wonderful with fish but also tasty as a dip for tortilla chips.

Makes 3 cups

2 cups dehydrated sliced peaches
1 tablespoon dehydrated chopped green onions
1½ teaspoons crushed dehydrated peppermint
Pinch of crumbled dehydrated chile pepper
1 teaspoon sugar
2½ cups boiling water

1. With kitchen scissors, cut the dehydrated peach slices in quarters. Put the peaches, green onions, mint, chile pepper, and sugar in a sterilized 1-quart canning jar. Pour in the boiling water, stir, put the lid on, and let cool.
2. Shake the jar and refrigerate for 24 hours. The salsa will keep in the refrigerator for up to 2 weeks.

Pineapple-Cranberry Salsa

Sweet, tangy, and tart—perfect with chicken, turkey, or fish.

Makes 3 cups

1 cup dehydrated cubed pineapple, chopped
½ cup dehydrated cranberries, crushed
2 tablespoons dehydrated chopped green onions
¾ cup firmly packed brown sugar
3 cups water

1. In a medium saucepan, combine all the ingredients and bring to a boil, stirring until the brown sugar dissolves. Reduce the heat to medium-low and simmer for 3 to 5 minutes.
2. Ladle into a sterilized 1-quart canning jar, adding more boiling water if needed to cover the solids. Put on the lid, let cool, and refrigerate for 24 hours. The salsa will keep in the refrigerator for up to 2 weeks.

Tomato Salsa

There are two ways to use the dehydrator to make salsa: You can make the salsa from fresh ingredients and then dehydrate it into a leather (see page 98) that you can later reconstitute, or you can make salsa using ingredients from your dehydrated pantry. This is my go-to recipe for the second option.

Makes 3 cups

> 1½ cups dehydrated chopped tomatoes
> ½ cup dehydrated chopped green onions
> 2 tablespoons crushed dehydrated cilantro
> 4 dehydrated lime slices, crumbled
> 1 dehydrated chile pepper, crumbled
> ¼ teaspoon coarsely ground black pepper
> 2½ cups boiling water

1. Put the dehydrated ingredients and black pepper in a sterilized 1-quart canning jar. Pour in the boiling water, stir, put on the lid, and let cool.
2. Shake the jar and refrigerate for 24 hours. The salsa will keep in the refrigerator for up to 2 weeks.

18

Desserts

We all love dessert! No matter what's for dinner, it's just not complete if it's not followed by a little sweetness. This chapter will help you create delicious desserts your whole family will love. Adding dehydrated fruit can help you bring your desserts to the next level. Plus, we will show you how to sneak in some extra nutrition by adding veggies that will naturally sweeten your cakes and muffins. Shhh! Don't tell the kids!

Fast Leather Pastry Sticks

This is a fun cookie that kids can help with.

Makes 8 to 9 cookies

> 1 (9-inch) frozen pie crust, defrosted
> 1 tablespoon butter, softened.
> 2 fruit leathers of your choice (page 88)
> 1 tablespoon half-and-half
> 1 tablespoon sugar

1. Preheat the oven to 350°F.
2. On a lightly floured work surface, roll out the pie crust to a circle about 12 inches in diameter. Use a 3-inch cookie cutter to cut out circles as close together as possible. Lightly butter each circle.
3. Unroll the fruit leather. With kitchen scissors or a small cookie cutter, cut into circles slightly smaller than the pastry circles. Dip the cut leather circles into a small bowl of warm water for 5 seconds. Place a fruit leather circle on each pastry circle, roll it up

into a stick, and place on a large nonstick cookie sheet 1 inch apart. Brush the sticks lightly with the half-and-half, then sprinkle with sugar. Bake until golden brown, about 20 minutes. Let cool.

Very Snappy Ginger Cookies

I developed this recipe just for use with dehydrated ginger. If you make these cookies with store-bought ground ginger, they will be way too strong. If you like ginger cookies, please try these—dehydrated ginger has its own special flavor, which I think is far superior to store-bought.

Makes 24 cookies

2 ¼ cups all-purpose flour
2 teaspoons baking soda
1 teaspoon ground cinnamon
¾ cup (1½ sticks) butter, softened
1¼ cups plus ⅓ cup sugar
½ cup blackstrap molasses
1 large egg
1 tablespoon coarsely ground dehydrated ginger

1. Preheat the oven to 350°F. Spray a large cookie sheet with cooking spray.
2. In a medium bowl, combine the flour, baking soda, and cinnamon.
3. In a large bowl, beat the butter and 1¼ cups of the sugar together until creamy. Add the molasses, egg, and ginger and beat until smooth. Add the flour mixture in three additions, mixing well after each.
4. Roll the dough into 1-inch balls, then roll in the remaining ⅓ cup sugar to coat. Place on the cookie sheet 2 inches apart. Press down on each with the palm of your hand to make a thick disk. Bake until the edges are light golden brown, 10 to 12 minutes. Let cool on the cookie sheet for 5 minutes, then remove to a wire rack to cool completely. Store in an airtight container.

Stained Glass Fruit Leather Cookies

This is such an easy way to make beautiful holiday cookies.

Makes 18 cookies

1 cup (2 sticks) butter, softened
½ cup firmly packed light brown sugar
¼ cup granulated sugar
2 cups all-purpose flour
3 fruit leathers of your choice (page 88)
¼ cup confectioners' sugar

1. In a large bowl, beat the butter, brown sugar, and granulated sugar together until smooth. Add the flour in two additions, mixing well after each.

2. Form the dough into a ball, wrap in plastic, and refrigerate for 30 minutes to an hour.
3. Preheat the oven to 350°F.
4. Remove the dough from the refrigerator and roll the dough ⅛ inch thick on a lightly floured work surface. Using a cookie cutter, cut out the cookies. Re-roll any scraps and cut out more cookies. Take half of the cut outs and cut a circle or other design in each one (you can use a smaller cookies cutter to do this, if you like).
5. Lay the fruit leathers out flat. Using the same cookie cutter (or the larger one, if you're using two sizes), cut out shapes from the leather.
6. Place the uncut cookies on an ungreased cookie sheet. To assemble the cookies, dip one fruit leather cutout in warm water for 1 to 5 seconds, then place it on one of the cookie cutouts on the cookie sheet. Repeat with the other cutouts. When all of the fruit-leather cutouts have been positioned, set the remaining cookie dough cutouts (with the windows cut into them) on top of the fruit leather layer. Bake until light golden brown about the edges, about 15 minutes.
7. Let cool on the cookie sheet for 5 minutes, then remove to a wire rack, sprinkle with the confectioners' sugar, and let cool completely. Store in an airtight container.

Apple-Zucchini Cookies

The perfect (sneaky!) way to get your child to eat their vegetables!

Makes 36 cookies

> 2½ cups all-purpose flour
> 1 teaspoon baking soda
> 1 teaspoon cream of tartar
> 1½ cups confectioners' sugar
> ½ cup (1 stick) salted butter, softened
> 1 large egg
> ½ cup water
> ¼ cup applesauce
> 1 teaspoon vanilla extract
> ½ teaspoon almond extract
> ¾ cup dehydrated chopped apples (or dehydrated sliced apples, crushed)
> ½ cup dehydrated shredded zucchini

1. In a medium bowl, combine the flour, baking soda, and cream of tartar.
2. In a large bowl, beat the sugar and butter together until smooth. Beat in the egg until smooth. Add the water, applesauce, and extracts and beat until smooth. Add the flour mixture in two additions and mix well. Stir in the dehydrated apples and zucchini until mixed well. Cover and refrigerate for 2 hours.
3. Preheat the oven to 350°F. Line a cookie sheet with parchment paper or use a nonstick sheet.
4. Roll the dough into 1-inch balls and place 2 inches apart on the cookie sheet. Flatten each with the palm of your hand into a thick disk shape. Bake until slightly brown around the edges, about 8 minutes. Let cool on the cookie sheet for 5 minutes, then remove to a wire rack and let cool completely. Store in an airtight container.

Apple-Cranberry Oatmeal Cookies

Satisfy your sweet tooth with these chewy good cookies.

Makes 24 cookies

    1 cup dehydrated chopped apples
    ¼ cup dehydrated chopped cranberries
    1 cup boiling water
    1½ cups (3 sticks) butter
    1¾ cups all-purpose flour
    1½ cups rolled (old-fashioned) oats
    2½ teaspoons baking powder
    ½ teaspoon salt
    ⅔ cup firmly packed light brown sugar
    ⅔ cup granulated sugar
    ½ cup lemon juice
    1 large egg

1. In a heatproof medium bowl, combine the dehydrated apples and cranberries. Pour the boiling water over, cover, and let sit for 15 minutes to rehydrate. Do not pour off any remaining water. Add the butter while the mixture is still warm and stir to mix well.
2. Preheat the oven to 350°F. Spray a large cookie sheet with cooking spray.
3. In a large bowl, combine the flour, oats, baking powder, salt, and both sugars until well mixed. Add the lemon juice and egg and mix well. Add the apple-cranberry mixture and mix well. Using a teaspoon, drop the mixture onto the cookie sheet 2 inches apart. Bake until light golden brown around the edges, 12 to 15 minutes. Let cool on the cookie sheet for 5 minutes, then remove to a wire rack and let cool completely. Store in an airtight container.

Cranberry-Orange Sugar Cookies

These cookies are tart and delicious.

Makes 36 cookies

    1⅓ cups sugar
    2 tablespoons dehydrated orange zest, divided
    2 cups all-purpose flour
    1½ teaspoons baking powder
    ¼ teaspoon baking soda
    1 cup (2 sticks) butter, softened
    1 large egg
    2 tablespoons water
    ½ cup dehydrated chopped cranberries

1. Preheat the oven to 350°F. Spray a large cookie sheet with cooking spray.
2. In a small bowl, combine ⅓ cup of the sugar and 1 tablespoon of the dehydrated orange zest. Set aside.
3. In a medium bowl, combine the flour, baking powder, and baking soda. Set aside.
4. In a large bowl, beat the butter and remaining 1 cup of sugar together until creamy, then beat in the egg and water. Add the flour mixture in three additions, mixing well after each. Stir in the cranberries and remaining 1 tablespoon orange zest. Refrigerate the dough for 1 to 2 hours to firm up.
5. Roll the dough into 1-inch balls, then roll in the orange sugar to coat. Place on the cookie sheet 2 inches apart and press down on each lightly with the tines of a fork to flatten a little. Bake until light golden brown around the edges, 10 to 12 minutes. Remove the cookies to a wire rack to cool completely. Store in an airtight container.

Cranberry Swirl Refrigerator Cookies

These cookies have a beautifully bright color.

Makes 36 cookies

> 1½ cups all-purpose flour
> ¼ teaspoon baking soda
> ¼ teaspoon salt
> ½ cup (1 stick) butter, softened
> ¾ cup granulated sugar
> 1 large egg
> 1 teaspoon vanilla extract
> ½ cup dehydrated chopped cranberries
> 1 tablespoon dehydrated orange zest
> ½ cup boiling water
> ¼ cup firmly packed light brown sugar
> 2 teaspoons milk
> ½ cup chopped walnuts

1. In a small bowl, combine the flour, baking soda, and salt.
2. In a large bowl, mix the butter and granulated sugar together until smooth, then add the egg and vanilla and beat until smooth. Add the flour mixture in two additions, mixing well after each. The batter should pull away from bowl, forming a ball. Wrap with plastic and refrigerate for 1 hour.
3. In a small heatproof bowl, combine the cranberries and orange zest. Pour the boiling water over, cover, and let sit for 15 minutes to rehydrate. Drain off any remaining water and stir in the brown sugar, milk, and walnuts.

4. Roll the chilled dough on a floured work surface into a 10-inch square. Spread the cranberry filling evenly over the dough, right up to the edges, then roll it up. Place it seam-side down on a plate and refrigerate until firm, about 1 hour.

5. Preheat the oven to 350°F. Spray a large cookie sheet with cooking spray.

6. Cut the roll across into ¼-inch-thick slices and place on the cookie sheet 2 inches apart. Bake until the edges are a light golden brown, 12 to 15 minutes. Let cool on the cookie sheet for 5 minutes, then remove to a wire rack and let cool completely. Store in an airtight container.

Coconut-Cranberry Cookies

These chewy cookies are perfect for the macaroon lover.

Makes 32 cookies

> 2 ¼ cups all-purpose flour
> 1 teaspoon baking powder
> 1 cup (2 sticks) butter, softened
> 1 cup sugar
> 1 large egg
> 2 teaspoons almond extract
> ½ cup dehydrated shredded coconut, finely chopped in a blender or food processor
> ¼ cup dehydrated cranberries, crushed

1. Preheat the oven to 350°F. Spray a large cookie sheet with cooking spray.

2. In a small bowl, combine the flour and baking powder.

3. In a large bowl, beat the butter and sugar together until smooth. Add the egg and almond extract and beat until smooth. Add the flour mixture in three additions, mixing well after each. Stir in the coconut and cranberries.

4. Using a teaspoon, place 1-inch pieces of dough on the cookie sheet 3 inches apart. Bake until light golden brown around the edges, about 15 minutes. Let cool on the cookie sheet for 5 minutes, then remove to a wire rack and let cool completely. Store in an airtight container.

Hawaiian Cookies

The warm flavors of Hawaii are combined to make this beautiful and flavorful cookie.

Makes 24 cookies

2½ cups all-purpose flour
1 teaspoon baking soda
1 teaspoon cream of tartar
1½ cups confectioners' sugar
½ cup (1 stick) butter, softened
1 teaspoon vanilla extract
½ teaspoon almond extract
1 large egg
1 cup water
¾ cup dehydrated steamed sliced pineapple, cut into small pieces with kitchen scissors
½ cup dehydrated shredded coconut
½ cup dehydrated maraschino cherries

1. In a medium bowl, combine the flour, baking soda, and cream of tartar.
2. In a large bowl, beat the confectioners' sugar and butter together until smooth. Add the extracts and beat until smooth. Add the egg and beat until smooth. Add the water and beat until smooth. Add the dehydrated pineapple, coconut, and maraschino cherries and stir to combine well. Cover and refrigerate for about 2 hours (this firms up the dough and allows the pineapple and coconut to rehydrate).
3. Preheat the oven to 350°F. Line a cookie sheet with parchment paper (or use a nonstick pan).
4. Roll the chilled dough into 1-inch balls and place on the cookie sheet 2 inches apart. Bake until the bottoms and tops of the cookies start to brown, about 8 minutes. Let cool on the cookie sheet for 5 minutes, then remove to a wire rack and let cool completely. Store in an airtight container.

Pumpkin Spice Cookies

These cookies have all the flavors of pumpkin pie—it's the ultimate fall cookie!

Makes 44 cookies

  1 cup hot water
  1/3 cup powdered dehydrated pumpkin
  1 3/4 cups sugar
  2 teaspoons ground cinnamon
  2 3/4 cups all-purpose flour
  2 teaspoons cream of tartar
  1 teaspoon baking soda
  1/4 teaspoon salt
  1/2 cup (1 stick) salted butter, softened
  1/2 cup vegetable shortening
  2 large eggs

1. In a small heatproof bowl, combine the hot water and powdered pumpkin, stirring well to combine. Cover and let sit 15 to 20 minutes to rehydrate into a thick puree.
2. In a small bowl, combine 1/4 cup of the sugar and the cinnamon. In a medium bowl, combine the flour, cream of tartar, baking soda, and salt.
3. In a large bowl, beat the remaining 1 1/2 cups sugar, the butter, and shortening together until smooth. Add the eggs one at a time, beating well after each one. Add the flour mixture in three additions, mixing well after each. Add the rehydrated pumpkin puree and mix well to combine. Refrigerate the dough for 20 to 30 minutes (this will make it easier to work with and create a nice round cookie).
4. Preheat oven to 375°F. Line a cookie sheet with parchment paper or use a nonstick sheet.
5. Roll the dough into 1-inch balls, then roll the balls in the cinnamon sugar to coat. Place them on the cookie sheet 2 inches apart. Press down on each with the palm of your hand into a thick disk shape. Bake until slightly brown around the edges, about 10 minutes. Let cool on the cookie sheet for 5 minutes, then remove to a wire rack and let cool completely. Store in an airtight container.

Cherry-Almond Bars

A wholesome way to satisfy your sweet tooth.

Makes 24 bars

> 1 cup dehydrated cherries, cut into small pieces with kitchen scissors
> ¼ cup boiling water
> 1 cup sliced almonds
> 2 cups all-purpose flour
> 2 teaspoons baking powder
> 2 cups firmly packed brown sugar
> ¾ cup (1½ sticks) butter, softened
> 2 large eggs
> ½ teaspoon almond extract
> ½ cup semisweet chocolate chips
> 1 teaspoon vegetable shortening

1. In a small heatproof bowl, combine the dehydrated cherries and boiling water, cover, and let sit for 10 minutes to rehydrate; do not drain any remaining water.
2. Preheat the oven to 350°F. Spray a 9 x 12-inch baking pan with cooking spray.
3. In a small bowl, combine the flour and baking powder.
4. In a large bowl, using an electric mixer, beat together the brown sugar and butter until smooth. Add the eggs one at a time, beating well after each one. Beat in the almond extract. Add the flour mixture and beat until smooth, about 2 minutes. Fold in the cherries with any remaining soaking water. Fold in the almonds. Pour the batter into the baking pan. Bake until golden brown on top, 30 to 35 minutes.
5. Meanwhile, melt the chocolate chips and shortening together in the microwave. Stir until smooth.
6. Remove the pan from the oven and drizzle the chocolate over the top in an attractive design. Let cool completely on a wire rack. Cut into 2¼ x 2-inch bars.

Lemon Bars

These tart and rich lemon bars make a wonderful summertime treat.

Makes 12 bars

> 1 cup all-purpose flour
> ¼ cup confectioners' sugar, plus more for dusting
> ½ teaspoon baking powder
> ¼ teaspoon salt
> ½ cup (1 stick) salted butter
> ¼ cup water
> 1 teaspoon powdered dehydrated sliced lemons
> 10 dehydrated lemon slices with the peel on
> 1 cup granulated sugar
> 2 large eggs

1. Preheat the oven to 350°F.
2. In a medium bowl, stir together the flour, confectioners' sugar, baking powder, and salt. Beat in the butter until smooth. Press the mixture evenly into an ungreased 9-inch square baking pan. Bake until slightly brown and firm, 15 to 20 minutes. Remove from the oven and set aside.
3. In a small bowl, whisk together the water and lemon powder and set aside, stirring occasionally.
4. Take the dehydrated lemon slices and crush or break to the desired size (the size of lemon pieces that you want visible in your lemon bars).
5. In a medium bowl, whisk the granulated sugar and eggs together (or use an electric mixer) until smooth and fluffy. Whisk or beat in the lemon water, then stir in the lemon pieces. Pour the mixture evenly over the crust. Bake until the lemon filling is firm to the touch, 20 to 25 minutes.
6. Remove from the oven and let cool completely on a wire rack. Cut into 2¼ inch x 3-inch bars, and dust with confectioners' sugar, if you like.

Crumb Plum Bars

These bars are always a hit with our friends and family. The plums can be swapped out for dehydrated apples or peaches.

Makes 12 bars

Crust

1½ cups all-purpose flour
½ cup confectioners' sugar
¼ cup granulated sugar
½ teaspoon salt
⅔ cup butter

Plum filling

16 dehydrated plum halves
1½ cups boiling water
2 tablespoons lemon juice
2 teaspoons cornstarch
½ teaspoon baking powder
1 large egg

1. Preheat the oven to 350°F. Spray a 10-inch square baking pan with cooking spray.
2. In a medium bowl, combine the flour, both sugars, and salt. Cut the butter in until the mixture is crumbly. Remove ⅔ cup of the crumble and set aside. Press the remaining crumble evenly in the bottom of the baking pan. Bake for 10 to 12 minutes (the crust will be half cooked at this point).
3. Combine the plums and boiling water in a heatproof medium bowl, cover, and let sit for 15 minutes to rehydrate; do not drain. Stir the remaining ingredients into the plum mixture. Transfer to a food processor and process for 1 minute into a rough puree. Pour evenly over the hot crust.
4. Sprinkle the reserved crumble evenly over the plum filling and bake until golden brown and the top springs back when touched, about 30 minutes. Remove from the oven and let cool completely on a wire rack. Cut into 2¼ x 3⅓-inch bars.

Toasted Coconut and Raspberry Bars

An easy-to-prepare recipe that is sure to delight your entire family.

Makes 12 bars

> 2 raspberry leathers (page 89)
> ⅔ cup boiling water
> ¾ cup (1½ sticks) butter, softened
> ⅓ cup plus ¼ cup sugar
> 1 large egg, separated
> 1⅔ cups all-purpose flour, sifted
> 2 large egg whites
> ½ cup dehydrated shredded coconut, finely chopped in a blender or food processor

1. In a small bowl, combine the leathers and boiling water, cover, and let sit for 15 minutes to rehydrate.
2. Preheat the oven to 350°F. Spray a 9-inch square baking pan with cooking spray.
3. In a medium bowl, beat the butter and ⅓ cup sugar together until creamy. Beat in the egg yolk until well combined. Stir in the flour until a soft ball of dough forms. Press the dough into the bottom of the baking pan. Set aside.
4. Stir the leathers and soaking water together until thick. Spread over the dough in the pan.
5. In a clean bowl, using an electric mixer, beat the two egg whites on high speed, slowly adding the remaining ¼ cup sugar as you beat. Continue to beat until soft peaks form. Spread the meringue over the raspberry filling, sprinkle with the coconut, and bake until the meringue topping is golden brown, about 25 minutes. Remove from the oven, let cool completely on a wire rack, and cut into 2 x 3-inch bars.

Apricot-Date Bars

Easy to make and loaded with fruit, coconut, and walnuts.

Makes 24 bars

> 1½ cups dehydrated apricot halves, cut into small pieces with kitchen scissors
> 3 cups water
> 1 tablespoon lemon juice
> 2 cups all-purpose flour
> ¼ teaspoon baking powder
> 1 cup sugar
> ¾ cup (1½ sticks) butter
> 1 large egg
> ½ teaspoon almond extract
> 1⅓ cups dehydrated shredded coconut
> ½ cup walnut pieces, chopped

1. Place the apricots, water, and lemon juice in a medium saucepan, bring to boil, cover, reduce the heat to a simmer, and cook until thick, 15 to 20 minutes, stirring occasionally. Remove from the heat and let cool a little bit.
2. Preheat the oven to 350°F. Spray a 9 x 12-inch baking pan with cooking spray.
3. In a small bowl, combine the flour and baking powder.
4. In a large bowl, beat the sugar and butter together until smooth. Add the egg and almond extract and beat until smooth. Add the flour mixture in two additions, mixing well. Stir in the coconut and walnuts. Press three quarters of the mixture evenly over the bottom of the baking pan. Spread the apricot mixture evenly over the crust. Crumble the remaining flour-and-coconut mixture and sprinkle that evenly over the apricot layer. Bake until golden brown, about 35 minutes.
5. Remove from the oven and let cool completely on a wire rack. Cut into 2¼ x 2-inch bars.

Oatmeal Date Bars

These classic oatmeal date bars are easy to make and a wonderful treat.

Makes 36 bars

> 2½ cups water
> 2 cups dehydrated chopped dates
> ¼ cup granulated sugar
> ⅓ cup walnuts, crushed (you can do this with a rolling pin)
> 1½ cups quick-cooking oats
> 1¼ cups all-purpose flour
> 1 cup firmly packed brown sugar
> 1 teaspoon salt
> ½ teaspoon baking soda
> ½ cup (1 stick) butter
> 1 tablespoon water

1. Preheat the oven to 350°F. Spray a 9 x 13-inch baking pan with cooking spray.
2. Combine the water, dates, and granulated sugar in a medium saucepan and simmer over medium heat, stirring frequently, until the mixture is thick. Stir in the walnuts and let cool.
3. In a large bowl, combine the oats, flour, brown sugar, salt, and baking soda. Cut the butter into the mixture until crumbly. Sprinkle over the water and mix in.
4. Press half of the oat mixture into the bottom the baking pan. Spread the date mixture over the oat layer. Sprinkle the remaining oat mixture over the date filling, covering it completely. Gently press down on the oat layer.
5. Bake until light golden brown around edges, about 40 minutes. Set the pan on a wire rack and let cool completely; cut into 2¼ x 1½-inch bars.

Banana-Raisin Oat Bars

These make a great snack or even breakfast-on-the-go.

Makes24 bars

> 1 cup honey
> ½ cup (1 stick) salted butter
> 2 cup rolled (old-fashioned) oats
> ½ cup dehydrated banana slices
> ½ cup dehydrated grapes

1. Preheat the oven to 375°F. Spray a 10-inch square baking pan with cooking spray.
2. Stir the honey and butter together in a medium saucepan over low heat until the butter is melted and the mixture blended.
3. Stir in the oats, bananas, and grapes. Press the mixture evenly over the bottom of the baking dish. Bake until golden brown, 25 to 30 minutes. Remove from the oven and let cool completely on a wire rack. Cut into bars.

Apricot-Oat Bars

This is a wonderful heart-healthy choice for snacking.

Makes 12 bars

> 1 cup dehydrated apricot halves, cut into small pieces with kitchen scissors
> ¾ cup (1½ sticks) butter
> ½ cup sugar
> ¼ cup honey
> 2½ cups rolled (old-fashioned) oats
> 2 teaspoons sesame seeds

1. Preheat the oven to 350°F. Spray a 10-inch square baking pan with cooking spray.
2. Combine the apricots, butter, sugar, and honey in a large saucepan and cook over low heat, stirring, until the butter has melted and everything is well combined; do not let boil. Remove from the stove and stir in the oats and sesame seeds.
3. Press the mixture evenly over the bottom of the baking pan. Bake until golden brown on top, 20 to 25 minutes. Remove from the oven, let cool completely on a wire rack, and cut into 2 x 4-inch bars.

Sweet Potato Brownies

These rich, chocolaty brownies are supermoist and delicious with or without the frosting.

Makes 16 brownies

> 1½ cups boiling water
> 1 cup dehydrated sliced sweet potatoes
> 1 cup all-purpose flour
> ½ cup natural unsweetened cocoa powder
> 1 tablespoon ground cinnamon
> 1 teaspoon baking powder
> ¼ teaspoon salt
> 4 large eggs
> ¼ cup vegetable oil
> 2 teaspoons vanilla extract
> ½ cup honey
> Pumpkin Cream Cheese Frosting (recipe follows)

1. Preheat the oven to 350°F. Spray a 9-inch square nonstick baking pan with cooking spray.
2. Pour the boiling water over the sweet potato slices in a medium heatproof bowl, cover, and let sit 15 to 20 minutes to rehydrate. Do not drain off any remaining water.
3. In a small bowl, combine the flour, cocoa, cinnamon, baking powder, and salt.
4. In a large bowl, whisk together the eggs, oil, and vanilla until smooth. Add the flour mixture and mix until well combined. Add the honey to the bowl with the sweet potatoes and any remaining water and whisk until smooth. Add to the batter and stir until well blended.
5. Pour the batter into the baking pan and spread to fill evenly. Bake until a toothpick inserted in the middle comes out clean, about 30 minutes. Remove from the oven and let cool completely on a wire rack before spreading the frosting over the top, if using. Cut into 2¼-inch squares.

Pumpkin Cream Cheese Frosting

Spread this on top of the brownies for an extra treat, or place it in a pastry bag and make decorative designs on the individual brownies.

Makes 2 cups

> ¾ cup boiling water
> ¼ cup powdered dehydrated pumpkin
> 1 tablespoon sugar
> ½ teaspoon ground cinnamon
> ½ teaspoon pumpkin pie spice
> 1 (8-ounce) package cream cheese, softened

1. In a medium bowl, whisk together the water and powdered pumpkin, cover, and let sit for 15 minutes to rehydrate into a thick puree.
2. Whisk the sugar and spices into the pumpkin, then beat in the cream cheese until well combined and the frosting is smooth.

Dehydrated Fruitcake

A holiday favorite, this fruitcake is packed with a delicious combination of fruits and nuts.

Makes one 8-inch cake; 10 servings

2 1/3 cups dehydrated green grapes
1 1/2 cups dehydrated red grapes
3/4 cup dehydrated apricot halves, cut into small pieces with kitchen scissors
2/3 cup dehydrated chopped dates
1/3 cup dehydrated maraschino cherries
2 tablespoons dehydrated orange zest
1 cup orange juice
1 cup (2 stick) butter, softened
1 cup firmly packed brown sugar
1/4 cup blackstrap molasses
4 large eggs
1/2 cup chopped blanched almonds
1 2/3 cups all-purpose flour
1 tablespoon coarsely ground dehydrated ginger
1 teaspoon ground allspice

1. In a large bowl, combine the dehydrated grapes, apricots, dates, cherries, and orange zest and orange juice. Cover and refrigerate overnight to rehydrate, stirring a few times.
2. Preheat the oven to 300°F. Spray the bottom and sides of an 8-inch cake pan with 3-inch sides with cooking spray. Line the bottom and sides with parchment paper and spray again.
3. In a large bowl, beat the butter and brown sugar together until creamy. Beat in the molasses, then beat in the eggs, one at a time, beating well after each. Stir in the fruit and any remaining orange juice, the almonds, flour, and spices and mix well.
4. Pour the batter into the cake pan and bake until the cake pulls away from the pan, about 2 1/2 hours. Let cool on a wire rack for 1 hour before removing the cake from the pan.

Date Cake with Caramel Sauce

This moist, rich cake is topped with deliciously sticky caramel sauce.

Makes one 8-inch cake; 10 servings

Cake

> 1 cup dehydrated chopped dates
> ½ cup dehydrated grapes
> 1 teaspoon baking soda
> 3 cups boiling water
> 2 tablespoons butter
> 2 large eggs
> 1 cup firmly packed light brown sugar
> 1 tablespoon dehydrated orange zest
> 1⅔ cups all-purpose flour
> 2½ teaspoons baking powder

Caramel Sauce

> 1 cup firmly packed light brown sugar
> ¾ cup heavy cream
> 2 tablespoons butter

1. Preheat the oven to 350°F. Spray an 8-inch cake pan with 3-inch sides with cooking spray.
2. In a medium heatproof bowl, combine the dates, dehydrated grapes, and baking soda and pour the boiling water over. Cover and let sit for 15 minutes to rehydrate. Drain off any remaining water.
3. In a large bowl, beat the butter, eggs, brown sugar, and orange zest together until smooth. Add the flour and baking powder and mix until well blended. Fold the dates and raisins into the batter. Pour the batter into the cake pan, spreading it evenly. Bake until golden brown and the center springs back when pushed down, about 40 minutes. Let cool on a wire rack before removing the cake from the pan.
4. Make the sauce. Heat the brown sugar, cream, and butter together in a small saucepan over medium-low heat, stirring, until thick and creamy.
5. Serve the cake slightly warm or at room temperature with a spoonful of the warm sauce drizzled over each slice.

Chocolate-Beet Bundt Cake

Naturally sweet, beets are often processed into sugar. Here their sweetness marries wonderfully with the richness of the chocolate, resulting in a deeply delicious dessert. Experiment with different ways to gild this lily—powdered sugar, chocolate drizzle, or cherries with syrup (pie filling).

Makes one 10-inch Bundt cake; 16 servings

⅓ cup powdered dehydrated beets
1 cup boiling water
2¼ cups all-purpose flour
⅔ cup natural unsweetened cocoa powder
1¼ teaspoons baking soda
1 teaspoon salt
¼ teaspoon baking powder
1⅔ cups sugar
¾ cup vegetable shortening
2 large eggs
1 teaspoon vanilla extract
1½ cups water

1. Preheat the oven to 350°F. Spray a 10-inch Bundt cake pan with cooking spray.
2. In a small heatproof bowl, whisk together the beet powder and boiling water, cover, and let sit 15 to 20 minutes to rehydrate into a thick puree, stirring occasionally.
3. In a medium bowl, combine the flour, cocoa, baking soda, salt, and baking powder.
4. In a large bowl, beat together the sugar and shortening until smooth. Beat in the eggs, one at a time, beating well after each. Beat in the vanilla. Alternate mixing in the flour mixture and water in several additions. Add the beet mixture and stir until well blended. Pour the batter into the Bundt pan and bake until a toothpick inserted in the center comes out clean, 40 to 45 minutes. Let cool on a wire rack for 15 minutes, then invert the pan onto a serving plate to remove the cake. Serve slightly warm or at room temperature.

Variations: For a quicker version you can use your favorite chocolate cake or devil's food cake mix (prepare it as directed on the package) and stir in the beet mixture along with the wet ingredients called for. You can also make it as a layer cake. Divide the batter evenly between two 8-inch layer cake pans and adjust the baking time accordingly. Frost with your favorite icing.

Peach Upside-Down Cake

Peaches take the place of pineapple in this new twist on upside-down cake.

Makes one 10-inch cake; 10 servings

5 tablespoons butter
¼ cup firmly packed brown sugar
2 cups dehydrated peaches, rehydrated in 3 cups water overnight in the refrigerator and drained
16 dehydrated cherries
1½ cups all-purpose flour
2 teaspoons baking powder
¼ teaspoon salt
⅔ cup granulated sugar
¼ cup cream cheese, softened
1 large egg
1 large egg white
1 (6-ounce) can pineapple juice
1 teaspoon vanilla extract

1. Preheat the oven to 350°F.
2. Melt 2 tablespoons of the butter in a 10-inch cast-iron skillet over medium heat, tilting to coat the bottom of the pan completely with the melted butter. Sprinkle the brown sugar evenly in the skillet. Remove from the heat. Arrange the peach slices over the bottom of the pan. Arrange the cherries around the peach slices. Set the skillet aside.
3. In a small bowl, combine the flour, baking powder, and salt. In a large bowl, beat the granulated sugar, cream cheese, and remaining 3 tablespoons butter with an electric mixer at medium speed for 3 minutes. Add the whole egg and egg white and beat well. Add the flour mixture to the egg mixture alternately with the pineapple juice, beginning and ending with the flour mixture; mix well after each addition. Stir in the vanilla. Spoon the batter into the center of the skillet and gently spread it over the fruit.
4. Bake until the cake springs back when lightly touched in the center, about 35 minutes. Remove from the oven and let cool on a wire rack for 10 minutes. Run a knife around the edge of the cake. Place a plate upside down on top of the skillet; invert onto the plate. Let stand 2 minutes before removing the pan. Serve warm.

Fruit Leather Jelly Roll Cake

This cake is sweet, with a light and fluffy cream middle.

Makes 8 servings

Cream cheese filling

1 (8-ounce) package cream cheese, softened
½ teaspoon almond extract
¼ cup heavy cream
¼ tablespoon confectioners' sugar
¼ teaspoon vanilla extract

Cake

6 large egg whites
1 teaspoon lemon juice
¼ teaspoon salt
¼ cup granulated sugar
½ cup all-purpose flour

Fruit filling

2 fruit leathers of your choice (page 88)
1 cup water
1 tablespoon lemon juice

Topping

2 tablespoons confectioners' sugar

1. In a small bowl, beat the cream cheese and almond extract together. In another small bowl, with an electric mixer, whip the heavy cream, confectioners' sugar, and vanilla together until soft peaks form. Fold into the cream cheese. Set aside.
2. Preheat the oven to 350°F. Line a 15 x 10-inch rimmed baking sheet with parchment paper.
3. In a large bowl, using an electric mixer, beat the egg whites, lemon juice, and salt on low speed until foamy. Slowly add the granulated sugar, turn the speed to high, and beat until soft peaks form. With the mixer on low, slowly blend in the flour. Pour the batter evenly over the baking sheet. Bake until the center springs back when pushed down, about 15 minutes. Remove from the oven and cover with a clean kitchen towel.
4. Combine the fruit leathers, water, and lemon juice in a small saucepan and bring to a boil, stirring constantly. Reduce the heat to a simmer and continue to simmer, stirring, until thick, about 2 minutes. Remove from the heat and let sit until the cake cools down enough so you can handle it.
5. Remove the towel from the cake and spread the cream cheese filling over it. Spread the fruit filling over the cream cheese filling. Very carefully roll up the cake from one of the short ends, removing the parchment paper as you roll. Wrap the roll in waxed or parchment paper, twisting the ends closed. Place seam-side down in the refrigerator and chill for an hour.
6. Sift the confectioners' sugar over the top, slice across into spirals, and serve.

Pineapple-Coconut Cupcakes

The flavors of your favorite tropical drink turned into your favorite sweet indulgence!

Makes 18 cupcakes

Cupcakes

1 cup boiling water
¼ cup dehydrated steamed cubed pineapple
½ cup granulated sugar
½ cup (1 stick) butter, softened
2 large eggs
1 cup all-purpose flour
1½ teaspoons baking powder

Frosting and toppings

½ cup (1 stick) butter, softened
½ cup cream cheese, softened
2¼ cups confectioners' sugar
1 cup dehydrated shredded coconut, finely chopped in a blender or food processor
¼ cup dehydrated chopped pineapple

1. Preheat the oven to 350°F. Line a regular-size muffin tin with 18 cupcake liners.
2. In a small heatproof bowl, combine the boiling water and dehydrated pineapple, cover, and let sit for 15 minutes to rehydrate. Drain off any remaining water.
3. In a medium bowl, beat the granulated sugar and butter together until smooth. Add the eggs, one at a time, beating well after each. Add the flour and baking powder and beat until smooth. Stir the pineapple into the batter. Spoon the batter evenly into the cupcake liners, filling them no more than three quarters full. Bake until the tops are golden brown, about 15 minutes. Remove from the oven and let cool in the tin on a wire rack.
4. Make the frosting. In a medium bowl, beat the butter and cream cheese together until smooth. Add the confectioners' sugar and beat until smooth. Place the coconut in a blender and chop into fine pieces. Pour into a small bowl.
5. Swirl the frosting on top of the cupcakes, then dip each one into the coconut and sprinkle with some of the chopped pineapple.

Pumpkin Cheesecake

What could be better than pumpkin pie and cheesecake? Pumpkin cheesecake!

Makes one 10-inch cheesecake; 10 servings

Crust

3 cups finely crushed graham cracker crumbs (about 20 whole crackers)

3 tablespoons light brown sugar

½ teaspoon ground cinnamon

½ cup (1 stick) salted butter, melted

Filling

2 cups boiling water

¼ cup powdered dehydrated pumpkin

3 (8-ounce) packages cream cheese, softened

3 large eggs

1 large egg yolk

¼ cup sour cream

1½ cups granulated sugar

1½ teaspoons pumpkin pie spice

2 tablespoons all-purpose flour

1 teaspoon vanilla extract

1. Preheat the oven to 350°F.
2. Make the crust. In a medium bowl, combine the graham cracker crumbs, brown sugar, and cinnamon. Add the melted butter and mix until thoroughly combined. Pour the mixture into a 10-inch springform pan and press evenly to cover the bottom. Set aside.
3. Make the filling. In a small heatproof bowl, combine the boiling water and powdered pumpkin, cover, and let sit for 15 minutes, stirring a few times, to rehydrate into a thick puree.
4. In a large bowl, beat the cream cheese until smooth. Add the rehydrated pumpkin puree, whole eggs, egg yolk, sour cream, granulated sugar, and pumpkin pie spice and beat until smooth. Add the flour and vanilla and beat until smooth. Pour the filling into the crust. Spread it out evenly with a rubber spatula. Bake until the filling is firm to the touch, about 1 hour.
5. Turn the oven off, crack open the door, and leave the cheesecake inside for 15 more minutes. Remove from the oven and let cool for 15 minutes. Cover with plastic wrap and refrigerate for 4 hours before removing the springform ring and serving.

Deep-Dish Apple Pie

There is nothing more comforting than warm apple pie, and now you can make it in a snap, with all the ingredients you need right at your fingertips.

Makes one 9-inch deep-dish pie; 8 servings

> 6 cups dehydrated sliced apples
> Boiling water
> 1 cup sugar, plus more for sprinkling on top
> 3 tablespoons cornstarch
> 1 tablespoon apple pie spice
> 1 cup water
> 2 (9-inch) pie crusts (store-bought or homemade)
> Milk

1. Place the dehydrated apples in a large heatproof bowl and fill with enough boiling water to completely cover them. Cover and let sit for 15 minutes to rehydrate. Drain the apples, reserving 1 cup of the soaking water.
2. Preheat the oven to 350°F.
3. In a small saucepan, whisk together the sugar, cornstarch, and apple pie spice. Add the water slowly, whisking constantly. Turn the heat to low and cook, stirring constantly, until the mixture is thick. Remove from the heat and let cool.
4. Fit one of the crusts into a 9-inch deep-dish pie plate. Arrange the apples in the crust, then pour the sugar-and-cornstarch mixture over. Set the other crust on top, trim the edges, and then seal the two crusts together, fluting the edge. Cut a few steam vents in the top crust and, if you like, decorate the top with pastry cutouts. Brush the top with a little milk and sprinkle with sugar. Bake until the crust is nicely browned and juice bubbles from the vents, about 40 minutes. Let the pie cool to room temperature before slicing.

Banana Cream Pie

Light, fluffy, and loaded with bananas.

Makes one 9-inch pie; 6 to 8 servings

> 1 (9-inch) pie crust (store-bought or homemade)
> 1 cup dehydrated sliced bananas
> 1 cup hot boiling water
> 1 tablespoon lemon juice
> ½ cup sugar
> ¼ cup cornstarch
> 4 large egg yolks
> 1 teaspoon vanilla extract
> 2 cups milk

1 cup heavy cream
1 tablespoon confectioners' sugar
1 teaspoon vanilla extract

1. Preheat the oven to 400°F.
2. Fit the pie crust into a 9-inch pie plate. Prick the bottom with a fork in several places. Fit a sheet of parchment paper inside and fill the crust with dried beans or pie weights. Bake for 15 minutes, remove from the oven, and let cool.
3. In a small heatproof bowl, combine the dehydrated bananas, boiling water, and lemon juice, cover, and let sit for 15 minutes to rehydrate.
4. In a small bowl, combine the sugar and cornstarch. Whisk the egg yolks and vanilla together in a medium saucepan. Add the sugar mixture and whisk until smooth. Whisking constantly, slowly pour in the milk. Cook over medium heat, whisking constantly, until the mixture thickens. Remove from the heat.
5. Drain the water from the bananas and arrange the bananas in the pie crust. Pour the custard evenly over the bananas. Refrigerate for 2 hours.
6. In a medium bowl, using an electric mixer, whip the cream until firm peaks form. Add the confectioners' sugar and vanilla and beat in briefly just to combine; be careful not to overbeat. Swirl the whipped cream over the custard and serve.

Pumpkin Pie

The classic.

Makes one 9-inch pie; 6 to 8 servings

1 (9-inch) pie crust (store-bought or homemade)
¼ cup powdered dehydrated pumpkin
2 cups boiling water
1 (12-ounce) can evaporated milk
1 cup sugar
3 large eggs
1 teaspoon coarsely ground dehydrated ginger
1 teaspoon ground cinnamon
¼ teaspoon ground cloves
¼ teaspoon ground nutmeg

1. Preheat the oven to 350°F. Fit the crust into a 9-inch pie plate.
2. In a small heatproof bowl, whisk the pumpkin and boiling water together, cover, and let sit for 20 minutes, stirring a few times, to rehydrate into a thick puree.
3. In a blender, combine the evaporated milk, sugar, eggs, ginger, cinnamon, cloves, nutmeg, and pumpkin puree and blend until smooth. Pour the filling into the crust and bake until the crust turns a golden brown and the filling firms up, about 50 minutes.
4. Let cool on a wire rack, then cover with plastic wrap and refrigerate until chilled.

Strawberry-Rhubarb Pie

With dehydrated strawberries and rhubarb in your pantry, there's no need to wait for spring to roll around to make this treat!

Makes one 9-inch pie; 6 to 8 servings

> ¾ cup dehydrated cubed rhubarb
> Boiling water
> 2 cups sugar
> 1 cup water
> 3 tablespoons cornstarch
> ½ teaspoon vanilla extract
> 1 cup dehydrated sliced strawberries
> 2 (9-inch) pie crusts (store-bought or homemade)
> Milk or beaten egg

1. Place the rhubarb in a 24-ounce canning jar or other heatproof, airtight container and fill with boiling water. Let cool, then refrigerate for 8 hours.
2. Remove the jar from the refrigerator, drain off any remaining water, and pour the rhubarb into a large saucepan. Add the sugar, 1 cup water, cornstarch, and vanilla and whisk together until very well combined. Bring the mixture to a boil and cook, stirring constantly, until thickened.
3. Remove from the heat and gently fold or push the dehydrated strawberries into the hot mixture. DO NOT STIR. Let cool for 30 minutes.
4. Preheat the oven to 350°F. Fit one of the crusts into a 9-inch pie plate.
5. Pour the filling into the pie crust, arrange the other pie crust on top (or you can cut it into strips and weave a lattice-top pattern), trim the edges, and flute them together into an attractive edge. Cut steam vents into the top if necessary. Brush the top with milk or beaten egg. Bake until the top crust is golden brown, about 45 minutes. Let cool to room temperature, then refrigerate to firm up the filling, 2 to 3 hours, before serving.

Peach Custard Pie

This summertime pie is sweet, creamy, oh so easy, and ready to make whenever you want it!

Makes one 9-inch pie; 6 to 8 servings

> 1 (9-inch) pie crust (store-bought or homemade)
> 2 cups dehydrated sliced peaches, each piece cut into quarters with kitchen scissors
> 4 cups boiling water
> ½ cup sugar
> 1 teaspoon salt
> 1 teaspoon ground nutmeg
> 1 teaspoon almond extract
> 4 large eggs
> 2½ cups half-and-half

1. Preheat the oven to 350°F. Fit the crust into a 9-inch pie plate.
2. In a large heatproof bowl, combine the peaches and boiling water, cover, and let sit until the water cools to rehydrate; drain off any remaining water. Drain the peaches on paper towels (but do not squeeze the water out or pat the slices dry).
3. In a large bowl, whisk the sugar, salt, nutmeg, almond extract, and eggs together until smooth. Whisking constantly, slowly pour in the half-and-half. Place the hydrated peaches in the bottom of the pie crust, then evenly pour the custard over. Bake until the filling firms up and the crust is golden brown, about 50 minutes. Remove from the oven, let cool, then chill before serving.

Fast and Easy Tarts

With fruit leathers in your pantry, these are a snap to make!

Makes eight 2-inch tarts

> 1 cup water
> 1½ teaspoons cornstarch
> 1 fruit leather of your choice (page 88)
> ¼ cup dehydrated chopped or thinly sliced fruit of your choice
> 8 (2-inch) prebaked tart shells (store-bought or homemade)

1. In a small bowl, whisk the water and cornstarch together until the cornstarch dissolves. Place the fruit leather in a small saucepan. Pour in the cornstarch and water. Turn the heat to medium and cook, stirring constantly, until the mixture is thick and creamy, 2 to 3 minutes. Remove from the heat.
2. Fold in the dehydrated fruit of your choice, then pour the filling evenly into the tart shells. Let cool, then refrigerate 2 hours before serving.

Strawberry Cream Puffs

Light and airy, these are always a perfect choice for dessert!

Makes 18 cream puffs

Pastries

1 cup water
½ cup (1 stick) butter
1 teaspoon granulated sugar
¼ teaspoon salt
1 cup all-purpose flour
4 large eggs

Filling

1 cup heavy cream
1 teaspoon vanilla extract
1 cup dehydrated sliced strawberries
½ cup granulated sugar
2 tablespoons crushed dehydrated peppermint leaves

Topping

¼ cup confectioners' sugar

1. Preheat the oven to 400°F. Spray a large cookie sheet with cooking spray.
2. Make the puffs. In a medium saucepan, bring the water, butter, granulated sugar, and salt to a boil. Add the flour and stir until smooth, then remove from the heat and let cool for 5 minutes. Blend in the eggs one at a time until the dough is smooth and shiny.
3. Drop the dough onto the cookie sheet using a large soupspoon, spacing them about 3 inches apart. Bake until golden brown, about 30 minutes. Remove from the oven and let cool.
4. Make the filling. In a medium bowl, using an electric mixer, whip the cream until firm peaks form. Briefly beat in the vanilla; be careful not to overbeat. Fold the strawberries, granulated sugar, and mint into the whipped cream.
5. Cut the cooled puffs in half and fill each with a heaping spoonful of cream. Place the tops back on and sprinkle with the confectioners' sugar.

Caramelized Dehydrated Fruit

With this method, you are rehydrating and caramelizing the fruit at the same time. The finished fruit makes a wonderful topping for puff pastry, crepes, or ice cream. The method is the same, the ingredients slightly different for the five fruits that follow.

Makes 1½ cups of each type of fruit

Mangoes

8 dehydrated thin mango slices, each cut in half with kitchen scissors

½ cup boiling water

¼ cup corn syrup

2 tablespoons lemon juice

2 teaspoons butter

1 teaspoon coarsely ground dehydrated ginger

1 tablespoon crushed walnuts

Apples

16 thin dehydrated apple slices (with the peel on)

½ cup boiling water

¼ teaspoon ground cloves

¼ cup corn syrup

2 tablespoons lemon juice

2 teaspoons butter

1 tablespoon crushed walnuts

Pears

16 thin dehydrated pear slices (with the peel on)

⅔ cup boiling water

¼ cup corn syrup

2 tablespoons lemon juice

2 teaspoons butter

1 teaspoon dehydrated peppermint leaves

1 tablespoon crushed walnuts

Peaches

16 thin dehydrated peach slices

½ cup boiling water

¼ cup corn syrup

2 teaspoons butter

1 tablespoon crushed walnuts

Bananas or Plantains

   32 thin dehydrated banana or plantain slices
   ¹⁄₃ cup boiling water
   2 tablespoons honey
   2 tablespoons butter
   2 tablespoons lemon juice
   1 tablespoon crushed walnuts

1. Place all the ingredients, except the walnuts, in a medium saucepan and simmer over low heat until the fruit is soft and the syrup has taken on a nice golden-brown color.
2. Stir in the walnuts.

Christmas Apples

Combining apples with sweet cherry juice, tart lemon juice, and spices creates a sweet snack with a heady aroma. Eat these on their own or use them to make the Marshmallow Christmas Apple Dessert on this page.

Makes 1 quart

   1 cup dehydrated sliced apples
   1 cup water
   ¹⁄₂ cup maraschino cherry juice
   2 tablespoons lemon juice
   2 whole cloves
   1 dehydrated ginger slice
   1 cinnamon stick

Place all the ingredients in a 1-quart canning jar or other airtight container, cover, and refrigerate for 24 hours and up to 2 weeks.

Marshmallow Christmas Apple Dessert

Try this sweet apple treat for something different this holiday season.

Makes 6 servings

   1 quart Christmas Apples (recipe above)
   1¹⁄₂ tablespoons cornstarch
   18 large marshmallows

1. Preheat the oven to 350°F.
2. Pour the Christmas Apples in a large saucepan; remove the cloves and slice of ginger and discard. Stir in the cornstarch and cook, stirring, over medium heat until thick.
3. Remove from the heat and place about ½ cup of the mixture in each of six 4-inch-diameter pudding dishes. Top each with 3 marshmallows. Bake until the marshmallows are golden brown, about 10 minutes. Let cool for 5 to 10 minutes and serve.

Baked Candied Cinnamon Apples

This fall and winter favorite can be enjoyed all year long. It'll fill your house with a heavenly aroma while baking.

Makes 8 servings

> 6 cups boiling water
> 3 cups dehydrated sliced apples
> 1 cup water
> ¾ cup sugar
> ⅓ cup red cinnamon candies
> ¼ cup (½ stick) butter
> ¼ cup lemon juice
> 1 tablespoon cornstarch

1. In a large heatproof bowl, combine the boiling water and dehydrated apples, cover, and let sit for 15 minutes to rehydrate. Drain off any remaining water (do not squeeze the water out or pat the apples dry).
2. Preheat the oven to 350°F. Spray a 10-inch square baking dish with cooking spray.
3. In a small saucepan, bring the 1 cup water, sugar, and candies to a boil, stirring constantly. Reduce the heat to a simmer and cook until thickened, 3 to 5 minutes. Remove from the heat and set aside.
4. Add the butter to the apples and stir to coat the apples evenly with the melted butter. Add the lemon juice and cornstarch and stir to combine. Pour the mixture into the baking dish. Drizzle the candy sauce over the apples and let sit for 15 minutes; do not stir. Bake until the apples are golden brown, about 35 minutes. Enjoy warm.

Apple Crisp

Serve this with vanilla ice cream for sweet perfection.

Makes 9 servings

> 6 cups boiling water
> 5 cups dehydrated sliced apples
> 1½ cups firmly packed brown sugar
> 1½ cups all-purpose flour
> ¾ cup (1½ sticks) butter

1. Preheat the oven to 350°F.
2. In a large bowl, combine the boiling water and dehydrated apples, cover, and let sit for 15 minutes to rehydrate; do not drain off any remaining water. Pour into a 9 x 12-inch baking pan.
3. In a medium bowl, combine the brown sugar and flour, then cut in the butter until you have a crumbly mixture. Sprinkle it evenly over the apples. Bake until golden brown and bubbling, about 40 minutes. Enjoy warm.

Brown Sugar-Almond Peach Crumble

An old-fashioned favorite.

Makes 4 to 6 servings

>   4 cups dehydrated sliced peaches
>   2 cups boiling water
>   1 cup firmly packed brown sugar
>   ½ cup whole wheat or all-purpose flour
>   ½ cup butter or butter-flavored shortening
>   ½ cup chopped almonds
>   1 teaspoon ground cinnamon

1. Preheat the oven to 375°F
2. Place the peaches in an 8-inch square baking dish. Pour the boiling water over the peaches and let sit while mixing the topping to rehydrate.
3. In a medium bowl, combine the remaining ingredients with a large fork until crumbly. Sprinkle the topping evenly over the peaches. Tap the baking dish to settle the crumbs. Bake until golden brown, 45 to 55 minutes.

Pineapple Bread Pudding

A tropical twist on bread pudding.

Makes 6 servings

>   1 cup dehydrated chopped pineapple
>   3 cups boiling water
>   1 cup sugar
>   ½ cup (1 stick) butter
>   4 large eggs
>   ½ cup milk
>   4 cups cubed (1-inch) fresh white bread

1. In a heatproof medium bowl, combine the pineapple and boiling water, cover, and let sit 15 to 20 minutes to rehydrate. Drain off any remaining water.
2. Preheat the oven to 350°F. Spray a 10-inch square baking pan with cooking spray.
3. In a medium bowl, beat the sugar and butter together until creamy. Add the eggs, one at a time, beating well after each. Stir in the pineapple, then the milk.
4. Spread the bread cubes over the bottom of the baking pan. Pour the pineapple mixture over the bread. Bake until it puffs up and turns golden brown, about 1 hour. Enjoy warm or cold.

Individual Peach or Raspberry Bread Puddings

Made with croissants, loaded with fruit, and sweetened with maple syrup, these little puddings will delight your guests.

Makes 4 servings

> 2 cups milk
> ½ cup maple syrup
> 3 tablespoons butter, softened
> 2 large eggs
> 1 teaspoon almond extract
> 4 croissants, cut into cubes
> 1 cup dehydrated sliced peaches or dehydrated raspberries

1. Place the milk, maple syrup, butter, eggs, and almond extract in a blender and blend until smooth.
2. Place the cubed croissants and your choice of dehydrated fruit in a large bowl and pour the milk mixture over. Use your fingers to lightly toss everything together. Divide the mixture between four 1½-cup ovenproof baking dishes. Let sit for 10 minutes.
3. Preheat the oven to 350°F.
4. Place the dishes on a cookie sheet and bake until the puddings puff up and the tops turn golden brown, about 35 minutes.

Mixed-Fruit Bread Pudding

Add dehydrated fruits to your bread pudding for extra flavor and sweetness.

Makes 12 servings

> 1 cup dehydrated sliced apples
> 1 cup dehydrated sliced peaches
> 1 cup dehydrated grapes
> ¼ cup dehydrated cranberries
> 3 cups milk
> 2 cups firmly packed brown sugar
> 1 tablespoon ground allspice
> ½ teaspoon ground nutmeg
> ¼ teaspoon ground cloves
> 16 slices white bread, cut into 1-inch cubes
> 2 large eggs, beaten
> 1 teaspoon dehydrated lemon zest
> Bread Fruit Pudding Sauce (recipe follows)

1. Preheat the oven to 350°F. Grease a 9 x 13-inch baking pan.
2. In a large saucepan, combine the dehydrated fruits, milk, brown sugar, and spices. Cook, stirring, over medium heat until heated through and the brown sugar has dissolved.

3. Remove from the heat. Fold in the cubed bread and let stand for several minutes until cooled. Fold in the eggs and lemon zest.

4. Pour the mixture into the baking pan and bake until the pudding puffs up and turns golden brown on top, about 1½ hours. Serve hot or cold with the sauce.

Mixed-Fruit Bread Pudding Sauce

Makes 1½ cups

> ½ cup (1 stick) butter, melted
> 2 tablespoons milk
> 1 teaspoon almond extract
> 1 cup confectioners' sugar

In a small saucepan, melt the butter over medium heat. Stir in the milk and almond extract, then beat in the confectioners' sugar until smooth. Serve warm.

Caribbean Rice Pudding

Enjoy the tropical flavors of mango, papaya, pineapple, and coconut mixed into creamy, comforting rice pudding.

Makes 4 servings

> 3 cups milk
> 2 large eggs
> ¼ cup sugar
> ½ teaspoon almond extract
> ¼ cup dehydrated chopped papaya
> ¼ cup dehydrated chopped mango
> ¼ cup dehydrated cubed pineapple
> ¼ cup dehydrated sliced coconut, chopped in a blender or food processor
> 2 cups cooked long-grain rice

1. In a large saucepan, whisk the milk, eggs, sugar, and almond extract together. Heat through over low heat, then stir in the dehydrated fruit and coconut. Stir in the rice until the mixture thickens.

2. Transfer to a serving dish, cover with plastic, and refrigerator for 2 to 3 hours to chill before serving.

Individual Banana Tapioca Puddings

Sweet nursery food at its best!

Makes 6 servings

> 36 dehydrated banana chips
> 2 cups milk
> ¼ cup sugar
> 3 tablespoons tapioca
> 2 large eggs, beaten
> Whipped cream
> Ground cinnamon

1. Preheat the oven to 350°F. Lightly spray a 6-cup muffin tin with cooking spray. Place 6 dehydrated banana chips in the bottom of each muffin mold.
2. In a small saucepan, heat the milk, sugar, and tapioca over medium heat for 5 minutes only. Let cool, then whisk in the beaten eggs. The mixture may look a little loose, but that's okay. Spoon the tapioca over the dehydrated bananas in the muffin tin and bake until the puddings firm up, 20 to 25 minutes.
3. Let the puddings cool a little bit, then remove from the muffin tin. Serve warm or chilled, topped with a little whipped cream and a sprinkle of cinnamon.

Mixed Berry Gelatin

A tart kick of flavor.

Makes 4 servings

> 1 (3-ounce) box raspberry gelatin
> 2 cups boiling water
> 2 tablespoons dehydrated blueberries

In a medium bowl, mix the ingredients. Let sit outside of the refrigerator for 30 minutes. Pour into a mold if you like, then refrigerate until firm, about 6 hours. This gelatin will turn dark blue.

GELATIN AND DEHYDRATED FRUIT

Gelatin and dehydrated food go together like kids and the word "why"!

Why? When you make gelatin with fresh fruit, the gelatin will become watery and look unappealing after a period of time. When you use dehydrated foods, your gelatin will hold its figure longer in the refrigerator.

Why? Why? You can even use items that you would normally not be able to use in gelatin, like kiwi, papaya, and pineapple, which contain enzymes that in their fresh state would keep gelatin from gelling. In the case of papaya and pineapple, though, the fruit needs to be cooked before dehydration to turn off those protein-degrading enzymes if you're going to use them with gelatin

Why? Why? Why? Dehydrated foods hydrate in gelatin like magic, creating a fun and tasty dessert that takes only a minute to prepare. Enough said!

Strawberry Gelatin

A perfect summertime snack for the kids.

Makes 4 servings

> 1 (3-ounce) box strawberry gelatin
> 2 cups boiling water
> ½ cup dehydrated sliced strawberries

In a medium bowl, mix the ingredients. Let sit outside of the refrigerator for 30 minutes. Pour into a mold if you like, then refrigerate until firm, about 6 hours.

Strawberry-Banana Gelatin

Everyone's favorite flavor combination, in a delectable gelatin dessert.

Makes 4 servings

> 1 (3-ounce) box strawberry gelatin
> 2 cups boiling water
> ½ cup dehydrated sliced banana

In a medium bowl, mix the ingredients. Let sit outside of the refrigerator for 30 minutes. Pour into a mold if you like, then refrigerate until firm, about 6 hours.

Cherry-Apple-Orange Gelatin

Makes 4 servings

- 1 (3-ounce) box cherry gelatin
- 1 tablespoon dehydrated sliced orange with peels cut into small pieces (6 per slice)
- 1 tablespoon dehydrated sliced apples with peels cut into small pieces (6 per slice)
- 2 cups boiling water

In a medium bowl, mix the ingredients. Let sit outside of the refrigerator for 30 minutes. Pour into a mold if you like, then refrigerate until firm, about 6 hours.

Green Kiwi Gelatin

This looks impressive, with its brilliant green color and beautiful kiwi slices.

Makes 4 servings

- 1 (3-ounce) box lime gelatin
- 2 cups boiling water
- ¼ cup dehydrated sliced kiwi

In a medium bowl, mix the ingredients. Let sit outside of the refrigerator for 30 minutes. Pour into a mold if you like, then refrigerate until firm, about 6 hours.

Glow-in-the-Dark Dragon Gelatin

The tonic water makes this exciting gelatin glow when placed under a black light! Great for any party! Dragon fruit has a flavor somewhat like that of kiwi.

Makes 4 servings

- 1 (3-ounce) box lime gelatin
- 2 cups boiling tonic water
- 4 slices dehydrated dragon fruit, each cut into quarters with kitchen scissors

In a medium bowl, mix ingredients. Let sit outside of the refrigerator for 30 minutes. Pour into a mold if you like, then refrigerate until firm, about 6 hours.

Orange and Green Apple Gelatin

A fun blend of colors and flavors.

Makes 4 servings

- 1 (3-ounce) box orange gelatin
- 2 cups boiling water
- 2 tablespoons chopped dehydrated orange slices with peel on
- 2 tablespoons chopped dehydrated green apple slices with peel on (each cut into 3 pieces with kitchen scissors).

In a medium bowl, mix the ingredients. Let sit outside of the refrigerator for 30 minutes. Pour into a mold if you like, then refrigerate until firm, about 6 hours.

Hot and Chilly Gelatin

A surprising new take on gelatin, guaranteed to excite the taste buds.

Makes 4 servings

- 1 (3-ounce) box orange gelatin
- 2 cups boiling water
- 1 tablespoon crumbled dehydrated chile peppers

In a medium bowl, mix the ingredients. Let sit outside of the refrigerator for 30 minutes. Pour into a mold if you like, then refrigerate until firm, about 6 hours.

Tropical Gelatin

A classic summer gelatin packed with fruit.

Makes 4 servings

- 1 (3-ounce) box orange gelatin
- 2 cups boiling water
- ¼ cup dehydrated steamed cubed (½ inch) papaya
- ¼ cup dehydrated steamed cubed (½ inch) pineapple
- ¼ cup dehydrated shredded coconut

In a medium bowl, mix the ingredients. Let sit outside of the refrigerator for 30 minutes. Pour into a mold if you like, then refrigerate until firm, about 6 hours.

Lemon-Papaya-Pineapple Gelatin

Makes 4 servings

  1 (3-ounce) box lemon gelatin
  2 tablespoons dehydrated steamed chopped pineapple
  2 tablespoons dehydrated steamed chopped papaya
  2 cups boiling water

In a medium bowl, mix the ingredients. Let sit outside of the refrigerator for 30 minutes. Pour into a mold if you like, then refrigerate until firm, about 6 hours.

Lemon-Cherry Gelatin

Sweet and sour, like a refreshing cherry lemonade!

Makes 4 servings

  1 (3-ounce) box lemon gelatin
  2 cups boiling water
  2 tablespoons dehydrated maraschino cherry halves
  2 tablespoons 1-inch pieces dehydrated honeydew slices

In a medium bowl, mix the ingredients. Let sit outside of the refrigerator for 30 minutes. Pour into a mold if you like, then refrigerate until firm, about 6 hours.

Orange Creamsicles

Makes 6 popsicles

  3 tablespoons powdered dehydrated oranges
  3 dehydrated stevia leaves, crumbled (or substitute 3 tablespoons granulated sugar)
  ¼ cup boiling water
  2 ¾ cups plain yogurt
  6 dehydrated thin orange slices with the peel on

1. In a small heatproof bowl, combine the orange powder and crumbled stevia and pour the boiling water over. Stir, cover, and let sit for 15 minutes to rehydrate; do not drain.
2. Whisk the yogurt into the orange puree until smooth.
3. For each popsicle, fill a ½-cup mold with the mixture, then push one dehydrated orange slice down the side of each mold. The orange slice will be visible when the popsicles are removed from the molds. Place the popsicle sticks and lids on the molds and freeze for 8 hours.

POPSICLES

This is another inexpensive and healthy treat you can make using your dehydrated foods! Make it interesting, make it colorful, and make it cool! Let's face it, store-purchased popsicles are just plain boring—where's the fruit?

Homemade popsicles are so much better, and lots of fun to make with kids. With your pantry of dehydrated fruits, you'll always have ingredients for making them on hand.

All you do is fill a popsicle mold with your favorite juice or yogurt and then add your favorite dehydrated fruits. Refrigerate overnight to allow the fruits to rehydrate. Then, transfer the pops to the freezer until frozen. Another way to create popsicles is to freeze fruit smoothies in popsicle molds—check out our smoothie recipes on pages 188–91.

Date Sugar and Apple Popsicles

Makes 6 popsicles

> 3 tablespoons dehydrated apple slices cut in thirds with kitchen scissors.
> 2 tablespoons date sugar
> ¼ cup boiling water
> 2¾ cups plain yogurt

1. In a small heatproof bowl, combine the apple powder and date sugar and pour the boiling water over. Stir, cover, and let sit for 15 minutes to rehydrate; do not drain.
2. Whisk the yogurt into the apple puree until smooth.
3. For each popsicle, fill a ½-cup mold with the mixture. Place the popsicle sticks and lids on the molds and freeze for 8 hours.

Mint Chocolate Chip Popsicle

Makes 6 popsicles

> 2½ cups plain yogurt
> ½ cup chocolate chips
> 1 tablespoon dehydrated mint, crumbled

1. Place the yogurt in the freezer until very cold but not frozen.
2. Melt the chocolate chips in the microwave, add the crumbled mint, and stir for 1 minute to combine.
3. Remove the yogurt from the freezer, lightly swirl in the minted chocolate. Be careful to lightly stir it in; you don't want it to be completely blended together. The cold yogurt will cause the chocolate to harden, creating a minty chocolate crunch. Place back in freezer for 5 minutes.

4. For each popsicle, fill a ½-cup mold with the mixture. Place the popsicle sticks and lids on the molds and freeze for 8 hours.

Pineapple and Coconut Popsicles

Makes 6 popsicles

2 tablespoons boiling water.
¼ cup dehydrated steamed chopped pineapple
2½ cups plain yogurt
2 tablespoons dehydrated shredded coconut

1. In a small bowl, sprinkle the boiling water over the dehydrated pineapple and let sit for 5 minutes. Do not drain.
2. Add the yogurt and coconut and mix everything together. For each popsicle, fill a ½-cup mold with the mixture. Place the popsicle sticks and lids on the molds and freeze for 8 hours.

Fruit Leather Pop

You can mix up different types of fruit leather or even cut the leather into fun shapes.

Makes 6 popsicles

2¾ cups plain yogurt
¼ cup honey
1 fruit leather of your choice (page 88), cut into small squares like confetti

1. In a small bowl, blend the yogurt and honey together, then fold in the leather pieces.
2. For each popsicle, fill a ½-cup mold with the mixture. Place the popsicle sticks and lids on the molds and freeze for 8 hours.

Loads of Fruit Pops

Makes 6 popsicles

2 tablespoons dehydrated maraschino cherries
2 tablespoons chopped dehydrated peaches (use kitchen scissors)
2 tablespoons dehydrated banana chips
¼ cup boiling water
2½ cups plain yogurt

1. In a small heatproof bowl, combine the dehydrated fruit. Pour the boiling water over, cover, and let sit for 15 minutes to rehydrate; do not drain.
2. Stir in the yogurt, then scoop into ½-cup-sized popsicle molds. Place the popsicle sticks and lids on the molds and freeze for 8 hours.

Juice Pops

Choose your favorite fruit juice and dehydrated fruit, and the rest is easy!

Makes 6 popsicles

> 3 cups fruit juice of your choice
> 1 cup chopped dehydrated fruit of your choice (small berries and sliced strawberries can remain whole)

1. Heat the juice in a microwave until hot but not boiling.
2. Add the dehydrated fruit to the juice, cover, and let sit for 15 minutes to rehydrate.
3. For each popsicle, fill a ½-cup mold with the mixture. Place the popsicle sticks and lids on the molds and freeze for 8 hours.

Lemon and Stevia Infused Water Pop

A wonderfully refreshing and guilt-free freezer treat!

Makes 6 popsicles

> 3 dehydrated lemon slices, cut in half with kitchen scissors
> 3 dehydrated stevia leaves, cut in half with kitchen scissors
> 3 cups water

1. In a small saucepan, combine the ingredients, bring to a boil, and let boil for 1 minute. Strain out the solids.
2. Let cool, then use tongs to put one stevia leaf half and one lemon slice half into each of six ½-cup popsicle molds. Pour the infused water evenly into the molds. Place the popsicle sticks and lids on the molds and freeze for 8 hours.

OTHER GREAT DEHYDRATED COMBINATIONS FOR INFUSED WATER POPS

- Orange and ginger
- Chile pepper and lemongrass
- Rosemary and rose petals
- Tarragon and lime
- Peaches and thyme
- Cranberries and stevia leaves
- Beets and a cinnamon stick
- Watermelon and peppermint leaves
- Honeydew and cantaloupe

Terms & Techniques to Know

Blanching: Some foods require blanching before dehydration (for certain other foods it is optional). This involves placing the items in boiling water for 1 to 2 minutes, then briefly dipping them into ice water to abruptly halt the heating process. This flash heating serves a few purposes. First, it destroys enzymes that play a role in causing particular foods to discolor and/or develop an odor or unwelcome taste over time. Blanching doesn't eliminate these processes but does considerably slow them. It also helps to soften a vegetable or fruit, allowing for the easy removal of unwanted skins, as is the case with peaches and tomatoes.

Boiling: This is used to cook a food all the way through prior to dehydrating. Some items you may wish to boil before dehydrating include potatoes, squash, beans, corn, carrots, beets, rutabaga, and rhubarb.

Broiling: Broiling a food prior to dehydrating will give it a roasted look when it is rehydrated. Do not use oil in this process, as oil impedes dehydration.

Building your pantry: Your pantry refers to your stock of vacuum-sealed and stored dehydrated items. Some people prefer to build their pantry with enough foods to sustain them in case of a weather emergency, others store food to last multiple years, and some build a pantry just large enough for immediate use in the kitchen for everyday recipes. The preference is yours!

Dehydrated foods: The terms "dehydrated" and "dried" are often used interchangeably in the dry-food business. However, there are subtle differences. Dehydration is a near-complete removal of water from foods, and implies the usage of some sort of dehydration device. Ideally, dehydrated foods should be 95% devoid of water, though we cannot actually measure this percentage quantitatively at home but rather must use our judgment.

Dehydrated foods should not be sticky or moist in any way, and are often crisp, though they can also be chewy and pliable.

Dried foods: The term "dried" is broader than "dehydrated." A dried food simply implies that some degree of water has been removed from the food, typically by means of air- or sun-drying. For example, the food industry often sells dates and raisins as "dried" foods. Dates and raisins are soft and chewy and moist, still containing a significant amount of water. When you handle raisins and other "dried" fruits, your hands will become moist and sticky. Dehydrated foods, by comparison, have had nearly all of the water removed, and therefore dehydration can be thought of as the extreme end point of "drying." For this reason, all dehydrated items are technically "dried" items, but not all dried items are dehydrated. But in this book, for the sake of simplicity, both "dried" and "dehydrated" are used to refer to dehydrated foods.

With a home dehydrator, you can dry foods to any degree you wish. If you remove grapes from your dehydrator before they are completely dehydrated, you will have "dried" grapes, or raisins. These will still be moist and chewy. If you place the raisins back into the dehydrator until they are no longer moist, you will have "dehydrated" grapes.

Freeze-dried foods: Much different from dehydration or drying, freeze-drying (also called *cryodessication*) uses extreme low temperatures to flash-freeze food items, and then a subsequent rapid reduction in pressure to sublimate the frozen water molecules directly into gas. The process is common in the food industry and the items are often packaged and sold in "dried" fruit mixes, pre-packaged soups, cereals, and more. Although a convenient and cost-effective method for companies, freeze-drying cannot be performed at home, and has some nutritional downsides.

Compared to dehydrated foods, freeze-dried foods are often lighter in color and crunchier, and can easily be crumbled with your fingers into a powder. The dry fruits in cereals, for example, are often freeze-dried.

Grilling: As with broiling, you can grill food to give it a roasted look prior to dehydration. Do not use oil in this process, as it impedes dehydration.

Heat seal: This is the process used to seal Mylar bags, which cannot be vacuum sealed. Heat sealing simply melds the bag shut, without removing any air. Many vacuum sealers have a heat seal-only setting. Alternatively, you can purchase a handheld heat seal, or simply use a hair straightener or a clothing iron and a metal edge, such as the side of a carpenter's level.

Powdering: Once dehydrated, you can throw any of your fruits and vegetables in a blender and reduce them to a flavor powder that can be used in rubs, breadcrumbs, soups, stews, and fruit sugars, or sprinkled over cookies or muffins. See page 80 for more information on this.

Rehydration: Rehydration puts water back into your dehydrated item, often restoring it to its original state. The methods used in this book are:
- *Quick soak:* This is when you take a dehydrated item and dip it into a bowl of boiling water for 1 to 60 seconds before using it in a recipe.
- *15-minute soak:* This is how you will rehydrate certain foods prior to cooking and baking. Simply place your dehydrated item in hot or boiling water to soak for around 15 minutes, drain the excess water, and then use the item in your recipe.
- *Rehydration by refrigeration:* Add to a 24-ounce canning jar 1½ cups of dehydrated sliced items such as beets, apples, peaches, or zucchini (if using small chopped items such as peas, corn, onions, etc., you would only require approximately ⅔ cup of the dehydrated items). For dehydrated vegetables, fill the jar to the top with boiling water or a brine (if you'd like pickled vegetables). For dehydrated fruits, fill to the top with room-temperature water, fruit juice, or a spiced water. For the vegetables, after the water cools, place the jars in the refrigerator for 24 hours (put the fruit immediately in the fridge). The rehydrated items are a delicious snack right out of the jar. The rehydrated vegetables can also be heated and served, and the rehydrated fruits can easily be made into a fruit salad or pie filling.

Sanitation: Although the process of dehydrating foods and vacuum storing kills most harmful bacteria, it is still important to practice proper sanitation in your kitchen. Thoroughly wash your food items with soap and water prior to dehydration, especially if you are planning on dehydrating the outer skins to use for cooking or teas.

Storage, long term: Long-term storage typically refers to items stored from 6 months to many years.

Storage, short term: Short-term storage refers to items stored less than 6 months.

Vacuum seal: When storing food in vacuum bags, you will close them using a vacuum sealer, which will remove all surrounding air, creating a suction-tight seal. This is different from a heat seal, which is used with Mylar bags.

Metric Equivalents

WEIGHTS

1 ounce = 28 grams
4 ounces (¼ pound) = 113 grams
8 ounces (½ pound) = 227 grams
16 ounces (1 pound) = 454 grams

VOLUME MEASURES

¼ teaspoon = 1.25 ml
½ teaspoon = 2.5 ml
1 teaspoon = 5 ml
1 tablespoon = ½ fluid ounce = 15 ml
2 tablespoons = 1 fluid ounce = 30 ml
¼ cup = 2 fluid ounces = 60 ml
⅓ cup = 3 fluid ounces = 80 ml
½ cup = 4 fluid ounces = 120 ml
⅔ cup = 6 fluid ounces = 160 ml
¾ cup = 6 fluid ounces = 180 ml
1 cup = 8 fluid ounces = 235 ml
1 pint = 16 fluid ounces = 475 ml
1 quart = 32 fluid ounces = 945 ml
1 gallon = 128 fluid ounces = 3,755 ml
   (3¾ liters)

LENGTH MEASURES

1 inch = 2.5 cm
1 foot = 30.5 cm

TEMPERATURE EQUIVALENTS

(rounded to the nearest 5)

°F	°C	Gas Mark
90	30	
100	40	
110	45	
125	50	
135	55	
250	120	½
275	135	1
300	150	2
325	165	3
350	175	4
375	190	5
400	205	6
425	220	7
450	230	8
475	245	9
500	260	10

Index

Page numbers in italics indicate sidebars.